BEFORE MODERNISM

Before Modernism

INVENTING AMERICAN LYRIC

VIRGINIA JACKSON

PRINCETON UNIVERSITY PRESS

PRINCETON & OXFORD

Published by Princeton University Press
41 William Street, Princeton, New Jersey 08540
99 Banbury Road, Oxford OX2 6JX

press.princeton.edu

All Rights Reserved

Names: Jackson, Virginia, author.
Title: Before modernism : inventing American lyric / Virginia Jackson.
Description: Princeton : Princeton University Press, 2023. | Includes bibliographical references and index.
Identifiers: LCCN 2022019918 (print) | LCCN 2022019919 (ebook) | ISBN 9780691232805 (paperback) | ISBN 9780691232799 (hardback) | ISBN 9780691233116 (ebook)
Subjects: LCSH: Lyric poetry—History and criticism. | American poetry—18th century—History and criticism. | American poetry—19th century—History and criticism. | American poetry—African American authors—History and criticism. | Poetics—History. | LCGFT: Literary criticism.
Classification: LCC PS309.L8 J33 2023 (print) | LCC PS309.L8 (ebook) | DDC 811/.0409896073—dc23/eng/20220722
LC record available at https://lccn.loc.gov/2022019918
LC ebook record available at https://lccn.loc.gov/2022019919

British Library Cataloging-in-Publication Data is available

Editorial: Anne Savarese and James Collier
Production Editorial: Ellen Foos and Jaden Young
Jacket/Cover Design: Katie Osborne
Production: Lauren Reese
Publicity: Alyssa Sanford and Charlotte Coyne
Copyeditor: Jennifer Harris

Jacket image: Engraving depicting a view of the night sky showing the milky way. Dated 19th century. World History Archive / Alamy Stock Photo

This book has been composed in Arno (Classic)

10 9 8 7 6 5 4 3 2 1

to Martin, Sadye, Walker & Yopie

and in memory of Elizabeth Wanning Harries

Though other stars may round thee burn,
    With larger disk and brighter ray,
And fiery comets round thee turn,
    While millions mark their blazing way;
And the pale moon and planets bright
Reflect on us their silvery light.

Not like that moon, now dark, now bright,
    In phase and place forever changing;
Or planets with reflected light,
    Or comets through the heavens ranging;
They all seem varying to our view,
While thou art ever fixed and true.

—JAMES MONROE WHITFIELD,
"THE NORTH STAR," 1849

CONTENTS

ILLUSTRATIONS

A NOTE ON NAMES

THE NAMES of some of the poets in this book may be unfamiliar to many readers. I am happy to introduce them here, but I am not happy to reintroduce the names of the two poets who frame this book, names that may be all too familiar to my readers. The name of the poet known for the last two and a half centuries as "Phillis Wheatley" poses a notorious problem: "*The Phillis*" was the name of the ship that compelled her through the Middle Passage, and "Wheatley" is the name of the family who thought they could buy her in 1761. How can we continue to use such a name? I am persuaded by recent attempts to rename Phillis Wheatley "Phillis Wheatley Peters," since at least "Peters" is the name of the Black man the poet chose to marry rather than the name of her White enslavers. Yet literary history has referred to her as "Phillis Wheatley," and since this book is about literary history, I have retained that name here. I recognize this as a bad choice. The name dictated by patriarchy is better than the name dictated by slavery, but adding patriarchy to slavery does not solve the problem.

The problem of the patronym persists in literary history's name for Frances Ellen Watkins Harper. Since Frances Watkins did not marry Fenton Harper until 1860, the poems I discuss here were written by Frances Watkins, not by Frances Harper. Fenton Harper died in 1864, and Frances Watkins Harper lived until 1911. Yet again, we have come to recognize this poet's work by an improper name, so in these pages I toggle back and forth between her patronyms. In an important sense, these Black women poets will never have names of their own—or as Sylvia Wynter might say and this book will argue, though these poets invented American lyric, the genres of their proper names have not yet been invented.

Preface

MNEMOSYNE

IN A POEM she wrote when she was in her teens, Phillis Wheatley gave memory a nickname. Enslaved in a fancy house in Boston, prompted by a White girl who said she had never encountered a poem "upon RECOLLECTION," the poet began,

> Mneme, begin; inspire, ye sacred Nine!
> Your vent'rous *Afric* in the deep design.[1]

Asking the mother of the muses to help her describe the act of remembering, this poet (who never mentions any memories of her own) pretends to be so intimate with the goddess Mnemosyne that she can abbreviate her name and claim to belong to her and her daughters (rather than to John and Susanna Wheatley and their children). Yet it turns out that Mneme may not be so familiar after all: not only do none of the poet's personal recollections surface in this poem, but ten lines later, she changes Mnemosyne's gender, referring to our dreams as "*his* secret stores," writing that "*he* wings his way / Thro' *Phoebe's* realm," as if all identities, including that of this "vent'rous *Afric*," were imaginary and transitive, as if real and fantastic persons could all disappear or be changed at any moment. If lyric poems are elevated forms of self-expression addressed to everyone at once and to no one in particular, this poem is a lyric only if what the poet wanted to express was her erasure from the forms that expression took. And why wouldn't she want everyone and no one to witness her disappearance? Isn't the pathos of unrealized self-expression also what lyric poetry is all about? "Thou still unravished bride of quietness," "Bright star, would I were stedfast as thou art," "Hail to thee, blithe Spirit!," "Ethereal minstrel! pilgrim of the sky!,"

"Tyger Tyger, burning bright": poets are always invoking imaginary beings who promise more than they can deliver, that reveal less than the poet wants to hear and more than the reader wants to know, that pretend to say what the poet can't quite manage to say.[2] Yet unlike the White male British Romantics who wrote those lines, Wheatley was not asking Mneme to stand in her place, to be the better poet. She was asking memory to tell a story that has yet to be told: the story of the invention of American lyric.

This book takes memory's place by tracing the historical poetics of American lyric from Phillis Wheatley to Frances Ellen Watkins Harper, from the late eighteenth to the middle of the nineteenth century. Why remember decades not usually considered important in the history of either lyric poetry in general or of American poetry in particular? While in the history of British poetry, those years span the rise of Romantic then Victorian poetics, and in the history of French poetry, those years are considered the prelude to the new modern poetry of Baudelaire, how can we describe a history of American poetry that has not been so conveniently periodized? And why refer to that history as "the invention" of a genre that would become so completely modern after the nineteenth century that poetry became another name for it? Of the many answers this book will give to those large questions, the most important is the one Wheatley gave herself: "the deep design" of American poetry began in the work of an ambitious Black poet and has continued to depend on the work of Black poets for the past two hundred and fifty years.

Because understanding the history of American poetry in this way means that accounts of American lyric as an ethno-nationalist, triumphally modernist project that began with the Puritans and culminated in the achievement of T. S. Eliot, or as Emerson's twin Transcendental brainchildren Walt Whitman and Emily Dickinson, or as a transatlantic anglocentric rainbow bridge stretching from Shelley to Stevens, or as the self-involvement of Romantic and modern poets that gave way to a post-lyric avant-garde, or as a return to lyric in reaction to that avant-garde, can all be understood as the fictions of racial continuity they always were.[3] Even comparative histories of American poetics that trace the break between cosmopolitan modern poets and an earlier provincially nationalist tradition have remained continuously and conspicuously White.[4] Meanwhile, Wheatley and Paul Laurence Dunbar have served as bookends for accounts of nineteenth-century African American poetry, which tend to suggest that, as Joan R. Sherman writes, "black poetry began with Phillis Wheatley, disappeared for over one hundred years, and only reemerged with Paul Laurence Dunbar."[5] But as Sherman and Ivy Wilson and Matt Sandler and other scholars have insisted, Black poets in the nineteenth century did not just disappear.[6] They were actively disappeared from literary history, from the history of poetics, and from the disciplines of English, American, and Comparative Literature as those histories and poetics and disciplines were constructed on the basis of default-White canons surrounded by segregated non-White canons at the end of the nineteenth century and throughout the twentieth. Attempts to undiscipline our twentieth- and twenty-first-century disciplines of literary studies have begun, but they have not yet reoriented our assumptions about the deep design of American poetics.[7]

This book tries to do just that—to give an alternative account of the ways in which early Black poets inspired the direction that American poetics has taken over the past two and a half centuries. Though it ends in the middle of the nineteenth century, its title is *Before Modernism* because the story I want to tell revises the British-and-European-Romanticism-to-American-modernism narrative that has dominated the literary critical understanding of American poetics. It also challenges the familiar idea that modern American poetry began in and as Walt Whitman's first edition of *Leaves of Grass* in 1855. As this book will show, the American poets left out of those stories influenced the very structures of poetics that Whitman celebrated and that modern literary criticism has relied on to make them disappear. When Wheatley wrote "Recollection" (later, "On Recollection") in 1771, her poem ended up in the *London Magazine; or, Gentleman's Monthly Intelligencer* in March 1772; by that time, she had already published poems in the *Boston Evening-Post* and as broadsides that were reprinted in newspapers on both sides of the Atlantic, and she had published her first poem in a shipping paper, the *Newport Mercury*, in 1767, when she was in her early teens. Actually, "Recollection" may have been printed as part of a campaign to gather subscribers for her proposed first volume of poetry, which was eventually published in London in 1773.[8] This is to say that American poetry began as something it no longer is: popular literature addressed to print publics that crossed genres and media and nations and genders and races and educations and classes. Toward the end of the eighteenth and for most of the nineteenth centuries, those publics recognized poems as particular genres (in the case of "Recollection," as a lesser ode in heroic couplets invoking a classical figure), rather than as representative expressions of particular persons. In the course of the nineteenth century, genres of poems became less important than the genres of the persons represented in and by them. As that shift began to happen, American poetry was gradually lyricized: ballads and songs, elegies and odes, hymns and epistles, epyllions and circuit-of-Apollo poems, georgics and locodescriptive poems that depended on miscellaneous forms of address gradually and unevenly merged into one big genre of address associated with the genre of the person rather than with the genre of the poem. All poetry (or almost all poetry) became lyric poetry.

In Wheatley's invocation of Mneme, you can see one beginning of that process. As a "vent'rous *Afric*," Wheatley's person upstaged her poem. Or at least her abstract persona did: when the woman whose first name was taken from the name of the ship that brought her to the dock at which the people with what became her last name paid for a girl in cash, called herself an "*Afric*," she was reclaiming the continent she came from. Yet this was also a name given to that place and those people by the people who thought they owned her, their way of distinguishing her from themselves. In the note that preceded "Recollection" in the *London Magazine*, an anonymous letter writer explains that,

> There is in this town a young *Negro woman*, who left *her* country at ten years of age, and has been in *this* eight years. . . . The following was occasioned by her being in company with some young ladies of family, when one of them said she did not remember, among all the poetical pieces she had seen, ever to have met with a poem upon RECOLLECTION. The *African* (so let me call her, for so in fact she is) took the hint, went home to her master's, and soon sent what follows.[9]

Here are the things we know about the person who wrote "what follows": that she is eighteen years old (she was probably actually younger), that she is a she, that her home is "her master's," that she is a "*Negro*," but not a native of either Boston or London but of "*her* [unnamed] country," which must be in Africa, because "*African*" is the one thing she can be called, since it is the one thing "in fact she is." All of this information is generic rather than personal, and its effect is to make us want to fill in the personal details. While it may be true that (as we will see in chapter 3) the poet whom June Jordan renamed "Phillis Miracle" did manage "nonetheless, to write, sometimes, toward the personal truth of her experience," it is also true that her experience is not the most obvious subject of her poems.[10] The subject of "Recollection" is the mental operation designated by the title, the act the poet asks Mneme to help her describe. The ode does not reward our curiosity about the poet (though at one point in it she alludes to "past follies and past crimes" the reader can only imagine), but after the prefatory setup, it is impossible to read the poem without thinking about the person who wrote it. The complaint about Wheatley's poetry that would become familiar by the time that J. Saunders Redding wrote in 1939 of the "negative, bloodless quality in Phillis Wheatley" is the consequence of the personal revelations that "Recollection" withholds. It is the reader's and not the poem's (or the poet's) desire to reveal more about this *African*. "In this sense none of her poetry is real," Redding concludes, and in a way that's true: if you think "real" poetry is personal expression, then "Recollection" is not poetry at all.[11] Yet it is this central negation, this empty (or really, crossed-out) space where personal expression should be that would expand over the next two and a half centuries to become the *prima mobile*, the animating force of the poetry so intimately defined by personal expression, the definition of American lyric.

This eloquent absence is not what Theodor Adorno had in mind when he wrote in 1957 that "the lyric work is always the subjective expression of a social antagonism," yet the negative dialectics of Wheatley's opening couplet suggest as much.[12] The four syllables of "Mneme, begin" at the beginning of the first line square off against the four syllables of "the deep design" that is the poet's and not Mneme's at the end of the second line; the invocation of "ye sacred Nine!" at the end of the first line is set against the assertion of "Your vent'rous *Afric*" at the beginning of the second line. The opening trochee of the invocation turns the iambs that ensue upside down; the internal rhymes of the first three syllables of those two feet make that reversal almost invisible; the two iambs that close the couplet repeat that internally rhyming long *e* but close on an accented identification with rather than difference from the "Nine." Not only do the beginnings and endings of the lines oppose one another, but the two lines are also unlike one another in their phrasing: while the first line marks the first four beats as distinct by *almost* stopping with a semicolon, it continues with an imperative ("inspire") that changes the direction of the apostrophe and doubles the caesura—yet the second line is a textbook bifurcated pentameter line, cut right down the middle. The nicknamed goddess and her daughters are both indistinguishable from and structurally at odds with the Black poet in the semantic and prosodic details of the lines themselves, as of course that poet was at odds with the structure of the Anglophone couplet, with the people publishing her poem, and with most of the people reading her poem. This antagonism is not a formulaic balancing of binary oppositions; it's an algorithm. The result of the chiasmus that aligns those antagonisms as if they were rhymed agreement is a charged yet empty center where they cross, a marked (and remarked) absence that speaks more loudly than words. This is the sense in which Wheatley's work is one beginning of a poetics that developed over the next century and more, as the person who both overshadows and is missing from this poem became the focus of all lyric reading. Black poets after Wheatley inspired the direction of American poetics—the direction of *lyricization*—not because they wrote the most influential poetry of the period—though as we shall see, Wheatley *did* influence the direction of Anglophone Romanticism, and many nineteenth-century Black poetic genres *were* appropriated by White Romantic poets, and Black Romantic poets *did* influence the development of modern American poetics—but because the deep design of the racialized social antagonism foundational to America (and not just to America) became the deep design of the poetry that, over the course of the long nineteenth century, became American lyric.

We might also say of Wheatley's couplet what J. Paul Hunter says of Pope's couplets, that "the route" by which it

> blurs and reconfigures binaries and develops a rhetoric of complex redefinition is circuitous; it challenges the transparency of the apparent rhetoric and blurs and bleeds images of plain opposites into one another. The effect, though, is not to fog or muddy or obscure—much less to deconstruct meanings to nothing stable at all—but to use the easy opposition as a way of clarifying the process of deepening qualification and refinement. It is a demonstration of how to read as an exercise in how to think.[13]

But here's the thing: if Wheatley is using Pope's couplet technology as Hunter so well describes it, she has thoroughly rewired it—or, to shift to a more contemporary metaphor, she has replaced its software. *Pace* Redding and the many historians of Black poetics who have found Wheatley's couplets "bloodless" because Popean, she does blur and bleed apparent opposites into one another, and in so doing she does refine the terms of the couplet's structuring oppositions (why *can't* the Muses respond to an *Afric*? Why *can't* this poet's deep design take precedence?). Yet the refinement of this couplet does not challenge "the transparency of the apparent rhetoric" that dictates these oppositions because nothing about that rhetoric is transparent. In Wheatley's poetics, the process of deepening qualification and refinement is indeed a demonstration of how to read as an exercise in how to think, and though I called that process "negative dialectics" in my last paragraph, it is not, like Adorno's theory of poetics, Hegelian, so does not share the commitment to historical progress that Hegel and Marx envisioned.[14] There is no synthesis of opposites in this couplet, no affect that sutures Mneme to the poet (despite the endearing possessive pronoun), no logic that attaches the genre of the ode to the person that everything about that genre misrecognizes. If a genre is, as Lisa Gitelman has suggested, most basically "a mode of recognition instantiated in discourse," then the problem for Wheatley's couplet is that the discourse that makes it recognizable as a genre also makes the person who wrote it unrecognizable.[15] The process of refinement by which the couplet works to foreground that unrecognition is not progressive, or utopian, or world-making. If we see it as a demonstration of how to read as an exercise in how to think, then what we're left thinking about is an elaborate frame around something that has been refined into airy thinness, around nothing at all—or at least around nothing for which we have had a name.

The pages that follow will suggest many names for that lyrical, abstract, ephemeral person. By the 1930s, this figure would be called "the speaker" of the poem—a person characterized by a definite article rather than by a race or a gender or a pronoun or a proper name. A missing person. But let's begin by following Wheatley in calling this abstract person *Mnemosyne*—or maybe even "Mneme." The slow readings in this book often try to piece together poems and people and personifications (or imaginary people) that are hard to remember (or at least hard to *read*), so I'll start, slowly, with this one. I take the phrase "slow reading" from the mid-twentieth-century literary critic Reuben Brower, though while Brower used the phrase to describe the way in which close attention to the language of the text itself could "show exactly *who* is speaking in a poem," revealing the poem's "dramatic situation," in this book I pay sustained attention to the ways in which the question of "who is speaking in a poem" became a question in the first place, to the ways in which the circumstances of poetry's many different genres of address were reduced and resolved into a genre defined by a fictional dramatic situation, and to the ways in which this imaginary drama came to define what Brower calls "the voice we hear in a lyric."[16] That slow reading can be close, surface, distant, reparative, or paranoid, but it is always both formal and historical—or, since form is an abstraction of genre (as the dramatic situation is always an abstraction of the poem's historical situation), slow reading primarily attends to how and why generic abstraction happens. Often, prosody stages the abstraction of genre into form, as poets adapt modes of recognition instantiated in the smallest details of a given prosodic discourse—for example, as Wheatley adapted the rhythm and rhyme of the iambic pentameter "heroic" couplet to her own purposes. The abstraction of genre into form is also the function of the rhetorical figure of apostrophe with which "Recollection" begins, a figure of address often considered quintessentially lyric (as we shall see in chapter 2), since in appealing to what is absent or inanimate, such figures of address tend to bring addressees like Mneme to imaginary life (thus personifying them, as we shall

see in chapter 3). So slow reading is a technique derived from historical pros-
ody and historical poetics, and unlike the modes of close reading developed
by "new" critics like Brower who made "the speaker" their primary focus, it
often focuses on unspoken incidental or eccentric details that tend to emerge
from poems when you linger with them long enough. In the case of Mnemo-
syne, that emergence turned out to be unspoken, incidental, and lingering
indeed.

   In the many years of research in which this project shape-shifted from an
almost-all-White book about nineteenth-century American poetry in public
to a book about late eighteenth- and early nineteenth-century Black poets'
interventions in American poetry in public, I often had trouble figuring out
what poems or people or fake people I was reading—either because most
nineteenth-century poems were printed anonymously or pseudonymously,
or because the names are now so obscure that it's hard to track them down, or
because the personifications or figures in them meant something very different
to readers in, say, 1772 or 1832 or 1854 than they meant to people in 1969 or 1988
or 2023. In tracing Wheatley's reception and transmission in the nineteenth
century, I came upon a volume that all Wheatley scholars quickly discover. In
1838, *Memoir and Poems of Phillis Wheatley, A Native African and a Slave. Also,
Poems by a Slave*, was published by Isaac Knapp in Boston. As Max Cavitch
writes, "this volume not only had strategic uses for contemporary abolition-
ism, but implications as well, for Wheatley's broader reception history, from
the mid-nineteenth century, to the more recent and contemporary eras of
black publishing history."[17] The preface to the volume identifies it as an aboli-
tionist publication, including Wheatley's only published book, *Poems on Vari-
ous Subjects, Religious and Moral* (1773) and the additional booklet *Poems by a
Slave*, which turns out to be a retitled version of *The Hope of Liberty*, the first
collection of poems published by the enslaved poet George Moses Horton
(one of the subjects of chapter 2), originally printed in 1829. In 1838, Wheatley
had been dead for over fifty years, and Horton would continue to be enslaved
for another twenty-seven. As M. A. Richmond wrote in 1974, Knapp's 1838
volume "was not meant to praise poetry but to advance the Abolitionist cause"
(as one can tell, since this "purpose is suggested by the cumbersome title").
Yet Richmond also suggested that even for later readers of Wheatley and Hor-
ton, "their poetry as poetry is not the main thing," since

   Their influence on American poetry is closer to nil than negligible, and if
   your interest is in poetry as such, you need pay them no more mind than

those other minor poets who clutter to the footnotes of literary histories. What is important about the poetry is what it reveals or suggests of the slaves who wrote it, and, by extension, what it reveals about the institution of slavery. Because of the censorship implicit in the slave condition, quite often what is left unsaid is more significant than what is said, and even what is said may be more important for what it masks than for what it lays bare.[18]

But what if Wheatley's and Horton's poetry *was* "the main thing"—what if their (and other early Black poets') importance to the history of transatlantic Anglophone poetics is enormous precisely because the idea that "what is left unsaid is more significant than what is said" is one way of describing the surplus value accorded to *all* (lyricized) poetry for the past two hundred and fifty years? What if these poets and others worked in poetic genres and discourses that rendered their work a record of the ways in which the racialized social antagonism that is modernity's foundation made "subjective expression" the precise "locus of impossible speech" that came to define the alienated modern lyric subject?[19] That impossible speech is not the result of explicit censorship, exactly, but it may well be the basis for later emphases on the fiction of "the speaker" as an imaginary person who says what the reader of lyric poetry wants to hear. The White appropriation of the pathos of this impossible speech animated the transformation of the neoclassical and Romantic poetic genres in which Wheatley and Horton wrote into modern lyric forms. But just as that process was happening, nineteenth-century Black poets reframed those forms *as* White appropriations.

This book will trace that dialectical process by focusing first on the work of Black poets in the late eighteenth and the first half of the nineteenth centuries, then by turning its focus to the early nineteenth-century poetics of whiteness, and then by interlacing the racialization of Black and White poetics in the 1840s and early 1850s. This structure places the poetics of whiteness in a secondary rather than a primary position, emphasizing the ways in which the lyricization of early American poetics was an uneven and unfinished process. As Ronald Judy has shown, "the multifarious possibilities of expression that constitute the historical legacy of this 'New World'" form "a body of work that contradicts, and so disrupts the integrity of, the dominant discourse of American cultural history"—which means that reading eighteenth-and-nineteenth-century Black poetics means rereading eighteenth-and-nineteenth-century White poetics.[20] This tripartite structure is meant to be more symphonic than Hegelian: the abstraction of verse genres into lyric was certainly the result of opposing forces, but it was not ideally synthetic.[21] As I was struggling to articulate the outlines of the complex historical poetics those complex sentences index, the Knapp volume suddenly offered me an image for that doubly silenced yet also doubly voiced double-consciousness, for the metalyrical abstraction of genre into form that has shaped the history of American poetics but that I could not quite name.

When I ordered the book online, I knew I wasn't buying a first edition, but when I turned to the copyright page (figure P.1), I wasn't sure what edition it was that I had received. The page is a palimpsest of the original Knapp publication (itself a reprinting of an 1834 edition of Wheatley's poems, accompanied by the "Memoir" to which we will return in chapter 3), and of two reprintings: one by the Ayer Company in Salem, New Hampshire, in 1988 and another by the Mnemosyne Publishing Company in Miami, Florida, in 1969. If, as Meredith McGill has shown, all printings and reprintings mark the ways in which "the public investment in printed texts transforms them into something less and something more than ordinary commodities," surely this particular record of reprinting documents the uneven history of many layers of investment, of many different publics, or perhaps of what Marx called "the mystical value of the commodity" that transcends (or multiplies) its immediate use-value.[22] In 1838, the volume of Wheatley's poems that was published in London in 1773 and the volume of Horton's poems that was published in Raleigh, North Carolina, in 1829 were, as Richmond insisted, published together in Boston as an abolitionist tract; the poems in it were written by people who were treated as commodities and their poems were valued by people who objected to that political economy. As Honorée Fanonne Jeffers has pointed out, the emphasis on Wheatley as *African* in abolitionist reprintings of her poems in the 1830s gestures "to American Colonization Society ideology that blacks in America were only temporarily displaced from their African homeland(s), and should return."[23] Wheatley's status as "*Native African*" could thus serve that ideology's ends, which is to say that the value of her self-identification as "vent'rous *Afric*" operated in a very different economy—a very different discourse—in 1838 than it did in the discursive economy of her poem in 1772.

But in the 1988 reprint of the 1838 volume, it seems to be the one-hundred-and-fifty-year-old book itself that the Ayer Company considered valuable. Or perhaps what the 1988 reprint marked a "public investment in" was the earlier public investment in that nineteenth-century publication demonstrated by the 1969 reprint, because Mnemosyne Publishing Co. was begun that year by University of Miami English professor Frank Willis in collaboration with librarians

Reprint Edition, 1988
Ayer Company, Publishers, Inc.
382 Main Street
Salem, New Hampshire 03079

Entered, according to an Act of Congress, in the year 1838, by
ISAAC KNAPP,
in the Clerk's office of the District Court of Massachusetts.

First Mnemosyne reprinting 1969

**Reprinted from a copy in the
Fisk University Library Negro Collection.**

Copyright © 1969   Mnemosyne Publishing Co., Inc.   Miami, Florida

Library of Congress Catalog Card Number:
76-83898

ISBN 0-8369-8686-5
Printed in the United States of America

FIGURE P.1. Copyright page, *Memoir and Poems of Phillis Wheatley, A Native African and a Slave. Also, Poems by a Slave.* Boston: Isaac Knapp, 1838. Reprinted by Mnemosyne Publishing Co., Inc., Miami, Florida, 1969, and Ayer Company, Publishers, Inc., Salem, New Hampshire, 1988.

at Fisk University as "a collection of original black history and literature books that [Willis] knew every African-American student should have access to but didn't."[24] In that case, what the Ayer Company was valuing was the extant tradition of Black literary history made available to students at that historically Black university and to later scholars of Black literary history. While I share Jeffers's skepticism of the antiblack abolitionist politics of the 1830s editions, and though I am grateful to Frank Willis and the Fisk librarians for reprinting the Knapp edition, for me the value of this record of several different economies of literary value at the moment I saw it (over thirty years after its most recent reprinting, which will also probably be its last, now that the book is digitally available in several electronic archives) was also the uncanny appearance of the muse Wheatley had summoned, as if in belated answer to her call. There she is, Mnemosyne herself, a feminine figure personifying centuries of public investment, shifting categories of poetic value, changing circumstances of mediation and transmission, an apparently White representative of Western civilization signifying a Black counter-tradition and counter-public, a far from simple abstraction. She looked back at me from that cluttered printed and reprinted page, a graphic impersonation of a century of poetics worth remembering. A generic figure taking the place of a person, definitely not a commodity (though used as logo for "something less and something more than commodities"), Mnemosyne, like a poem, cannot speak for herself. This book does not give her voice, but it does invoke "her secret stores," the forgotten history of the many iterations and reiterations of her adventurous silence, the history of American lyric. *Mneme, begin.*

1

What History Does to Us

"We do view"

"*As Greece had a Plato why may we not have a Platoess?*" So James W. C. Pennington, Pastor of the Colored Congregational Church in Hartford, Connecticut, artfully introduces Ann Plato's *Essays; Including Biographies and Miscellaneous Pieces, in Prose and Poetry*, printed for the author in June, 1841.[1] By "we," Pennington means that "our young authoress justly appeals to *us*, her own people, (though not exclusively,) to give her success" (xix). Why "not exclusively"? "I am not in the habit of introducing myself or others to notice by the adjective 'colored,' &c.," Pennington writes, "but it seems proper that I should just say here that my authoress is a colored lady" (xvii). Because Pennington launches in print the print debut of "*our* young authoress," he acknowledges that the signature anonymity of publication, the fact that the objects of his and her address are by definition indeterminate, may not work in their favor: *we* may know who we are, but *you* could be anyone.[2] Simultaneously avowing and disavowing the genres of personal and impersonal address that Pennington understands the book's readers will attribute to both of them, he also introduces the enduring problem of racialized and sexualized reading: whoever you are opening Plato's book in the nineteenth century or inside this book in the twenty-first, you may or may not be one of *us*. Despite the fact that, as Frances Smith Foster writes, Plato probably "wrote for, and her book was marketed to, black people, especially young black girls," what Pennington's introductory remarks (and my introductory remarks) emphasize is not only the wayward address of print publication but the grammar of unremitting predication that Fred Moten describes as the "particular kind of failure" associated with blackness: "a constant economy and mechanics of fugitive making where the subject is hopelessly troubled by, in being emphatically detached from, the action whose agent it is supposed to be."[3] That predication and alienation of personal agency is also, of course, a classic description of the particular kind of failure associated with being a woman. Prefacing a book full of prefaces, Pennington imagines his subject as a new female philosopher of color who might be able to imagine in turn what no one else yet has: a scene of reading that would not be a scene of subjection, a way to suspend the economy and mechanics instantiated in fictions of race and gender, a genre of address or even a pronoun that could include all of us, a world in which things would be different.[4]

But that imaginary, intimately common world is not this one, and not even poetry—*especially* not poetry—can make it so.[5] As Pennington writes, warming to his subject, "the opinion has too far prevailed, that the talent for poetry is *exclusively* the legacy of nature" (xviii). Again, whatever is posited "exclusively"—race, tradition, individual talent, nature, sex, publicity— necessitates further qualification, and that necessity is infuriating. According to Pennington (echoing Wordsworth, Mill, Hegel, and a host of other theorists of Romantic poetics), "there is no doubt that the talent for poetry is in a high degree *attainable*," but the balance between nature and art is tricky: while Plato "has done well by what nature has done for her, in trying what art will add . . . the fact is, this is the only way to show the fallacy of that stupid theory, that *nature has done nothing but fit us for slaves, and that art cannot unfit us for slavery!*" (xviii). This *us* is not an us like the others. This *us* is the subject and object of stupid theories of poetics (and of nature and of personhood of everything else) that your misreading of us makes possible. This *us* is not something even a Platoess can redeem. Can any poet escape the perils of lyric reading?

If to read lyrically is to confuse the poem with the person, then what Pennington is saying—and what Plato will exemplify—is that we have a problem. Whatever we think of the then teenaged Ann Plato (whoever *we* are) will determine what we think of her poems. Yet few of us now think about Ann Plato or her poems at all, and few of us ever have. As Kenny J. Williams writes, Plato's poems are hard to recover (though the Schomburg Library of Nineteenth-Century Black Women Writers 1988 edition of Plato's book that Williams introduces is evidence of the attempt to do so) because "to some readers they might seem to be simply exercises in versification" (xlvii).[6] On this view, Plato was too young and too early and too undeveloped to make the transition that Mary Loeffelholz has described as the signature move of nineteenth-century women poets "from school to salon": "a shift from reading, reciting, writing, and publishing poetry in the didactic context of primary and secondary schooling to reading, reciting, and publishing poetry in the emergent later nineteenth-century venues of autonomous high culture."[7] Unlike the even earlier teenaged "'colored,' &c" Wheatley, whose poetry she read and rehearsed, Plato did not become an international or national or even local sensation on the basis of her first and only published book. As far as we know, she became a schoolteacher, at least for a while, and never published anything again. In any case, the book she did publish was slight (about six by four inches), cost about twenty-five cents, seems not to have been advertised, and it is unlikely that many of the limited number of copies "printed for the author" in Hartford were ever sold.[8]

There are definitely limitations to reading nineteenth-century American poems—especially abolitionist poems—"as if they were written or somehow destined for the readers of a *book*," as McGill has stressed.[9] There are also limitations to reading all books of poems as if they were written or somehow destined to be the same kind of thing, not least because, as Joanna Brooks has written, nineteenth-century books were not created equal, since "conditions of chronic discontinuity and disruption endemic to communities of color by reason of political and economic exploitation affect books and book cultures as well."[10] Plato's local publication for her community cannot be compared to the fancy London publication and transatlantic circulation of Wheatley's volume or, on the other hand, to the pamphlets, newspaper pages, broadsides, speeches, and manuscripts that, as McGill also emphasizes, were the popular media of poetry's nineteenth-century circulation. Yet part of the reason that Plato's poems may have failed to achieve the success for which Pennington prepared them is also that they are so generically impersonal, so tailor-made for the print public sphere. If Plato was a practitioner of "black aesthetics" in Evie Shockley's sense of a poet "whose subjectivity is produced by the experience of identifying or being interpellated as 'black' in the U.S.," a poet "actively working out a poetics in the context of a racist society" (and she was), the invisibility of that subjectivity within the aesthetically conventional, often feminized nineteenth-century genres of her work has made that practice hard to see.[11] Pennington may have been anxious that readers would judge Plato's book by the age, race, and sex of its "authoress," but later readers have worried that the book makes Ann Plato impossible to find. In Plato's twenty poems, the subject is so emphatically detached from the action whose agent it is supposed to be that she hardly seems to be there at all.

Consider the first stanza of "To the First of August," a poem so generic that one of the few critics who has commented on it is reduced to saying that Plato "certainly exhibits no passionate or elated response in writing about the end of slavery in the British Caribbean," the event that is the poem's occasion:[12]

> Britannia's isles proclaim,
>   That freedom is their theme;
> And we do view those honor'd lands
>   With soul-delighting mien.[13]

One reason that this is such a difficult poem to read is that it looks so easy. Its difficulty is nothing like the difficulty associated with British Romantic lyric (say, with Keats's great odes), since Plato's poem is difficult because it poses little hermeneutic challenge and neither expresses nor solicits much emotion. Whoever *we* are in the quatrain's third line, the reason that our identity is confusing is neither interpretive nor affective, exactly. This difficulty feels historical, but not Romantic. The common meter lines appear so metrically facile that their very facility becomes their difficulty, and if the assonance, or off-rhyme between "theme" and "mien" is hard to read, that is not because one is moved by it or wonders what it means. (Even Britannia seems to be doing a school assignment here.) That difficult facility is thus also nothing like the exacting and fragmented modern poems that Charles Bernstein jokingly ascribes to "the early years of the last century, when a great deal of social dislocation precipitated the outbreak of 1912, one of the best known epidemics of difficult poetry."[14] As literary critics became professional interpreters of sophisticated Romantic bafflement and doctors tending to the modern outbreak of broken form, they left everyday poems like Plato's behind in the American nineteenth century where they belonged.[15] The British-Romanticism-to-American-modernism-to-post-modernism, Shelley-to-Stevens-to-Ashbery narrative of the history of American poetry is still so common that not only relatively obscure poets like Plato but also famous poets like Wheatley, Sigourney, Bryant, Horton, Longfellow, Jackson, Harper, and Dunbar have been left out of it.

Of course, all-White-mostly-male histories of American poetry that pretty much skip the nineteenth century have been and are still being written, and when Terrance Hayes begins one of his *American Sonnets for My Past and Future Assassin* with the lines, "The black poet would love to say his century began / With Hughes, or God forbid, Wheatley," he invokes a century of histories of African American poetry that struggle to incorporate Black poets writing before 1900.[16] Almost half a century ago, Sherman wrote that, despite the foundational histories of Black poetry written in the twentieth century by Benjamin Brawley, James Weldon Johnson, Redding, Sterling Brown, Jean

Wagner, and others, "Afro-Americans of the nineteenth century are the invisible poets of our national literature"—and, as I began this book by suggesting, as far as the stories we tell about the history and theory of American poetics go, this is still very much the case.[17] Rarely if ever is the intricate relation between the poetics of the nineteenth century and the poetics of the twentieth and twenty-first centuries narrated in its raced and gendered complexity. This book puts late eighteenth- and early nineteenth-century American poetics back into the transatlantic history and theory of poetics, but not by nationalizing that poetics or by aligning it with Romantic lyric theory or by making nineteenth-century American poets harbingers of modern "social dislocation," and not by separating poets into raced and gendered traditions. Transatlanticism, nationalism, Romanticism, modernism, the Black radical poetic tradition, the apparently dominant tradition of American poetic whiteness, the emergence of the category of World Poetry, and feminized and masculinized poetics are intertwined in this book, difficult to extricate from one another because their development was so mutually informing, so collaterally formed.

And *that* is because Ann Plato and the poets who preceded and succeeded her in the United States in the late eighteenth and first half of the nineteenth centuries made retroactive ideas of national poetics and Anglophilic Romantic poetics and comparative modern poetics and definitely raced and gendered poetics possible in the first place by inventing the modern poetic genre we now think of as lyric—or, since almost all poetry is now understood as lyric, by inventing the genre we now think of as poetry by inventing the idea that poetry (unlike prose) could *be* a single genre.[18] Not incidentally, the American nineteenth century also witnessed the invention of the idea that White, Black, Indigenous, Spanish American, Asian American, and many other people could be single genres (or kinds, or races, or cultures, or ethnicities), which is why those terms are capitalized throughout this book. As Kwame Anthony Appiah writes, the point of such capitalization is to emphasize that race is a social rather than a natural entity: "White people don't deserve a lower-case *w* and shouldn't be allowed to claim it," Appiah quotes the philosopher Sally Haslanger as arguing; since "racial identities were not discovered but created . . . we must all take responsibility for them. Don't let them disguise themselves as common nouns and adjectives." While capitalizing White risks echoing the practice of White supremacists, Appiah argues that "you could argue that it's the other way around: If the capitalization of *White* became standard among anti-racists, . . . Supremacists would have to find another way to ennoble themselves."[19] This is not to say that capitalization solves the problem.

Far from it! Capitalization emphasizes the intransigent mess of the discourses attached to race in America. It is also not to say that there were not lyric poems before the nineteenth century or before America or before modern racialization—of course there were. It is only to say that as all racial designations have been historically constructed in relation to the discourse of White supremacy, so all poetic designations have been historically constructed in relation to a lyricized idea of what poetry is and was. Neither whiteness nor lyric naturally or inevitably became a transcendent idea about people or poems.

On the contrary, while most poetry is now thought of as lyric, not all poetry has always been understood as lyric, and lyric has not always been understood exclusively (as Pennington might say) as *our* personal expression. As I wrote in my definition of lyric for the most recent edition of *The Princeton Encyclopedia of Poetry and Poetics* (2012),

> In Western poetics, almost all poetry is now characterized as *lyric*, but this has not always been the case. Over the last three centuries, *lyric* has shifted its meaning from adjective to noun, from a quality in poetry to a category that can seem to include nearly all verse. The ancient, medieval, and early modern verse we now think of as lyric was made up of a variety of songs or short occasional poems. Since the eighteenth century, brevity, subjectivity, passion, and sensuality have been the qualities associated with poems called *lyric*; thus, in modernity the term is used for a kind of poetry that expresses personal feeling (G.W.F. Hegel) in a concentrated and harmoniously arranged form (E. A. Poe, S. T. Coleridge) and that is indirectly addressed to the private reader (William Wordsworth, John Stuart Mill). A modern invention, this idea of lyric has profoundly influenced how we understand all poetic genres.[20]

The encyclopedia entry calls for such general claims, though these claims may seem to have more to do with the long and uneven process of lyricization than with *the lyric* as such. I do think that ideas of lyric are differential and historically contingent, made rather than given, and in the entry I pointed to some of the complexity of those differences and contingencies in various European and especially anglocentric periods and places. I now realize that since the *Princeton Encyclopedia* is an American publication devoted to a comparative perspective, my definition also inherited a racist idea of lyric from the nineteenth-century American poetics that definition said nothing about.

This is partially because, as you will have noticed from the smattering of men's names in the definition's first paragraph, part of that inheritance means thinking of *the* lyric (especially "in Western poetics") as White, or really on not acknowledging that such thinking is racialized (which comes to the same thing), even when one is trying to complicate the definite article. In this book, I will show that this very White idea of lyric is in fact a raced illusion that was composed in response to Black and Indigenous figures in late eighteenth- and early nineteenth-century American poetics, but it was also an illusion firmly grounded in a history of American lyricization in which Black poets framed it as a raced and gendered imaginary. Indigenous poets did, too, especially by the end of the nineteenth century, as did Spanish American and, later, Asian American poets, but I focus here on the dialectical relation between Black and White poetics because that dialectic was so foundational to the poetry of the early nineteenth century—and because I cannot claim to make this book comprehensive. As Kirsten Silva Gruesz has shown, nineteenth-century Latinx poetic identities were "grounded in a larger web of transamerican perceptions and contacts" rather than in "lost texts from the Spanish borderlands," and in this book I also hope to show that many versions of Black poetics were internal rather than marginal to the larger web of American poetics.[21] As we shall see in chapters 4 and 5, Hispanophiles William Cullen Bryant and Henry Wadsworth Longfellow laid much of the institutional groundwork for nineteenth-century White American poetics, and transamerican, Indigenous, and Black "perceptions and contacts" were entwined with one another from the beginning. Manu Samitri Chander has called the nineteenth-century colonial poets writing as subjects of the British Empire "Brown Romantics," and has suggested that "the formal characteristics of Brown Romanticism that initially struck the critics as derivative and imitative actually served to expose the Eurocentric racism informing the very tradition in which they wrote."[22] I would like to suggest something similar here about BIPOC (Black, Indigenous, and people of color) American Romanticism, but especially about the poets involved in what Matt Sandler has called "the Black Romantic revolution" in the nineteenth century. While the history of American racialization certainly cannot be reduced to an image in black and white, in this book I am concerned with the ways in which "the afterlife of slavery" (to use Saidiya Hartman's phrase) emerged from and in and as the history of American poetics that began when slavery was still very much alive.

I take Stephen Best's point that while "attempts to root blackness in the horror of slavery" may feel "intuitively correct," they also invite us "to long for the return of a sociality" most modern readers may never have experienced, especially not as a collective that can be designated in and as the first-person plural.[23] But late eighteenth- and early nineteenth-century Black poets were often even more skeptical of the communal identity assumed by that first-person plural than later readers may be. Because they participated in a history in which collective identities and the poetic genres attached to them were in the process of being formed, poets were the architects as well as the critics of raced versions of collective representation—and those versions often responded to and included writers composing in Spanish and French or were racialized by way of Indigenous and Orientalized figures. Racialization and lyricization worked hand in hand to become Black and White, but neither the history of poetics nor the history of race began as a coherent genre of either poems or persons.

That is because in the first half of the nineteenth century, when slavery was not yet in its afterlife, many poets gradually and unevenly, at different times and in different places and for a variety of reasons, modified popular verse genres that addressed a wide range of real and imaginary publics (ballads that invoked and addressed a "folk"; hymns that addressed a congregation; "sorrow songs" that addressed the enslaved; national anthems that addressed White male citizens; elegies that addressed mourners; odes that addressed monuments, occasions, parks, stars, or the wind; gallows confessions that addressed witnesses to the execution; drinking songs that addressed drunkards or antidrunkards; epistles that addressed real or fictive correspondents, and so on and on), collapsing (or blurring, or combining, or abstracting) them into a literary, lyricized idea of poetry as the expression of a fictive speaker addressing him/her/their/itself to everyone and no one, that replaced the genre of the poem with the genre of the person (or, as in the case of birds or stars, with personified nonpersons). Black poets and women poets saw early and often that lyric's abstract communal subjective tendencies came at their expense. They pushed back by demonstrating the alienation of that abstraction from historical persons, and it is this response that has shaped modern ideas of lyric as what Adorno would call "the expression of a social antagonism." Of course, though this is the second time I have invoked Adorno's useful idea, a German Marxist philosopher did not sum up the poetics of the American nineteenth century. Actually, the social antagonisms that informed nineteenth-century American poetics made the modern lyric Adorno had in mind pale in comparison, which is why we need a Platoess to show us the way back to them. The invention of American lyric may have begun as a White supremacist project, as White poets in the nineteenth century constructed a lyricized poetics of universal personal representation, but American lyric was actually shaped and delivered to modernism by poets who had more in common with Ann Plato than with, say, Ralph Waldo Emerson. This is because it was the inherent conflict, the dialectical relation between Black and White poetics in the nineteenth century that came to shape the history and theory of American poetry for the next two hundred years. As that conflict eventuated in the transformation of many genres of verse address into one speaking genre, Black poets like Plato transformed the default whiteness of that genre's capacious speech.

"The rising race"

The genres of Plato's address in "To the First of August"—hymn, ode, anthem, "First of August" abolitionist poem, transatlantic Romantic poem— don't merge into a song of herself, into the utterance of a single speaker or a singular collective. Mae Gwendolyn Henderson's theory that Black women writers "speak in tongues" in the sense that they "speak in a plurality of voices as well as in a multiplicity of discourses" helps to explain why not, but it is also not clear that Plato is the one speaking here at all.[24] Unlike Frederick Douglass's fierce abolitionist Fourth of July address marking the date to which the popular genre of "First of August" poems were an antithetical response, Plato's poem never explicitly says, "The blessings in which you, this day, rejoice, are not enjoyed in common."[25] Instead, the poem makes what is common more difficult to locate. In the first stanza, it seems safe to assume that this quasi-Pindaric ode commemorating a public occasion addresses a public the poet also represents: as people considered "'colored' &c.," we know that while some of us (members of the Talcott Street, or Colored Congregational Church in Hartford, for instance) may be free, most of us in the United States in 1841 were not. But as the poem goes on, the stability of this *we* begins to waver:

> And unto those they held in gloom,
>   Gave ev'ry one their right;
> They did disdain fell slavery's shade,
>   And trust in freedom's light.
>
> Then unto ev'ry British blood,
>   Their noble worth revere,
> And think them ever noble men,
>   And like them, hence appear.

The possible allusion to Wheatley in Plato's use of "gloom" to characterize the state of enslavement makes that state seem bygone and poetic (since in Wheatley's "To the University of Cambridge, in New-England," "The land of error, and *Egyptian* gloom" describes the poet's free life in Africa rather than her enslaved life in America), but the cancelled rhyme between "gloom" and "shade" is enough to let us know that this history is unfinished (and in any case, in both the eighteenth and nineteenth centuries, "gloom" was common poetic parlance for enslavement). As "they" have the power to issue proclamations that "give ev'ry one" the right everyone should already have had, "we" seem to have no such power.

Or no such personhood. The personification of "Britannia's isles" means that not only can they "proclaim" their "theme," but they can also change their collective mind. And what can *we* do? "Fell slavery" shamefully possesses "shade," freedom redemptively possesses "light," but what do *we* possess? We are asked to pay tribute to "ev'ry British blood" (to every Anglo person?), but how could we "like them, hence appear"? Perhaps this is an instance of what Ivy Wilson calls Plato's "latent concern with tone"; perhaps it is an instance of what Frank Wilderson III calls (after Orlando Patterson) "social death," the in-between state that Claudia Rankine describes as a way of being "there-but-not-there . . . in a historically antiblack society"; perhaps it is a symptom of what Joseph Rezek calls "the racialization of print."[26] Perhaps what Sylvia Wynter would have called "this referent-*we*" has shifted from naturally to poetically marked (though "blood" blurs such literal/figural distinctions), since to be like these White British men, White American men would need to abolish slavery.[27] Yet "hence appear" stops short of action, and in the next two stanzas our collective agency leaps across the Atlantic in a single bound:

And when on Britain's isles remote,
　　We're then in freedom's bounds,
And while we stand on British ground,
　　You're free,—you're free,—resounds.

Lift ye that country's banner high,
　　And may it nobly wave,
Until beneath the azure sky,
　　Man shall be no more a slave.

This *we* appears continuous with the *we* of the first stanza, so rather than viewing British emancipation from afar, either we have emigrated to the British

West Indies or we can fancy ourselves there. But even in this fantasy future, it is not our voice but someone else's (Britannia's? the voice of the islands themselves? a sound emanating from "British ground"?) that says we are free. All we can do in response is to become British citizens of the mind, since this speech act only works within those "bounds," as if "that country's banner" did not signify an empire but an "azure," impersonal human condition in which "Man shall be no more a slave."

This line is jarring because of the ontological shift entailed in its exchange of personal pronouns. "It must be seen that the ordinary definition of the personal pronouns as containing the three terms *I, you,* and *he,* simply destroys the notion of 'person,'" the linguist Émile Benveniste avers, since "'person' belongs only to *I/you* and is lacking in *he.*"[28] The address that enacts emancipation (*"You're free—you're free—"*) happens a world away from the categorical statement about what "Man shall be." Can a man be "a slave" and a person? What about a woman who, like Ann Plato, was not enslaved but was also not a legally recognized person? And what about the first-person plural? If emancipation is enacted only in "that country," then are *we* persons, or are we like *he,* some version of pronoun that "simply destroys the notion of 'person'"? Or is Plato suggesting that what Zakiyyah Iman Jackson (after Sylvia Wynter) has called "the violence of humanization or the burden of inclusion into a racially hierarchized universal humanity" is too great an imposition, that the land of "the azure sky" may be preferable to being rendered such a legally designated emancipated person?[29] The least we can say is that whoever or whatever utters this categorical universal proclamation, it is not the voice that speaks in the poem's last two stanzas:

And oh! When youth's extatic hour,
    When winds and torrents foam,
And passion's flowing noon are past,
    To bless that free born home;

Then let us celebrate the day,
    And lay the thought to heart,
And teach the rising race the way,
    That they may not depart.

If we have no voice to "proclaim" our own freedom, then perhaps in a generation we will be able to "celebrate the day" that slavery ended an ocean and a lifetime away, in turn "teaching" the next generation—what, exactly?

Katherine Clay Bassard suggests that "as a member of a truly autonomous community of free blacks, Plato envisions the transformation of society as a function of time."[30] "The way" certainly sounds promising, and given the hymnal meter, decidedly Congregationalist. But are *we* "the rising race"? If so, why and how have we become "they"? There is something stranger than history in this further pronominal shift, especially because the reason we are teaching them the way is so "they may not depart." Depart from where? Where to? Again, we are caught between pronouns that personalize and depersonalize at the same time. Are "they" now in the British Empire or in America? Has emancipation leaped back across the ocean in this speculative future? If the "us" in the first line of the final stanza is held at a temporal arm's-length distance by that line's "Then . . . ," the "they" of that stanza's last line is held at a much greater epistemic distance from "us." Are *we* or *they* "the rising race"? Both our pedagogical position and the definite article disidentify *us* from this abstraction, though the introduction of "race" into what has so far been a discourse of nationalism, slavery, unnamed whiteness, and freedom is enough to shake us up. "Race" is a term that Pennington went out of his way not to use, and for good reason: his invocation of the surplus adjective "colored &c." emphasizes the arbitrary imposition of racialization and its proliferating definitional qualifications, while "race" was a term newly essentialized by all kinds of theories by 1841. As Nicholas Hudson writes, over the long eighteenth century, "'race' gradually mutated from its original sense of a people or single nation, linked by origin, to its later sense of a biological subdivision of the human species." By the mid-nineteenth century, according to Hudson, "'race' meant more than just a 'lineage' or even a variation of the human species induced by climate or custom. It meant a fixed disparity in the physical and intellectual make-up of different peoples."[31] In other words, by 1841 "race" was a racist term, a symptom of what James Brewer Stewart calls the "harsh new spirit of modern racial essentialism."[32]

That point has been made many times in many ways, but as history would have it, James Pennington was one of the first Black intellectuals to make it in print. Pennington escaped from enslavement at nineteen, was active in abolitionist circles in Brooklyn, New York, was the first Black student to attend Yale, was involved in the *Amistad* case, performed the marriage between Frederick Douglass and Anna Murray shortly after Douglass's escape, and, like William Wells Brown, later took refuge from the consequences of the Fugitive Slave Law in Scotland, England, and Europe, lecturing widely (and thus enacting the transatlantic divide that was the subject of Plato's poem). In 1841, the same year that he introduced Plato's writings, Pennington published *A Text Book of the Origin and History, &c. &c. of the Colored People*, in which he is at pains to disprove what Ibram Kendi calls "the curse theory" that claimed that Africans were descendants of Hamm or Cain, and thus "stamped from the beginning."[33] Then, as Britt Rusert has shown, Pennington moves from the older biblical defense of slavery and monogenesis to the new theories of polygenesis, crafting "an ethnology" of Africanness that runs counter to the racial science that emerged in the 1830s.[34] Though it begins as a biblical refutation and scientific critique, Pennington's book ultimately becomes an ambitious challenge to the idea of race itself. But that did not make Pennington an advocate for what might now be called the category of the post-racial—far from it. Pennington would agree with Ta-Nehisi Coates that "race is the child of racism, not the father," but one hundred and seventy-five years before Coates wrote that sentence, Pennington was worried about the implications of such genealogical metaphors for critical race theory.[35] The book joined a growing chorus of responses by Black thinkers to the antiblack theories embedded in Jefferson's *Notes on the State of Virginia*, but as Rusert suggests, the most striking thing about Pennington's book is its "highly imaginative and speculative act of reconstructing kinship," its pitched refusal of the tenets of racialization and at the same time its construction of a web of intimate social relations for the collective vulnerability of people whose lived experience was structured by those theories.[36] We will return to responses to Jefferson's racism and to those theories in chapter 3 of this book, but for now the important point is that for his part, Pennington was devoted to defining a *we* that our Platoess could represent between or in spite of them.

So why does the last line of Plato's poem embrace the "fixed disparity" of the racial concept Pennington so strenuously argued against? I don't think it does, exactly, but this line does tell us a lot about the desire for such categories, for the poetic voice of "a people" represented by an exemplary person, for variations on what Katie Trumpener has called a "bardic nationalism."[37] As Best has written, "a communitarian impulse runs deep within black studies," and a communitarian impulse certainly runs deep within the history of poetics.[38] But that impulse should not lead us to think that the *we* of Plato's poem is racially or poetically continuous with, well, with *us*. Since as Hortense Spillers writes, "the personal pronouns are offered in the service of a collective function," the trick is to understand the collective they represent.[39] Because in 1841 the twinned processes of lyricization and racialization were taking their mutually informed shapes but were not yet fully accomplished, Plato's poem was not a bardic performance of what everyone with whom she identified or whom she represented felt or believed, nor was it made of a set of strategies the poet adopted in order to express her personal objection to and departure from received ideas. While Pennington and others were trying to unravel the new scientific racial essentialism in their speculative versions of what Rusert calls "fugitive science," Plato and others were subtly making the racist discourses embedded in poetic genres themselves more fugitive.

Common meter was itself a discourse that divided popular from elite verse, folk from literary composition in 1841.[40] By Plato's time, it was associated with both Black and White psalmody. As her poem took the meter of congregational song, so Plato's discourse addressed the shifting collective identities that metrical discourse itself made manifest. "They may not depart" because the plural third person in that discourse could not be aligned with the plural first person, at least not securely. The lines echo the language of Proverbs 22:6, which in the King James reads, "Train up a child in the way he should go / And when he is old he will not depart from it." This biblical echo takes over the sense of the lines, making them seem obedient to scripture, but again, that echo comes at the expense of any sense of definite agency. If "the rising race" is in its infancy and "we" have grown old, then has the abolition of slavery in the British colonies made race something it was not before? Over the course of the poem as a whole, nation, colony, country, liberty and slavery give way to the newly coined idea of a "rising race," but that race is divided from *us*, divided from "the notion of 'person.'" This may be because, as Hartman writes, "The slave is neither civic man nor free worker but excluded from the narrative of 'we the people' that effects the linkage of the modern individual and the state," but it is also because the individual was never what was at stake in this poem.[41] The fifth stanza's categorical trimeter assertion that "Man shall be no more a slave" is not only an experiment in what freedom will "then" feel like "on Britain's isles remote," but an experiment in the category best matched to this new category of person: "Man"? "British blood"? "Azure sky"? "Rising race"? Whoever we are, our collective identity can only be named as what we are not.

As it happened, the representation of the First of August as what *we* were not was on spectacular display in two issues of *The Colored American* where we do view the scene that seems to have inspired Plato's poem. In the summer of 1840, when Plato was preparing her book for publication, that newspaper (in which she would publish her first poem in September of that year) printed two announcements of the "Emancipation of the Slaves in the British West-India Islands," accompanied by illustrations of Britannia's personified power (figures 1.1 and 1.2).

BRITANNIA GIVING FREEDOM TO HER SLAVES.

FIGURE 1.1. "Britannia Giving Freedom to Her Slaves," from *The Colored American*, May 9, 1840.

FIRST OF AUGUST.

FIGURE 1.2. "First of August," from *The Colored American*, August 1, 1840.

In the May announcement (figure 1.1), "Britannia Giving Freedom to Her Slaves," a White goddess (a latter-day Mnemosyne) reminiscent of second-century Roman rule in ancient Britain, complete with Corinthian helmet (a figure for Western empire popularized in eighteenth-century British land-grabs) hands a small book to a shirtless Black man while cradling a long spear. With her other hand, the goddess points to the sky, and with his other hand, the man holds the scythe of a field laborer. Behind the man is a woman holding a baby and at least one other child. The woman looks at the viewer/reader sideways, and behind her another man and woman raise their hands in grati-tude or prayer. Beneath Britannia's feet, remnants of whips and chains lie next to her cornucopia and her shield. In the later issue, titled "First of August" (figure 1.2), a gigantic White figure of a more modern unarmed woman, her now unhelmeted hair flowing, gestures toward a group of people while she holds her book aloft; to her left (our right), an American flag stands behind another group, including a White man who may be preaching, a man carrying a whip, and a young White woman surrounded by Black children learning their ABCs. Both illustrations feature a singular, luminously white, finely etched, larger-than-life feminized figure of Anglo power set against compli-cated groups of multiple darkly shaded, practically featureless human-shaped figures variously gendered and aged. Both Britannias personify and ventrilo-quize a long multiply populated gloomy juridico-political history as a su-premely singular White divine gift.

The May announcement tells some of that history, stating that "by an act of the British Parliament passed in 1833, slavery was to cease in all British West India Islands on the 1st of August, 1834, and a system of apprenticeship to be sub-stituted in its place till the 1st of August, 1840; when that system was to terminate, and entire freedom to be consummated." So despite its portrayal in Plato's poem and in the illustrations addressed to readers of *The Colored American*, emanci-pation in the British West Indies was not a punctual event, and it was certainly not an act performed by a supernatural woman. Or maybe it was: as the May issue goes on to explain, "twenty millions sterling, or about ninety millions dollars" (money that bore the imprint of the goddess Britannia) was paid by Parliament "to the masters" in exchange for the people they claimed to own. The "masters" in Antigua and Bermuda took the money and released enslaved people in 1834, but "in the other Islands, the apprenticeship system was adopted." Yet

> contrary to general expectation, entire abolition was found to operate far
> better than the other plan; insomuch that there began ere long to be no

little stir in relation to the subject. The cry for complete emancipation in all the Islands arose from all quarters; the tables of the British Parliament were heaped with petitions; the country was agitated from end to end. In this state of things, when all was commotion, uncertainty, anxiety, and suspence, the Colonial Governments put an end to the matter of abolishing the apprenticeship themselves, to take effect on the 1st of August, 1838. To give the finishing touch to this work of emancipation, the British Government, on learning these movements of the Colonial Legislatures, proceeded to abolish the system in the remaining Colonies that had no Legislatures. (vol 1, no. 10, 4)

What really happened between 1833 and 1840 was that Britain purchased enslaved Africans in the West Indies from the men who thought they owned them, thus upholding these men's legal claim. The British Parliament then devised its own version of temporary enslavement in the form of indentured servitude. When there was a "cry . . . from all quarters" and several instances of violent resistance objecting to such continued violation of natural rights, some colonies took matters into their own hands. After much "commotion, uncertainty, anxiety, and suspence"—that is, on the brink of another colonial revolution—"the British Government . . . proceeded to abolish the system" several years after it first promised to do so.

In fact, as the writers of this article in *The Colored American* and Ann Plato and everyone else knew, the First of August had been trying to happen for a long time. After the Haitian Revolution of 1789–1804, which C.L.R. James succinctly and memorably dubbed "the only successful slave revolt in history," the British Empire knew its days in "the sugar islands" were numbered.[42] That knowledge was an open secret, since as Marlene Daut has argued, the "transatlantic print culture of the Haitian Revolution" broadcast it far and wide in "hundreds, perhaps even thousands, of written texts that took the form of eye-witness accounts, letters, memoirs, history, novels, poetry, plays, and newspaper articles."[43] Actually, as Cedric Robinson has shown, African resistance to the Slave Registry had already destabilized British colonial power by the early nineteenth century, and the sugar plantations had been losing money for a long time.[44] And as Julius S. Scott has made clear, "by 1793, the continuing rebellion of blacks and people of color in Saint-Domingue provided a rallying point for would-be revolutionaries in other areas, and curtailing the movement of people and ideas had become a paramount issue for the rulers in English- and Spanish-speaking territories."[45]

This is all to say (or to let the experts say) that the most visible historical events in the late eighteenth-century Black Atlantic—the obscene mass murder on board the *Zong* in 1781 and before that what the historian David Waldstreicher has called "the Mansfieldian moment" of the 1770s, when Lord Mansfield, the chief justice of the Court of the King's Bench, decided in favor of James Somerset's right not to be returned from England to enslavement in the West Indies, and after that, the Haitian Revolution—all punctuated an ongoing and unsustainable extractive racial capitalism that underwrote repeated proclamations of British enlightenment.[46] The Mansfield decision in particular "immediately set off a wave of speculation about the end of slavery in England that was framed by the black community there," Waldstreicher writes, "because it politicized slavery and slavery-ized politics" (534). We will return to the slavery-izing of late eighteenth-century colonial politics and poetics in chapter 3, but it's important to note here that after the supposedly revolutionary Mansfield decision and even after the spectacularly violent *Zong* case, it took Parliament seven decades to abolish slavery in its colonies and it took ninety-five more years for its former North American colony to do so. History is violent and unjust and messy and uneven and populous and racist and misogynist and compromised and everyone celebrating the First of August in 1840 knew that. As J. R. Kerr-Ritchie has written, "public celebrations of West Indian emancipation in the Atlantic World" drew attention to the way in which "between 1834 and 1861, slavery became abolished in the British Empire but expanded in the United States."[47] Ann Plato lived and wrote in a former British colony in which the disarray of history had eventuated in slavery's expansion rather than even a piecemeal form of abolition, so why did her poem embrace the White Goddess fantasy version of events?

An Imaginary Person

I wish I could urge us to read Plato's poem as an instance of what Lauren Berlant dubbed "Diva Citizenship," which they described as "a moment of emergence that marks unrealized potentials for subaltern political activity."[48] Berlant wrote that these glimpses of unrealized potential tend to emerge when "acts of language can feel like explosives that shake the ground of political existence. . . . In remaking the scene of collective life into a spectacle of subjectivity," such moments "can lead to a confusion of willful and memorable rhetorical performance with sustained social change itself" (223). But Plato's poem was not such a performance, since the only diva in it is a giant feminized White su-

premacist being. Plato's poem does not remake the scene of blurred and si-
lenced collective life into a scene of subjectivity (as, for example, M. NourbeSe
Philip did in her 2008 *Zong!*); instead, Britannia bestows social change on a
scene of collective life that Britannia cannot represent.[49] How could she? Since
personifications by definition have no subjectivity, this White Britannia is a
perfect foil for the individual and distributed subjectivities the poem evokes
by not being able to articulate: not national, not colonial, not racial, not gram-
matical, not gendered or sexualized, not even Christian discourse can consti-
tute a first-person plural pronoun—an *us*—that will stick, let alone achieve
imaginary citizenship or construct a national fantasy of spectacular
subjectivity—except, again, as what *we* do not have, as what looms over and
withholds in order to pretend to bestow ourselves to *us*.

Yet I have been suggesting that Plato's poem (like Wheatley's "Recollec-
tion") is for that very reason both a corrective to and an exemplary instance of
a history in which poetry has embraced such fantasies so intimately that po-
etry has become another name for them. Just as one epistemic beginning of
transatlantic concepts and histories of race emerged over the nineteenth
century, so one epistemic beginning of transatlantic concepts and histories of
poetics emerged then, too. As McGill has written, "slavery is not just one
theme among others in a poetic tradition that remained stable across the cen-
turies it took to abolish the trade, emancipate the enslaved, and petition for
some measure of acknowledgement and redress. The history of Anglo-
American poetry was itself transformed by its encounter with the slave sys-
tem."[50] As we shall see in chapter 3, as early as the 1770s, Wheatley (in what
Waldstreicher has called "the Wheatleyan moment") was attributing "silken
fetters" and "soft captivity" to acts of a feminized poetic imagination: ideas
about collective identity and ideas about poetry emerged together in and as
ideas about race, slavery, settler colonialism, the Atlantic world, gender, and
sexuality over the long nineteenth century, and in this book I try to show you
how that happened, poem by poem.[51] Since, as Simon Gikandi has written,
"in the American and West Indian colonies . . . ideals of taste could not be
imagined or secured except in opposition to a negative sensorium associated
with slavery," we will see how American poetics came to depend on an ideal
of individual poetic freedom from "slavish" meter's "silken fetters" (which is
one reason you may not like poems like Plato's, or indeed, why you may not
like most of the poems in this book).[52] As Meredith Martin writes, "the
conventional narrative of English meter's evolution from 'regular' to 'free'
maps usefully onto ideas of progress and expansion, of empire as well as of

social democracy" as well as onto the sophistication of aesthetic sensibility, but the very language we use for the origin and aim of this conventional narrative also maps onto the "sensorium associated with slavery."[53] As Cavitch puts it, "it should come as no surprise that nineteenth-century prosodic discourse is broadly inflected by the language of slavery."[54] Yet that obvious inflection does continue to surprise literary historians, since it has not been understood as the racialization of the structure of American poetics itself.

Like McGill and Cavitch and Martin, I am a scholar of historical poetics, and, as I have already suggested, I consider prosodic and rhetorical genres part and parcel of the long process of lyricization that began in the eighteenth century and continues into the twenty-first. In that process, those genres have become increasingly abstract and at the same time increasingly identified with an imaginary rather than a historical person. In the figure of that imaginary person, we can see the economy and mechanics of racialization writ large. If by the 1930s, that imaginary person would come to be called "the speaker" of the poem, that may be because the definite article tells you all you really need to know about just how abstract (literally, removed, or taken out of place) that speaker came to be. When we read a poem as an address on the part of "the speaker" to any and all of us who can put ourselves in his/her/their place (since the definite article makes sure that speaker has no definite pronoun), we make ourselves into a choral *we* performing a readerly karaoke that solves the problems of collective identity that Plato's poem so eloquently poses. This is to say that the figure of the speaker allows us to make ourselves into a public, a notion that, as Michael Warner writes, "enables a reflexivity in the circulation of texts among strangers who become, by virtue of their reflexively circulating discourse, a social entity."[55] The lyric speaker functions as a metadiscursive phenomenon, doing all the things a person does (including addressing us as if that address were personal) without actually being one, thus organizing *us* around that abstraction.

But Plato's poem was addressed to a public that was still in the process of forming itself around such figurative persons, that more often formed itself as a social entity on the basis of the genre of the poem rather than the genre of the person. We know from the title that the poem joins a long eighteenth-century tradition of "Pindaricks," of variations on choral song for public occasions, and as have seen, we know from the meter that this choral ode is also a choral hymn. The last line of the penultimate stanza locates our "free born home" in a particular hymn that may well have been sung in Hartford's Talcott Street Congregational Church but that later became a Confederate marching song (and even later, a "free trade" labor-organizing song). That slide from Black spiritual to White Christian national anthem to portable secular song is also evident in Plato's poem, but the diva meta-citizenship of Britannia is just what the choral performance of "To the First of August" cannot claim. Pindaric ode, Black hymn, White hymn, "sorrow song," "spiritual," abolitionist poem, First of August poem, ekphrastic response, newspaper poem, workers' song, proverb poem, Bible lesson all blur into a genre that merges these dissonant parts, if it does, under the aegis of a hovering figure of a very abstract person that bears a striking resemblance to Britannia and that provided the rhyming template for Pennington's "Platoess."

In the nineteenth century, that figure would have been recognizable as the *Poetess*, a "generic figure," as Yopie Prins writes, "with a long and various history, often connected to popular poetry with broad national and international circulation."[56] In several parts of this book, but especially in chapter 5, I elaborate some of the ways in which that generic figure was adopted by various poets, but first it's important to note that the Poetess is capitalized because it is a fabricated abstraction, and in the nineteenth century especially, it was acknowledged as a larger-than-life fictional public person, a cartoon "authoress," an imaginary performance rather than a particular woman poet, which is why women and men, straight poets and queer poets and trans poets could all inhabit the figure. Eliza Richards has written of Edgar Allan Poe's Poetess performances, of "a male genius figure who impersonates women poets, and women poets who personify mimesis," and we could extend Richards's insight to consider the construction of the figure of the Poetess as well as Longfellow's learnedly capacious and Walt Whitman's capaciously queer embrace of the Poetess pose.[57] "As a detachable figure that exceeded the work of any actual woman poet," Prins explains, "the Poetess became a repeatable trope, a personification" (1052), and that personification became another genre that could contain (or, like Britannia, overwhelm) popular genres of address that were often in conflict with one another. As Pennington's rhyming pun indicates, Plato's poem would be associated with this figure (as indeed, all poems by women poets tended to be), but it also keeps its distance from it. Just as Plato's poem is almost but not quite an ode or a hymn, it is almost but not quite Poetess verse.

Indeed, because nineteenth-century American poetics turned the genre of the poem into the genre of the person, the fact that the Poetess was already a genericized person means that Poetess verse gives us a view into the economy and mechanics of lyricization, the process under way but not yet realized in

Plato's poem. As a figure made to order for the poetics of vicarious feeling, the Poetess herself was often depicted as silenced, wounded, or dead, and even her themes tended toward self-sacrifice (picture the nightingale with her breast upon a thorn, the boy on the burning deck, the tribe driven from its land, the enslaved mother whose baby is sold, the angelic child who dies very young). As Alexandra Socarides has written, self-cancellation rather than self-promotion was the secret strategy that made Poetess verse so popular, since "erasure . . . was not just something done to women poets, but the result of a set of conventions that once made the circulation of their poetry possible in the first place."[58] When Pennington introduced Plato's book as the work of "a colored lady, a member of my church, of pleasing piety and modest worth" (xvii), he was making sure that Plato fit those conventions. Prins and I have written that the figure of the nineteenth-century Anglo-American Poetess was so modestly self-effacing that she was "not the content of her own generic representation . . . not a speaker, not an 'I,' not a consciousness, not a subjectivity, not a self."[59] I still think that's true, but in this book I am interested in how and why the racialized figure of the Poetess became a flashpoint for such negation, thus paving the way for the figure of the inherently negated, generic lyric speaker.

"Who made the Poetess white? No one, not ever," Tricia Lootens has passionately insisted, invoking a long history of Black Poetess performance, from Wheatley to Felicia Morris.[60] As Lootens has so eloquently demonstrated, it's true that because the figure was made (especially in the United States) on the work of poets of color, the Poetess does not always look like Britannia. But the figure of the Poetess as empty vehicle of cultural transmission was made to represent so many things and absorb so many genres that it did tend to become as White as Britannia by default, even or perhaps especially when it was represented by Black poets. While the figure that Lootens calls "the Political Poetess" allowed many Black and Indigenous poets to write deeply committed, even revolutionary poems that made their Diva performances seem like social change, the Poetess was always a multiply divided, ventriloquized figure, at once the modest, almost invisible woman poet and the candid personification that hovered over her. "To the First of August" stops short of bringing the young woman poet of color and the macro-personification of the Poetess together—in fact, the poem pushes the person and the personification toward opposite poles of representation. The "detachable figure that exceeded the work of any particular woman poet" is so detached in "To the First of August" that she is in the background rather than the foreground of the poem, a mass print illustration rather than a voice or a subject. The public detachability of the Poetess was a forerunner of the trans-racialized, trans-gendered modern lyric speaker. We have already begun to see how Wheatley became an early template for this figure, and we will go on to see how later Black practitioners of Poetess poetics like Plato and Frances Ellen Watkins Harper framed the Poetess as White, distancing their verse from the whiteness of the feminized figure that they, like most nineteenth-century American poets, also appropriated. If the nineteenth-century Poetess seems as dated as the horsehair sofa, that is because it is that multiply ventriloquized, distanced version of the Poetess that remains.

That may seem like an elaborate way to come to terms with the pronominal confusion, alienated figuration, and impersonal feminized passivity that characterizes Plato's "To the First of August," and it may take me the rest of this book to convince you that such elaboration is warranted—indeed, that it is central to the history of American poetics. Plato's biographer Ron Welburn offers a much more straightforward rationale for the poem's flat affect when he suggests that the reason that "To the First of August" appears so "dispassionate" is that Plato was not actually African American and thus was simply not personally invested in the event the poem celebrates. Welburn nominates "The Natives of America," another Plato poem very much in the Poetess genre, as the poem that gives us the "real" Ann Plato, "a Native American within a black community."[61] "On 'The Natives of America' rests the hypothesis of Plato's Native ancestry and the foundation of her voice as a young female leader of her city's urban Indian community," Welburn writes (34). While I have suggested that the Poetess is a generic figure, Welburn reads this figuration quite literally. Welburn gives the writer her first and only book-length consideration, and much of the book makes a fascinating case for *Ninni-missinuok* (Algonquian) survivance in Northeastern US urban communities and specifically in the Talcott Street Congregational community. Yet his case for what he calls Ann Plato's "Native identity" depends on a reading of a single poem as "voiced" by Ann Plato (and to support that reading, on a detail in the 1870 Iowa census and some indications that the four biographies in Plato's book are of young women who were also "part of the fluctuating *Missinuok* world" [184]). Plato may very well have shared Indigenous ancestry with other diasporic people considered "'colored' &c." in Hartford in 1840 (as indeed, many BIPOC people in the nineteenth century did), but what is remarkable about her biographer's conviction is that he understands the two "speakers" in "The Natives of America" as historical persons rather than as fictional poetic *personae*, and he thinks that the story they tell is the history of a single "race."

Because "To the First of August" and this poem are "her only two poems concerned directly with racial and historical themes," according to Welburn, the "contrasts in cultural investment" between the two poems prove that Plato was "Native" and not "Black" (33). All of the problems with the communal *we* that we noticed in "To the First of August" (that is, all of the problems inherent in the history and theory of gendered and racialized lyric reading) appear to this reader to be solved by "The Natives of America," a poem that restores the agency of singular and plural subjects, that doubles down on the race concept, that makes a clear distinction between us and them, Black and Indigenous, she and he, then and now:

> Tell me a story, father please,
> Then I sat upon his knees.
> Then answer'd he—"what speech make known
> Or tell the words of native tone,
> Of how my Indian fathers dwelt,
> And, of sore oppression felt
> And how they mourned a land serene,
> It was an ever mournful theme." (Plato (1841/1988), 110.)

After this beginning, the daughter implores her father to tell her their family's "history," and the father recounts the ravages of settler colonialism. "We were a happy race," he begins, emphasizing that "when we no tongue but ours did trace," this race's sense of communal identity was intact. Yet English rhymed couplet by English rhymed couplet and stanza by stanza, that monocultural, monolingual identity is dismantled, until "My daughter, we are now diminish'd, unknown, / Unfelt." That last word is the Poetess's signature sentimental appeal, but just as we begin to share the intimate pathos of this vanishing people, the father affirms that, after all,

> I love my country, and shall, until death
> Shall cease my breath.

What can this singular personal possessive pronoun possibly mean after the (by 1841, generic) tale of genocidal destruction? This Indian father's words echo Sir Walter Scott's *The Lay of the Last Minstrel* (1805), in which the exiled bard returns to "the vile dust, from which he sprung, / Unwept, unhonored, and unsung." Is the father in Plato's poem a spokesman for his race or for nineteenth-century Anglophone poetry? The question is left hanging fire in Plato's poem in the only stanza that contains a single couplet, yet Welburn concludes that the poem is "Ann Plato's most incisive political and historical statement. Its speaker oratorically sustains its tone by impressing his daughter with the wisdom of his pride in all its wounded passion and the rightful history he relates to her; these speak for themselves" (43).

But history is not what speaks in Plato's poems. History is the mute, messy, racist, brutal, banal, sentimental, accidental, incidental, monumental, state-sponsored, national, everyday, revolutionary, colonial, global, economically driven, sexualized, and gendered substrate that poems and people make their ways in and through. "History, as no one seems to know, is not merely something to be read," James Baldwin wrote in 1965, over a century after Plato's poetry suggested something similar. "On the contrary, the great force of history comes from the fact that we carry it within us, are unconsciously controlled by it in many ways, and history is literally present in all that we do. It could scarcely be otherwise, since it is to history that we owe our frames of reference, our identities, and our aspirations."[62] From Baldwin's (and, I am suggesting, Plato's) perspective, history cannot eventuate in a totality because *we* are inseparable from "the frames of reference" that determine what history has made of us. While "The Natives of America" does not convince me that history made Ann Plato the daughter of a proud Indigenous father, Welburn's deeply invested lyric reading of the poem does speak volumes about the racializing of poetics and the poetics of racialization, about the desire for a racially representative poetic speaker, for a singular identifiable figure who can dissolve the difficulty of poems like "To the First of August."

As we shall continue to see in every part of this book, the frames of reference that conferred Indigenous and Black identities were intimately entwined in nineteenth-century history and poetics, so the fact that a modern lyric reader of Plato has belatedly discovered that she represents both at once makes a lot of sense. Such analogy and displacement tell an old and period-appropriate story, since, as Ezra Tawil has shown, the antebellum American attachment to the literature of "racial sentiment" tended to confuse and align "New World Indians" with African Americans.[63] As Tiffany Lethabo King has argued, "at the stress points and instantiations of Black fungibility and Native genocide, the violence moves as one," and in the nineteenth-century literary imaginary, as we shall see especially in chapter 4, the one-ness of that violence served White supremacist poetic ends.[64] While Welburn knows that what he calls "dying Indian-theme poems" constituted one of the most popular American genres of the late eighteenth and early nineteenth centuries, and that White Poetesses like Plato's famous Hartford predecessor Lydia Huntley Sigourney specialized in such poems, and while he does not seem to know that the New York City White celebrity poet William Cullen Bryant famously made such poems all about the genealogical claims of vanishing fathers, it is the oratorical performance of Plato's "speaker" that he takes to separate her poem from that early genre. This book will consider many poems like "The Natives of America" because, as in the case of Poetess verse, so many nineteenth-century poets used the genre for their own purposes. But the great force of these and other genres common to the nineteenth-century poetic commons is the fact that our ways of reading poetry (since Welburn is far from alone here)—our *poetics*—tend to attribute to them the desire for "the speaker": for an abstract, ahistorical, singular, publicly shared, and structurally feminized voice that can deliver the poetry of the future to us in order to make history disappear.

An American Lyric

I hope that by this point in this book I have made you reasonably suspicious of that shared pronoun and of such a sweeping claim about our shared poetics. By *us*, I mean readers who have been shaped by modern literary criticism, by the tendency to think of a poem as the utterance of a fictional persona called "the speaker," and that probably means most of us who learned to read poetry in high school and college in the United States over the past century or so. "The pedagogy of lyric poetry is constantly insisting (and readers are constantly forgetting) that the 'I' in a poem should be called the 'speaker,' or the 'persona,' and should not be conflated with the biographical author," Barbara Johnson writes, adding that "many poets have made a point of considering this 'speaker' as a function of the poem, and not the other way around."[65] On the view that Johnson takes to be normative, "the speaker" is a fiction (as both the definite article and quotation marks tell us) on which not only "the pedagogy of lyric poetry" came to depend by the middle decades of the twentieth century, but also a fiction born of the nineteenth-century poems on which that pedagogy itself was built and which it shaped in turn.

This is to say that the fiction of the speaker was not invented one day over breakfast in 1937 by Cleanth Brooks or another day over dinner in 1941 by John Crowe Ransom or another day in 1951 by Reuben Brower—nor was it dissolved one day in 1914 by Gertrude Stein or another day in the 1960s by the Black Arts Movement or another day in the 1970s by a group of White mostly male Language poets. Herbert Tucker has made the case that "the thirst for intersubjective confirmation of the self, which has made the overhearing of a persona our principal means of understanding a poem," emerged from "an anxiety of textuality" that twentieth-century literary criticism inherited from the nineteenth-century Victorian dramatic monologue's framing of "overheard" Romantic lyric, an "anxiety over the tendency of texts to come loose from their origins . . . that the New Critics half acknowledged and half tried to curb under the regime of a now avowedly fictive self."[66] The nineteenth-century American chapter of those origins was even more important to Southern Agrarian critics like Brooks and Ransom and to Black critics like James Weldon Johnson and Sterling Brown than were the British origins Tucker traces, since, as Caroline Gelmi has written and we have begun to see, in the United States, the idea of a poetic speaker was "a racial and ideological formation, an invention of particular reading practices" that emerged from late-eighteenth-and-nineteenth-century American poems like the ones considered in this book.[67] Sonya Posmentier has suggested that there was a specifically Black history of lyric reading and lyricization (institutionalized by Du Bois, Zora Neale Hurston, and Brown, among others) that ran parallel to and challenges my theory of lyricization as the "transformation of multiple folk materials into a singular poetic voice" in American literary criticism.[68] I think she is right, and this book will show that what happened in the nineteenth century was that many different verse genres, only some of them identified with a "folk," were transformed into an imaginary lyric voice detached from those genres. The retro-projection of those genres as "folk materials" began in the nineteenth century and continued well into the twentieth, and like all nostalgic fantasies, the racialization of that backward glance was part of its ideological formation. We have also begun to see how that formation was shaped by particular modes of impersonally personal address in many different varieties of print. Modernism's inheritance of the highly mediated racial and ideological folk fantasy—the ways in which print was accompanied by fictions of poetry before or after or to the side of print—was surprisingly direct. But a century earlier, it is already clear that the figure of the speaker that is nowhere in evidence in "To the First of August" is nascent in it—and by extension in nineteenth-century American poetics more generally—as a racialized abstraction that in turn produces the abstraction of lyric reading. As Phillip Brian Harper has argued, if we think of abstraction as "the cognitive mechanism by which persons of African descent were conceived as enslavable entities and commodity objects," we might also think of abstraction as the generic mechanism by which kinds of poems were reified into kinds of people.[69] I have begun to describe and will have a lot more to say about the complicated logic of that double abstraction in the pages that follow, but first I should say more about what I mean by "lyric reading," an idea that has led to a lot of confusion since it appeared in my first book, *Dickinson's Misery: A Theory of Lyric Reading* in 2005 and was extended in the small book I wrote with Yopie Prins inside *The Lyric Theory Reader: A Critical Anthology*, the large book we co-edited in 2014.

In *Dickinson's Misery*, I took up the example of Emily Dickinson, another nineteenth-century American poet who sometimes posed as a Poetess and who, like Ann Plato, favored hymnal meter, and I used this example to demonstrate the distance that separated Dickinson's verse practices and circumstances of address from later editorial, popular, and critical readings of her poems as "feeling confessing itself to itself, in moments of solitude." You will recognize that last phrase as John Stuart Mill's: Mill uses it to distinguish interested public address from sincere poetic self-address; as he wrote in 1833, "eloquence is *heard*, poetry is *overheard*. Eloquence supposes an audience; the peculiarity of poetry appears to us to lie in the poet's utter unconsciousness of a listener."[70] As a reclusive woman who published very few of her poems while she was alive, Dickinson literalized Mill's ideal of lyric address as the antithesis of public speech. Yet as Warner writes, this ideal was always a fiction, since "poetry is not actually overheard; it is read as overheard. And similarly, public speech is not just heard; it is heard (or read) *as* heard, not just by oneself but by others" (81). So why have readers adopted the fiction of this false opposition for the past two hundred years?

As Tucker argues, something like Mill's nineteenth-century distinction has prejudiced twentieth- and twenty-first-century poetics against explicitly political poems like Plato's "To the First of August" (which definitely supposes an audience, even if it may not have had much of one) in favor of poems like

> My Life had stood—a Loaded Gun—
> In Corners—till a Day
> The Owner passed—identified—
> And carried Me away—[71]

Dickinson's poem, perhaps composed toward the beginning of the Civil War, found with her manuscripts after her death in 1886 and never (as far as we

know) sent to anyone or published during her lifetime, shares the abcb com-
mon meter quatrain structure of "To the First of August," but although its
subject is also hopelessly troubled by, in being emphatically detached from the
action whose agent it is supposed to be with a vengeance, that pathos of un-
certain agency is individualized, is itself the subject of the poem, a subject
announced in the poem's first word as a singular possessive pronoun. While
few critics have bothered with Plato's poem, "My Life had stood" became, as
I wrote in *Dickinson's Misery*, "the *ars poetica*, the zero-sum game of interpreta-
tion, for nearly all accounts of Dickinson's poems as *lyrics*" in the late twentieth
century.[72] While Plato's use of common meter contributes to our sense of her
poem as generic and impersonal, for the critic Susan Stewart, writing in 1995,
Dickinson's "use of hymn meters makes us hear the individuality of her voice
and the specificity of her words because of their dissonance from the habits of
tradition."[73] This is a better example than Welburn's reading of Plato for what
I mean by "lyric reading": whenever a "speaker" or a "voice" can be distin-
guished from "the habits of tradition," whenever we can discover "dissonance"
between individual form and communal content, what Tucker felicitously
calls "the intersubjective confirmation of the self," the desire to substitute the
intimate address of the private person for the public address of the poem, is
fulfilled. But where does this desire come from, and why has modern poetics
been constructed in response to it?

It will take me the rest of this book to answer that question. The short ver-
sion of an answer is the one I gave in *Dickinson's Misery*: "While it is beyond
the scope of this book to trace the lyricization of poetry that began in the
eighteenth century," I wrote, "the exemplary story of the composition, recov-
ery, and publication of Dickinson's writing begins one chapter, at least, in what
is so far a largely unwritten history" (6). This book is my attempt to fill in more
chapters in that still largely unwritten history, but those chapters are not the
ones I thought I would write when I wrote that sentence about Dickinson.
Dickinson became a privileged subject of lyric reading and Plato did not, not
only because Dickinson was a rich White woman shut up in a big house who
published very few of the poems that continue to be made into the lyrics that
editors and critics want them to be, not only because Dickinson knew impor-
tant people who connected that editorial and critical history to powerful in-
stitutional homes at Amherst and Harvard, not only because those institutions
fostered and continue to foster Dickinson's distribution as popular poet in
addition to maintaining rights to scholarly editions of her work, not only
because Dickinson, like Plato, composed in a meter that was one of the toggle

switches between elite and popular reading practices in the nineteenth century, not only because Plato was a Black and/or Indigenous "'colored' &c." schoolteacher whose institutional access (at least in her lifetime) was limited to Pennington and the Talcott Street Congregational Church, not only because what "Britannia's isles proclaim" in Plato's poem is transatlantic history and the time and place when and where "My Life had stood" remains indeterminate and portable, not only because the collective personal pronoun is so hard to pin down in Plato and the definite singular possessive is so easy to appropriate in Dickinson, but because by 1890 (when the first volume of Dickinson's poems was posthumously published), the subject hopelessly troubled by, in being emphatically detached from, the action whose agent it is supposed to be was the subject of racialized reading that Plato's poem prefigures. Mill's "feeling confessing itself to itself, in moments of solitude," British Romantic poetics more generally, Dickinson, modern Anglophone poetics, modern American literary criticism, modern American comparative literature, and postmodern, post-lyric American avant-garde poetics all owe their prized versions of the genre of the radically abstracted solitary subject to the predicament of the colonized, enslaved, feminized, free, compromised, "'colored' &c." figures with whom the nineteenth century—well, with whom the twentieth and twenty-first centuries—could not and still cannot come to terms.

In *Dickinson's Misery*, I defined lyric reading in relation to Mill, but located it in the twentieth- and twenty-first-century literary criticism that made Dickinson into an exemplary lyric poet. While I did invoke Emerson and I did associate Dickinson with the nineteenth-century Poetess, the Mill-to-New-Criticism-to-feminism-to-post-structuralism-to-historical poetics trajectory of my critical argument there omitted (as all literary critics are trained to omit) the mid-nineteenth-century American poetics of which Plato's poems are such common examples. This is to say that my definition of lyric reading and my version of American poetics in that book were (like Dickinson, Mill, New Criticism, post-structuralism, a lot of feminism, and most American academic versions of poetics, even the historical kind) very White. But nineteenth-century American poetics and the history of literary criticism built on that poetics did not emerge like a White goddess out of the head of Emerson—or out of the heads of Dickinson or Whitman, for that matter. They came out of the crucible of racialized reading I have invoked by beginning this book with Phillis Wheatley and Ann Plato, the latter a forgotten woman poet of color who was in fact a Platoess, if we read her dialectically. If Dickinson was the perfect fit for lyric reading, it is Plato's bad fit that makes her work so symptomatic of our desire for it: the dissociative logic that characterizes the first-person plural pronoun's associations in "To the First of August" invites resolution in a singular figure, a representative person, but that person is (like race itself) an outsized fiction at odds with the poem. This fiction satisfies the desire for collective resolution to the extent that it is racist: Britannia singularly personifies a common transatlantic dream of White supremacy, while the multiple, indistinct figures to whom she delivers "freedom" shade into the background, and that shade defines her whiteness as her whiteness defines their shade.

This dynamic sounds like an inversion of Hurston's famous comment in "How It Feels to Be Colored Me" (1928): "I feel most colored when I am thrown against a sharp white background."[74] In *Citizen: An American Lyric* (2014), Claudia Rankine adopts Hurston's line, and then adopts Glenn Ligon's 1992 graphic adaptation of that line (figure 1.3), commenting that Ligon "used plastic letter stencils, smudging oil sticks, and graphite to transform the words into abstractions."[75] In nineteenth-century American poetics, a similar logic of racialization-as-abstraction was already on full display in the smudged genres and plastic pronouns that transformed the abstract genre of the poem into the abstract genre of the person.[76] As Posmentier writes, "as Glenn Ligon has shown us in the thick oil—black on white, or is it white on black?—with which he letters Hurston's 'I do not always feel colored,' the background and the foreground are not distinguishable in Hurston's racial theory," nor are they distinguishable in the racialized history of poetics.[77]

Let's follow Rankine and Posmentier in calling that abstraction "American lyric," and let's also follow them in identifying that lyric imaginary with a racial imaginary. "What we mean by a racial imaginary is something we all recognize quite easily," Beth Loffreda and Rankine write,

> the way our culture has imagined over and over again the narrative opportunities, the feelings and attributes and situations, the subjects and metaphors and forms and voices, available both to characters of different races and to their authors. The racial imaginary changes over time, in part because artists get into tension with it, challenge it, alter its availabilities. Sometimes it changes very rapidly, as in our own lifetimes. But it has yet to disappear. Pretending it is not there—not there in imagined time and space, in lived time and space, in legislative time and space—will not hurry it out of existence. Instead our imaginings might test our inheritances, to make way for

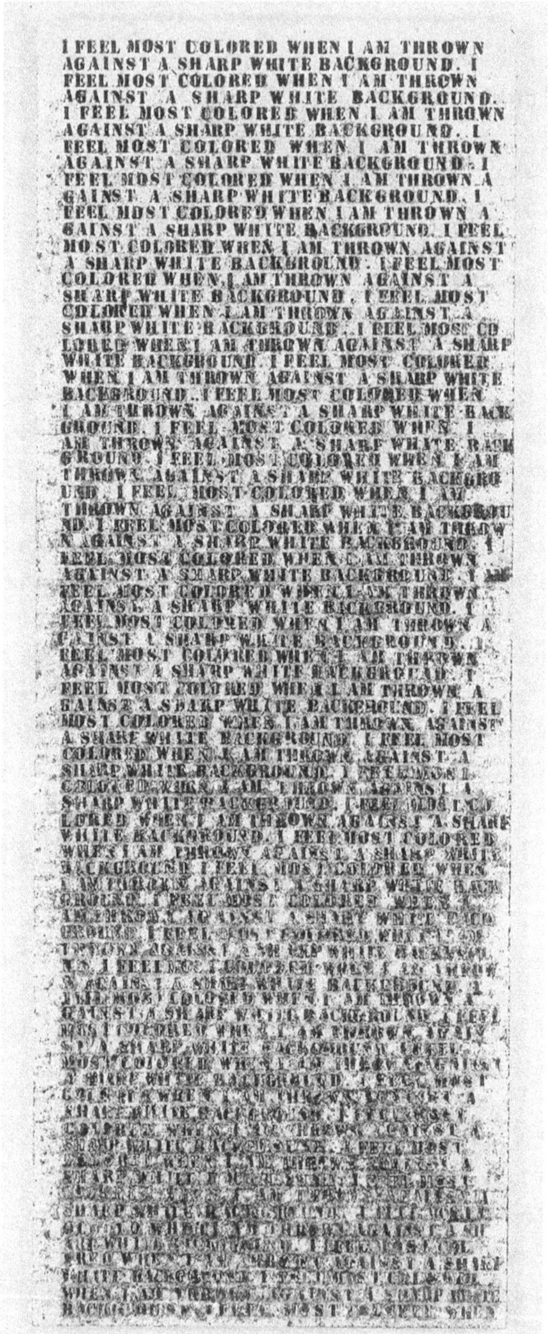

FIGURE 1.3. Glenn Ligon, *Untitled (I Feel Most Colored When I Am Thrown Against a Sharp White Background)*, 1990. Oil stick, gesso, and graphite on wood. 80 × 30 inches. © Glenn Ligon; courtesy of the artist, Hauser & Wirth, New York, Regen Projects, Los Angeles, Thomas Dane Gallery, London, and Galerie Chantal Crousel, Paris.

a time when such inheritances no longer ensnare us. But we are creatures
of this moment, not that one.[78]

This book is about a version of the racial imaginary that has been difficult to
recognize because it is instantiated in the lyric imaginary that has shaped the
history and theory of American poetics. In 1841, James Pennington imagined
a Platoess who could "make way for a time when such inheritances no longer
ensnare us," and Loffreda and Rankine are still trying to imagine such a time
in the second decade of the twenty-first century. Their assurance that the racial
imaginary "is something we all recognize quite easily" on one hand reminds
us that race is a fiction made real by the social relations that Baldwin calls "the
force of history," and on the other hand that this aggressive historical fiction
has become generic.

When Gitelman defines genre as "a mode of recognition instantiated in
discourse," she continues by explaining that "schoolbooks have long sug-
gested, by contrast, that genre is a question of ingredients or formal
attributes—sonnets have fourteen lines, for instance, while comedies end in
marriage and tragedies end in death," yet "a different perspective" might focus
"on recognition that is collective, spontaneous, and dynamic."[79] It is no acci-
dent that Gitelman's examples of the canned idea of genre in "schoolbooks"
are literary, and it is also no accident that Loffreda and Rankine's examples for
what racial recognition that is collective, spontaneous, and dynamic feels like
are also literary. As the literary was invented on the basis of genre, it was also
invented on the basis of race. The lyric imaginary and the racial imaginary are
both genres embedded in and formed by historical discourses that uncon-
sciously control how easily we recognize poems and persons, and they are so
intimately entwined with one another that telling them apart becomes a duck-
rabbit illusion (or what Wittgenstein called *seeing that* versus *seeing as*), since
what we all recognize quite easily quickly becomes hard to distinguish from
the genres of which we are made.

And who are *we*? "We are creatures of this moment" that has lasted for a
long time. Ann Plato's imaginary *we* was on the brink of something that re-
mains unfinished. In *Dickinson's Misery*, I wrote that "the (only) apparently
contextless or sceneless, even evanescent nature of Dickinson's writing at-
tracted an increasingly professionalized attempt to secure and contextualize it
as a certain kind (or genre) of literature—as what we might call, after Charles
Taylor, a lyric social imaginary" (6–7). I now see that the racial social imagi-
nary that informs that lyric social imaginary is something we do all recognize

quite easily: Dickinson's writing was especially susceptible to lyric reading because she was a White diva like Britannia, but also because such reading always assumes Britannia's position, granting the poetic subject a freedom predicated on its previous revocation. As Moten writes, "freedom is in unfreedom as the trace of the resistance that constitutes constraint."[80] Dickinson's unfreedom made her an attractive White feminized version of the lyrical pathos of racialized unfreedom that characterized the nineteenth century, so for this literary history, Dickinson is at best a negative example of the lyric imaginary I have in mind. She will not make another appearance here; her poetics were not important to the process of lyricization in the late eighteenth or early nineteenth centuries, though she became a poster child for that process in the twentieth.

I have begun with Plato because an ordinary woman poet of color best represents the nineteenth-century formation of a large idea of lyric that she did not actually practice, an idea that emerged at her expense. I have tried to frame her as a Platoess who would agree with Rankine that the first-person speaking subject is split down the middle: "No 'I' in my mind's eye is the whole of anything," Rankine wrote in 2001, "I am a part and so, torn apart by the aggression of the uninterrupted . . . , I look around and see the illusion of wholeness and surety inciting the Crusades, slavery, the Battle of Little Big Horn, *Shoah*, Hiroshima, Pearl Harbor, Vietnam, etc."[81] Like Plato in "To the First of August," Rankine asks how a personal pronoun can be part of a collective that "does not harbor the illusion of wholeness," that does not pit *us* against *them*, and, like Plato, she implies that this *we* is possible only as "an inchoate desire for a future other than the one that seems to be forming our days."[82]

Kamran Javadizadeh has suggested that Rankine's unremitting predication of personal pronouns exposes what he calls "the whiteness of the lyric subject."[83] In defining what he means by "the lyric subject," Javadizadeh cites my description of the consequences of lyricization: "the progressive idealization of what was a much livelier, more explicitly mediated, historically contingent and public context for many varieties of poetry had culminated by the middle of the twentieth century in an idea of lyric as temporally self-present or unmediated," as I wrote in *Dickinson's Misery* (9). Javadizadeh continues,

Race has not, so far, been a central preoccupation of "the new lyric studies," but Jackson's account of the historical consolidation of a normative lyric as "temporally self-present and unmediated" resonates with whiteness's implicit claims to universality and unmediated identity, whereby to be white in the United States is to be, apparently, without race and without a role in the erasure of whiteness's racialized others. (476)

It is a good point, and a general one. The lyric social imaginary that has dominated American poetics for the past two centuries is racialized to its core, but not entirely because of its claims to universality and unmediated identity. The very idea of "the lyric subject," like the idea of "the lyric speaker," supposes a normative definite article, and that norm has its own history. Javadizadeh offers a great reading of Rankine's ambivalence when it comes to personal pronouns, linking the difficult, endlessly predicated "I" in *Don't Let Me Be Lonely* (2009) and the difficult, endlessly predicated "you" in *Citizen* to "the new forms of lyric subjectivity that are allowed by Rankine's recognition" of "the whiteness of the lyric subject," especially as that subject is represented in and by the late modernist poetics of Robert Lowell. "For Rankine, Lowell especially has seemed representative not only of confessional poetics but also of a (mostly White, mostly male) post-Romantic lyric tradition for which confessionalism has long seemed the denouement," Javadizadeh writes (476).

Rankine does seem to have a close attachment to Lowell's poetics, but the version of the history of American poetics in which her critic places this attachment (here Wordsworth-to-Lowell-to-Rankine rather than Shelley-to-Stevens-to-Ashbery) omits any consideration of nineteenth-century American poetics before modernism. That omission is important not because Rankine claims a debt to nineteenth-century American poetics, but because the internal alienation that characterizes the concept of "the speaker" emerged from the racial imaginary of nineteenth-century American poetics, and thus it makes sense that it was fully realized a century later in confessional poetics, in which, as Rankine writes in *Citizen*, "your ill-spirited, cooked, hell on Main Street, nobody's here, broken-down, first person could be one of many definitions of being to pass on" (72). Good literary critics (and even good poets like Rankine) have been trained to think of this first person as the legacy of "the Romantic lyric tradition," but Rankine's version of "An American Lyric," in which that first person is endlessly troubled by, in being emphatically detached from, the action whose agent it is supposed to be (lest that action turn into "slavery or the Battle of the Little Big Horn") is ensnared by her inheritance of the lyric racial imaginary bequeathed to modernism by the nineteenth-century American poetics that later poets and critics have tried hard to forget in order to "make way for a time when such inheritances no longer ensnare us." According to Shockley, in *Citizen*, Rankine's poetics actively dissolve the coherence of that *us*, in much the way I have suggested that Ann Plato's poetics so passively did almost two centuries earlier. What results from the conflicting modes of racial identification solicited by *Citizen*'s shifting forms of address, Shockley writes, "may be less a challenge to the coherence of the lyric speaker than to the coherence of many readers. Rankine's relational lyric-*You* may challenge us . . . to retheorize the lyric genre."[84] This book is an attempt to accept that challenge. Robert Lowell's poetry-writing "Brahmin" ancestors Maria White and James Russell and Amy Lowell may represent one vividly literalized genealogy of White American poetic inheritance, but Rankine's projects demonstrate the ways in which the nineteenth-century racially incoherent lyric imaginary is still an unacknowledged creature of this moment.

At this moment in the history and theory of American poetics, it is past time to acknowledge that past. We need to change the White Romanticism-to-modernism narrative of "the lyric subject" as well as the White modernism-to-avant-garde narrative of "the post-lyric subject" in order to write a new history and theory of poetics that does not reduce nineteenth-century American poetics to Emerson and Dickinson and Whitman, that gives Ann Plato her due. Since indeed we are creatures of this moment that has not yet been redeemed by a Platoess, we need to change our ways of telling the history and theory of American poetics because those ways have been thoroughly racist. And wrong. They have been racist not only because Javadizadeh is right that they tend to depend on a default-White universalizing idea of "the lyric subject" unmarked by race or gender, but more importantly because they have not been antiracist—and they have not been antiracist because of the ways in which that lyricized idea of poetry came into being in the United States in the late eighteenth and early nineteenth centuries in the first place. As *we* became a personal pronoun contingent on racialized definition and as *we* simultaneously became an imagined community that only the poetry of the future could redeem—as *we* became a genre, what Sylvia Wynter would call a "referent-we"—the first-person plural came to be represented by a first-person singular fictive person who embodied both that discursive dissonance and the utopian hope for its resolution. To Pennington, Plato's poetry seemed to promise that future (or perhaps he was just good enough to say so), but now that future is our past. It is true that the process of lyricization in nineteenth-century American poetry eventuated in a White supremacist version of modern poetics, but it is also true that poets of color, and especially Black poets, had the last word in this process: they made the lyricized poetics that modernism inherited by throwing that White fiction against a racialized background, by making what became the publicly private lyric speaker into an abstract figure of representational alienation.

So now we can return for the third time to what Adorno said in 1957: the modern lyric "is always the subjective expression of a social antagonism" because

> a poem is not merely an expression of individual impulses and experiences. Its universality is no *volonté de tous*, not the universality of simply communicating what others are unable to communicate. . . . It anticipates . . . spiritually, a situation in which no false universality, that is, nothing profoundly particular, continues to fetter what is other than itself, the human.[85]

Adorno was actually belatedly responding to a similar claim Walter Benjamin had made twenty years earlier in relation to Baudelaire, who, according to Benjamin, "envisaged readers to whom the reading of lyric poetry would present difficulties" because of "a change in the structure of their experience" in modernity.[86] While I am suggesting that modern lyric is itself a product of a long history of racialized social antagonism (note that even in Adorno's German, the subject-verb phrase for what divides humanity is *das Menschliche fesselte*: "fetter," in English translation, a nineteenth-century remnant of imprisonment and enslavement, here modifies the category of "the human," or, literally, "the men"), in Benjamin's view, Romantic lyric took an alienated (or as Baudelaire would say, *hypocritical*) form in response to modernity (specifically, to life on the streets of Paris in the nineteenth century). Adorno was correcting Benjamin, because Adorno's version of modern lyric contained the alienation of the subject within its own formal negative dialectal "false glitter" rather than in its scenes and themes (Adorno [1957/2014], 344). While Adorno and Benjamin may have disagreed on the location of the modern lyric's alienation, neither questioned the stability of the genre itself, because for both the definition of lyric was essentially Hegelian. For Hegel in the first decades of the nineteenth century, *Lyrik* represented the most difficult of aesthetic genres, since in it the poet "must identify *himself* with this particularization of himself as with himself, so that in it he feels and envisages *himself*."[87] On the view that Benjamin and Adorno and most later lyric theorists have shared, the nineteenth century may have been able to afford Hegel's ideal of a self-expressive sincerity until Baudelaire and the readers for whom he wrote lost faith in it, but after a certain moment (1854 or 1865 or 1900 or 1903 or 1912 or 1922 or 1945 or 1973 or 2001, depending on who is telling the story), the lyric lost faith in itself.[88]

Yet for Benjamin and Adorno both, and indeed for a long history of poetics that has descended from Herder and Hegel (often without knowing it and without sharing a Frankfurt School Marxist utopian horizon), because that alienated modern lyric reflects the spirit of the age, it, too, is a figure of and for a progressive history. As Adorno writes, "this very lyric speech becomes the voice of human beings between whom the barriers have fallen."[89] As Paul de Man once quipped, "this scheme is so satisfying to our inherent sense of historical order that it has rarely been challenged, even by some who would not in the least agree with its potential ideological implications."[90] Whether we trace lyric modernity from Hegel through Marx to Benjamin and Adorno or from Hugo to Rimbaud or from Goethe to Stefan George or from Whitman to Williams or from Johnson to Brown to Brooks or from Poe to Valéry to Eliot or from Elizabeth Bishop to Morgan Parker or from Bryant to Tommy Pico or from Wordsworth to Anne Spencer to Harryette Mullen to Danez Smith, the stories we tell about modern lyric indeed remain remarkably consistent: Once upon a time, *before modernism*, lyric poetry was the expression of *our* inner subjectivity, but after *x* happened, lyric came to be and will every after remain at odds with itself. And so will *we*.

Minstrel Reading

Jonathan Culler thus joins a long and distinguished critical tradition when he laments the fact that the conception of lyric "as representation of subjective experience, while widely disseminated and influential, no longer has great currency in the academic world."[91] He continues,

> It has been replaced by a variant that treats the lyric not as the mimesis of the experience of the poet but as the representation of the action of a fictional speaker: in this account, the lyric is spoken by a persona, whose situation and motivation one needs to reconstruct. This has become the dominant model in the pedagogy of the lyric in the Anglo-American world, if not elsewhere. (2)

Culler does not say when or why this replacement came about, perhaps because we all recognize quite easily that it did. The history of the shift does not interest him, but Culler's *Theory of the Lyric* (2015) is deeply invested in showing how "extraordinarily limited and limiting" this "variant" has become, since "it leads to neglect of the most salient features of many lyrics, which are not to be found in ordinary speech acts" (2). In order to discover the lyric's extraordinary transhistorical formal features, *Theory of the Lyric* surveys a wealth of examples "in the Western lyric tradition" (3), including hundreds of poems that demonstrate "the nature of lyric and its range of possibilities" (6). Culler's aim is to do "justice to the possibilities inherent in the tradition. In sum, the theory of the lyric is an enterprise of correction and rectification that offers resources for future engagement with lyric poetry" (9). Culler's theory of the lyric indeed introduces a welcome "correction" to the narrative of sincerity-to-alienation that has dominated modern and post-modern poetics, and its "rectification" of that narrative leans heavily on "the most canonical lyrics of the Western tradition: from Sappho, Horace, Petrarch, Goethe, Leopardi, Baudelaire, Lorca, Williams, and Ashbery" (9). For Culler, this is "our tradition," and it offers "us reproducible experiences of pleasure and puzzlement, as we speak them to ourselves and to others—as we should do more often" (353). By the end of *Theory of the Lyric*, the fiction of the lyric speaker has been replaced by our communal lyric speech. And *we* all seem to be White.

But this version of *our* whiteness, too, is an old story in the history of poetics. As we shall see in chapter 5 of this book, this story is not just Eurocentric but originates with Henry Wadsworth Longfellow, the most popular poet in the United States in the nineteenth century. Longfellow invented the American version of Comparative Literature at Harvard in the 1840s in order to make Goethe's *Weltliteratur*, or concert of world literatures, into a lyricized White Western (and emphatically New World) poetic voice that speaks for all of us. But my allusion to the history in which *Theory of the Lyric* participates is out of keeping with the spirit of Culler's book, since Culler positions his celebration of communal comparative lyric against the background of what he calls "the modern historicist critique of the category of lyric, often known as 'the new lyric studies'" (83). He attributes this critique to me and to Prins, claiming that in *The Lyric Theory Reader* (2014), we "argue that the category of lyric is an illicit imposition of modern criticism on various poems that we have, willy-nilly, made into lyric through lyrical reading" (83). Since "the historicist critique apparently seeks to dissolve the category of lyric to return us to a variety of historical practices" (84), Culler's *Theory of the Lyric* responds by offering an antihistoricist defense of lyric form as our rightful cultural inheritance. And who are *we*? Culler makes an excellent point when he writes that

> The two models of lyric—lyric as expression of the feelings of the poet and lyric as the representation of a fictional poetic speaker or persona—arise at different historical moments and have quite discrete functions. To lump them together as "lyricization" seems historically irresponsible. (84–85)

That certainly does seem to be the case from the perspective of the broadly comparative Western history of poetics on which Culler's lyric theory depends. But if we place Culler's project against the racialized background of nineteenth-century American poetics, we can see that lyricization did not happen "willy-nilly": instead, the history of American poetics has been expertly constructed as a bridge that connects ideas of the expressive lyric to ideas of the fictive lyric speaker, since this forgotten chapter in that history so explicitly racialized the relation between the two. What has been historically irresponsible has been the omission of nineteenth-century American poetics (aside from the usual nods to Whitman and Dickinson) from theories of the lyric.

In *The Lyric Theory Reader*, Prins and I chose to exhibit the past one hundred years or so of theories of the lyric for what they have been, and Culler is not alone in mistaking that exhibition of influential modern critical theories for our own critical lyric theory. Apparently, like the Poetesses about whom we write, we have been better at serving as vehicles for cultural transmission than we are at representing our own views. Immediately upon the anthology's publication in 2014, John Keene expressed dismay at its "racist blindness," since "what else do you call an approach which erases almost completely the very presence of people whose existence [is] constitutive of the thing being discussed, which is to say, lyric poetry in the Anglophone world, which by its very nature involved, as countless literary scholars and others have pointed out, colonialism, chattel slavery, imperialism, white supremacy, ethnocentrism, and so much more?"[92] Keene is right that whatever insight *The Lyric Theory Reader* might offer into the twentieth-century formation of lyric theory should be placed against the background of what the anthology omits. There were then and are now, as Keene insists, "any number of Asian American, Latino/Latina, Native American, mixed race, and white critics, let alone African American scholars, who have written on lyric poetry and race," but we did not include them in our anthology. Because we wanted our anthology to demonstrate the blind spots that have characterized lyric theory over the past century, we did not want to be in the position of pointing out that much work on lyric and race does not change the essentially racist categories, the modes of reading, that have made lyric theory so White.

Instead, we chose fifty influential essays (forty of them by White men) that formed and extended modes of lyric reading that Keene called out as the cast of academic business as usual. As Dorothy Wang writes, "critics look at the work of [John] Ashbery as contributing to 'universal' questions of subjectivity and poetics while [John] Yau, with rare exception, is seen as occupying a narrower historical or partisan niche," and this

> double standard extends to how we read works of poetry. Critics are more likely to think about formal questions when thinking about Ashbery's poems but almost certainly to focus on political or black "content" when examining the work of Amiri Baraka, a poet who has pushed the limits of formal invention for more than a half century—certainly as long as Ashbery has.[93]

Wang, like Keene, makes it clear that by anthologizing essays that think through lyric theory by relying for the most part on White American, British, and Western European poets, we were recapitulating "the Western lyric tradition" I have just accused Culler of promoting as *the* tradition of lyric theory. As Posmentier sums it up, "Jackson and Prins define the history of modern lyric reading almost entirely as a product of 'Anglo-American' (by which, it seems, they mean *white* American and European) criticism."[94] What were we thinking? By showing and telling the twentieth-century history of lyric reading that has been adopted as normative, part of what we ended up reaffirming is its dominant whiteness and we ended up practicing what Wang calls its "double standard." "The whiteness of the lyric subject" is a product of the history of lyric reading that our anthology traces, not an immutable poetic landscape. I, too, wish that the default-White history of lyric theory that *The Lyric Theory Reader* documents had not happened, and that we had included more alternatives to it in our anthology.

Before Modernism tries to show some of the reasons why that history did happen, but also why the modes of reading that Wang describes so well have been hard to shake, since it is no accident that her concerns echo Pennington's. That's because the abstract, fictive lyric speaker was made abstract and fictive in and through the racialized process of lyricization in the late eighteenth and early nineteenth centuries. By the twentieth century, when modern literary criticism and *The Lyric Theory Reader* begins, that process had led to the substitution of an unmarked persona who indeed replaced the gendered, raced, classed, and variously marked poets those personae represented. While influential White poets like Bryant and Longfellow institutionalized this process of abstraction, and popular White Poetesses impersonated it, they often did so by making non-White figures their subjects. Poets of color and especially Black poets reacted by inventing the genre we now recognize as lyric in response to that abstraction, though this does not mean that lyric is simply a reaction formation, or that Black poets were reactive rather than proactive in their inventions. In order to see how and why Black poets invented modern lyric in the late eighteenth and first part of the nineteenth centuries, we need to undiscipline the modern lyric theory represented in our anthology, and that process of undisciplining starts with telling the story of how American lyric theory came about. As Anthony Reed has suggested, just as lyric reading determines "which poems come to be canonized and which poets and forms come to be neglected," so "racialized reading . . . effectively sidesteps or precludes other forms of analysis."[95] I do not want to defend our choices in *The Lyric Theory Reader*, since the truth is we should have seen then what has become much clearer to me while writing this book: modern lyric theory—and especially modern lyric *reading*—has been racist, and a great deal of the whiteness of lyric theory can be traced to the history of American poetics before modernism that *Before Modernism* begins to tell.

My aim in *Before Modernism* is to retell the history of American poetics as the history of gendered and racialized lyricization. What do I want that history to do to us? I certainly do not want it "to dissolve the lyric," though it must be clear by now that I think such definite articles should make us all nervous. In an early piece called *what I want history to do to me* (figure 1.4), the artist Kara Walker has drawn a cartoon version of the answer I want to give to this question. What kind of appropriation am I practicing by making Walker answer for me? Can a Black woman artist speak for a White woman literary critic? That's not exactly the question posed by Walker's line drawing, but it comes close, and it also comes close to the question all modern lyric reading poses. As Zadie Smith eloquently articulates Walker's drawing's challenge to the viewer,

> What might I want history to do to me? I might want history to show me . . . that we create oppositions—black white male female fat thin beautiful ugly virgin whore—in order to provide definition to ourselves through contrast. I might want history to convince me that although some identities are chosen, many are forced. Or that no identities are chosen. Or that all identities are chosen. That I feed history. That history feeds me. That we starve each other. All of these things. None of them. All of them in an unholy mix of the true and the false.[96]

Notice that Smith's response to Walker's use of the first-person singular pronoun is to appropriate it for her own purposes, as indeed the image asks us to do. Notice also that Smith's appropriation of Walker's lyric question results

FIGURE 1.4. Kara Walker, *what I want history to do to me*, 1994. Ink on paper. 18 × 12 inches. © Kara Walker, courtesy of Sikkema Jenkins & Co., New York; Sprüth Magers, Berlin.

in the personification of history, as if history could answer the questions that history itself has posed. Notice, too, that Smith, herself a British woman of color, bounces back and forth between the parodically racialized, parodically sexualized figures in the drawing without being able to locate any resolution of this brutal dialectic, until the image becomes "an unholy mix of the true and the false." In this way (as in so many others), the relation between the two figures is dialectical but it is not Hegelian, and therefore (*pace* Benjamin and Adorno) is not susceptible to a reading that supposes a synthetic utopian horizon when their struggle will cease. It is also not (*pace* Culler) susceptible to a reading in which lyric address would make either "I" in our mind's eye the whole of anything, especially not the whole of the Western lyric tradition. Notice how sick (or maybe just offended or annoyed) this image makes you feel, whether you feel caricatured, as I do, as the corseted White Diva (a Scarlett O'Hara version of Britannia) or you feel dragged back like the Angel of History, whose face is turned toward the nineteenth-century past that both figures perform in exaggerated silhouette. Where we see a lyric tradition, she sees a catastrophe that keeps piling wreckage upon wreckage and hurls it under her feet. The angel would like to stay, awaken the dead, and make whole what has been smashed. But she cannot do that because she is bound with such force that she cannot depart. The rope irresistibly propels her into the future to which her back is turned, while the page she reaches toward is blank.[97] On that page is American lyric, and it was invented in the late eighteenth and early nineteenth centuries by poets like Ann Plato, who learned how to use it to throw a voice we have mistaken for our own.

That appropriated, printed voice that we have come to call "the speaker" has always been a minstrel performance. Earlier in this chapter, I called that lyric voice a "karaoke" experience, but Walker's image makes this kind of cultural appropriation look like the blackface minstrelsy it always was. Like Culler, I would like to "correct and rectify" this "extraordinarily limited and limiting" figure, as indeed I believe the history of American poetics has been trying to do since it became fixed as a genre (as a mode of recognition instantiated in discourse) in the first decades of the twentieth century. Culler is right that "a distinctive mode of reading poems as the utterance of a fictional persona" was crystallized by the New Criticism of "the mid-twentieth century" (85), but New Criticism did not invent lyric reading and the many sequels to New Criticism over the past many decades have not undone lyric reading. As we write in *The Lyric Theory Reader*, "New Criticism and the Practical Criticism may be understood as parts of a longer history of the abstraction or collapse of various verse genres into a large idea of poetry as such," and that large idea just keeps getting larger (159). *Before Modernism* is about an untold American part of that longer history, in which various verse genres that supposed various modes of communal address began to gradually collapse into a fictional persona whose gendered and racialized abstraction (the very abstraction emphasized in Walker's drawing) was further abstracted by the definite article attached to that fiction. One of the many great things about Walker's image is the way it racializes whiteness by hyper-gendering it. Misogyny and racism, as we all recognize quite easily, are often joined at the hip. This book argues that these now-grotesque antebellum characters—the hoop-skirted (or hoop-slipped) White Diva who can't stand on her own two feet and the larger-than-life woman of color (Black? Indigenous? Caribbean? Maroon? Nanny of Jamaica? Nanny of Barbados? Unnamed revolutionary?) who supports and defines her while dragging her back into history—remain immanent in the internal division inherent in the figure of the impersonally personal speaker in modern poetics. That immanent frame is what makes the figure so easy to appropriate, since the unholy mix it holds in tension convinces us that no identities are chosen and yet, in the impersonally personal lyricized genre that poetry has become, all may be. As Stephanie Burt writes, according to the logic of modern lyric reading, "poems let us imagine someone else's interior life, almost as if it were or could have been ours":

> they project a voice and embody a compelling or attractive individual consciousness, which we can then hear, or speak, or sing, or try on, or try out, as if it were our own. . . . It's a very traditional goal, one sometimes given the slightly confusing name of "lyric." . . . It entails what look like contradictions—how can you see yourself in someone else, adopt as your own someone else's words?[98]

How indeed? My hope is that this "traditional goal" of American lyric will come to feel less compelling once you learn where it came from and at whose expense you continue to perform it.

The Continuity of American Poetry

This is not to say that you should not enjoy reading poems in whatever ways you want to read poems! Discouraging you from doing so would be perverse, especially at a time when we are so often told that most people don't read much poetry at all. The Chicago-based Poetry Foundation's mission "to raise poetry to a more visible and influential position in our culture" reflects a general contemporary concern that poetry is no longer central to "*our* [American] culture" in the ways that it was central to everyday life in the nineteenth century, when poems graced the upper left hand column of every newspaper and a new book-length poem by Longfellow was more like a Taylor Swift album or a new season of an HBO series than like a new book of poetry by Jericho Brown. While it may be true that, as Michael Cohen writes, "the many ways in which people in the past engaged with poetry in their daily lives" often had as much to do with *not* reading poems as with what we now mean by *reading* them, since "nonreading . . . can also be a productive enterprise, one that takes many forms, from ignoring, forgetting, and suppressing to copying, transcribing, reciting, memorizing, collecting, exchanging, and mimicking," it is also true that modes of reading were changing rapidly in the nineteenth century and that those changes eventuated in the version of personal lyric appropriation that Burt describes so well.[99] As Roger Chartier writes, reading "rarely leaves traces, is scattered into an infinity of singular acts, and purposely frees itself from the constraints seeking to subdue it," but that does not mean that we cannot trace the history of how and why and when and where genres of reading have taken shape.[100] As we have begun to see and will continue to see throughout this book, as the fantasy of "our culture" was invented in response to the reality of proliferating versions of *us*, popular genres of collective verse (ballads and hymns, odes and elegies, drinking songs and sorrow songs and First of August poems) that addressed particular communities gradually merged into a very different genre of privatized public address, a very different mode of recognition instantiated in the discourse of an all-inclusive "imagined community" (a phrase originally coined for American poetry in the first decade of the twentieth century by the American scholar of poetics Francis Barton Gummere).[101] It is this shift from generic to generically personal address that has changed the "position of poetry" from apparently central to apparently marginal, since the phenomenology of hearing or speaking or singing or trying on or trying out an "attractive individual consciousness . . . as if it were our own" is something we can now each do in our solitary cells rather than something we often do in concert with other people (unless we are attending a spoken-word or poetry-reading performance). As we have begun to see, that individuation of verse address also means pretending that those personalized exchanges add up to one big, shared exchange, that "our culture" is commonly distributed, that the same personal pronoun applies to all of us.

But "pretending" is the wrong word for this now normalized reading prac-
tice, since what really happens when we read poems this way is that a com-
munal horizon of shared sociality is projected out of a radical privatization of
experience (the school of poetics that Gummere inaugurated in the early
twentieth century was actually called "communalism"). In order to dwell in
that contradiction, the "attractive individual consciousness" represented in the
poem must be made abstract, must be made into a fictive individual without
a name or a race or a gender, must be made available to *us*. How did the poetry
of the many become the poetry of the one over the course of the late eigh-
teenth and first decades of the nineteenth centuries? In the chapters that fol-
low, I pose a series of answers to that question in slow readings of a few poems
by a single poet or group of poets. These chapters cover a specific historical
period, but they are not arranged in a specific chronological sequence, exactly;
instead, they draw lines back and forth between the late eighteenth and mid-
nineteenth centuries, cross-hatching the period but certainly not filling in all
the gaps. Because my argument here is not only about these poets but also
about the historical formation of a poetics, I have arranged each chapter in
relation to a particular poetic structure, though both "poetic" and "structure"
are very general ways to describe the organizing figures I have in mind.

This first chapter has surrounded Plato's poem with a larger consideration
of the role of personal abstraction in lyric theory and historical poetics. In
chapter 2, I emphasize apostrophe, the Romantic figure of address that has
been so central to modern lyric theory, in the work of Plato's fellow American
Romantics John Pierpont, Frederick Douglass, James Monroe Whitfield, and
George Moses Horton (the poet identified only as "a slave" in the title of that
1838 Isaac Knapp edition in which his poems were published with Wheat-
ley's). Apostrophe, "the direct address to an absent, dead, or inanimate being
by a first-person speaker," as Barbara Johnson so usefully defined it, creates
fictions of both speaker and addressee. Such fictions may appear benign or
even world-making, but as Johnson argued, in apostrophic poetic address
(such as "Mneme, begin"), "the absent, dead, or inanimate entity addressed
is therefore made present, animate, and anthropomorphic. Apostrophe is a
form of ventriloquism through which the speaker throws voice, life, and
human form into the addressee, turning its silence into mute responsive-
ness."[102] For Black poets in the nineteenth century, such interpellation felt—
for good reason—like erasure rather than expression. In their different ways,
these poets recognized that, as Brent Hayes Edwards writes, "the lyric is not
a timeless, universal form; it is marked by history—and its history couches a

threat to the enunciation of black subjectivity."[103] The reason this is true is because American lyric was invented in the nineteenth century on the basis of that threat. As Black poets wrote poems that foregrounded the hazards of interpellation that Romantic apostrophe posed, poems that often took the figure of apostrophe itself as their subject, they signified on the process of lyricization as it was unfolding, changing the direction of that process by making it metalyrical from the beginning.

Or perhaps even before the beginning. I began this book by introducing Phillis Wheatley's metalyrical creation of a poetics of personal abstraction in the late eighteenth century, and in chapter 3 I return to Wheatley, and specifically to the poem that became "On Recollection," in order to consider the many ways in which her poetics saw the threat of Romantic apostrophe coming in the privileged eighteenth-century figure of personification. The result of this figure in Wheatley's poetics is not animation or "mute responsiveness," but silence, disintegration, vanishing, dissemination, scattering, disappearance, and refinement into evanescence. It is as if her personifying figures literalized and realized the dangers of figurative personhood that later Black Romantic poets perceived before they happened. Yet as we shall also see, that may be because the pathos that aligned Wheatley's poetics with her self-characterization as the "last and meanest of the rhyming train," the poet and the poetry "all beautiful in woe," influenced the Anglo-American Romantic poetics that later Black poets recast as inherently antiblack. Wheatley's poetics thus prefigured both Romanticism and the Black nineteenth-century critique of Romanticism that together formed American lyric.

This is to say that in the first three chapters of this book, I attempt a history of what Moten calls a "mode of lyricism that has been explored and cultivated precisely by folks who have both *been refused* access" to "normative [Hegelian] lyric subjectivity" as well as a history of the ways in which Black poets "have also *refused* that normative subjectivity themselves."[104] Yet in my account, early Black poetics was also formative of what eventually became the "normative lyric subjectivity" of personal abstraction, since those refusals were internal to rather than rejections of that norm. But of course the racialization of lyric in the nineteenth century did not just affect Black and non-White poets; the poetics of whiteness was also an emphatically racialized historical formation. This book's chapter 4 is devoted to the poetry of William Cullen Bryant, and especially to the Romantic prosody that Bryant borrowed from the British Romantics, a debt that earned him a reputation as "the American Wordsworth." Bryant's use of the stanzaic and metrical structures made famous by

Wordsworth, Robert Southey, and other Lake School poets made him into an institution of a new American Romantic poetics, "the father of American poetry." Bryant was also a maker of new American cultural institutions: The New York Public Library, Central Park, and the Metropolitan Museum of Art were all Bryant's ideas, but his other influential idea was the creation of the transatlantic White Romantic lyric in the 1820s and 1830s in poems like "To a Waterfowl" (1818), "An Indian at the Burial-Ground of His Fathers" (1824), and "The Prairies" (1833). Though Bryant was ostensibly a liberal antislavery activist, like many nineteenth-century abolitionists, he was also a racist, and his racism became evident in his support of Andrew Jackson's genocidal removal policies. It also became evident in his prosody: the abstract person that emerges in Bryant's Romantic poetics is a feminized White male speaker thrown against a non-White background, and the whiteness of that speaker is guaranteed by the iambs, dactyls, amphibrachs, trochees, and enjambments of his lines.

In chapter 5, I organize an unlikely comparison between the Black feminist activist poet Frances Ellen Watkins Harper and the White Harvard Professor and best-selling poet of the nineteenth century, Henry Wadsworth Longfellow, under the sign of the popular nineteenth-century figure of the Poetess. Unlike apostrophe or personification or prosody, the Poetess is not a figure many lyric theorists still associate with the structure of poetics, but perhaps we should. As I have already begun to suggest, in the nineteenth century, the Poetess was a figure intimately associated with the work of women poets, but it was also, like apostrophe and personification and prosody, a figure that was detachable from the work of any particular poet. Nineteenth-century White male poets like Poe and Whitman (or, for that matter, Bryant) employed Poetess poetics, and that was possible because the Poetess was not consubstantial with the author's gender or sexuality. Yet using the figure of the Poetess was not like using poetic genres such as the elegy or the epistle; since the Poetess was more like a trope than a genre, it could be as definite and slippery as a turn of phrase, turning through many prosodic and rhetorical genres at once. For Watkins Harper, that slipperiness made the figure adaptable to a poetics that joined the poetics of Plato, Whitfield, Horton, and Wheatley in reimagining the antiblack poetic discourses they worked and lived within. Watkins Harper recognized the whiteness of feminized abstraction in the poems of famous Poetesses like Elizabeth Oakes Smith and took it apart, piece by piece and poem by poem. She also very clearly recognized the coalescence of that abstraction in a representative lyric voice, and like Adorno, she understood the reification, the "false glitter" of the illusion of that singular lyric expression as the index of a social antagonism.

At around the same time, Longfellow seems to have recognized much the same thing, but he adopted the figure of the Poetess in order to create an influential poetics that appeared to resolve all social antagonisms in the feminized voice of poetry itself. The Poetess poetics of self-sacrifice and self-erasure proved central to all of Longfellow's best-selling poetry, which turned particular verse genres into open-access abstractions of those genres. It was also central to his World Literature project at Harvard, which turned all Western literary traditions into one big, lyricized tradition of White poetics. By appropriating the trope of the Poetess as figure for his own authorship, Longfellow managed to make that authorship and that tradition appear to belong to everyone and no one rather than to the man Poe liked to print-shout at as "PROFESSOR LONGFELLOW." In contrast, Watkins Harper disowned the feminized lyric impersonation her poetry seems to perform by intimating an alternative poetics not based on apostrophe or personification or either accentual or quantitative prosody or the speaking figure of the Poetess. While Longfellow may be said to have realized the ambitions of nineteenth-century White poetics by institutionalizing a way of reading poetry as shared communal expression, Watkins Harper realized the ambitions of Black Romantics like Wheatley, Plato, Horton, Douglass, and Whitfield by imagining a poetry that could dissolve such inherently racist and antifeminist communal fictions. Though this way of understanding nineteenth-century Black poetics risks casting that poetics as a project of "rejoinder, protest, or commentary, figuring black writing as reactive rather than productive," as Reed cautions, my argument is that this reframing of American poetics *was* productive.[105] The chapters of *Before Modernism* begin with Wheatley and end with Watkins Harper in order to propose a new literary history, a new historical poetics, a new account of the invention of American lyric.

This book does and does not end with its last chapter, since the process of lyricization is uneven and unfinished. While I have described these chapters as a developmental history, honestly, there is too much left out here for me to make that claim. Because slow reading takes time, I don't include enough poems per poet, or enough poets, to call this book an accurate representation of the poetics of the late eighteenth and entire first half of the American nineteenth centuries. The only glancing background presence of Emerson and Poe here, for example, will surprise some readers, not to mention the absence of Whitman. Since Emerson has been the focus of most discussions of nineteenth-century American poetics, I have intentionally displaced that focus in order to tell a story that does not make Transcendentalism the central event of the 1840s and 1850s. As for Whitman, well, the brief history of the invention of American lyric that I recount here allowed him to do what he would do. If I had included more or different poems and poets (and there are so many others I *could* have chosen), I might have narrated a different version of American poetics "before modernism"—though even if all of the poems and poets represented here were replaced by others, the trend of the century would still be toward lyricization, toward an increasingly capacious and increasingly indeterminate version of poetry as lyric by the middle of the nineteenth century. But that new lyric form was of course itself subject to change, and for the past two centuries, it has been anything but stable. How could it be? While Plato's First-of-August ode in common meter addressed very specific and very general publics, the gradual abstraction of lyric address into the fictive speech of an imaginary person has occasioned a proliferation of lyric and post-lyric poetic genres that address everyone and no one, that speak to you in the voice of an impossible person born of what history has done to us.

2

Apostrophe, Animation, and Racism

PIERPONT, DOUGLASS, WHITFIELD — AND HORTON

"O poets to come"

Do poems speak to you? Think of what happens when you read poems unlike Plato's, poems that use the personal "I" rather than the generic "we," poems in which you encounter the signature version of excited Romantic poetic address that begins with a single letter adorned with its own exclamation mark: "*O!*" Don't you imagine that someone is *saying* (or shouting or whispering or gasping) "O!"? Does it matter that you don't know who that person might be? Or do you not think this is a person at all, since you know this is a poetic convention? Do you feel moved to respond anyway, if only silently? Don't you want to imagine that overseeing or overhearing that address brings you into its range, thus making you feel as if you were joining a collective of such responsive silences?[1]

Nineteenth-century American poets often hoped you would feel this way. Think of Whitman! It is hard to imagine a poet who more wanted to be the one to speak to and for the many. A poem that he included only in the 1860 edition *Leaves of Grass* ends with the lines,

> O Death! O you striding there! O I cannot yet!
> O heights! O infinitely too swift and dizzy yet!
> O purged lumine! you threaten me more than I can stand!
> O present! I return while yet I may to you!
> O poets to come, I depend upon you![2]

That's a lot of exclamation marks and a lot of Os, and this poem contains almost a hundred more. The poem is, in fact, titled "Apostroph." (in a typically Whitmanian pseudo-French affectation), and it demonstrates the ambition of the Romantic figure-become-genre through sheer excess.[3] As Anahid Nersessian writes of British Romanticism, such apostrophic excess may lead us to see that Romantic "lyric, in contrast to more plainly referential genres like epic or satire, is where figuration can really show its gift for making the phenomenology of attenuated life credible and conspicuous." If readers "have been tempted to identify apostrophe with lyric itself," Nersessian explains, "that may be because apostrophe so explicitly concerns the activity of things that seem hardly to exist at all," things that stand a chance of being called into being by being addressed.[4] Is that what Whitman's apostrophes demonstrate? What are these strange things that have not "yet" appeared, that seem hardly to exist at all, these things that apostrophe so explicitly—and repeatedly—concerns?

In Whitman's poem, Death, heights (of Death?), "lumine" (a nominative form of illumine? Also Death, when "purged"?), the "present" (life, not Death), and future "poets to come" are the objects of this recursive apostrophic address, but not because they do not exist or because their existence is "attenuated." On the contrary, it is because Death is certain and the poet "cannot yet" accept that certainty that there is the need for so much over-the-top O-ing, as well as the need for the culminating invocation of "the poets to come," since those future poets will keep the O-ing going when these apostrophes no longer keep Death at bay. Whitman's apostrophes are forms of protest against the dying of the light, against things that "threaten *me* more than I can stand" (emphasis added). While the post-structuralist and formalist critical view of lyric-as-animating-apostrophe shares the fantasy of a communal horizon of shared sociality projected out of a radical privatization of experience (since it allows us all to dwell in the fiction of this lyricized speech situation), Whitman characteristically exaggerates the ominous potential of apostrophe, emphasizing the threat such hyper-figurative address poses to the addressee.[5] What Whitman's apostrophes want to make disappear is the mortality that threatens him, but it's worth asking why apostrophe might be supposed to have such destructive power. If poetic address calls absent or invisible things into being, how (and why, and when) can poetic address also make things disappear? And why might it be important to do so in public, especially in print? Whitman (laureate of print that he was) is as usual onto something here, since as it turns out, there is another side to the "gift" of apostrophic figuration in the history of American poetics. Because in the nineteenth century especially, apostrophes tended to overwhelm other genres of verse address (as Whitman's poetics were so spectacularly designed to do), they indeed performed a disappearing act by blending those genres together into an abstract, imaginary genre, into a communal poetry of the future that could solve the conflicts of the present by locating those conflicts in an imaginary person (as Whitman's poetics were also so spectacularly designed to do).

For Whitman's contemporary Black American Romantics, that new imaginary lyric genre and its new imaginary generic person made the personal costs of such abstraction, such disappearing acts, such blurring, vertiginously high, since apostrophe's "gift for making the phenomenology of attenuated life credible and conspicuous" came to seem like White Britannia's gift of a way of being that White Romantic poetics (well, that White America) had rendered attenuated, incredible, and inconspicuous in the first place. When Whitman invoked the destructive potential of apostrophe in 1860, he was drawing on anxieties repeatedly expressed in the work of his Black contemporaries, though the history and theory of American poetics have both been premised on an ignorance of this debt. During the 1840s and early 1850s, the decades in which Whitman was busy inventing his version of apostrophic lyric address, Plato was not the only Black poet to recognize that the lyricizing ambition of apostrophic address threatened to make us all credibly and conspicuously White, even (or especially) when, because of what history has done to us, *we* continue to be in danger of hardly existing at all.

Two in One

How did the nineteenth-century American process of lyricization work to shift the phenomenology of verse address from the generic mode of Ann Plato's "To the First of August" toward the phenomenology of modern lyric reading? How and why did nineteenth-century Black poets in particular turn the publicly private lyric speaker into an abstract figure of representational alienation at the same time that speaker was being invented by nineteenth-century transatlantic White poetics? While the point of this varied history is that there is no single response to those questions, consider a few concentrated examples of the many ways in which apostrophe became one common thread stitching the twinned processes of racialization and lyricization so tightly together that for the past two hundred years it has been difficult to tell them apart.

In Boston in 1843, John Pierpont, a White poet, lawyer, merchant, minister, and the maternal grandfather of J. Pierpont Morgan (patriarch of the US banking industry), published what became an immensely popular volume of *Anti-Slavery Poems* that included "Hymn for the First of August," dated 1842. Pierpont's version of the genre begins,

> Where Britannia's emerald isles
>   Gem the Caribbean sea,
> And an endless summer smiles,
>   Lo! The negro thrall is free!
> Yet not on Columbia's plains.
>   Hath the sun of freedom risen:
> Here, in darkness and in chains,
>   Toiling millions pine in prison.
>
> Shout! ye islands disenthralled,
>   Point the finger, as in scorn,
> At a country that is called
>   Freedom's home, where men are born
> Heirs, for life, to chains and whips,—
>   Bondmen, who have never known
> Wife, child, parent, that their lips
>   Ever dared to call their own.[6]

Like Plato's poem, "Hymn for the First of August" is in common meter, and the title specifies a specific subgenre of that meter (as does its echo of Plato's echo of the particular hymn associated with "Freedom's home"). While the rhyme scheme in Plato's poem is irregular and strategic (abcb in the first three stanzas, though in the first stanza the rhyme is slant, abbb in the fourth stanza, though again with slight variation, abab in the fifth and seventh stanzas, another abcb in the sixth stanza), Pierpont's rhymes emphasize the neat fit of two quatrains within each octave (ababcdcd). For American readers in 1843, Pierpont's heavily enjambed octaves might have recalled the British Romantics' use of *ottava rima* that was all the rage after Plato's fellow Connecticut poet Fitz-Greene Halleck ("the American Byron") published his long poem *Fanny* in 1819, though both Pierpont's title and the embedded quatrains identify his poem with popular rather than high literary verse. This is to say that what Plato's poem *is*, Pierpont's poem is *like*—which is not to say that Plato's poem is what Pierpont is copying, exactly. His source is not a particular poem but a genre of poetry, not only the genre of the popular hymn but the genre of the political hymn, not only the genre of the political hymn but the genre of the abolitionist hymn, not only the genre of the abolitionist hymn but the celebration of the first of August in such hymns by free Black writers, not only the Black celebration of the first of August in such hymns but the communal source of address embedded in these genres, the *we* that in Plato's poem indexes such raced solidarity and such raced disparity.

There is no *we* in Pierpont's poem, and there is no "lyric I"; of the pronouns to which Benveniste insists "person belongs," there is in Pierpont's cover version of Plato's generic hymn only the apostrophically addressed second-person pronoun, "ye islands." Whereas Plato's odic apostrophe seems to emanate from "British ground" to address *us* (*"You're free—you're free—"*), Pierpont's "Hymn" addresses the British West Indies directly, asking "Britannia's emerald isles" to be the ones to apostrophize America, "a country that is called / Freedom's home." Whereas Plato's apostrophe brings a fictive speaker and collective addressee into focus for just a moment, in Pierpont's poem that speaker has been established from the beginning as the apostrophic point of origin, as the stand-in for the White abolitionist poet. That poet is categorically disidentified with "the negro thrall" and "toiling millions," with the inheritance of "chains and whips," with the "bondmen" who have no heirs "to call their own." The personal pronoun that "destroys the person," as Benveniste would say, here creates an imaginary person who is antiblack, who is not *them*. Though "free," Plato merges in and out of the enslaved and/or emancipated pronominal collective her poem invokes, and thus does not become such an imaginary person, does not become a speaker singled out to represent that collective. Yet I have suggested that everything in her poem tells us where the desire for such a figure came from, and I have also suggested that modern lyric reading was gradually made in answer to that desire. In Pierpont's poem, written just a year after Plato's poem was published, we can see how at least one White poet used the figure of apostrophe to frame that speaker as structurally antiblack.

"Now it is certainly beyond question that the figure of address is recurrent in lyric poetry," Paul de Man wrote, with declamatory assurance. In fact, de Man declares, apostrophe occurs so often in lyric that it should be considered constitutive of "the generic definition of, at the very least, the ode (which can, in its turn, be seen as paradigmatic for poetry in general)."[7] De Man thus makes a figure into the defining feature of a genre, rather than the other way around. We might think that the fact that Pierpont's line, "Shout! ye islands disenthralled" occurs in a poem might determine our sense that such address is imaginary, but that is not de Man's point. For de Man, it is the figure that generates the genre, and a capacious genre it is, embracing lyric from "the ode" to "poetry in general." This book tries to fill in some of the missing two centuries glossed over by de Man's two-sentence slide from ode to lyric to a general, lyricized idea of poetry. But the idea that the figure of apostrophe generates the lyric imaginary is not just a post-structuralist pose that needs to be historicized; it has been taken to be common sense. As Culler wrote in 1976, "Imagine a man standing on a corner in the rain cursing buses: 'Come on, damn you! It's been ten minutes!' If he continues apostrophically when other travelers join him on the corner, he makes a spectacle of himself; his apostrophe works less to establish an I-Thou relation between him and the absent bus than to dramatize or constitute an image of self . . . the vocative of apostrophe is a device the poetic voice uses to establish with an object a relation that helps to constitute him."[8] This is to say that apostrophe does not just conjure the imaginary presence of an absent, dead, or inanimate addressee but also conjures the addresser, the *speaker* ("the poetic voice") in a fictive dramatic situation ("a relation that helps to constitute him"). While the man on the corner in the rain "makes a spectacle of himself," the poetic speaker comes into being through "the vocative of apostrophe"; what would be "embarrassing" on a street corner becomes "poetry" when lineated on a printed page. *O rose! O tree! O America! O wind! O ye islands disenthralled! O you!*: lyric apostrophe changes what Erving Goffman calls "the footing" of the speaker, suspending the everyday sociality of address in view of a poetic relation that may be indeterminate yet intimate, close yet unsettled, partial yet complete, and that is why de Man says that it is the figure that generates the genre.[9] Johnson thus followed both de Man and Culler when she defined apostrophe as "the direct address to an absent, dead, or inanimate being by a first-person speaker."[10] But Johnson was more worried than either de Man or Culler about the cause-and-effect relation assumed by the figure that still seems to define lyric address. Which came first, the poem or its genre of address? That genre of address or its speaker? That speaker or his/her/its/their "image of self"? That self or its vehicle of mass transport?

When Johnson writes that the figure of apostrophe "has come to seem almost synonymous with lyric voice" (529), the emphasis on *come to seem* and *almost* means that we should be careful when investing in that synonymy. As Johnson explains, because "apostrophe manipulates the I/thou structure of direct address in an indirect, fictionalized way . . . the absent, dead, or inanimate entity addressed is therefore made present, animate, and anthropomorphic. Apostrophe is a form of ventriloquism through which the speaker throws voice, life, and human form into the addressee, turning its silence into mute responsiveness" (530). When the addressee is a rose or an urn or a skylark, such ventriloquism seems harmless enough (though both Blake's rose and Keats's urn are ventriloquized as victims of potential sexual violence, and so is Shelley's skylark, in at least a few of its variations), but Johnson's critique of the ways that apostrophe "manipulates the I/thou structure of direct address" occurs in her essay "Apostrophe, Animation, and Abortion" (1987), the essay from which this chapter takes its title, and there she is particularly interested in the question that preoccupied the nineteenth-century Black American poets that Whitman echoed: what happens when the rhetorical questions that apostrophe poses are literalized?

As Berlant put it, "Johnson tracks the political consequences of apostrophe for what has become fetal personhood":

> a silent, affectively present but physically displaced interlocutor (a lover, a fetus) is animated in speech as distant enough for a conversation but close enough to be imaginable by the speaker in whose head the entire scene is happening. But the condition of projected possibility . . . creates a fake present moment of intersubjectivity in which, nonetheless, a performance of address can take place. . . . Apostrophe therefore . . . is actually a turning back, an animating of a receiver on behalf of the desire to make something happen *now* that realizes something *in the speaker*, makes the speaker more or differently possible, because she has admitted, in a sense, the importance of speaking for, as, and to, two—but only under the condition, and illusion, that the two are really (in) one.[11]

What Berlant elaborates in the "form of ventriloquism" that Johnson attributes to lyric apostrophe is its intersubjective expense, since apostrophic intersubjectivity can only be a fantasy that constitutes "an image of self" rather than a conversation. The political consequence of Johnson's analysis of apostrophic poems about abortion means that the "fake moment of intersubjectivity" that the logic of apostrophe makes possible condemns women having or considering abortions to the position of murderer or sufferer, since the fetus is always already animated by virtue of being addressed. In Pierpont's poem, the ventriloquized animation of "ye islands disenthralled" creates a present moment of intersubjectivity between Britain and the White abolitionist poet, a moment in which the poet speaks for Britannia ("Lo! The negro thrall is free!") and "ye islands disenthralled" speak for the poet, denouncing the laws of "a country" that is in fact the poet's own.

The political consequences of this version of White anglocentric American lyric allow Pierpont to create a shared poetic world—a genre—that we all recognize quite easily. That world may be "fake," but because it occurs in a poem, it performs an illusion of agency embodied by the speaker who not only gives British colonies voice but who speaks for and as Britannia herself. That performance looks even more White and gendered when placed against the background of Plato's poem. In Plato's "To the First of August," apostrophe does not become synonymous with lyric voice, and a performative present moment of intersubjectivity never happens, not even for *us*, as "we do view those honor'd lands" with which Pierpont so easily identifies. That is because the full-throated apostrophic ease on which the post-structuralist lyric theory I just traced briefly through de Man, Culler, Johnson, and Berlant depends has an uneasy history. That ease allows de Man to equate apostrophe with lyric and lyric with "poetry in general" and allows Culler to make apostrophe what separates the lyric poet from "a man standing on a corner." But apostrophe doesn't seem so easy to Johnson and Berlant, who both separate genre from figure in order to show how a political issue ("an issue like, say, abortion") and the politicized lived condition of "cruel optimism . . . a relation of attachment to compromised conditions of possibility whose realization is discovered either to be impossible, sheer fantasy, or too possible, and toxic" tally the literal costs of figurative intersubjective apostrophic fictions.[12] De Man and Culler both assume a long arc in which the figure of Romantic lyric address becomes increasingly poetic and transhistorical; Johnson and Berlant both take apostrophe out of poetry, returning it to the poetics of contemporary lived experience. In fact, the figure of apostrophe does have a long history of turning genres into people, as we shall see in every chapter of this book. By creating an illusion of intersubjectivity (what Tucker calls "the intersubjective confirmation of the self"), apostrophic address facilitates the metapragmatic subsumption of a variety of poetic speech genres into a lyricized genre identified with and by the two-in-one apostrophic speaker.[13] In Pierpont's poem, that intersubjective fiction makes the abolitionist poet doubly White, since the pronouns that "destroy the person" are attributed to "the negro thrall," to "toiling millions" in "darkness," while the apostrophe to the British West Indies is an affirmation of mutual White solidarity that subordinates the collective genre of the hymn to the personal voice of the White, Anglo-identified male abolitionist.

The Night Sky

Actually, Pierpont's most famous Garrisonian abolitionist poem, "The Fugitive Slave's Apostrophe to the North Star," literally made a genre of its titular rhetorical figure, and that genre went viral in the 1840s and 1850s, perhaps

because, as the title also affirms, the speaker of the poem is not the apostrophi-
cally interpellated White poet but that poet's blackface performance of the
nameless, generic "fugitive slave"'s fictive apostrophic interpellation of what
Jared Hickman has called "the North-Star cult in African American litera-
ture."[14] The metapoetics of this double, already-doubled apostrophic address
are clear from the poem's title, and become even clearer in its first stanza:

> Star of the North! though night-winds drift
>   The fleecy drapery of the sky,
> Between thy lamp and me, I lift,
>   Yea, lift with hope, my sleepless eye,
> To the blue heights wherein thou dwellest,
> And of a land of freedom tellest.[15]

The form of ventriloquism that Johnson describes as apostrophe's mechanical
effect is on full display here—so much so that one wonders whether such
display isn't the stanza's point. In that last couplet's punch line, the star tells
the fugitive exactly what he wants to hear, thus making his fugitivity more or
differently possible, since such a speaking star might give him the ability to
guide himself to a "land of freedom." Whereas the two-in-one intersubjective
fiction of apostrophe in Pierpont's impersonation of a favorite genre of
nineteenth-century Black poetics in "Hymn for the First of August" makes the
White American poet as White as Britannia, the two-in-one intersubjective
fiction of apostrophe in "The Fugitive Slave's Apostrophe to the North Star"
explicitly makes the White poet a Black impersonator—thus again racializing
him as White. Since the poem first appeared in 1839 and was massively re-
printed through the 1840s and 1850s, it both prefigured and, in its reprintings,
responded to the Fugitive Slave Law, especially because by the end of the
poem that "land of freedom" is colonial Canada, "of England's Queen and En-
glish law. / Queen, that hath made her islands free." This poem thus joins the
First of August poems in casting the empire from which America had so re-
cently claimed republican freedom as an example of the freedom America
could not offer. In using this large, generic version of apostrophe as a way to
conjure the enslaved fugitive's voice, Pierpont's poem emphasizes that fiction's
portability, its dislocation from its historical circumstances of address (per-
haps even from the planet), and of course its dislocation from a definitely ra-
cialized historical body, a body the poet claims as his own.

The prosody of the poem underwrites this claim to ownership, since the
stanza in which Pierpont appropriates the fiction of that racialized body is a

sestet he took from Bryant that Bryant had borrowed from Wordsworth and Wordsworth had adapted from Shakespeare. The Venus and Adonis stanza (ababcc) was named for Shakespeare's 1593 verse epic but was widely used in the early modern period as an iambic pentameter heroic quatrain joined to a couplet.[16] By the time that Wordsworth adapted the stanza for "I wandered lonely as a cloud" (1804–7/1815; the poem now known as "Daffodils"), a tetrameter version had become popular, and, as we shall see in chapter 4, it was Wordsworth's version of the stanza that Bryant further adapted in his popular 1824 poem "An Indian at the Burial-Place of His Fathers" and in "The Indian Girl's Lament" in 1825, making the last inset quatrain line in the sestet a trimeter rather than a tetrameter in both poems, thus adding a folksy twist to the British model.[17] It was Bryant's version of the stanza that would have been closest to Pierpont, so it's interesting that Pierpont does not copy Bryant's fourth-line trimeter, instead extending the tetrameter couplet lines by an extra beat. That extension emphasizes Pierpont's sympathy with the British rather than the "American Wordsworth," but Bryant's use of the stanza in poems that feature a lone survivor of colonial violence does help Pierpont frame his fugitive as a New World literary theme, and the attraction of that theme for White readers was its pathos of endangerment. This framing is what Lethabo King calls "the black shoals" of two-in-one historical analogies between enslavement and Indigenous genocide.[18] Like Bryant's generic, nameless "Indian" who is a survivor of the violence inflicted by "the pale race, who waste us now," and like the generic, nameless "Indian girl" who builds a burial-place for herself and her dead warrior-lover, Pierpont's implicitly Black (because enslaved) fugitive is alone in a world bent on his extinction. Bryant's 1825 "Hymn to the North Star" also stands somewhere in the background of Pierpont's poem, since "the sad and solemn night" that is the scene of the poet's apostrophe to "Star of the Pole!" in that 1825 poem is also Pierpont's apostrophic scene. But in Bryant's poem, the speaker of the apostrophe is not an endangered Black fugitive but the well-situated White New York poet, who addresses the star as

> A beauteous type of that unchanging good,
> That bright eternal beacon, by whose ray
> The voyager of time should shape his heedful way.[19]

This is to say that just as the structure of Pierpont's apostrophe hailed a White public, the structure of the poem itself is made of layer upon layer of Anglo-American White poetics. Because the nameless fugitive designated by the definite article represents that history of poetics, Pierpont's White abolitionist public could be reassured that though he may be framed by Indigenous and Black signifiers, he remains the White poet's sympathetic persona, a figure that speaks to and for but also as that public.[20]

Pierpont's version of blackface minstrelsy is and is not like the "love and theft" that Eric Lott describes as "an emergent social semantic figure highly responsive to the emotional demands and troubled fantasies of its audiences" in the performance culture of the antebellum period.[21] While it is true that the vanishing Indians and enslaved fugitives of antebellum poetics represented all kinds of sadistic White fantasies, the genres and media of address on which those figures depended entailed their own social semantics. In his *North Star* newspaper, Frederick Douglass wrote that blackface performers were "the filthy scum of white society, who have stolen from us a complexion denied to them by nature, in which to make money, and pander to the corrupt taste of their white fellow citizens" (October 27, 1848). Lott calls this "a denunciation that nicely captures minstrelsy's further commodification of an already enslaved, noncitizen people," but argues "that there was a range of responses to the minstrel show which points to an instability or contradiction in the form itself" (15). There certainly seems to have been a range of responses pointing to an instability or contradiction in the form of lyricized blackface print performance featured in Pierpont's poem, so much so that Douglass appears not to have considered the poem as addressed to the corrupt tastes of White readers but as addressed—or at least addressable—to the new Black public his newspaper hoped to create. Whether or not he actually named the paper for Pierpont's poem, Douglass printed the poem in the paper's first issue on December 3, 1847, and the poem and the paper remained close kin, since in later issues (when the paper could afford it) an image of the fugitive addressing the star claimed center stage on the paper's masthead (figures 2.1 and 2.2).

I have accused Pierpont of writing a racist abolitionist poem that allowed a White public to disidentify with and perhaps even enjoy his subject's suffering, but if so, why would Frederick Douglass (hardly a pushover!) have so closely associated his paper with this poem? As Ann Stoler has phrased a similar question, "How could racism serve such a wide spectrum of political agendas at the same time?"[22] Perhaps just as Douglass disagreed with his co-editor Martin Delany about the usefulness of Harriet Beecher Stowe's racist abolitionist celebrity to the cause of Black emancipation, Douglass appropriated Pierpont's popular apostrophic poem as his paper's hieroglyphic because in that way Pierpont's generic apostrophic fiction could be resignified as Douglass's lived experience.[23] I mean "signified" in Henry Louis Gates's sense of the

FIGURE 2.1. Detail of masthead, *North Star*, Friday, February 22, 1850.

FIGURE 2.2. Masthead, *North Star*, Friday, February 22, 1850.

Black aesthetic operation in which "the sign itself appears to be doubled, at the very least, and (re)doubled upon ever closer examination," but I also mean to suggest that since Douglass was "signifyin(g)" on the *already* doubled structure of apostrophe, he was attempting to take that doubleness back in order to translate it into singleness.[24] Frederick Douglass was not "the" fugitive slave but a particular person who was enslaved, who became a fugitive, and then became one of the most important public intellectuals of the nineteenth century. What for Pierpont was impersonation for Douglass was his own ordeal—the life of an individual whose very name was a racialized impersonation.[25] Daniel Hack has suggested that Douglass's later serialization of Dickens's *Bleak House* in what was by the 1850s called *Frederick Douglass' Paper* "makes newly visible and meaningful certain aspects of the novel even as it calls into question the power of such features to determine the cultural work the novel—and by extension, any text—performs."[26] I am saying something less tentative and more specific about the difference that genre makes to Douglass's reprinting of Pierpont's lyric: Douglass's appropriation of this apostrophic fiction literalized the figure in a way that did not just "call into question" the "cultural work" of the White abolitionism Douglass broke with when he broke with Garrison. Instead, his paper resignified apostrophic lyric address as an inherently racialized fiction. Essentially, the speech act that Douglass was performing in and as print was something like, "That fugitive slave is not *your* 'fugitive slave'; that figure is *me*!" I do not want to further ventriloquize Douglass by putting words in his mouth, since he let his paper do the talking for him, but Douglass's graphic version of Pierpont's ventriloquism did in effect recast racialized poetic abstraction as racialized personal experience.[27]

In this way, Douglass's individuation of the figure of apostrophe attempted to check the development of modern lyric reading just as that logic was beginning to take shape. Because we have not included nineteenth-century American Romantic apostrophes—and especially not Black American Romantic apostrophes—in our consideration of the figure taken to define the lyric as a genre, both the racialized history of the figure (and thus of the lyric) and the public exposure of that racism have gone unnoticed.[28] Both have also gone unnoticed in recent celebrations of nineteenth-century American poetry's public popularity: a recent post on the Library of Congress website titled "Discover Poetry in Old News!" begins with the example of Pierpont's poem's appearance in the first issue of the *North Star*, explaining that "poetry was a regular feature of many anti-slavery newspapers, one of the tools to inspire readers to deepen their support for the abolitionist cause."[29] What this national celebration of poetry in public forgets to say is that what Douglass's placement of the poem also made public was what he stated in his opening editorial, "Our Paper and Its Prospects," in that first issue of the paper on December 3, 1847: that his Black newspaper would do "what it would be wholly impossible for our white friends to do for us," or more pointedly, that "the man who has *suffered the wrong* is the man to *demand redress.*" That lyric stance may be one way to answer the question recently posed by Rowan Ricardo Phillips: "how, if at all, did the poetic climate affect the man who would come to be known as the most famous black in the world"?[30] As Douglass's biographer David Blight writes, "irony was often Douglass's principle rhetorical weapon; now he boldly offered himself as its very embodiment."[31]

If that irony has sometimes been lost on later readers, it was not lost on the Black counter-public that Douglass's paper did manage to create.[32] In 1849, the great Black poet James Monroe Whitfield did what Douglass stopped short of doing when he rewrote Pierpont's poem and published it in Douglass's paper. Titled simply "The North Star," omitting the first phrase of Pierpont's title but repeating his apostrophe's initial signature exclamation, Whitfield's poem explicitly revises Pierpont's:

> Star of the north! whose steadfast ray
> > Pierces the sable pall of night,
> Forever pointing out the way
> > That leads to freedom's hallowed light:
> The fugitive lifts up his eye
> To where thy rays illume the sky.[33]

Whereas the fugitive is the fictional speaker of Pierpont's poem, Whitfield's revision retains the shape of the Venus and Adonis stanza but makes its speaker indeterminate. In fact, it turns out the poem's title has been abbreviated because this apostrophe is not the fugitive's at all. Whose is it? Notice that Whitfield omits the word "slave," and notice, too, that someone or something has taken the faux-fugitive's place in addressing the star. It would be easy to say that it is the poet who speaks here, but if so, then he speaks in tongues. The first half-line is Pierpont's, so we could say its "voice" is that poet's blackface performance. The second line's cliché, "sable pall," was common to literary descriptions of scenes of death in the nineteenth century (it appears in Dickens's *Martin Chuzzlewit*, for example, which was first serialized between 1842 and 1844), but the first line of the working-class White British Poetess Eliza Cook's 1842 "The Poor Man's Friend" ("No sable pall, no waving plume") might be especially relevant here, since as a Chartist poet, Cook was writing political verse, and this particular poem (about the obscure grave of a man so impoverished that "the mourning dog that starves and dies" is its only attendant) became an enormously popular broadside ballad.[34] In the echo of Cook, Whitfield evokes the social death of the fugitive that the North Star's "steadfast ray / Pierces," thus establishing the political agency of both the star and of the newspaper named after it. The fourth line intensifies the emphasis on the star/paper's purpose on behalf of the oppressed, as "freedom's hallowed light" reverses John Quincy Adams's refutation of "tyrants" in "freedom's hallowed shade," and perhaps also recalls the early nineteenth-century popular Scottish poet Thomas Campbell's famous poem "Hallowed Ground" ("Is't death to fall for Freedom's right? / He's dead alone that lacks her light!").[35]

My point is not that these are exact literary allusions in Whitfield's poem, but that such associations constellate (so to speak) to form an echo chamber of progressive political poetic discourse—so much so that it is this public poetic discourse that becomes the "speaker" of these lines.[36] Both the form of the stanza itself (in its American iterations) and all of these associations are taken from White writers generally sympathetic to those in need, including those enslaved. So perhaps we could say that the "speaker" of these lines is the discourse of liberal White political poetics, a suggestion that makes sense of the poem's second stanza:

> That steady, calm, unchanging light,
>   Through dreary wilds and trackless dells,
> Directs his weary steps aright
>   To that bright land where freedom dwells;
> And spreads, with sympathizing breast,
> Her aegis over the oppressed.

Just as Whitfield's retention of the Venus and Adonis stanza signals his recognition of Pierpont's debt to Bryant's Anglophilic poetics, his second stanza invokes a particular couplet in Bryant's "Hymn to the North Star": "And they who stray in perilous wastes, by night, / Are glad when thou dost shine to guide their footsteps right." Actually, Whitfield is doubling down on echoes of Bryant here so that we will be sure to hear his source in the background: the last line of "To a Waterfowl" (1818), Bryant's most popular single lyric, is "Will lead my steps aright." This emphasis on Bryant as the surround sound of "The North Star" would have ensured that Whitfield's readers in Douglass's North Star understood this discourse as White liberal poetics, but also, since Bryant was most famous by this point in the nineteenth century as the poet who was also the editor of the New-York Evening Post, as White print poetic culture, especially White newsprint poetic culture. As we will see in more detail in chapter 4, Bryant's paper (and his use of the Venus and Adonis stanza itself) was supportive of Jackson's genocidal settler colonialism, but the paper was also explicitly antislavery. Thus, we could say that if Douglass reprints Pierpont's lyric in order to reclaim its blackface apostrophic fiction as the newspaper editor's own personal experience made public, Whitfield rewrites Pierpont's apostrophic lyric for Douglass's paper as a depersonalized chorus of inherently discordant, even contradictory White poetic-political public discourse that spoke "for" variously disempowered groups, including those enslaved. While Douglass revoked Pierpont's fictional speaker by undoing its fictionality, Whitfield revoked Pierpont's speaker by exposing it as White communal poetic public speech. That revision makes it clear that this impersonal, inchoate, only vaguely politically empowering, structurally antiblack transatlantic White poetics did not belong to *us*. The feminization of the star's "sympathizing breast" risks catachresis in order to echo an eighteenth-century nonconformist British hymn popular in nineteenth-century America: known as "Charity," the hymn begins, "O may our sympathizing breast / The generous pleasure know," and includes the stanza,

> When the most helpless sons of grief,
>   In low distress are laid:
> Soft be our hearts their pains to feel,
>   And prompt our hands to aid.[37]

The idea that such Christian sympathy could be an "aegis," or protective shield for "the oppressed" may have inspired White liberal transatlantic discourse with the satisfaction of its own Britannia-like generosity (especially since in the Iliad, the *aegis* belongs to the goddess Athena), but after this culminating invocation of such discourse as the inheritance of Western literary history, Whitfield's poem turns away from these feminized mythologies of White protection by shifting its apostrophe to the star into a different discursive register and a different poetics altogether.

The third and fourth stanzas of "The North Star" begin with a *volta* meant to turn our attention away from the genre of Pierpont's poem, away from the mode of recognition instantiated in the discourse of White Christian liberal literary political poetics of which both Pierpont's poem and Whitfield's first two stanzas are made, toward a mode of recognition instantiated in a discourse that at first appears otherworldly:

> Though other stars may round thee burn,
>   With larger disk and brighter ray,
> And fiery comets round thee turn,
>   While millions mark their blazing way;
> And the pale moon and planets bright
> Reflect on us their silvery light.

Not like that moon, now dark, now bright,
    In phase and place forever changing;
Or planets with reflected light,
    Or comets through the heavens ranging;
They all seem varying to our view,
While thou art ever fixed and true.

Unlike the poem's first two stanzas, these lines do not apostrophize the star as if the star were a White savior but instead address the star as the centerpiece of a cosmography we are being taught how to read. Such scenes of instruction were common in slave narratives; indeed, two years before Whitfield's poem was published, Andrew Jackson's narrative of escape described the ability to read the night sky as a commonly shared form of racialized literacy:

> I am sometimes asked, how we learn the way to the free States? My answer is, that the slaves know much more about this matter than many persons are aware. They have means of communication with each other, altogether unknown to their masters, or to the people of the free states. . . . There is scarcely one, who does not understand the position of the "north star," although that is about the extent of their knowledge of Astronomy.[38]

As Hickman writes, "Jackson's revelation deliciously insinuates the existence of a network of subaltern astronomical knowledge, a secret society of African learning whose full content cannot be known by the white observer," but this Black network does not seem so much insinuated as simply acknowledged in Jackson's account.[39] Whitfield's apostrophe to the one star that does not "seem varying to our view"—that is not the effect of reflected light or the momentary explosion of "fiery comets"—invokes a first-person plural that bears comparison to Plato's "we do view": as Plato's first-person plural pronoun was unstably constituted through distributed attention to British Caribbean abolition, so Whitfield's first-person plural is constituted by our attention to a "fixed" star. And who are *we*? Though apostrophes to the north star were the common stuff of slave narratives and slave impersonations, Whitfield's cosmographic apostrophe translates Pierpont's "toiling millions" into starry "millions," thus translating blackness out of the afterlife of slavery into the punctuated darkness of the night sky. Whitfield's poetics literalize apostrophe's political consequences, agreeing with Pennington that poetry may be "the only way to show the fallacy of that stupid theory, that *nature has done nothing but fit us for slaves, and that art cannot unfit us for slavery!*" Though Whitfield's night sky guides a fugitive to freedom, it is also a recoding of what such freedom might be, since as Hartman writes, racialized freedom may be "a glimpse of possibility, an opening, a solidification without any guarantee of duration before it flickers and is then extinguished," and in this sense freedom and slavery did not form an ancipital pair, though blackness and antiblackness surely did.[40]

As Wilson emphasizes, all of Whitfield's projects were dedicated to discovering such an optimistic opening in the fabric of racist America, since they were "premised on a desire that continually imagines an imminent—but tragically never immanent—future lingering on the precipice of arrival."[41] The night sky in "The North Star" is a vision of blackness as a cosmos unlike anything to be found in the nineteenth-century United States and especially unlike the versions of blackness imagined by White liberal poetics. As a committed emigrationist and Black nationalist, Whitfield and his friend and fellow Prince Hall Freemason Martin Delany broke with Douglass over the possibilities for full American citizenship for Black men, developing, as Wilson and Robert Levine write, "a hemispheric vision of 'America' as offering possibilities for a black nationality beyond national borders, and a conviction that emigration differed considerably from colonization precisely because it was a matter of political choice."[42] Rejecting what David Kazanjian describes as "the colonizing trick" of an equality always already located elsewhere, Whitfield and Delany also rejected America's hypocritical promise of national racial equality on the basis of citizenship, an idea Whitfield set on apostrophic fire in his most famous poem, "America":

> America, it is to thee,
> Thou boasted land of liberty,—
> It is to thee I raise my song,
> Thou land of blood, and crime, and wrong.[43]

As Wilson writes, "echoing and ultimately parodying Samuel Francis Smith's 'America' (1831), popularly known as 'My Country, 'Tis of Thee,' Whitfield illuminates the contrast between the America of the free celebrated in the song and the America of slavery at the heart of his poem. . . . The poem's opening visceral lines lull the reader with a degree of familiarity and anticipation only to have that familiarity immediately undercut."[44] That is certainly true, but since it is also true that Smith's song used the melody of "God Save the Queen," the British national anthem, Whitfield's parody was multilayered, and not just addressed to "a reader" but to a particular public attuned to those transatlantic layers.[45] While Smith's song apostrophizes America in its own White-identified communal voice, Whitfield's "America," like Whitfield's "The North Star," addresses that Anglo-identified White voice itself. The last stanza of Whitfield's version of the First of August poem, "Stanzas for the First of August," repeats his apostrophic accusation in "America" but changes the racialization of both the subject and the object of that apostrophe's address:

> And from those islands of the sea,
>   The scenes of blood and crime and wrong,
> The glorious anthem of the free,
>   Now swells in mighty chorus strong;
> Telling th'oppressed, whe'er they roam,
> Those islands now are freedom's home.[46]

"The scenes of blood and crime and wrong" common to both America and the colonized Caribbean give rise to an "anthem of the free" that is not the expression of a single voice and that is not addressed only to those enslaved. Like Plato (and unlike Pierpont), Whitfield uses the First of August genre (and its hymnal echo of "Freedom's home") to imagine an emerging free Black genre of verse address, a genre by definition alienated from the poetic stuff of which it is made, and he also tries to imagine that this new genre could have the courage of its convictions. The stanzas addressed to the night sky in "The North Star" position their object of address in a speculative cosmic horizon of blackness set free of the fiction of a single White lyric voice (though both poems retain the legacy of that voice in the Venus and Adonis stanza), but in "The North Star," Whitfield's object of address is not only not White but is also potentially free of White discourses infused with antiblackness—a freedom that Whitfield himself sought in Central America and in Haiti and finally in California, a freedom he never found. As he wrote to Douglass in 1853, "I believe it is the destiny of the negro, to develop a higher order of civilization and Christianity than the world has ever seen," but in order to do so, "they must show a powerful nation in which the black is the *ruling* element," no longer subject to "a white aristocracy."[47]

In the last stanza of "The North Star," that Black supremacist planetary and interplanetary vision turns on a pun that brings it back to earth and to the Black print public sphere that Douglass's newspaper created:

> So may that other bright North Star,
>   Beaming with truth and freedom's light,
> Pierce with its cheering ray afar,
>   The shades of slavery's gloomy night;

And may it never cease to be
The guard of truth and liberty.

The apostrophic shift here from an address to the heavens to an address to a newspaper ("that other bright North Star") is so abrupt it is almost comic (as puns always are). If the stanzas that track the constellations imagine a liberated Black cosmology aligned with Black Freemasonry's worship of the star Polaris and a free Black public no longer constrained by White supremacy, then this last stanza shrinks that cosmic, revolutionary horizon to the size of the secular constellations visible on the *North Star* masthead.[48] The gesture is a tribute to Douglass, but the vision of a version of blackness no longer constrained by "slavery's gloomy night" or by the inherent antiblackness of White America overshadows the wit of this final stanza. Between the voice of White liberal print poetics in the poem's first stanzas and the emerging voice of a new Black print public in its final stanza, another alternative has begun to appear, but that free Black heavenly world is too "varying" to have one voice. Pierpont's apostrophe assumes the fictive voice of the fugitive slave, but Whitfield's apostrophic turning parodies Pierpont's lyricizing figure of apostrophe itself, since Whitfield's poem demonstrates that the speaker created by the figure of apostrophe is (unlike the night sky) always already personified, and thus always already raced. In this sense, Whitfield's poem also exemplifies a generic feature of White apostrophic lyric, since, as Carolyn Williams writes, "parody performs the conservative function of historical preservation, effectively creating repaired continuity while making a break with the past. In this way, parody becomes the negative moment of a historical dialectic in tradition building."[49] In order to imagine the horizon of a Black radical tradition not subject to apostrophe's racialized subjective frame, Whitfield parodically repeats that frame, thus making its whiteness recognizable.[50]

Surplus Lyricism

Actually, Pierpont had already demonstrated the structurally White, personifying principle of apostrophe when he composed a companion piece to "The Fugitive Slave's Apostrophe to the North Star" titled "Slaveholder's Address to the North Star," a poem that begins

Star of the North, thou art not bigger
    Than is the diamond in my ring;
Yet every black, star-gazing nigger
    Stares at thee, as at some great thing!

Yes, gazes at thee, till the lazy
And thankless rascal is half crazy.[51]

The "Slaveholder's Address" certainly characterizes this ugly proslavery speaker as virtually illiterate (despite his repetition of the Venus and Adonis stanza) next to the fugitive speaker who so eloquently addresses "the fleecy drapery of the sky," but the explicit antiblackness of this parodic apostrophe is also an exaggeration of the implicit antiblackness of Pierpont's sympathetic impersonation of the fugitive slave's address, since Whitfield's "The North Star" helps us see that what the extremity of Pierpont's dialectically opposed personifications exposes is the racializing, lyricizing, personifying power of the figure of apostrophe itself.[52] Perhaps this is why it is Pierpont's "Slave-holder's Address" and not Pierpont's "The Fugitive Slave's Apostrophe" that appears in Delany's revolutionary Black nationalist novel *Blake or, The Huts of America* (1859–1862) as "the apostrophe of an American writer to the sacred orb of Heaven" when the novel's fugitives are being given "an explanation by which you can tell the North Star."[53] Because, as Jerome McGann writes, "*Blake* is arguing the necessity of emigrating from white racist America, emi-grating 'to Afraka' . . . (an orthographic sign that there is 'a world elsewhere' of black actualities and black truth)," Delany uses the more obviously antiblack version of Pierpont's poem to make his point.[54] But where is this world else-where? As Rusert has brilliantly demonstrated, "*Blake* draws widely on as-tronomy to link the subterranean science of fugitivity to speculative sciences that were themselves resistant to the accounting methods of racist science and statistics," including "a veritable instruction manual on locating the North Star. . . . Ultimately, the narrative embraces a syncretic form of science that is further shaped by the mysticism and science and knowledge production in freemasonry."[55] Delany in effect thus created an alternative Black cosmography in order to imagine a Black "world elsewhere," and he articulates his own ver-sion of such a world by positioning another of Whitfield's apostrophic poems as the antithesis of Pierpont's parodic antiblackness, but he attributes Whit-field's poem to Placido, a fictional Cuban revolutionary leader modeled on the martyred Black Cuban revolutionary poet Plácido, thus realizing in literature the principled political rejection of White America that Whitfield could not realize in life.[56]

Whitfield/Placido's poem is not a parody but is instead an affectively charged meta-apostrophic performance, since in it the poet addresses not only the figure of apostrophe and the White poetic discourses of which it was made but actually proleptically addresses a new, yet unrealized, transformed lyric genre that apostrophe would bring into being. This amazing poem asks this imaginary lyric genre to do the impossible, to remain in what Williams calls "the negative moment of a historical dialectic" in order to suspend that dialectic's synthesizing power of racialization. The poem, in deceptively simple quatrains, begins,

> YES! Strike again that sounding string,
>> And let the wildest numbers roll;
> Thy song of fiercest passion sing—
>> It breathes responsive to my soul![57]

In the context of Delany's novel, the poem is sung by Placido (without the accent), two other men and "six ladies," who, "taking their stand on the orchestra prepared for the occasion at the extreme end of the drawing-room, commenced in the most striking strains the following ballad composed for the evening and the event" (286). The "ballad" convinces the assembled crowd "that the western world had been originally peopled and possessed by the Indians—a colored race—and a part of the continent in Central America by a pure black race," since the tendency of ballad discourse to form a racialized folk provides a discursive platform for their collaborative revolt (287). Yet though Whitfield's poem, first published in Douglass's *North Star* on March 15, 1850, may be in the tetrameter quatrains that came to be associated with ballads, it does not tell any particular balladic story or describe any world "originally peopled and possessed," and it does not mention slavery or race or Indians or America or Cuba. In fact, in its original version in Douglass's paper, Whitfield's poem seems to be addressed *to* a poet *by* a potential reader or listener rather than addressed *by* a poet *to* a potential listening audience or reading public. That reversal amounts to a pitched exemplification and inversion of Berlant's argument that apostrophe "is actually a turning back, an animating of a receiver on behalf of the desire to make something happen *now* that realizes something *in the speaker*, makes the speaker more or differently possible, because she has admitted, in a sense, the importance of speaking for, as, and to, two—but only under the condition, and illusion, that the two are really (in) one." Whitfield's "YES! Strike Again That Sounding String" passionately embraces this promise of poetic power only to render its object powerless, only to make such a two-in-one, fictively intersubjective speaker less or differently *im*possible—at least in the inclusive, fictive form conferred by lyric apostrophe.

This poem thus works in some of the ways that Moten associates with the Black radical tradition's "ongoing improvisation of a kind of lyricism of the surplus," as its generic quasi-Virgilian invocation of poetic song turns into a series of directions to a hypothetical poet to make that song into an address to the equally hypothetical speaker of the poem, a speaker that would come into being as an effect of that address, were that address ever to happen:

> If thou wouldst soothe my burning brain,
>   Sing not to me of joy and gladness;
> 'T will but increase the raging pain,
>   And turn the fever into madness.[58]

As Sandler writes, "the poem's quatrains echo the musicality of its subject, but also retain a sense of the lyric poem as somehow more interior, more intellectual, more deliberative than song."[59] The point is compelling, but where is the subject here, exactly? If lyric apostrophe creates a fictional scene of speech and listening "that makes the speaker more or differently possible," Whitfield's poem (unlike Delany's use of it in his novel) refuses to locate such a scene, instead amplifying the stakes of lyrically constructing one:

> Sing of the battle's deadly strife,
>   The ruthless march of war and pillage,
> The awful waste of human life,
>   The plundered town, the burning village!
>
> Of streets with human gore made red,
>   Of priests upon the alter slain;
> The scenes of rapine, woe and dread,
>   That fill the warriors' horrid train.
>
> Thy song may then an echo wake,
>   Deep in this soul, long crushed and sad,
> The direful impressions shake
>   Which threaten now to drive it mad.

I agree with Sandler that these lines articulate "the period's most condensed statement of revolutionary Black lyric theory" (100), but they do so precisely because they amount to a metapoetic framing of apostrophe's lyricizing agency (complete with exclamation point!), an example of the way a poem that looks like a ballad becomes a scene of personal expression and personal address, an object lesson on how apostrophe's two-in-one intersubjective fiction shifts the genre of the poem toward the genre of the person. And what is the genre of this person? If Pierpont's poems perform one version of the way forms of address can make poems into racialized people, Whitfield's hypothetical Black lyric performs an inversion of that antiblack act of address, or an unmaking of it. Everything in the poem tells us that apostrophic lyric address creates the fictional identities of its subject and its object, yet everything in the poem insists on the dangerous conditionality of those fictions, since this poem longs for a form of address that it never achieves—or more precisely, this poem longs for a form of address that would address *it*. If, to return to Johnson's definition, "apostrophe is a form of ventriloquism through which the speaker throws voice, life, and human form into the addressee, turning its silence into mute responsiveness," then Whitfield's apostrophe ventriloquizes that act of ventriloquism, cancelling both speaker and addressee, turning mute responsiveness into an angry pathos of future possibility predicated on present violence and silence. This apostrophe is indeed a "particular kind of failure": "a constant economy and mechanics of fugitive making where the subject is hopelessly troubled by, in being emphatically detached from, the action whose agent it is supposed to be." It is also an uncanny precursor of Whitman's "O Death! O you striding there! O I cannot yet!" This affectively overdetermined apostrophe is a specter haunting the history of poetics, the specter of American lyric. In *this* poetry of the future, the subject remains tentative, since it "may" appear only as "an echo," may register "deep in this soul" that remains unnamed and unidentified, remains so alienated that in the last line it shifts from subject to object, becomes not an individual lyric *I* or a generic communal *we*, but instead reverts to an abstract, inanimate *it*. *It* waits for apostrophe's rhetorical animation to shake it up, since in Whitfield's radical Black lyric theory, by 1850, this is what history has done to us.

For Whitfield, Douglass, and Plato, public verse genres had not yet collapsed into the single genre of personal, apostrophic lyric, but all three writers saw that large genre and its signature invitation to "adopt as your own someone else's words" coming toward them. Plato's response was to become a feminized vehicle of cultural transmission, a laureate of inconspicuously shared disidentification, while Douglass's and Whitfield's responses were masculinized assertions of counter-signification, at once oriented toward a new Black public sphere and turned toward a (barely imaginable) future in which the barriers between separate publics will have fallen. All three produced a poetics of uncertain agency that has proven far more influential in literary history than has the nineteenth-century White apostrophic poetics exemplified by Pierpont and Bryant that these and other nineteenth-century poets of color framed and changed. Or let me put this differently: the gendered and raced social antagonism that modern American lyric would express emerged from both the minstrel performance of nineteenth-century White poetics and the under- and overdetermined, radically alienated response of nineteenth-century Black poetics. The synthesis of the two that was accomplished over the late eighteenth and nineteenth centuries formed a shape-shifting persona attached to a definite article, an abstract person that eventually took the place of popular genres of raced address but that also retained the legacy of that racism in its apostrophic and prosodic structure, since its dialectic of power and powerlessness continues to measure what we think poems are and do. But that dialectic did not begin in Black poets' responses to the lyric minstrelsy of White poets like Pierpont, though the nested examples from 1839–1850 we have just surveyed may make it look that way. While free mid-nineteenth-century Black Romantic poets channeled, parodied, and refused White apostrophic lyric address, at least one earlier notable enslaved Black Romantic poet became so entangled in White lyric apostrophe's antiblack two-in-one intersubjective fictions that both his poetry and his person came to serve as models of why and how such signifying would become so necessary and so antithetical, of why and how lyric reading would eventually come to replace the genre of the poem with the genre of the person.

Individual Influence; or, Catachresis

Consider the Shelleyan apostrophic address of "On Liberty and Slavery," an ode written in North Carolina in 1828, over a decade before any of the poems we have considered so far:

> Come Liberty, thou cheerful sound,
>   Roll through my ravished ears!
> Come, let my grief in joys be drowned,
>   And drive away my fears.[60]

The poet is George Moses Horton, a man born in the late eighteenth century and enslaved for sixty-eight years. In 1828 in North Carolina, Horton was not, like Douglass, literalizing the abstraction of apostrophic address, nor was he, like Whitfield, refusing and undoing apostrophe's racialized intersubjective illusion. By calling those negations of White lyricism a "specter haunting the history of poetics, the specter of American lyric," I just echoed Marx rather dramatically in order to cast his Black American contemporaries as fellow revolutionaries, but Horton's antecedent lyrical spectral presence makes that poetry of the future and that theory of history seem less promising—or let's just say that Hegelian historical progression is not the deep design of the poetics that the man who became known as "the slave poet" bequeathed to American lyric. By 1838, when Horton's 1829 book of poems was reprinted as a companion to Wheatley's only book in the compound volume published by Pierpont's friend and fellow Garrisonian abolitionist Isaac Knapp, Horton's name had been replaced by the violent noun used to identify the genre of both his poetry and his person. Horton was himself the dehumanized human form whose social death lent a spectral animation to the apostrophic figures of Romantic poetics. In his poetics, "figuration can really show its gift for making the phenomenology of attenuated life credible and conspicuous" indeed. He is the too-perfect answer to Johnson's question, "If apostrophe is said to involve language's capacity to give life and human form to something dead or inanimate, what happens when those questions are literalized?"[61] Horton's poetry thematizes the apostrophic turn away from the bondage that his own Romantic apostrophes end up enforcing. As Sandler writes, "through the seeming anomaly of his Romantic sophistication, Horton advanced a caustic revolutionary vision of Black modernity"—yet perhaps Horton's poetics were less revolutionary and visionary than they were the articulate delineation of the conditions for that revolution.[62] Perhaps it is this poet's impossible discursive position, his radical alienation, that appears so retrospectively "modern," since his surplus lyricism—his reiterated apostrophe to a freedom that keeps never arriving—invites his readers to embrace fantasies of liberation on his behalf. Anglo-American Romanticism may have been suffused with metaphors of slavery and imprisonment, but the tenor of those metaphors was always hidden in plain sight.

Or for Horton, not hidden at all, and that is the challenge his poetry poses to modern literary criticism, to later nineteenth-century Black replies to White apostrophic Romantic fictions, and to those fictions themselves. As McGill has written in eloquent understatement, "Horton's early printed poetry often takes the frustrations of the slave experience as its subject, though not with the kind of autobiographical specificity that students schooled in lyric reading have come to expect."[63] The Romantic Promethean poet was often metaphorically enslaved, but Horton's apostrophe to Liberty is an elaborately figured but also very literal appeal to be released from the illicit imposition of bondage. Like Whitfield, Horton used the discourse of Romantic poetics to frame his appeal, but while Whitfield directly challenged that discourse, for Horton the inadequacy and incongruity of that frame itself is his apostrophe's stunning point: the Shelleyan animation of Liberty as "cheerful" music, the figuration of the poet's own body as a Keatsian feminized object of Liberty's lyrical ravishment, the hyper-figurative and very Shelleyan drowning "in joys," and the invocation of all that figuration as a corporate agent that might "drive away" the poet's "fears" are all the sorts of strategies that tend to be ascribed to Romantic lyric apostrophe's special liberating superpowers. White abolitionist poets have often been described as Shelleyan, but the borrowed figures of liberation and self-abandonment they favored have no such powers for Horton, despite—or really, because of—his assertion that they do. These lines are about the violence inherent in apostrophe as dangerous intersubjective illusion, as the promise of a transcendence that apostrophe cannot actually accomplish. Horton's lines literalize what Paul Fry describes as the Romantic "ode's will to escape the bondage of its own hell": whatever constrains the poet, his verse will not resolve it—in fact, the more this poet apostrophizes, the more dire his predicament appears.[64] Deidre Shauna Lynch has written of "romantic readers' investments . . . in the proposition that loving literature goes hand in hand with losing literature," and in Horton's poetry we can see an extreme literalization of this early nineteenth-century tendency to "love literature to death": by apostrophizing a receding ideal, Horton confuses the familiar figures invoked by British Romantic poets with his own attenuated life.[65] That confusion refigures their metaphors as abstractions that share the pathos of his enslaved condition without sharing its consequences.

Horton's invitation to Liberty was thus both deeply literary and not at all metaphorical: when it was published in the Lancaster *Gazette* on April 8, 1828, as "Liberty and Slavery" and in Horton's first booklet of poems *Hope of Liberty* in Raleigh the next year as "On Liberty and Slavery," and in the Knapp volume in 1838, and in abolitionist newspapers in the 1850s, it was meant to stand as a reiterated odic appeal to the poem's readers to somehow urge the person who thought he owned Horton to grant him his freedom (probably by purchasing it). That appeal never worked; Horton was not emancipated until after Lincoln's assassination in the spring of 1865, when he joined a Cavalry Corps unit as a refugee. My point is that Horton's ode is not only a metalyrical poem but also, like Whitfield's odes, one of those "eloquent" political poems that were so common on both sides of the Atlantic that Mill thought that by 1833 "lyric poetry" needed to be defended from them. But unlike the political appeals of White liberal political poetics that Whitfield parodied, Horton's appeal, like that of his North Carolina contemporary David Walker, not only did not work but also did not generalize oppression. Instead, Horton's poem searched for figures specific to, as Walker wrote, "the most degraded, wretched, and abject set of beings that ever lived since the world began."[66]

As his ode develops, Horton asks Liberty to become the poet composing a political appeal on those beings' behalf:

> Say unto foul oppression, Cease:
>   Ye tyrants rage no more,
> And let the joyful trump of peace,
>   Now bid the vassal soar.

The apostrophic twistings and turnings are complex here, though the illusory simplicity of the quatrains' metrical protocol makes that complexity hard to see. The poet's attempt to ventriloquize Liberty, to make Liberty be the one to "say unto foul oppression, Cease," doesn't work. Such a general futile complaint against tyranny is indeed Romantic, but rather than becoming an unacknowledged legislator writing his way into a better world, this poet exchanges his own apostrophe to Liberty for the apostrophic address "the joyful trump of peace" directs toward "the vassal." Since figuratively and materially mediated address is the problem rather than the solution in this ode, both the fiction of the speaker and the fiction of the listener keep changing shape. Now not liberty but "the trump of peace" seems to speak, as the poet imagines a poetic instrument that could inspire a historically indeterminate bondman complete with definite article to "soar"—an apostrophic effect even less likely than Liberty's literal manifestation in response to a poem. The uncertain agency of this apostrophe within an apostrophe allows Horton to condense Shelley's "Ode to Liberty" (1820) into five stunning quatrains:

> Soar on the pinions of that dove
>   Which long has cooed for thee,
> And breathed her notes from Afric's grove,
>   The sound of Liberty.
>
> Oh, Liberty! thou golden prize,
>   So often sought by blood—
> We crave thy sacred sun to rise,
>   The gift of nature's God!

Bid Slavery hide her haggard face,
    And barbarism fly:
I scorn to see the sad disgrace
    In which enslaved I lie.

Dear Liberty! upon thy breast,
    I languish to respire;
And like the Swan unto her nest,
    I'd like to thy smiles retire.

Oh, blest asylum—heavenly balm!
    Unto thy boughs I flee—
And in thy shades the storm shall calm,
    With songs of Liberty!

To understand these quatrains' inhabitation of the apostrophic basis of Romantic lyric address that Whitfield and Douglass parodied and rejected, place those common-meter stanzas next to the elaborate metrical performance of the last fifteen-line stanza of Shelley's "Ode to Liberty," in which Shelley, too, refuses the lyrical apostrophe on which his poem is based:

Paused, and the spirit of that mighty singing
    To its abyss was suddenly withdrawn;
Then, as a wild swan, when sublimely winging
    Its path athwart the thunder-smoke of dawn,
Sinks headlong through the aerial golden light
      On the heavy sounding plain,
      When the bolt has pierced its brain;
As summer clouds dissolve, unburthened of their rain;
    As a far taper fades with fading night,
      As a brief insect dies with dying day,
    My song, its pinions disarrayed of might,
      Drooped; o'er it closed the echoes far away
Of the great voice which did its flight sustain,
    As waves which lately paved his watery way
    Hiss round a drowner's head in their tempestuous play.[67]

If we think of Horton's lines as entwined with Shelley's, we can see that apostrophic fictional intersubjectivity is a problem for both poets. We can also see that Shelley's breathtaking singular surrender to that problem cannot be Horton's. Horton's multiplying, shifting apostrophes stand in stark contrast to the decisive turn away from apostrophe in the last stanza of Shelley's ode. In his penultimate stanza, Shelley addresses Liberty one last time:

> If thine or theirs are treasures to be bought
> By blood or tears, have not the wise and free
> Wept tears, and blood like tears?

Like Horton, Shelley fails to make Liberty show up; unlike Horton, he and the history of appeals he recounts are "free" to keep trying.

Shelley's ode's last stanza is the jarring non-answer to the question of whether anyone *should* keep trying, and here the repeated attempts at European revolution the poem has narrated come to an end in what Fry calls a "becalmed westering."[68] Whatever we may think of Shelley's comparison of the end of his poem's own "mighty singing" to the "wild swan" that plunges to its death when someone shoots it and "the bolt has pierced its brain," Horton translates the "pinions" of Shelley's song back into the literal "pinions of that dove" that figures the peace that Liberty would offer if it were to arrive, and which in turn apostrophically addresses ("which long has cooed for") Liberty. Now an apostrophe within an apostrophe within an apostrophe, Horton's metalyric riff on Shelley's metalyricism turns the "westering" European history of Shelley's poem toward a different Atlantic history in which the insertion of the lost peace "of Afric's grove" reverses both Shelley's Eurocentric account and the "westering" Universal History on which it was based. If the "pinions" of poetic apostrophic address were to be inspired by ("breathed . . . from") Africa rather than (as in Shelley's poem) a vague primitivist history that leads to ancient Greece, then what might Liberty become? If the peace that "breathed her notes from Afric's grove" had not been disrupted by the Atlantic slave trade, then what and where might Liberty have remained? Horton condenses Shelley's ode's despairing invocation of "blood or tears" into an apostrophic turn on an idea "so often sought by blood" or invoked as divine gift. That Eurocentric idea of Liberty needs not to see the ongoing violence that is not represented in Shelley's ode or in Hegel's philosophy or in eighteenth- and nineteenth-century accounts of historical progress, and so cannot see the people who were not "wise and free" but were literally pinioned. In the only stanza of Shelley's ode that sketches a pre-European chaotic "palace and pyramid, / Temple and prison," the poet tells Liberty that "thou wert not" in that barbarous prehistory, so the "congregator of slaves / Into the shadow of her pinions wide" gathered "many a swarming million." Horton borrows Shelley's violent metaleptic pun,

in which what flies becomes what binds, and the violence inside that pun oc-
casions the turn of the last stanzas of Horton's ode away from the "golden
prize" of Liberty and toward the "haggard face" of Slavery. As in Shelley, the
fictional person of Slavery is feminized, a feminization that makes Horton's
last three quatrains "disarrayed of might" sink headlong into the poet's literally
enslaved situation of address.

The shame that surrounds this turn toward literal binding is hard to de-
scribe. It is possible to read the stanza as Liberty's ventriloquized triumph over
Slavery, in which case the personified Slavery shamefully hides "her haggard
face" in deference to Liberty, and Liberty makes the "barbarism" of an out-
worn stage in historical progress "fly" away in shame, a counterpoint to "the
vassal" bid to "soar" by "the trump of peace" that originated in Africa. But the
two lines that follow cancel that optimistic reading by literalizing it: the shame
of slavery does not belong to a personification but to a person. This person
cannot deny "the sad disgrace" of his enslaved condition, and so his figurative
protection is exposed as soon as it is invoked. Whereas Shelley's song takes
the form of the dying swan in its final beautiful dive, Horton's "pinions disar-
rayed of might" seek the shelter of a final apostrophe to Liberty as a maternal
figure whose "breast" becomes a haven only when the poet also assumes the
feminized form of a swan not plunging to its death but retiring "unto her nest,"
a nest that is somehow also a figure for Liberty's "smiles." Since Liberty cannot
grant the poet liberty, the best the surplus lyricism of this apostrophic *mise en
abyme* can offer is the temporary refuge of figuration itself. Shelley's "Ode to
Liberty" may drown in the "tempestuous play" of its own figures, but Horton's
ode shifts the figuration of its appeal so often that by the last quatrain, the
"shades" that the asylum-balm-sound-prize-sun-breast-nest-tree catachresis
provides hang by a tetrameter line, and that thread's stitch of the human to the
nonhuman is far from empowering. The ending figure is so tenuous that the
last two lines seem to reverse Shelley's last fifteen lines in a sudden swoop:
whereas in Shelley's lines the figure of the dying swan takes over and becomes
clouds, taper, insect, song, and "drowner's head," Horton's apostrophic cata-
chresis is itself drowned out by the pathos of uncertain agency that follows the
poet's retreat into Liberty's temporary "shades," a pun on the spectral condi-
tion of enslavement that frames the entire poem. The "storm" raging outside
those "shades" is all too real, and the attempt to calm it "with songs of Liberty"
addressed to Liberty has exposed the person who sought refuge in the Romantic
apostrophic ode to the catachresis (the "bad use") of his literal situation of
address.

That literal situation did not change until Horton was sixty-eight, and it's not clear that "liberty" is the word for the changes he weathered over the last twenty years of his life. After 1866, he seems to have lived in Philadelphia, where he wrote a poem about racism on the city's streetcars; after that, he may or may not have emigrated to Liberia. In 1867, he wrote a poem about his hopes to leave the city of brotherly love (the city the poem calls "a friendless place" and "nothing but a strife") for a place "where milk and honey flow along."[69] The poem was published in *The African Repository*, but as far as we know, Horton wrote no poems about reaching the Africa of milk and honey or about achieving the liberty his verse apostrophized for forty years. The truth is, though he became famous in abolitionist circles in the 1830s and 1840s as "the Slave Poet," and in the South as "the Colored Bard of North Carolina," most of Horton's poems were not about slavery at all. After the 1829 publication of *Hope of Liberty*, the first volume of poems published by a Black poet in the South, North Carolina's slave laws became much harsher and more restrictive in response to Walker's *Appeal*, Nat Turner's rebellion, and a range of enslaved people's liberation fronts along the North Carolina border. Horton's work continued to circulate in abolitionist circles in the North, but when his second book was published in North Carolina in 1845, it contained no explicitly antislavery verse. Titled *The Poetical Works of George M. Horton, The Colored Bard of North Carolina*, what this second book did contain was a prefatory "Life of the Author, Written by Himself."[70] It is an astonishing self-portrait, especially as preface to his North Carolina publisher's introductory assurance that this poet "is deeply conscious of his own inferiority." In fact, Horton's autobiographical sketch is a testimony to his own interpellation by the discourses of antiblackness, and to his own consequent unwillingness to be a subject of representation. Written in response to "the importunate request of a few individuals," Horton's essay begins as a reluctant reply to a demand, a reply that promises to be only "a slight specimen entirely clear of exaggeration" (iii). After recounting some of the facts of his birth (though like Douglass, Horton writes that "to account for my age is beyond the reach of my power"), the focus of this "specimen" quickly becomes Horton's acquisition of the literacy his *Poetical Works* exemplify, literacy acquired (again like Douglass's) with self-defining effort in stolen hours from his enforced "disagreeable" occupation as a "poor cow-boy." But unlike Douglass's assertion of literacy as individual influence, Horton writes that when he finally "reached the threatening heights of literature, and braved in a manner the clouds of disgust which reared in thunders under my feet" (vii), he was overwhelmed. The self-making conventionally associated with the hard-earned acquisition of literacy turns in Horton's account to a scene of potential unselving, of forces that threaten the constitution of a single individual from above and from below.

In fact, another rare Horton prose piece recently discovered by Jonathan Senchyne in the New York Public Library is actually titled "Individual Influence," and in it Horton describes his subject as "a literary medley," as "a system of curiosity existent between a natural and supernatural feeling in man." What Horton saw clearly was that catachresis was the accurate expression of the individual whose interpellation conflated the "natural and supernatural," whose integrity could not be defined within the phenomenology of antiblackness. This extraordinary essay (if that's what it is) defines the "contrast between a terrestrial and a celestial power" as follows:

> The former is certainly dependent on the latter, which acts as an individual agent, and hence with an individual influence, with a thorough predominating appreciation, under a cloud of solemnity, it checks the stream of egotism, and dulls the enthusiastical blaze of the philosopher: it furls the wing of imagination, and binds conceit in the chain of compunction: it sets the heart on fire from the seeming friction of a variety of thoughts, and effuses a universal conflagration through the soul, and thus it supports an individual influence in earth, and in Heaven.[71]

Like Whitfield's and Delany's Black Freemasonic cosmographies, Horton's poetics of catachresis emphasizes what Sylvia Wynter would call the limitations of "the secular liberal monohumanist conception of our being human," exploring instead "our *genres of being human*," genres contingent on "our discursive *formations*, aesthetic fields, and systems of knowledge."[72] Horton mixes metaphors, genres, discourses, aesthetic fields, and systems of knowledge in order to articulate an inarticulable genre of being human and in that process he begins to invent a new genre of being poetic. As Joshua Bennett writes, such a poetics gives us one account of the phenomenology of "those who have historically not been able to, or simply not *desired* to, exert their will in things but have instead had to count themselves as among and *as infinitely more than things*."[73]

Thus, while nineteenth-century readers would have expected Horton's literacy to become his path to self-expression, to "freedom," to "individual influence," in his own account, something very different and very strange happens instead. He professes such a fondness for reading poetry that he claims to have picked up every piece he could find "written in that curious style ... and if it was, I as carefully preserved it as I would a piece of money" (viii). This fondness for the "curious style" of verse led Horton to compose verses "in my head," since it would be many years before his ability to read was matched by an ability to write. That mental composition "behind a plough" did actually turn into currency: when Horton began to visit the University of North Carolina campus "carrying fruit," the students discovered his "spark of genius" and "eagerly insisted" that he "spout, as they called it" (xiv). The students ended up paying Horton to compose acrostics and other love poetry for their sweethearts, and many of these poems appear in *Poetical Works*. Horton names several of the student-patrons who abused him as benefactors who provided money and more books, and he thanks the racist, proslavery patron "Mrs. Hentz of Boston" (for a time a faculty wife at the college, later a novelist) for getting his first book published and "for the correction of many poetical errors" (xvii). Even the last book of poems that Horton published in 1865 after marching toward emancipation with the Union cavalry was composed by commission of the captain of the regiment with which Horton traveled; this captain reported that Horton worked "both night and day composing poems for this book," while (in his late sixties) walking for several months.[74] All of Horton's poetry was addressed to those who addressed him as subject to their influence, within the economy of their antiblack interpellation. What are the genres of that way of being human?

No wonder modern literary critics have found it difficult to locate "the speaker" of Horton's poems. Faith Barrett suggests that Horton's miscellaneous, proliferating apostrophes are "dramatic voice-effects" that result "from the many ways in which he is restricted, as an enslaved black man, from writing and speaking." She concludes that he "demonstrates extraordinary skill as a poet by creating solitary romantic speakers who offer possibilities for identification to displaced American readers both white and black, Northern and Southern."[75] Certainly Barrett's observation is more generous than Redding's earlier opinion that "Horton appears dressed in motley," that he was "the forerunner of the minstrel poets," or than Sterling Brown's even earlier judgment that "Horton's works remain the hodge-podge of a clever slave."[76] But the attribution of a variety of "solitary romantic speakers" to Horton's poems adjusts those poems to the very protocols of lyric reading that his verse—as his undoing of Shelley and his self-narration both attest—deconstructed in advance. Though "deconstructed" may be the wrong word here; the reason that Horton's poetics simultaneously undid and generated the subject position of a lyricized abstract "speaker" is that he did not just write about but inhabited the impossibility of that two-in-one apostrophic fiction. Sandler argues that "the distance between poetry and the reality of enslavement gave Horton's work its dialectical quality," but I think that the negative dialectic Horton's work set in motion emerged from the identity rather than the distance between Horton's poetics and his enslavement, an anguished proximity that made Horton's poetry a reiterated articulation of the conditions for that revolution, a primer on the many ways in which lyric figures of address can unmake the very person who asks poetry (or the people reading it) to set him free.[77]

All of which brings us back to Shelley—or to Horton's transformation of Shelley's revolutionary poetics into a new American lyricism. That lyricism, like Shelley's, preceded the creation of "the speaker" as an unnamed, abstract, represented person, but in Horton's revisionary Romantic apostrophic poetics, you can see where that abstraction began. The book in which Shelley's "Ode to Liberty" was published in 1820 was *Prometheus Unbound, a Lyrical Drama in Four Acts; with other poems*. Like Shelley's Prometheus, George Moses Horton was eventually unbound. But his poetry was not. "On Liberty and Slavery" was, like all of his poems, a binding song, a song he was still singing in 1865 as he walked toward "freedom." In his last book, he included a poem originally published in April 1843 (just as Pierpont's *Anti-Slavery Poems* appeared in Boston) in the *Southern Literary Messenger*. Hardly an abolitionist publication, that paper featured the forty-six-year-old Horton's poem as merely the curious production of "a negro boy, belonging to a respectable farmer" (figure 2.3):

ODE TO LIBERTY

O! Liberty, thou dove of peace,
    We must aspire to thee,
Whose wing thy pris'ners must release,
    And fan Columbia free.

The title of Shelley's ode and the figuration of Liberty as a bird both reiterate Horton's earlier, more famous "On Liberty and Slavery" in even simpler common-meter form, but this simplicity is deceptive—not only because it always *is* in Horton's poetry but also because when he republished this second ode to Liberty in his last book, *Naked Genius*, Horton exposed the proslavery publication's mistake:

ODE TO LIBERTY

O! Liberty, thou dove of peace,
  We must aspire to thee,
Whose wings thy pinions must release,
  And fan Columbia free.

Horton's fondness for Shelley's violent metaleptic pun, in which what flies becomes what binds, was erased in the *Southern Literary Messenger*, where "wings" became "wing" and "pinions" became "pris'ners."[78] In correcting the misprision twenty years later, Horton insisted that the pun—and its internalized catachresis—indeed contained the problem no individual's apostrophe to Liberty could influence. For Shelley, the structure of poetic address itself may have beautifully enacted the impossibility of the state of liberation that address desired, but Horton's historical situation exponentially increased the stakes of that aestheticized inefficacy, the pathos of that uncertain Romantic agency. In a letter that Horton addressed directly to Garrison in 1844, the year after "Ode to Liberty" appeared in the *Southern Literary Messenger* and the year before *The Poetical Works* was published in Hillsborough, Horton wrote,

> I faithfully trust a sign that your examination into the facts of my condition will inspire your pleasure to open to the world a volume which like a wild bird has long lain struggling in its shell impatient to transpire to the eye, a dubious world.[79]

Horton asks Garrison to use his famous abolitionist influence in support of the poems that are here themselves figured as the "wild bird" they so often adopt as figure. This poetry-bird is not only not liberated into flight but "has long lain struggling" to merely appear. What might happen when it does? Is it the poet who is "dubious" about the reception of his work, or the world that is "dubious" about the poet? Horton's dangling modifier condenses into a single word the abject condition of the subject defined in and by an antiblack structure of address. These poems are pinioned by the shell of the very poetic genres and discourses that promise to set them free—as the person who wrote them was pinioned by the very people who promised to set him free. We cannot know if Garrison would have replied to Horton's appeal to promote his poems and to donate one hundred and forty-five dollars to purchase the poet's freedom because David L. Swain, the president of the University of North Carolina, to whom Horton entrusted the letter, never sent it. The letter was

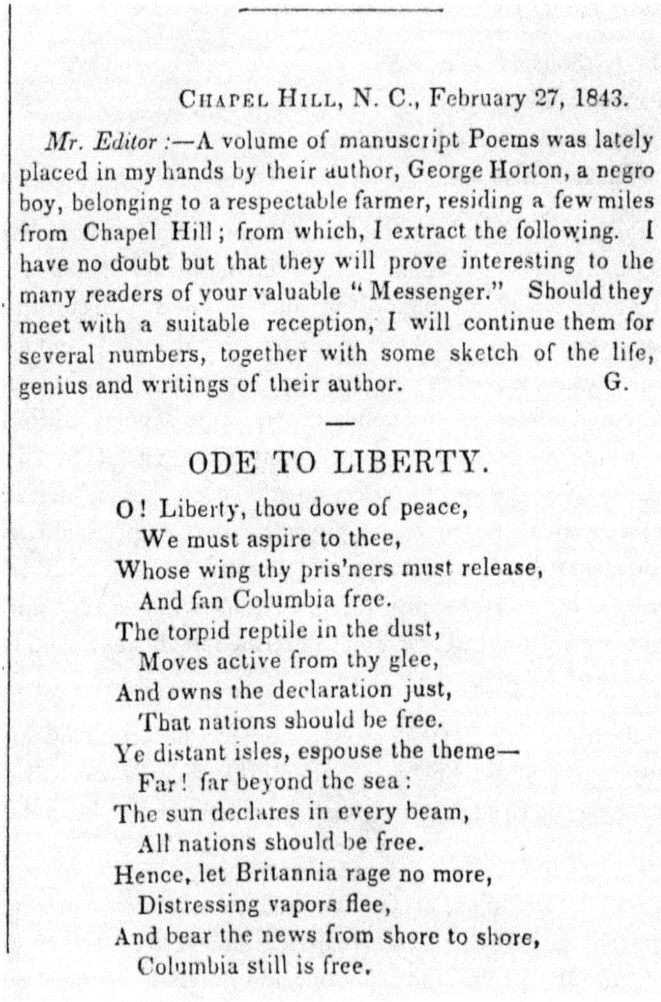

CHAPEL HILL, N. C., February 27, 1843.

Mr. Editor :—A volume of manuscript Poems was lately placed in my hands by their author, George Horton, a negro boy, belonging to a respectable farmer, residing a few miles from Chapel Hill; from which, I extract the following. I have no doubt but that they will prove interesting to the many readers of your valuable " Messenger." Should they meet with a suitable reception, I will continue them for several numbers, together with some sketch of the life, genius and writings of their author.   G.

ODE TO LIBERTY.

O ! Liberty, thou dove of peace,
    We must aspire to thee,
Whose wing thy pris'ners must release,
    And fan Columbia free.
The torpid reptile in the dust,
    Moves active from thy glee,
And owns the declaration just,
    That nations should be free.
Ye distant isles, espouse the theme—
    Far ! far beyond the sea :
The sun declares in every beam,
    All nations should be free.
Hence, let Britannia rage no more,
    Distressing vapors flee,
And bear the news from shore to shore,
    Columbia still is free.

FIGURE 2.3. George Moses Horton, "Ode to Liberty," *Southern Literary Messenger; devoted to every department of literature and the fine arts* 9, no. 4 (April 1843), 237.

found with a similar letter addressed to Horace Greeley in Swain's papers after his death. It is this literalization of the Romantic apostrophic dialectic of transcendence and constraint, of possession and dispossession, of self-making and self-loss that would eventuate in the lyricization of American poetry, since in order to become a form of address capacious enough to encompass Slavery as well as Liberty, the history of antiblackness as well as the genres of White flight, Horton's ode must substitute the figure of the person for the figure of the poem (not to mention an imaginary free "Columbia" for an actually carceral America).

"O! Liberty, thou dove of peace": Don't you imagine that someone is *saying* (or shouting or whispering or gasping) "O!"? Does it matter that you don't know who that person might be? Or do you not think this is a person at all, since you know this is a poetic convention? Do you feel moved to respond anyway, if only silently? Don't you want to imagine that overseeing or overhearing that address brings you into its range, thus making you feel as if you were joining a collective of such responsive silences? I hope your answers to those questions have changed since the beginning of this chapter, but if not, that's not surprising, since over the next two hundred years, the figure of that abstract person and its attendant collective silences would come to define lyric as a genre so capacious that poetry became another name for it, a genre that keeps offering each of us the hope of a liberty found in poetry alone.

3

Personification

ON PHILLIS WHEATLEY'S MEMORY

Phillis's Wake

Before Horton, before the nineteenth century, before "America," before either White or Black Romanticism, before modernism, there was the poet who came to be known as Phillis Wheatley. American lyric, Anglophone Romanticism, and modern poetics would all have been very different if not impossible without her, yet her memory's persistence would certainly have surprised the woman remembered for the past two and a half centuries by that improper name. It might have surprised her even more to learn that she has become the eighteenth-century poet most often read by students of American literature today. That woman was probably kidnapped as a small girl somewhere near Africa's western coast (Senegal? Gambia? Sierra Leone?), then delivered to colonial Boston and sold to a wealthy merchant's family who gave her a literate English education, their last name, and the first name of the ship that brought the captive child through the Middle Passage.[1] This familiar story is disturbing enough, yet every part of it—her importance to literary history, her pedagogical uses, her name, the geographical speculation across colonized space and time, the idea that racial capitalism can be reduced to incidents of kidnapping, the discourse that allows a child to be "sold," the assumption that an education is something the Wheatley family "gave" this child, the way the definite article attached to "*the* Middle Passage" can stand for so many different acts of violence—discloses another vertiginous disturbance. The fact that every account of this poet's work for the past two centuries has begun with such a memorial personal description speaks volumes about the roots and aftershocks of the stories that have made her poems so difficult to read and so foundational in, to, and for the history of American lyric.

In "The Difficult Miracle of Black Poetry in America or Something Like a Sonnet for Phillis Wheatley," June Jordan asks, "Why did they give her that name?" Christina Sharpe answers that "the Wheatleys made an experiment of her":

> Phillis Wheatley, daughter of a "bitterly anonymous man and woman" [as Jordan wrote], was "meager" (a meager, sickly child according to some accounts), never really a girl; at least not "girl" in any way that operates as a meaningful signifier in Euro-Western cultures; no such persons recognizable as "girl" being inspected, sold, and purchased at auction in the "New World." Likewise, to some, Phillis was never really a poet. Most famously not to Thomas Jefferson, who wrote in Query XIV of *Notes on the State of Virginia*, "Misery is often the parent of the most affecting touches in poetry.—Among the blacks is misery, God knows, but no poetry. . . . Religion indeed has produced a Phyllis Whately [sic]; but it could not produce a poet."[2]

The process of lyricization that replaced the genre of the poem with the genre of the person could hardly have found a more generative source than this person whose personhood was rendered both indefinite and overdetermined, this girl poet whose poetry continues to be both idealized and erased. Might it be possible to exchange the memory of Wheatley as the kidnapped and enslaved genius I have just repeated for another kind of literary memory that has been latent in that cover story all along? As I began this book by suggesting, once considered as constrained as the person who wrote it, Phillis Wheatley's miraculous verse has actually proven so unrestrained that, as Dana Murphy writes, it continues to inspire "nothing less . . . than everlasting literary life."[3]

There are by now hundreds of variations on the deceptively basic opening statement that "Phillis Wheatley was a native of Africa; and was brought to this country in the year 1761, and sold as a slave" (as a particularly influential account of the poet began in 1834), yet despite the obligatory reiteration of these apparently personal details, readers have found it even more difficult to locate the poet in her poems in Wheatley's case than in Plato's or Whitfield's or Horton's.[4] Many more have tried, since there has long been a consensus that, as each volume of *The Schomburg Library of Nineteenth-Century Black Women Writers* begins, "the birth of the Afro-American literary tradition occurred in 1773, when Phillis

Wheatley published a book of poetry."[5] Yet there has also long been a concern that, as James Weldon Johnson wrote in *The Book of American Negro Poetry* in 1922, "Phillis Wheatley has never been given her rightful place in American literature."[6] How could both of these things be true at once, and what would Wheatley's "rightful place" in literary history be? Must she remain an endless experiment in personal and literary interpretation, an experiment always already appropriated by editors, readers, and critics? Or can what Samantha Pinto describes as the "surprising, uneven directions" of the Black reception of Wheatley's biography and poetry (from nineteenth-century poets like Plato and Horton to the "Phyllis Wheatley" clubs of the 1890s to the multiplying literary texts about Wheatley that have been addressed to Black children since the middle of the twentieth century to the uptake of Wheatley as precursor by Black feminism and by modern Black women poets from Jordan to Shockley to Jeffers's renaming—or restoration—of the woman who became Phillis Wheatley Peters) change the legacy of that appropriation?[7]

There are as many answers to those questions as there are retroactive versions of the woman and her work—not to mention misspellings of her misbegotten name. I will continue to refer to her here as "Wheatley," though Jeffers has made a compelling case that if we are going to call this poet by a patronym, she should be known as Phillis *Peters*, the name of the Black man the adult woman chose to marry rather than the name of the White man who enslaved her as a child.[8] That seems right, though since in this chapter I am concerned with the reception of "Phillis Wheatley," with the ways in which Phillis Wheatley Peters has been remembered as well as with the ways in which she represented her own memory, I will continue to use the familiar name she never should have had. That dead name has been used in many places for many purposes, but one place the woman memorialized by it has not been granted is first place in the invention of American lyric, a position she deserves because the vexed relation between the genre of her person and the genre of her poems is not just the object of two and a half centuries of racialized literary appropriation and identification, but the constant, excruciating, dazzling subject of her poetics. Not incidentally, that vexed subject also became the subject of the genre that came to be known as the Romantic lyric. While Horton adopted the apostrophic figures of that genre in order to transform them into figures for his own enslaved condition, Wheatley set the terms for those figures in advance.

A lot of people have known this—among them, Ann Plato. In "Lines, Written Upon Being Examined in School Studies for the Preparation of a Teacher," another of the poems included in the only book she published in 1841, Plato wrote,

> Now fifteen years their destined course have run,
> In fast succession round the central sun;
> How did the follies of that period pass,
> I ask myself—are they inscribed in brass!
> Oh, Recollection, speed their fast return,
> And sure 'tis mine to be ashamed and mourn.[9]

In "On Recollection," the second version of the poem with which this book began and the seventeenth poem in *Poems on Various Subjects, Religious and Moral*, Wheatley wrote,

> Now eighteen years their destin'd course have run,
> In fast succession round the central sun.
> How did the follies of that period pass
> Unnotic'd, but behold them writ in brass!
> In Recollection see them fresh return,
> And sure 'tis mine to be asham'd, and mourn.[10]

Kenny J. Williams warns that "before it is assumed that Plato 'copied' from Wheatley or rushed into print in order to be considered the direct descendant of Wheatley, it must be remembered that her poetry in many ways is more varied than the strictness of Wheatley's adherence to the neoclassical tradition."[11] Katherine Clay Bassard responds to Williams by arguing that what is needed "is not a curt dismissal" of Plato's repetition of Wheatley's lines, "but a way of theorizing black women's subjectivity, authorship, and writing community that will allow a historical dialogue to emerge."[12] I agree with Bassard (not least because Plato's heroic couplets are less rather than more varied than Wheatley's), yet what seems to me most remarkable about Plato's appropriation of Wheatley's lines is that she turns the fifth line into an apostrophe to Recollection itself, thus lyricizing (or we might say, *romanticizing*) the genre of Wheatley's poem. While Wheatley's "On Recollection" is indeed a neoclassical lesser ode that begins with a Virgilian address to "Mneme," or Mnemosyne, that generic invocation seems a world away from the sudden sigh of Plato's plaintive "Oh, Recollection." If by the 1820s–1840s, as we have already seen in the work of Plato, Pierpont, Douglass, Whitfield, and Horton, the racialized figure of apostrophe blurred the genres of poetic address and the subjects of that address, Plato's apostrophe to Recollection responds to that threat of abstraction in both her own name and in Phillis Wheatley's (or perhaps in her own name *as* Phillis Wheatley). Notice that Plato has also changed Wheatley's "Unnoticed, but behold them writ in brass!" to "I ask myself—are they inscribed in brass!" varying the allusion to Shakespeare's adage, "Men's evil manners live in brass; their virtues / We write in water," by introducing doubt.[13] What *were* these "evil manners" both poets so feared in themselves? In literally recollecting Wheatley's lines, Plato's lines transform the personal secret that prompts the last line's reflexive "And sure 'tis mine to be asham'd, and mourn" into something that she and Wheatley have in common. Plato's Wheatley, like Plato, seems to possess a talent for dispossession, a Keatsian negative capability, her name not after all inscribed as a memorial to her captivity and enslavement but poetically "writ on water." Plato claims a transhistorical intimacy with Wheatley, and Plato's poem begins a lyric reading of Wheatley's poem, trying on the voice of "On Recollection" as if it were Plato's own, as if there were something between them that could go without saying.

Yet this act of ventriloquism does not result in what Berlant calls "a fake moment of intersubjectivity," does not eventuate in a communal identity made of "two in one." Plato's insertion of an apostrophe into Wheatley's lines does not end up accomplishing the purpose of the Romantic figure. Instead, the last lines of Plato's poem break into another voice, or at least into an interpolated (as well as interpellated) conclusion in quotation marks in lines that appear nowhere in Wheatley:

> "What shall I ask, or what refrain to say?
> Where shall I point, or how conclude my lay?
> So much my weakness needs—so oft thy voice,
> Assures that weakness, and confirms my choice.
> Oh, grant me active days of peace and truth,
> Strength to my heart, and wisdom to my youth,
> A sphere of usefulness—a soul to fill
> That sphere with duty, and perform thy will."

Is this Wheatley's ghostly response to being summoned? Is this the voice of Recollection, answering the poet's request to tell her what to do with her time? Is this Plato's own voice, reclaiming its independence from the "example of Phillis Wheatly [*sic*]," which Pennington's introduction to her book suggested that Plato "followed" (viii)? It seems more likely that these lines turn back to the devotional appeal that begins Plato's "Lines": "Teach me, O! Lord, the secret errors of my way." If so, then these concluding lines are the answer to a prayer, an answer that would be realized in Plato's future work as a teacher (since Plato, like Wheatley, was a good Congregationalist who would have understood the Lord's answer as her own inner voice). But in that case, why are these lines in quotation marks? Perhaps the questions in the first couplet of this last section ("What shall I ask, or what refrain to say? / Where shall I point, or how conclude my lay?") are the real questions here. What the recollection of Wheatley has raised for Plato is the specter of a person alienated from her own voice, a poet displaced within her own poem. What Plato's version of Wheatley allows us to see is that common descriptions of British Romantic lyric as an exemplary combination of "affective intensity" and "intrinsic formal difficulty" might also be descriptions of Wheatley's work. Yet such widely accepted definitions of Romantic lyric as a poetry that privileges moments of autonomous affective intensity and reflexive subjectivity never include Wheatley, since "the strictness of [her] adherence to the neoclassical tradition" and the (only) apparent reticence of her personal expression— which is all to say, her position as Black, enslaved, and colonial—have served to qualify her work as pre-Romantic, as at best a referent for the Romantics, as at most *almost* lyric.

But Ann Plato seems to have known better, since the question that her repetition of Wheatley poses is the question implicit in the compulsory rehearsal of Wheatley's memory in every reading of her poems and in each intentional or unintentional revision of her name: "What does it matter who is speaking?"[14] It is that question, rather than any of the gorgeous things that Wheatley's poems say or do not say, that makes her work so generative for the kind of poetry that only much later would be called Romantic lyric. Of course, because Wheatley's poetry was from the beginning "an experiment," it has always mattered a great deal that it is a young enslaved Black woman—a "sable prodigy"—who is speaking, just as it has always mattered a great deal that it is hard to understand what this person wants to say—or more to the point, what the poems *do* say. Do Wheatley's poems speak for themselves? What do we mean when we say a poem "speaks"? Do we mean that the poet expresses herself through the poem? Do we mean that the poem speaks for her? Or do we mean that the poem achieves a voice of its own? Plato's version of Wheatley emphasizes Wheatley's importance as an early model for the nineteenth-century Poetess, the figure that became an impersonated genre. As we have already begun to see in Plato's poetics and shall see in detail in chapter 5 of this book, that genre begged the question of poetic voice by feminizing it, and in Wheatley's case that feminization was, as I have written elsewhere, "so radically overdetermined that it allows us to see the emergence of the category that would be so central to nineteenth-century American poetics."[15] By "category," I meant the Poetess, but it is also true that in Wheatley's work we can see the emergence of the lyricized category of poetry that Wheatley and Plato and later Poetesses helped to make possible and would come to represent.

No wonder then that for over two and a half centuries, Wheatley's work has prompted male readers to raise such basic theoretical questions about poetic address. As Gates points out, while Jefferson's antiblack version of Wheatley (whose name he spelled "Phyllis Whately," perhaps inadvertently substituting the last name of the contemporary White Poetess Mary Whateley) inspired a range of eighteenth-century responses, nineteenth-century readers (including Martin Delany), "were fulsome in their praise of Wheatley and her poetry." Yet by the end of the nineteenth century, Gates notices, that praise turned to a complaint that persisted through the twentieth century:

> We can trace the anti-Wheatley tendency . . . to 1887, when Edward Wilmot Blyden, one of the fathers of black nationalism, wrote about her contemptuously, and the tone was set for the century to come. James Weldon Johnson, writing in 1922, complained that "one looks in vain for some outburst or even complaint against the bondage of her people, for some agonizing cry about her native land," finding instead a "smug contentment at her escape therefrom."
>
> But what really laid her low was ultimately a cultural critique of her work—less what she said than the way she said it.
>
> Wallace Thurman, writing in 1928, calls her "a third-rate imitation" of Alexander Pope. . . .
>
> By the mid-sixties, criticism of Wheatley rose to a high pitch of disdain. Amiri Baraka, a founder of the Black Arts Movement, wrote in 1962 that Wheatley's "pleasant imitations of eighteenth-century English poetry are far and, finally, ludicrous departures from the huge black voices that splintered southern nights with their *hollers, chants, arwhoolies,* and *ballits.*"[16]

Gates does not mention that between Thurman and Baraka, no less a scholar than Redding, "the veritable dean of Afro-American literary critics," made the complaint I cited in my preface about Wheatley's "negative, bloodless, unracial quality . . . that somehow cannot seem altogether real as the essential quality and core of one whose life should have made her sensitive to the very things she denies. In this sense none of her poetry is real."[17] Redding makes explicit what is implicitly at stake in Gates's quotations of others: Gates's defense of

Wheatley's poetry against "the anti-Wheatley tendency" of Thomas Jefferson and at least some twentieth-century Black male literary historians and figures in the Black Arts Movement urges us to move beyond such confusions between what Wheatley said and the way she said it in order to find the "real" woman in the poems, "to learn to read Wheatley anew, unblinkered by the anxieties of her time and ours." Gates's hope is that if we can just get past that history of "cultural critique," then "two and a half centuries after a schooner brought this African child to our shores, we can finally say: Welcome home, Phillis; welcome home" (89).

Gates himself thus completes the continuum that his chronicle of lyric reading traces, as he extends the very reading he rejects, fusing the poet and her poems together into a single feminized, infantilized entity, asking "us" to do so as well. While Plato channels, varies, and finally departs from Wheatley's lines, Gates places Wheatley firmly in the center of "our" attention, using her to consolidate a communal *we* that will welcome the apostrophically addressed Phillis "home" to an America that does not need to call her by John and Susanna Wheatley's last name, that does not "read white, or read black," that can become a humanistic imagined community greater than the sum of its racialized parts.[18] While the century of Black criticism by men that Gates traces wanted Wheatley to represent "her people," to add her (small, feminine) voice to (the implicitly masculine) "huge black voices" that found ways to register personally representative protest, Gates wants Wheatley to represent all of us, Black and White, male and female, now and then. From the beginning of the consolidation of lyric in the last decades of the nineteenth century to the high modernist framing of lyric in the 1920s to the identity politics of confessional, personal lyric in the 1960s, Gates's account of "the anti-Wheatley tendency" chronicles rather exactly the development of modern ideas of lyric as the alienated expression of the single subject who speaks for all of us. Yet to Gates's dismay, modern critics have not assimilated Wheatley's work to that version of lyric—so he makes a plea for that assimilation on an even more hyperbolically and intimately lyric basis. But perhaps the reason that the desire to read Wheatley lyrically has proven simultaneously irresistible and impossible is not that her work is insufficiently expressive. Perhaps Wheatley has been so attractive and so resistant to lyric reading because her work is actually an important but heretofore overlooked origin story in the development of the idea that representative personal expression is what the lyric is all about. Since Romantic lyric did not yet technically exist when Wheatley wrote her poems in the 1760s and 1770s, it would be difficult to pursue my earlier argument that Romantic lyric address "couches a threat to the enunciation of black subjectivity" in Wheatley's work, as I have suggested it did for Black poets writing in the nineteenth century, or as Edwards suggests it does for Black poets writing in the twentieth century. Didn't Wheatley write before the history of Romantic-to-modern lyric that couched that threat began?

Apparently not. Gates and the Black male critics his version of "Phillis" opposes all use the dialectic of desire and failure inherent in Wheatley's work to define a shared modernity, whether that modernity is what Wheatley is not or that modernity is what Wheatley can teach us so that "we" can practice lyric reading unencumbered by the "anxieties" (or really, the conflicts, the social antagonisms) of the past. While it may continue to be difficult to read Wheatley's poetry as part of "the specific counterculture of modernity produced by black intellectuals" that Paul Gilroy associates with the expressive double consciousness of the Black Atlantic, it is by now clear that this is the specific modern counterculture to which her work belongs—if only we could figure out how. Though Gilroy positions Wheatley at the origin of "an anti-hierarchical tradition of thought that probably culminates in C.L.R. James's idea that ordinary people do not need an intellectual vanguard to help them to speak or to tell them what to say," he does not consider Wheatley herself that intellectual vanguard.[19] The entire twentieth century seems to have wished that she had been, that Wheatley had given some account of her experience in the Middle Passage, of her early life in Senegambia or Ghana or wherever her life began, of her first given name and language, of her experience when enslaved, of what it felt like to survive. The century also seems to have wished that she had written revolutionary, Romantic, proto-modern lyrics as testimony to her survival, or as James Weldon Johnson put it in a judgment that Gates does not cite, "had she come under the influence of Wordsworth, Byron or Keats or Shelley, she would have done greater work."[20] But perhaps it was Wordsworth, Byron, Keats, Shelley, Bryant, Sigourney, Horton, Longfellow, Whitfield, Watkins Harper, Poe, Whitman, Dunbar and the modern history of Anglo-American poetics that came under *Wheatley's* influence, since affective intensity and reflexive subjectivity are not just aspects of her work. They are its subjects, the possibilities it brings into view only in order to foreclose. Perhaps Wheatley remains what David Scott has called a "conscript of modernity" because her work did not represent an exemplary new poetic voice but instead exemplified the conditions of lyric's advent, the basis for modern poetics.[21] While Wheatley has been accused of writing pre-Romantic, pre-modern, pre-lyric poetry, her work may be better understood in terms of the ways it "contains, implies, produces, generates, permits (or whatever aberrant verbal metaphor one wishes to choose) the entire possibility of lyric."[22] I am arguing that this was not an accident or a by-product of the "experiment" of Phillis Wheatley but was instead the intention of her poetics all along—though the version of lyric that has resulted from that intention is not something anyone could have foreseen.

On Recollection

Certainly, the stakes of who speaks and why in the poem that became "On Recollection" are, as Plato noticed, very high indeed. As I began this book by suggesting, this poem's first stanza invokes the mother of the muses as therapist or life coach for the poet's own memory lapse:

> MNEME begin. Inspire, ye sacred nine,
> Your vent'rous *Afric* in her great design.
> *Mneme*, immortal pow'r, I trace thy spring:
> Assist my strains, while I thy glories sing:
> The acts of long departed years, by thee
> Recover'd, in due order rang'd we see:
> Thy pow'r the long-forgotten calls from night,
> That sweetly plays before the *fancy's* sight. (76)

Before she can say anything, the poet needs to remember what it is she wants to say. Like Milton, who invoked the "Heav'nly Muse" as aid to his "adventurous Song," Wheatley asks for all nine muses' aid as a "vent'rous *Afric*" whose "great design" (the 1773 revision of the earlier version's "deep design") may be as ambitious in its way as *Paradise Lost*. Yet while the subject of Milton's epic is clear from the poem's first words ("Of Mans First Disobedience, and the Fruit"), the first lines of "On Recollection" are all about trying to figure out what "the acts of long departed years" that are the poem's subject could have been. For that, the poet needs all nine muses, a capacious invocation that is not quite like Byron's later romantically dismissive "Hail Muse! *et cetera*," but that does foreground the act of invocation of the muses as generic, that puts the neo- in neoclassicism.[23] Mneme and her daughters may have the power to recover things we cannot remember, but what is it that this poet is trying to recall?

It's not just the early and repeated use of the first-person singular pronoun that announces this poem as personally motivated, as lyric rather than epic; it is also the way in which the poem fits Anne Carson's definition of lyric as "a highly concentrated action in which every letter and syllable counts."[24] Carson's is of course a retroactive definition of lyric, a late twentieth-century idea based on a classical source (for her, Sappho), but it does describe the odd pressure on each generically odic moment of Wheatley's series of variations on *her* classical source: every line contains an appeal to be reminded of what it is that is "long-forgotten," of why it has been forgotten, of how long this forgetting has been going on, even of who it is that is doing the forgetting, but that concentrated action of recollection is a poetic action pure and simple, since it produces no result. It is this lack of result that puts so much pressure on the person the poem does and does not represent, the person responsible for the memories that never appear.

The genre of "On Recollection" would have been recognized even in its first lines as a lesser ode—not quite Horatian or Pindaric, and definitely not Great or Sublime—yet its generic gestures feel both mixed and strained. While Jesse McCarthy, who has recently joined the long history of lyric readers of Wheatley, imagines that she wrote love poetry in Sappho's wake in order "to reach back to the earliest and most primal function of poetry: the stitching of poetry to experience," this poem, at least, not only remixes distinctly modern genres but also unstitches poetry from experience with Penelope-like precision.[25] In the rest of the poem, the pathos of that personal and generic strain comes to replace recollection as the subject here—or perhaps it would be better to say that this pathos of uncertain personal and generic agency comes to define both the poem and this version of recollection itself. In the second stanza of the revised version, we are told that "*Mneme* in our nocturnal visions pours / The ample treasures of her secret stores," a statement that seems promising, since dreaming would be one way of remembering. On this view, Wheatley might be subscribing less to an eighteenth-century version of the unconscious than to what Jonathan Kramnick describes as "a countercurrent within the eighteenth-century dominant theory of perception." In the dominant account, Kramnick writes, "ideas or impressions provide an internal picture of an external object or event," but in the countercurrent, "what minds and works of art do is not so much represent things as make them present to us."[26] Can memory recover not just the images but the "acts of long forgotten years"? Are those acts never really in the past, since they are always with us?

While Wheatley's poem may state a desire for historical presence, what the muse of memory gives the poet is neither representation nor proximity, exactly, but something that hovers in between, as she

To the high-raptur'd poet gives her aid,
Through the unbounded regions of the mind,
Diffusing light celestial and refin'd.
The heav'nly *phantom* paints the actions done
By ev'ry tribe beneath the rolling sun. (77)

As a promise of enlightenment, this is a confusing scene. As Julie Ellison writes, "the chief power of recollection turns out to lie in its ability to see the simultaneous operation of different peoples from above."[27] While painted actions would belong to "an internal picture," to a representational mode, the shift into the high gear of Christian history ("ev'ry tribe beneath the rolling sun") is hardly representational. It is also not co-presence, though this panoramic history seems to have led to "the acts of long-departed years" that the poet wants to recall to the present moment. But the change in scale here makes history the wrong word for this mind-painting, since its context is biblical—specifically, Revelations 7:9: "After this I beheld, and, lo, a great multitude, which no man could number, of all nations, and kindreds, and people, and tongues, stood before the throne, and before the Lamb, clothed with white robes, and palms in their hands." This is not a memory; it is instead the grandest possible stage set for memory, whose personification in the third stanza ascends the throne of Judgment, sorting the saved from the damned:

Mneme, enthron'd within the human breast,
Has vice condemn'd, and ev'ry virtue blest.
How sweet the sound when we her plaudit hear?
Sweeter than music to the ravish'd ear,
Sweeter than *Maro's* entertaining strains
Resounding through the groves, and hills, and plains.
But how is *Mneme* dreaded by the race,
Who scorn her warnings and despise her grace?
By her unveil'd each horrid crime appears,
Her awful hand a cup of wormwood bears.
Days, years mispent, O what a hell of woe!
Hers the worst tortures that our souls can know. (77)

As the muse of memory takes the Lord's throne, Judgment Day becomes an everyday occurrence, a feminized, internalized drama "within the human breast." As Ellison puts it, "Mneme combines the prospective energy of fancy and the internalized, monitory voice of Christian conscience" (117). Now, this theological introjection could just be good Congregationalist practice with a classical twist, but it might be more interesting to think about it as an instance of what David Hall calls "lived religion"—here, the way the Protestant penchant for self-examination is lived in and as a poetics.[28] The idea that memory's "plaudit," or approval, might be "sweeter than" poetry—even Virgil's ("Maro's") poetry—suggests as much, but the second half of the stanza that turns on the "But" of memory's disapproval zooms out of this internal focus back to a panoramic overview of "ev'ry tribe," of "all nations, and kindreds, and people, and tongues." These multitudes cannot be supposed to be "within the human breast." "The race / Who scorn her warnings and despise her grace" must be one of these tribes or nations or kindreds or people, yet it would make more sense if the word were "person" rather than "race" here, since in that case the rest of the stanza could follow a logic of self-accusation and self-chastisement. Maybe "race" is just here for the rhyme with "grace"?

That seems unlikely, since as I noted at the very beginning of this book, in the version of the poem written in late 1771 and published in 1772 in the *London Magazine* and widely reprinted across the Atlantic, the third stanza contains a variation on the same couplet, but in this earlier version, *Mneme* is male and his relation to the poet's practice is even more intimate:

He, from his throne in ev'ry human breast,
Has *vice* condemn'd, and ev'ry *virtue* blessed.
Sweet are the sounds in which thy words we hear,
Coelestial musick to the ravish'd ear.
We hear thy voice, resounding o'er the plains,
Excelling Maro's sweet Meneliun strains.
But awful *Thou*! to that perfidious race,
Who scorn thy warnings, nor the good embrace;
By *Thee* unveiled, the horrid crime appears,
Thy mighty hand redoubled fury bears;
The time mis-spent augments their hell of woes,
While through each breast the dire contagion flows.
Now turn and leave the rude ungraceful scene,
And paint fair Virtue in immortal green.
For ever flourish in the glowing veins,
For ever flourish in poetick strains.
Be *Thy* employ to guide my early days,
And *Thine* the tribute of my youthful lays.[29]

Wheatley's biographer and editor Vincent Carretta notes that "Wheatley mis-identifies the goddess Mneme as male" in this early version, "an error she cor-rects in the 1773 *Poems*" (Wheatley [2019], 164). Does that mean that the rest of what is changed between the two versions also constitutes "an error"? While in the later poem the goddess exercises a divine power, in the earlier poem the poet apostrophically implores memory to do so, assuring this masculine figure that "we hear thy voice," a voice "excelling" that of Virgil, a voice that addresses us directly. These lines then apostrophize that source of address in turn, bring-ing his "awful" agency to bear on "that perfidious race, / Who scorn thy warn-ings," but also enlisting his agency as "guide" for Wheatley's own "poetick strains." These apostrophes to memory not only change the goddess's pronoun but also deliberately exceed the poet's initial generically classical invocation of him/her in order to modernize memory and tell this trans entity what to do. When Tucker writes of what he calls "the romantic calving of odes from epics," of the way classical invocation morphs in poems by Keats and Words-worth into "the embedding of invocatory verses within an episode of the ac-tion an epic narrates," he could be talking about Wheatley's first published version of "On Recollection."

This is to say that Tucker's point about the White British Romantic lyric that had not yet taken shape, in which "something about the manifestly incred-ible convention of invocation rescued it from discredit, prolonged its life, and suited it to the performance of a set of tasks that helped define poetic Roman-ticism as a traditionally grounded orientation toward the modern," accurately describes what Wheatley's multiplication of her invocation was already doing.[30] In Wheatley's poem, those tasks include turning, apostrophically, from "the horrid crime" that remains unnamed in the past toward a future in which modern (even "youthful") life and poetry "flourish." Recognizing that memory can be destructive, the poet asks memory to save that epic destruc-tion for others. Even more explicitly than the later version, these lines are about the relation of the many to the one, the distinction between history and poetry, the fine line that separates violence from regret—or really, they are about the difficulty of telling the difference between the ancient and the mod-ern, between the large scale of righteous judgment and the small scale of fallen existence, between a race's "horrid crime" and an individual's "time mis-spent," between the "dire contagion" that "flows" unseen and the "immortal green" that, poetically, covers it up. In the first version, "that perfidious race" might just mean all those other sinners on one side of these divides, but in the later version, far from being a random end rhyme, "race" designates those who dread memory, who are tortured by it, for whom memory leads to a "hell of woe." And who are they?

In both versions, this is where the lines that Plato repeats intervene. They actually make more sense in the first version, since the decision to "now turn" from "the ungraceful scene" of this unnamed race's "horrid crime" leads directly to the alternative of the poet's virtuous practice. In fact, in the version that would live on in Wheatley's famous book, the six lines that follow "O what a hell of woe! / Hers the worst tortures that our souls can know" seem to come out of nowhere, whereas the lines after the earlier precedent appeal, "Be *Thy* employ to guide my early days, / And *Thine* the tribute of my youthful lays," follow seamlessly:

> Now *eighteen years* their destin'd course have run,
> In due succession, round the central sun;
> How did each folly unregarded pass!
> But sure 'tis graven on eternal brass!
> To *recollect*, inglorious I return;
> 'Tis mine past follies and past crimes to mourn.
> The *virtue*, ah! unequal to the *vice*,
> Will scarce afford small reason to rejoice. (77)

Plato may have repeated these lines if this were the version she knew, but I doubt it. Whereas in the version she did know, the lines are all about poetry, the earlier version strains to make "the horrid crime" of "that perfidious race" align with the poet's own "past follies and past crimes." The later poem actually makes the relation between collective violence and individual shame more difficult rather than easier to understand because the sense that something is missing—whatever memory it is that makes the fifteen-year-old Ann and eighteen-year-old Phillis "asham'd, and mourn"—causes the lines to come untethered from the history that is their precondition in the later version. That untethering makes Plato's feminized lyric reading possible, as it makes possible the lyric reading of the personal consequences of antiblack racial violence I have been following Wheatley in circumventing but also tempting you to imagine.

The most spectacular instance of a reader of "On Recollection" cutting through these circumlocutions and giving in to such imaginings in print is, as far as I know, John C. Shields's confession in *Phillis Wheatley and the Romantics* (2010) that,

After a casual reading, one is inclined to think, because the poet declares that her memory causes those horrid crimes to return, hence provoking her "to be asham'd, and mourn," that the crimes are probably her own. Closer inspection, however, "paints" quite a different picture. Indeed what would an asthmatic, benign teenager closely supervised by her white owners know of "the worst tortures"? Recall that Phillis, gallingly and unimaginatively named for the slaver that brought her, was seven or eight years old when she was sold on the block, July 11, 1761, with nothing but a piece of dirty carpet to conceal her nakedness. So she was certainly old enough to have recorded implacably on her memory the horrors of the terrible Middle Passage. Acknowledging that the mores governing the behavior of young African girls would have universally demanded these female children exercise modesty, one can readily grasp why the young girl's piece of dirty carpet would have forced shame upon her. . . . As for her mourning, this innocent victim of slavery no doubt possessed a plethora of occasions for her grief, such as the loss of her parents, siblings, and other family members, not to mention the loss or possible deaths of those Africans who befriended her on the wretched journey from Africa to Boston. Viewed from this perspective, Wheatley's ostensibly sweeping prospect actually bespeaks an intensely personal experience.[31]

What Shields "is inclined to think" in this paraphrase is exactly what Wheatley's poem does not say. By filling in the missing narrative between her couplets, this critic makes "On Recollection" into the representation of "an intensely personal experience," into the Romantic lyric everyone has always wanted Wheatley to have written. To do so, he needs to ignore the ways in which the revised version (which Shields calls "the superior version") especially goes out of its way to render its omissions as what Geoffrey Hartman has called "traumatic knowledge," a kind of knowing that Hartman describes as "literary," as particularly "Romantic," and as "a contradiction in terms," since when a poet like Wordsworth "evokes the role of 'mute insensate things' in the growth of the mind," he means that their resistance to expression—even to consciousness—is part of what makes them so powerful.[32] One is inclined to think that what Shields is doing is answering the poem's invocation in Mneme's name, giving the answer memory never gives in either version of Wheatley's poem. But in answering the poem's apostrophe by supplying these missing memories, Shields makes the objects of shame and mourning that remain both overdetermined and indeterminate in the poem into one person's historical experience, and he documents this experience by repeating recollections of Phillis Wheatley that were invented in the nineteenth century, when Wheatley Peters was no longer alive. In place of the poet's traumatic knowledge, the critic supplies a screen memory—in this case, an oddly specific memory that has been hiding Wheatley's poetics from view for almost two hundred years.

Experience Uncounted and Unclaimed

We will get to that particular and repeatedly fictionalized memory in a moment, but first it's important to emphasize that this is not to say that Wheatley was not herself traumatized and did not have her own screen memories— obviously she was and did. The question that readers of Wheatley tend to raise and then avoid is the relation of that historical trauma—of that historical *person*—to her poetics. It is tempting to read Wheatley's poetics as an account of what Anne-Lise François calls "uncounted experience . . . a mode of recessive action that takes itself away as it occurs," but this uncounting, this lyrical recessiveness, is so overdetermined, so historically motivated in Wheatley's case that it feels wrong to say that her aesthetic entails what François describes as an intentional "ethical suspension of the subject's claims to mastery and appropriative powers." Was such suspension, for her, a choice? Yet it also feels wrong to simply align Wheatley's traumatic knowledge with "trauma itself, often described as entailing the loss of the ability to assimilate experience to first-person narratives."[33] It is obscenely easy to fit Wheatley into Cathy Caruth's model of "unclaimed experience" that is the result of trauma, since the way in which her poetry is invested "in the complex relation between knowing and not knowing" always begs the question of what really happened to her, of how what happened made her who she was and able to write what she did— that is, of how racial violence made her history and her poetics as well as over two centuries of readings of her poetics possible.[34] In any case, as Caruth writes, such experience does not tend to result in the kind of narratable memories that Shields attributes to Wheatley but is more often expressed in "insistently recurring words or figures" that "engender stories that in fact emerge out of the rhetorical potential and the literary resonance of these figures, a literary dimension that cannot be reduced to the thematic content of the text," that "stubbornly persists in bearing witness to some forgotten wound" (5).

But what if there are no stories that emerge out of the recurring figures of unbounded refinement, of scattering, of dispersal, of vanishing, of multiplicity that haunt Wheatley's poetics? What if those figures instead document un-counting itself, taking away the terms of rhetorical mastery and appropriation, since those were the only terms available? What if, as (Saidiya, not Geoffrey) Hartman writes, replacing such figures of undoing with narrative is by defini-tion "ongoing, unfinished," even "impossible"?[35] What if whereas Shields de-livers Wheatley's childhood memories as "innocent victim" apparently intact, their missing referents firmly located in a story that turns out (as we will see in a moment) to be not her own, the insistently recurring gaps and vanished referents in Wheatley's poems bear witness to forgotten wounds in a very dif-ferent way? We will never know what experiences those gaps mark, but in saying that Shields's account of that injury is a screen memory, I mean that his story makes the long history of lyric readings of Wheatley—the long history of making up stories that connect her memory to her experience and her ex-perience to her poetry and her poetry to a representative, feminized "speaker"—seem to have some basis in individual and defined rather than col-lective, undefined, and unfinished history.

That is just the distinction that "On Recollection" renders impossible. Like forgetting, screen memories for Freud represent a compromise between re-pressed pain and the psyche's defense against it.[36] When something is too pain-ful to remember, the unconscious puts a less threatening memory in its place to protect us. In the case of Shields's "closer inspection" of Wheatley's poem, it may be terrible to think of a naked child ashamed of her condition, of a hurt girl bereft of her family and companions, but it is much more challenging to see how the poem "On Recollection" beats—couplet by couplet, iambic foot by iambic foot—the representation of individual subjectivity into thin air. If history can be narrated as the story of a person, it can be contained and per-haps redeemed. In the hope of such redemption, such personal liberty, lyric reading turns this poem's elaborate instances of consent not to be a single being into a single person's story line, responding in Mneme's name to the poet's opening appeal for therapeutic restoration.[37]

But individual literary memories cannot heal collective historical trauma, and in any case readers' memories are notoriously unreliable. When Toni Mor-rison wrote about the problem of "history versus memory, memory versus memorylessness," she opened the distinction I am trying to describe—but Morrison was a twentieth-and-twenty-first-century novelist, and her cele-brated concept of Black communal "rememory" depended on both a mod-ern theory of consciousness and a modern theory of narrative (as well as a modern theory of blackness) that engendered stories that emerged out of the rhetorical potential and the literary resonance of recurring words or figures.[38] Those stories indeed address the metalepsis that characterizes the way those words and figures seem to travel across space and time on their own, but in Morrison's novel *Beloved*, for example, where the idea of rememory is first articulated, that metaleptic potential is embodied by Sethe, a literary character in a volume of historical fiction. Once, like Wheatley, enslaved, the trauma-tized Sethe admits that it is

> so hard for me to believe in time. Some things go. Pass on. Some things just stay. I used to think it was my rememory. You know. Some things you forget. Other things you never do. But it's not. Places, places are still there. If a house burns down, it's gone, but the house—the picture of it—stays, and not just in my rememory, but out there in the world. What I remember is a picture floating around out there outside my head.[39]

Sethe expresses the distraction and displacement symptomatic of traumatic knowledge, but she also lives through that trauma and that knowledge as a single being, as a fictional woman with a name and a personal history. In con-trast, at the end of "On Recollection," what we might call the poem's culminat-ing re-recollection scatters personifications and persons to the wind:

> Of *Recollection* such the pow'r enthron'd
> In ev'ry breast, and thus her pow'r is own'd.
> The wretch, who dar'd the vengeance of the skies,
> At last awakes in horror and surprize,
> By her alarm'd, he sees impending fate,
> He howls in anguish, and repents too late.
> But O! what peace, what joys are hers t'impart
> To ev'ry holy, ev'ry upright heart!
> Thrice blest the man, who, in her sacred shrine,
> Feels himself shelter'd from the wrath divine! (77)

If for Morrison's Sethe, re-memory is an out-of-body experience, Wheatley's personified re-*Recollection* has no body or history of her own. She is not an actual person, so of course she can have no experience—but the persons who "own" her are also figurative rather than actual persons, since their experiences merely serve as examples of Recollection's "pow'r." According to Barbara John-son, "personification purposely represents an abstraction as a person. A quality that might form part of a whole person becomes the whole around which a person is shaped."[40] As a personification "own'd" by everybody, a "pow'r" distributed to each and all, the collective yet singularly experienced abstraction of Recollection shapes each person differently: "the wretch" recognizes his crimes "in horror and surprise," while the man of "upright heart" is "shelter'd" from such "anguish." And the poet? Is Recollection the whole that makes her whole?

In the short stanza that prefaces this final stanza, the poet invokes a different personification as model:

O *Virtue*, smiling in immortal green,
Do thou exert thy pow'r, and change the scene;
Be thine employ to guide my future days,
And mine to pay the tribute of my praise. (77)

This is the stanza that follows the stanza that Plato repeated—a revision of the lines that prefaced that stanza in the earlier version of the poem. The end of that stanza, we recall, hinges on the poet's decision to "now turn" from "the ungraceful scene" of an unnamed race's "horrid crime" toward her own virtuous practice. So the apostrophe to Virtue in this penultimate stanza might be read as a use of personification to shape an effort of personal compensation for collective historical violence. But what is the effect of that compensation? As Johnson writes, unlike apostrophe, personifications "are figures of being, not address. What matters in them is their predicates, not their voices. Instead of the phenomenalization of human speech [as in apostrophe], they endow the world with meaning centered around the representation of human being."[41] Yet Virtue's predicate, "smiling in immortal green," is not a human being, exactly. Even Virtue's desired employment as "guide" is not necessarily humanizing, especially when its "pow'r" shape-shifts into Recollection's "pow'r" over a lot of unnamed proxies for human beings in the last stanza. By the end of the poem, it is not just Phillis Wheatley's memory that is gone; Recollection has replaced her with several anonymous, representative men.

That vanishing act makes it all the more remarkable that Shields is only one of many modern readers to find the poet's own story fully recollected in this poem. And he is also not alone in narrating that story biographically, in the precise language of the *Memoir and Poems of Phillis Wheatley, A Native African and a Slave*, the influential account first published in 1834 and included in the 1838 collection of Wheatley's poems with Horton's, an account ascribed to one Margaretta Matilda Odell. That memoir begins, "Phillis Wheatley was a native

of Africa; and was brought to this country in the year 1761, and sold as a slave."
It continues by narrating that sale:

> She was purchased by Mr. John Wheatley, a respectable citizen of Boston. . . .
> Mrs. Wheatley wished to obtain a young negress, with the view of training
> her up under her own eye, that she might, by gentle usage, secure to herself
> a faithful domestic in her old age. She visited the slave-market, that she
> might make a personal selection from the group of unfortunates offered for
> sale. There she found several robust, healthy females, exhibited at the same
> time with Phillis, who was of slender frame, and evidently suffering from
> change of climate. She was, however, the choice of the lady, who acknowl-
> edged herself influenced to this decision by the humble and modest de-
> meanor and the interesting features of the little stranger.
>
> The poor, naked child (for she had no other covering than a quantity of
> dirty carpet about her, like a "fillibeg") was taken home in the chaise of her
> mistress, and comfortably attired. She is supposed to have been about seven
> years old, at this time, from the circumstance of shedding her front teeth.
> She soon gave indications of uncommon intelligence, and was frequently
> seen endeavoring to make letters upon the wall with a piece of chalk or
> charcoal.[42]

Whose memory is this? It is certainly not the recollection of the woman who
came to be known as Phillis Wheatley. At the end of her memoir, Odell identi-
fies herself as "a collateral descendant of Mrs. Wheatley," adding that she "has
been familiar with the name and fame of Phillis from her childhood" (35).
Carra Glatt has recently confirmed that genealogical records indicate that
Odell was (Mrs.) Susanna "Wheatley's great-grandniece through her mother,
[who was] the granddaughter of Susanna's older sister Elizabeth Wheeler Mar-
shall."[43] So the story repeated as memoir—the story that has been used to
introduce the poet to readers for almost two hundred years—is at best family
lore transmitted over several generations and varied for half a century across
several removes.

Yet as Jennifer Rene Young writes, "Odell's biography may be responsible
for the majority of myths that still exist about Wheatley today."[44] Both Odell's
tenuous connection to the poet and her considerable distance from any per-
sonal knowledge serve to explain why the emphasis here (as in the memoir as
a whole) is on the kindness of Susanna Wheatley as the "respectable" compas-
sionate woman willing and able to buy a child for "gentle usage," and on that
child as object rather than subject of White "selection." "Slender," "suffering,"

"humble and modest," a "little stranger," a "poor, naked child" covered by "a quantity of dirty carpet," "shedding her front teeth," this person is indeed a pitiful figure, as she is designed to be, since Odell's memoir was intended to solicit White sympathy, a condescension modeled on that of her ancestress herself. The memoir thus extends the long history that Joanna Brooks has shown began as "the story of Wheatley and her white female patrons in Boston," a story which Brooks suggests "makes plain the evasions, responsibilities, and betrayals at the heart of white sentimentalism and its racialized divisions of emotional labor."[45] We will return to those evasions and betrayals when we return to the racialization of the sentimental Poetess in chapter 5, but here it's worth noting that the editor of the 1838 volume adds his own male republican challenge to Odell's feminized appeal when he writes that this child "was sold and bought like a beast in the market! and that in the same land where, shortly after, the people rose in their indignation against oppression, and asserted, in the face of a frowning world, that 'All men are born free and equal.'"[46]

This very nineteenth-century complaint about this child's dehumanization in a proto-revolutionary Boston full of demands for natural rights contrasts rather starkly with Odell's also very nineteenth-century focus on the provenance of the child's attire: if colonial Bostonian hypocrisy is the object of the editor's irony, Odell draws our attention to the child's cultural displacement, to another version of alienation that solicits the sympathy of "the lady" and of the reader. Whereas Shields emphasizes that the child's odd garment would have "forced shame" upon the African girl, Odell compares the "dirty carpet" to a "fillibeg," a Gaelic word for "little quilt." Why would an African child be wearing Scottish tartan fabric? According to the *OED*, "fillibeg" is a word that circulated for a brief period in the late eighteenth and early nineteenth centuries, a word notably favored by Robert Burns ("His Philibeg, an' Tartan Plaid"). The word marks Phillis as literary on first sight—a displaced minstrel, cast on foreign shores (it may also unconsciously register Scotland's participation in the slave trade).[47] In Odell's account, Boston's shores are not hostile but instead offer a haven in which the already-poetic child—the child attired in and as poetry on first sight—can become "comfortably attired," can be in a position to receive Odell's relative's charity and thus become the "genius in bondage" that readers in 1838 already knew as "Phillis Wheatley." Those readers also knew that this child's rudimentary "marks upon the wall" were the rehearsals for that genius's transatlantically famous poems. There would be a long historical association between Black American poetics and Scottish minstrelsy (you can see it in Douglass's story of being named for a character in Sir

Walter Scott, and in Dunbar's Scots dialect verse, to cite just two famous examples), but the remarkable thing about the screen memory that Odell probably heard as family tale is that it makes this recollected person "of slender frame" a miniature Poetess, a personification of poetry from the beginning—or perhaps this small Phillis is less a personification than she is poetry's very person.

Since the difference between a personification and a person—as Johnson puts it, the difference between the representation of a human being and a human being—would become the central preoccupation of Wheatley's poetics, it's important to notice that stories like Odell's (or really, many reiterated versions of Odell's story) have made that central preoccupation hard to see. Readers since the nineteenth century have been so preoccupied with the status of the person the poetry is taken to represent that they have been unable to see through that invented person to her poems. You will have noticed that this way of putting the difficulty of reading Wheatley is exactly the opposite of the difficulty that Gates and the history of criticism he recounts describe: I am suggesting that Wheatley's poetry has been difficult to read not because she did not express herself in it but that, like Odell, lyric readers of Wheatley have substituted a defensive fiction of a poetic person for the poetics of uncertain personhood the poems do so extravagantly express.

In a much less often remembered part of her narrative, Odell comes close to acknowledging as much. While describing the poet's "habits of composition," she remarks a "circumstance . . . which peculiarly claims our attention":

> She did not seem to have the power of retaining the creations of her own fancy, for a long time, in her own mind. If, during the vigil of a wakeful night, she amused herself by weaving a tale, she knew nothing of it in the morning—it had vanished in the land of dreams. . . . It has been suggested that memory was in fault in this instance; but we have hesitated to account for this singular habit of mind in this manner; for, upon duly considering the point, we cannot suppose that Phillis could have made much rapid progress in various branches of knowledge, if she had not possessed a retentive memory—and still less, that she could have succeeded in the attainment of one of the dead languages. We are rather inclined to refer the fact in question to some peculiar structure of mind. . . . But the difficulty still remains. . . . Most persons are aware that, by a mental effort . . . they can recall scenes and events long since forgotten; but Phillis does not seem to have possessed this power. . . . We consider this statement of the case corroborated by the poem on "Recollection." In this little effusion, referring so directly to the

point in question, we find no intimation or acknowledgment of any defi-
ciency, but rather the contrary. (19)

Odell's prose struggles to account for the relation between a traumatized
young woman's memory lapses and an accomplished poet's extraordinary
mnemonic abilities; again, she avoids acknowledging the former while using
a poem as evidence of the latter. Since we have just lingered on the poem she
chooses as example, we are in a position to see that whatever it is that Odell
means by "the contrary" of an "acknowledgment of any deficiency," what this
poem actually does is to alienate personal memories from poetic ones, persons
from personifications. That alienation constitutes the drama of the poem, but
it has remained invisible to readers who often inadvertently follow Odell in
substituting a figurative person for a historical one.

Or really, the historical Phillis and her "peculiar structure of mind" remains
the referent for the figurative poetic person who becomes larger than life in
this and subsequent accounts. That figure has come to be known as "the
speaker," a fictional person who may participate in a narrative associated with
the historical poet, but whose voice transcends history. It is this figure that
allows Marsha Watson, for example, to conclude her passionate reading of "On
Recollection" with the claim that "Wheatley's speaker commands what 'ev'ry
tribe' fears most—the collective memory of, and so collective guilt for, the
individual crimes of an entire people. . . . Her very ability to remember the
'crimes' against her people inspired 'her great design,' creating this poem and
this volume and, once unleashed, will prove to be a potent weapon of ven-
geance."[48] Here, as in Odell's memoir, a poetic person—a poetic *speaker*—
assumes the agency that Wheatley herself could not assume, the agency that
everything about "On Recollection" undoes or renders uncertain. In this fa-
miliar version of lyric reading, this speaker manages to represent not only
Wheatley's memory but the memory "of an entire people" for whom she
speaks. This figurative consolidation is exactly what never happens in Wheat-
ley's poems, in which persons evaporate into personifications that dissolve
before our eyes, into figures of being that, over and over, cease to be.

Personifications But Not People

I wish I could prove that point by recollecting all of the extant poems, but since
that's not possible here (or anywhere, especially for such a slow reader), con-
sider in conclusion the small poem that marked Wheatley's advent in print, a
poem often forgotten because it is not included in *Poems on Various Subjects*.

Wheatley's remarkable talent for creating figures of depersonification—figures that characterize her entire poetics but for which I have been unable to find any established rhetorical term—apparently began early and emerged often. The lack of a term for these depersonifying figures is surprising, given Heather Keenleyside's observation that "the term 'personification' is newly invented in the eighteenth century: the *OED* identifies Samuel Johnson's dictionary entry [1755] as the first English use of the term. . . . Personification, Johnson writes, is 'the change of things to persons.'"[49] Since there seems to have been so much contemporary attention to the figure that it became important to name it, why not also name the change of persons to things that fall apart (which is of course not the same thing as objectification or reification, terms that did not appear until the mid-nineteenth century)? Against the post-Romantic (and especially post-Wordsworthian) view that has identified eighteenth-century poetic "personification with the old regime," a view that allowed writers from Marx to Freud to "turn to personification to establish their own modernity, repeatedly defining this modernity against a primitive confusion of persons and things," Keenleyside suggests that "the eighteenth-century fondness for personification [instead] reveals modernity to be marked less by the clear distinction between persons and things than by the persistent instability of these terms" (24). For Keenleyside, that instability makes personification the rhetorical figure "that appears peculiarly apposite to modernity itself" rather than the figure that defines poetic premodernity, since the questions this freshly minted term raised in the eighteenth century concerned what Steven Knapp describes as an "almost systematic ambivalence toward personification," or what Keenleyside understands as "the ways in which personification can appear duplicitous, cloaking ontological uncertainty in a rhetorical move" (27). Personification was a hot topic in the second half of the eighteenth century because, as Adela Pinch succinctly puts it, "personifications can suggest that we know what a person is."[50]

If the emerging eighteenth-century discourse of personification was all about worrying that this is exactly what no one knows, it is also true that (as Gilroy and Glissant and Hartman and Moten and Wilderson and others have made abundantly clear) the beginnings of this modern ontological uncertainty emerged in relation to the people whose personhood was being systematically revoked at an accelerating pace.[51] But "in relation" is much too weak and passive a prepositional phrase for the economy of that system; if personification is the figure "that appears peculiarly apposite to modernity itself," that is because it was in the interest of the triangular trade not to know what a person is. Surrounded by a discourse of personification based (like everything else in modernity) on the structuring principle of an antiblackness cloaked in and as a rhetorical move, at least one of those people developed a poetics that put the consequences of that motivated uncertainty on spectacular figurative display. Wheatley's consistent and often exhilarating habit of making personifications scatter and disappear places her work in the vanguard of "the specific counter-culture of modernity produced by black intellectuals" that Gilroy describes, though neither he nor anyone else, as far as I know, has attributed that coun-terculture to Wheatley. Not incidentally, her undoing of the figure that her contemporaries were so busy putting together also places her work in the van-guard of lyricization, since by negating the figure that anchored White dis-courses of poetic personhood, her poetry ends up tracing the lyric outlines of her own undoing, as well as the intimate relation of that undoing to both her own memory and to the ways in which she has been remembered.

This fatally generative facility first appeared in "On Messrs. Hussey and Coffin," a shipwreck-survival ode published in the *Newport Mercury* (a ship-ping paper) for December 14–21, 1767, when Wheatley was about fourteen, and not reprinted while she was alive (figure 3.1). As the note "To the Printer" indicates, the "on" in this title is not the abstract "on" attached to the second version of "On Recollection" but the marker of an historical occasion—or really, of two occasions: the first, "the narrow Escape" of the Wheatleys' dinner guests from a storm at sea that complicated their short trip from Nantucket to deliver whale oil to Boston; the second, the occasion on which the initially unnamed "Negro Girl" overheard their account while doing domestic forced labor ("'tending Table"). For good measure, the historicity of the poem is the subject of the note, which emphasizes that "the following Occasion, viz. Messrs Hussey and Coffin" took place in real time for real people, the "viz." (for the Latin *videlicet*, "that is" or "to wit," or literally, what it is permissible to see) underlining the identity of the people involved. While it is unlikely that this girl was directly addressed by those people, her poem begins by directly addressing *them* as "*Messrs.*" As it happens, this is a form of address also inven-ted in English at about this time in the eighteenth century. The *OED* gives examples of the designation used "chiefly in commercial and formal contexts" beginning in 1740 in Benjamin Franklin's *Philadelphia Gazette* to thank his sup-porters and in Sterne's *Tristram Shandy* in 1761 (the year Phillis landed in Bos-ton) to thank the monthly reviewers. The just barely teenaged Wheatley was thus quite *à la mode* not only in her focus on personification but in the title of her first published poem. This child who had no proper name was also ahead

[*NEWPORT MERCURY*, December 21, 1767]

To the P R I N T E R.

Please to insert the following Lines, composed by a Negro Girl
(belonging to one Mr. Wheatley of Boston) on the following
Occasion, viz. Messrs Hussey and Coffin, as undermentioned, be-
longing to Nantucket, being bound from thence to Boston, nar-
rowly escaped being cast away on Cape-Cod, in one of the late
Storms; upon their Arrival, being at Mr. Wheatley's, and, while
at Dinner, told of their narrow Escape, this Negro Girl at the
same Time 'tending Table, heard the Relation, from which she
composed the following Verses.

On Messrs. HUSSEY and COFFIN.

DID Fear and Danger so perplex your Mind,
As made you fearful of the whistling Wind?
Was it not Boreas knit his angry Brow
Against you? or did Consideration bow?
To lend you Aid, did not his Winds combine?
To stop your Passage with a churlish Line,
Did haughty Eolus with Contempt look down
With Aspect windy, and a study'd Frown?
Regard them not:—the Great Supreme, the Wise,
Intends for something hidden from our Eyes.
Suppose the groundless Gulph had snatch'd away
Hussey and Coffin to the raging Sea;
Where wou'd they go? where wou'd be their Abode?
With the supreme and independent God,
Or made their Beds down in the Shades below,
Where neither Pleasure nor Content can stow.
To Heaven their Souls with eager Raptures soar,
Enjoy the Bliss of him they wou'd adore.
Had the soft gliding Streams of Grace been near,
Some favourite Hope their fainting Hearts to cheer,
Doubtless the Fear of Danger far had fled:
No more repeated Victory crown their Heads.
  Had I the Tongue of a Seraphim, how would I exalt thy
Praise; thy Name as Incense to the Heavens should fly, and the
Remembrance of thy Goodness to the shoreless Ocean of Beati-
tude!—Then should the Earth glow with seraphick Ardour.
Blest Soul, which sees the Day while Light doth shine,
To guide his Steps to trace the Mark divine.
                                        Phillis Wheatley.

FIGURE 3.1. Phillis Wheatley, "On Messrs. HUSSEY and COFFIN,"
Newport Mercury, December 21, 1767.

of the curve in making the proper names of two White men (her enslaver's
business associates) into one corporate person, since doing so anticipated
nineteenth-century debates about the confusion between individual and com-
mercial agency.

So when her couplets begin asking that corporate fiction questions, do they
apostrophically animate it, turning its (or their) silence into mute responsive-
ness? Or, like Whitfield and Horton, does this young Black poet turn the ani-

mating fiction of apostrophe back on itself? If what matters in personifications "is their predicates, not their voices," as Johnson insists, then the question of animation so important to the structure of Romantic lyric apostrophe is not really the question here. As Plato and Douglass and Whitfield and Horton revised the apostrophic basis of nineteenth-century Romantic poetics, Wheatley revised the eighteenth-century fondness for poetic personification. The first couplet is addressed to the *Messrs.*, but it is a rhetorical question—a question that expects no answer—rather than an apostrophe to an absent, dead, or inanimate person, place, or thing that conjures that person, place, or thing into poetic life. Given the poem's emphasized and advertised occasion, we can assume that the people to whom this question was addressed were very much alive and around to hear it, even if it seems unlikely that they ever answered. It is indeed true that what is interesting about even this first very direct question is not its voice but its predicate, since the second line of the couplet begins to motivate the personification that directly follows it. After the first line's blunt evocation of the "Fear and Danger" that the two businessmen must have felt (feelings that themselves confuse cause and effect, subject and object), this question becomes not only "Weren't you *afraid* when 'one of the late Storms' almost wrecked your ship?" but "Did your fear lead you to imagine that 'the Whistling Wind' was a figurative being out to get you?" There is a doubling of apostrophe and personification for a moment here, but when the wind turns out to have a familiar name, the idea that "Boreas knit his angry Brow / Against you" becomes less threatening than the prospect of an unnamed whistling wind momentarily seemed to be.

That is because once the personification is named as a familiar literary character, Messrs. Hussey and Coffin become literary rather than historical characters, too, and their averted shipwreck becomes the property of a poetic rather than an historical genre. In that genre—part shipwreck-survival ode, part the genre that Norman Maclean dubbed "the personified lyric," part occasional tribute, part proleptic elegy, part versified newspaper report on current events, part evangelical public appeal, part the emerging genre of poems in White print media composed by diasporic Africans, free and enslaved— Boreas poses no real danger, and neither does Eolus, precisely because they *are* personifications. When in Pope's translation of the *Iliad*, "the piercing blasts of Boreas blow," we know we are reading poetry, not history.[52] This is the kind of purely poetic use of personification of which Lord Kames complained when (in 1762, five years before this poem was published), he described a "species of personification [that] must be referred to the imagination. The inanimate object is imagined to be a sensible being, but without any conviction, even for a

moment, that it really is so."[53] The problem for Kames was the lack of "convic-
tion" that such purely imaginative figures betray: no one needs to believe in
them, so no one needs to believe in that kind of *poetry*. This explicitly fictive
quality seems to be the problem to which personification has remained stuck,
as the figure increasingly became an index of the difference between what
Kames calls "passionate" poetry and merely "descriptive" verse: by the time of
the 1802 preface to *Lyrical Ballads*, Wordsworth's promise "to imitate, and as
far as possible, to adopt, the very language of men" was guaranteed by his
subsequent promise that "the Reader will find no personifications of abstract
ideas in these Volumes."[54] By 1956, Maclean could write an essay titled "Per-
sonification But Not Poetry," in which he confessed that although he was "one
of those who has attempted to throw some ray of historical understanding
upon the personified lyrics of the eighteenth century . . . I still do not like
them."[55] As Keenleyside makes clear, personification's bad reputation after the
eighteenth century runs deep, but what may seem surprising is that in the first
of several abrupt turns in Wheatley's poem, this young poet asks the Messrs.
to share this principled objection to the figure she has just employed, a now-
you-see-them-now-you-don't scene change from the emotionally expressive
faces of the personified winds to their dismissal: "Regard them not." Like
Kames, Wheatley encourages her readers to see that holding these fictive
blowhards in high regard would mean believing in them, and according to
good Congregationalist practice, of course our belief must not belong to pagan
gods but instead to "the Great Supreme," to a faceless source of animation that
cannot be personified or properly named. By its ninth line, this poem turns
out not to be a "personified lyric" after all—in fact, it rejects the premise of con-
ventional personifications altogether. What is it, then?

One thing it is not is an apostrophic lyric, since not only does the poem
warn against the attractions of mythical personifications, but it continues to
relentlessly deanimate the poem's titular addressees. By the tenth line,
Hussey and Coffin are dead—or at least their death becomes the poem's
speculative drama. Though the occasion of the poem is the pair's survival,
they are asked to

> Suppose the groundless Gulph had snatch'd away
> Hussey and Coffin to the raging Sea;
> Where wou'd they go? where wou'd be their Abode?

Where indeed? And why indulge in such a counterfactual fantasy, given Hussey
and Coffin's aforementioned "narrow Escape"? Though the poem directly ad-

FIGURE 3.2. Gaspard Marsy II and Anselme
Flamen. *Boreas and Orithyia (Allegory
of Air)*. Original marble 1677/1681 (Marsy)
and 1684/1687 (Flamen); bronze ca.
1693–1716. National Gallery of Art,
Washington, DC.

dresses these two men, in these lines their pronoun changes from "you" to "they,"
and wherever *you* might be, *they* are imagined as victims of the shipwreck that
did not happen. In this imaginary scene, Cape Cod Bay becomes "the groundless
Gulph" that has no face, no definition, and no name—in other words, whatever
this abyss is, it is the antithesis of a personification. Yet this antipersonification
does possess a terrifying agency, since in this fantastic drama it has "snatch'd
away" the poem's addressees. "The raging Sea" is also alive enough to be mad,
but like the Gulph's grasp, this madness emerges from an unknown source in
unknowable form. The purple-winged cold northern wind Boreas may have
been famous for abducting the young maiden Orithiya from her home, but
eighteenth-century readers like Wheatley would have known well exactly who
was responsible for that scene of fear and danger, of abduction and rape, a scene
that seventeenth- and-eighteenth-century writers, painters, sculptors, and por-
celain makers loved to represent in detail (figure 3.2).[56] In such representations,

the source of violence and violation is not in question. Yet after Boreas makes his exit in Wheatley's poem, the problem of where fear and danger begin and end, of who will snatch whom and why, becomes impossible to fathom, much less personify.

In a poem she wrote five years later, Wheatley makes a rare appearance as the person "snatch'd" by forces beyond personification's reach:

> I, young in life, by seeming cruel fate
> Was snatch'd from *Afric's* fancy'd happy seat:
> What pangs excruciating must molest,
> What sorrows labour in my parent's breast?
> Steel'd was that soul and by no misery mov'd
> That from a father seiz'd his babe belov'd:
>
> Such, such my case.[57]

Is this Phillis Wheatley's memory? One is tempted to agree with Paula Bennett that these lines suggest that "being kidnapped taught Wheatley all she needed to know about freedom and theft," but what do these lines really tell us about what this person knew or remembered?[58] What do they say about the "cruel fate" that "snatch'd" this soon-to-be poet from "*Afric's* fancy'd happy seat," about the "Steel'd" soul that "from a father seiz'd his babe belov'd"? Not much. Like the Gulph and the Sea in "On Messrs. Hussey and Coffin," fate and "that soul" are agents of destruction that lack faces and proper names. They are not personifications, exactly (neither is capitalized, neither attains even quasi-human form), but stand-ins for persons. The difference between these form-less agents and the Gulph and Sea is that they are historical rather than natural forces, but like the Gulph and Sea, they are indiscriminate: the person they attack is one among many.

In calling attention to her "case" (from the Latin *cadere*, to fall), Wheatley emphasizes that this is not something that happened only to her and her family; this violence may not have been as frequently represented as the drama of Boreas's rapaciousness, but it was so common as to be typical. While this singular moment in Wheatley's poetry has been understood as the personal memory that readers have long longed for the poet to disclose, it may be just the reverse: so many parents and children were "snatch'd from *Afric's* fancy'd happy seat" in the eighteenth century that what happened to this girl transforms the personal into the generic. Because she knows it happened to her, she can imagine what her parent "must" have felt, but whether or not this is the scene that Wheatley actually remembered, it is important precisely because her "case" was shared by millions of people who crossed the raging sea. This is not a defensive screen memory like Odell's "fillibeg," but it is hermeneutically defensive and self-concealing nonetheless, since, as in "On Recollection," personal memory here evaporates behind collective experience. We might call this moment a "case memory," a way of narrating the history common to many as individual experience. In this kind of memory, the distinction between what is and is not personal—as well as between what does and does not constitute a person—becomes the central question.

If personifications give human form to forces beyond our control, then case memories testify to the need for social control. "Such, such my case": this first-person testimony is in the service of a political argument, but that argument is not explicitly about the abduction that made this poem possible in the first place. Addressed and sent directly to William Legge, Earl of Dartmouth, on his appointment as Secretary of State for the Colonies in August 1772, the ostensible argument of the poem is on behalf of the enslavers rather than the enslaved, since the latter serve only as case studies for the former. Just after stating her own case, the poet asks, "And can I then but pray / Others may never feel tyrannic sway?" It may be true that, as Eric Slauter writes, such appeals "allowed white colonial readers to see themselves within the context of their own rhetoric—as slaves to British tyranny—but it also may have prompted them to reflect on their status as tyrants themselves."[59] Yet this particular appeal to the new British Secretary to side with the colonists' demands would be disappointed on both counts: Legge would not in fact support those claiming greater independence from British rule, and no law prohibiting the importation of slaves to the new republic would be enacted until 1808. Peter Coviello stresses that these lines are instead about Wheatley's own fitness to participate in that emerging republic, since they make "a clear argument, in the first place, about the nature of republican virtue—namely, that it requires a capacity for proper feeling"; Wheatley's obvious possession of such feeling, Coviello argues, is "a defense of the black citizen's very capacity for virtuous republican citizenship."[60] Such an argument seems closer to Wheatley's political aim, as well as to the aims of later abolitionists who used Wheatley's poetry in the service of appeals for a common sympathy, but Wheatley's object may also have been more personal, so to speak.

Waldstreicher has suggested that the more immediate occasion of Wheatley's poem was not only Dartmouth's appointment on the brink of revolution, but the Mansfield decision in England in May 1772 not to return James

Somerset to enslavement in the West Indies. That event was also, we recall, in the background of Plato's "To the First of August," but for Wheatley it was very much in the foreground, since as Waldstreicher writes, "when Wheatley wrote so boldly and optimistically to Lord Dartmouth about British freedom, liberty, God, and slavery, she could be so confident in part because [just a few months earlier] a blow seemed to have been struck against slavery at the very center of the empire."[61] When Wheatley traveled to London the next year, it is likely that she used the precedent of the *Somerset v. Stewart* decision that would have granted her freedom in England to negotiate her emancipation if she agreed to return to Boston. This is to say that Wheatley's "case" may have been a source of personal political agency, whether or not it changed the hearts and minds of her White readers or even if it actually was a particular rather than generic memory. As Joseph Rezek has suggested, it may also have been a source of personal literary agency, since in addition to the fact that "this passage from the poem to Dartmouth has long been recognized as a central moment in Wheatley's work because of her reflections about her father, Africa, and the slave trade," it may also be "the central moment in all of *Poems on Various Subjects* because it ties her consciousness of those things to a politics shaped by the medium that provides access to them"—that is, to the medium of the book itself, the book that Wheatley's presence in London aimed to promote.[62] That publication and that presence also allowed the young poet to forge political alliances with Black abolitionists like Somerset who, as fate would have it, was, according to Waldstreicher, "friendly with Sapho and Tombo, slaves of Steuart's Deputy Cashier Nathaniel Coffin" (536).

Thus while the last few paragraphs may have seemed to you a digression from our concluding focus on personification in Wheatley's first published poem, I assure you that has not been the case: at least one of the Messrs. Hussey and Coffin actively participated in the African-West Indian-North American traffic in persons that brought Wheatley to the room in which she served them dinner, and the other probably did as well. Charles Steuart, Coffin's boss, "acquired" James Somerset in Boston before bringing him to England in 1769, so Somerset was enslaved by Steuart at around the time that Wheatley met his Deputy Cashier Nathaniel Coffin and wrote her poem. In any case, Coffin was prominent enough in the trade to have crossed paths with the people who would become the two most famous abducted Africans in the Anglophone world of the 1770s, James Somerset and Phillis Wheatley. We cannot know if the fourteen-year-old Wheatley knew of this corporate entity's involvement with cases like hers when she wrote and published her first poem in 1767, but given the ample evidence of her later strategic circulation of her verses, that would not be surprising. If she did, then the poem's fantastic representation of Hussey and Coffin's demise and afterlife becomes even more pointed: *"Where wou'd they go? Where wou'd be their abode?"* If these people had died in the shipwreck in Cape Cod Bay that did not happen, would they have disappeared, as Phillis surely saw people die and disappear in the wake of her much longer, much more terrifying voyage? It is a child's question, but the traumatic knowledge that informs it is not childish. If Benveniste is right that "the ordinary definition of the personal pronouns as containing the three terms *I, you,* and *he,* simply destroys the notion of 'person,'" because "'person' belongs only to *I/you* and is lacking in *he,*" then this question rhetorically destroys the corporate entity that literally destroyed people. To return to Pinch's point that "personification can suggest that we know what a person is," this depersonifying question suggests that whether or not we not know what a person is, people can fall and be torn apart.

That is why the second half of the poem is all about the death and dissolution rather than the life and animation of its titular subjects. I like to think of this last movement as a revenge fantasy, but that desire is probably my own, not the poet's—and in any case in this fictive drama, these White men seem to end up in heaven. This long concluding turn no longer addresses the fashionable imaginary Nantucket corporation (which remains in the plural third person), but an imaginary scene of deanimation, of depersonification. The no-longer-corporate-person or persons tossed along these lines is or are like so much flotsam and jetsam on the surface: they drop down to "Shades below," then up to Heaven for a blissful moment, in a wild arc, as if their redemption were really Redemption and so a ticket into what Warner has begun to call "the Evangelical Public Sphere." That was the sphere that Wheatley's elegy for the evangelical minister George Whitefield entered so successfully and helped to make transatlantic, but in her first published poem, her public subject evaporates into the heavenly atmosphere where "Rapture soars." That disembodiment also eventuates in a dismemberment of the poem's or poet's "I" in the break into the prose interpolation in which "I" becomes one of many hypothetical Seraphim, or perhaps just a "Tongue" no longer contained in an iambic body.

In a way, this is the emancipation from pentameter couplets that Wheatley's modern lyric readers have always wanted to see her achieve, but it turns out that the couplets aren't what constrains this poet's verse after all. In fact, to recall J. Paul Hunter's point about Pope, the "route" by which each of these couplets

> blurs and reconfigures binaries and develops a rhetoric of complex redefinition is circuitous; it challenges the transparency of the apparent rhetoric and blurs and bleeds images of plain opposites into one another. The effect, though, is not to fog or muddy or obscure—much less to deconstruct meanings to nothing stable at all—but to use the easy opposition as a way of clarifying the process of deepening qualification and refinement.[63]

Hunter's description is so true of Wheatley's couplets that their oppositions deepen and qualify and refine their subjects out of existence. Are Hussey and Coffin above or below? Inert or winged? Enjoying "Streams of Grace" or still struck by "the Fear of Danger"? Does the rhyme between "Abode" and "God" mean that they have gone to heaven, or does the rhyme between "below" and "flow" mean that they have been caught in the undertow? And what are we to make of the last rhyme before the couplets' collapse into prose, the odd rhyme between "fled" and "Heads"?

Perhaps the prose is meant to settle the questions that the couplets multiply and suspend, but if so, it does not quite succeed. The first appearance of the first-person pronoun in this poem is not what anyone would call a "lyric I," not only because this first-person statement is not an expression of any one person's thoughts or feelings, but also because these are not statements but conditionals: "*Had* I the Tongue of a Seraphim, how I *would* exalt thy Praise," "thy Name *should* fly," "Then *should* the Earth glow." Whatever all these phrases amount to, their sum is a fantasy inside a fantasy, surplus lyricism within surplus lyricism. Wheatley would soon become famous for writing elegies that allowed her to share the afterlives of a lot of White people, but her earliest printed paean to eternal life celebrates an exaltation above scale even for White folks. Rather than an assertion of individual expression, this conditional "I" fogs and muddies and obscures the plain opposites that the preceding couplets so delicately hold in place. After this prose confusion, the final couplet,

> Blest Soul, which sees the Day while Light doth shine,
> To guide his Steps to trace the Mark divine,

is itself such a blur of monosyllabic reconfiguration that it polarizes rather than synthesizes the preceding couplets' insistent dialectic: who is the "Blest Soul"? What Day? What Light? This providential blur is the only "guide" that mediates between the Soul and "the Mark divine," than which nothing could be less personified. The only person left standing at the end of this poem is the one designated by the final signature: *Phillis Wheatley*. But the person named by that signature is not there, either. This epitaph marks the memory of the person who has survived for two and a half centuries between the lines that actually *were* writ on water, and wherever she remains, her own memories have dispersed in her wake.

Yet the reconfiguration of those memories into a speaking person continues to screen her poetry from view. To return to the version of the name that Thomas Jefferson recollected when he notoriously wrote in 1781 (three years before Wheatley's death) that "Religion indeed has produced a Phyllis Whately [*sic*]; but it could not produce a poet," we are now in a position to see that he was using Wheatley's case as proof that "among the blacks is misery enough, God knows, but no poetry."[64] While later readers have been quick to reject Jefferson's antiblack racism, they have actually hewed rather closely to the logic that continues to make Phillis Wheatley a case memory, a representation of a human being rather than a human being, a personified example of a person rather than a person. This is just the distinction that this poet devoted her career to exposing and undoing, since it is just the distinction that enabled the extractive racial capitalism that determined the course of her short life. Yet it is also the very distinction that almost all readers since Jefferson have enforced. The portrait of her misery, not her poetics, has guided the reading of her poems. I do not mean what Gates means when he writes that "if Phillis Wheatley was the mother of African-American literature, there is a sense in which Thomas Jefferson can be thought of as its midwife" (50). Gates's point is that "Blacks took on Jefferson's challenge" and produced a body of literature in response. That may well be true, but Phillis Wheatley was not only at the origin of Black American poetics but at the origin of Anglo-American Romanticism. For Gilbert Imlay, lover of Mary Wollstonecraft and illegitimate father of Fanny Imlay, Wheatley's example provided an opportunity to question "Mr. Jefferson's judgment" in 1793, and to argue that "Phillis appears much the superior. Indeed, I should be glad to be informed what white upon this continent has written more beautiful lines."[65] Imlay then cites Wheatley's "On Imagination" as evidence that her poetry can speak for itself. Shields thinks that Imlay's response to Jefferson was part of a network of early transmission of Wheatley's poetry to the British and German Romantics, and that she thus influenced the movement.[66] That may also well be true, but the more obvious conclusion is that Wheatley's poetics prefigured both the history of Black American poetics and of Anglo-American Romanticism not because either

Black or White poets took up her exemplary case but because like the Romantics, she pushed couplets and personifications to their breaking points, and like the Romantics, she made poems based on the traumatic knowledge of the self-alienated person. Yet like later Black American poets but unlike White Romantics, she withheld that knowledge and that person from the poems themselves, instead demonstrating over and over the destruction that antiblack discourses wrought on both persons and personifications.

It is this eloquent absence, this skill in dismantling figures of poetic personhood that became enormously influential in the history of American poetics, since that history has been devoted to the fabrication of poetic persons that generically screen the systemic violence that has made so many people vanish and fall apart. Jefferson's case was racist, but so was Imlay's—and some version of their exchange has been reiterated for over two hundred years. All lyric readings of Wheatley that substitute the personified person for the poems racialize that person, as her poem to Dartmouth warned that they would. The problem has always been that the poems gathered under the name "Phillis Wheatley"—the hymns, the circuit-of-Apollo poems, the Universe poems, all sorts of odes, the hurricane poems, the rebus, the famous elegies, the *apologeia*, the extraordinary ekphrastic epyllion on Niobe's loss of child after child after child after child, "all beautiful in woe," the infamous eight-line poem in which the very young Wheatley describes her abduction as a "mercy" and the fate of those abducted as a process of being "refin'd" into sugary angelic whiteness— have not been allowed to state the case they make over and over, the case of a person depersonified by the modes of recognition instantiated in the discourses in which she wrote and by means of which she continues to be read. Instead, the genres and figures and prosodies that blur together and dissolve in the poems themselves have been reconstructed in the name of a supposed person, a poetic "speaker" who has come to share Wheatley's memory without sharing her cruel fate. The genres and figures and persons and personifications and measures that Wheatley's poetics so artfully disarticulated have been rearticulated in her name, and the product of that refinement has in turn generated the lyricization of American poetics. Her poetry initiated this process not because of what the poems tell us about the woman who wrote them "but because of what lived on from this history."[67] In this sense, her poems indeed tell a very personal story, a history in which the consequences of antiblackness set a new poetics in motion, a version of American lyric that abides.

4

Prosody

WILLIAM CULLEN BRYANT AND
THE WHITE ROMANTIC LYRIC

The Poet's History

If Black poets set modern American lyric in motion in the late eighteenth and nineteenth centuries, their White contemporaries have been accused of bringing it to a halt. Sometimes, as we saw in Pierpont's poems, that retrograde impulse emerged when White poets appropriated non-White figures, but appropriation was just one of many ways in which nineteenth-century American poets countered the poetics of blackness with what may now seem an old-fashioned poetics of whiteness. Not only did the Black poets in the first part of this book not just react to White poetics, and not only did White poets not simply perform minstrel versions of Black poetics, but just as Black poetics was made within discourses that also made that poetics virtually impossible (and thus, as I have suggested, endlessly generative), so White poetics was made within received Anglophone prosodic genres. While the second part of that sentence may look like a recipe for racial continuity, that is not exactly how it worked out. On one hand, Spenserians and sonnets and Venus and Adonis stanzas did have the advantage of conferring the fiction of a hereditary whiteness; on the other, they were not distinctly *American*. In order to make them American, early nineteenth-century White poets often stressed their independence from the borrowed poetics on which they actually did depend, or placed their poems against non-White backgrounds, emphasizing the displacement of the Anglo poet in the wilderness.

If this account of American poetics sounds as if it came out of a textbook, that's because it did: the introduction to the 2003 edition of *The Norton Anthology of American Literature* for the decades between 1820 and 1865 explains that throughout the first half of the nineteenth century, "critics called for writers to celebrate the new country in poetry or prose, repeatedly going as far as to advise would-be writers on potentially fruitful subjects such as American Indian legends, stories of colonial battles, and celebrations of the American Revolution."[1] What the textbook does not say is that the reason such subjects were recommended is that they made sure that the figures in the foreground of this emerging literature were not only nationally identifiable as American but racially identifiable as White. What it also does not say is that the whiteness of these figures was not only a consequence of the structural racism of Anglophone poetics, but that it has (somewhat paradoxically) come to mark most nineteenth-century White American poetry as insufficiently American, insufficiently modern, and, especially, insufficiently lyric.

Or perhaps the point is too obvious to require comment. After all, *The Norton Anthology of American Literature* continues to feature a cover that may be worth a thousand words (figure 4.1).[2] *Kindred Spirits*, Asher Brown Durand's 1849 painting of the American poet William Cullen Bryant (the figure on the left) and his friend the painter Thomas Cole, takes its title from a sonnet by Keats. (And because Cole had just died and Bryant had written a sonnet for Cole twenty years earlier on "The Painter Departing for Europe," advising Cole to keep "the wilder image" of the New World "bright" while in the Old, the title's allusion was multilayered.) The painting hung for over a century in the New York Public Library, an institution that was Bryant's idea (which is why Bryant Park extends behind it).[3] Central Park and the Metropolitan Museum of Art were also Bryant's projects, and he served as editor of the *New-York Evening Post* for over half a century.[4] But the painting is no longer in New York since it was bought by Alice Walton, the Walmart heiress, in 2005 for more than 35 million dollars (the highest price ever paid for a pre-twentieth-century American painting).[5] It is now in her museum in Arkansas. As the *Norton* cover, the Manhattan landmarks, and the painting's value all indicate, Bryant remains symbolically central to institutions of American culture, even as those institutions themselves have forgotten or dismissed his influence. I will go on to argue that Bryant's poetics also remain central to institutions of American poetry, though those institutions also seem to have left Bryant behind. Despite his value as figurehead, Bryant's work has been categorically devalued by modern American literary criticism. Why? What is the relation between Bryant's cultural influence, his particular poetics of whiteness, and his antiquarian demise? And what does this odd combination tell us about the history of American lyric?

FIGURE 4.1. Cover, *The Norton Anthology of American Literature*, Shorter Eighth Edition: *Volume 1, Beginnings to 1865* (2012).

As early as 1917, the *Cambridge History of American Literature* relegated Bryant to a chapter titled "Bryant and the Minor Poets," and dubbed him (in a phrase that was used less dismissively in the nineteenth century) "the American Wordsworth."[6] This is the view Roy Harvey Pearce extended when he traced *The Continuity of American Poetry* in 1961: according to Pearce, the problem with Bryant was that he "taught and ministered to most of his readers" rather than, like Walt Whitman, calling "into question received definitions" of poetry.[7] Although it has become easy to point to F. O. Matthiessen's 1941 *American*

Renaissance: Art and Expression in the Age of Emerson and Whitman as a monu-
ment to this kind of nationalist canon formation and exclusion, Matthiessen's
dismissal of Bryant's poetry as symptomatic of "the want of male principle in
American genius" and of "the fatal imitation of Europe" in pre-Emersonian
American letters was enough to make Bryant's work seem at best a tributary
to the onward flow of American poetics—and at worst, an unnamed mother
rather than potent father—for the rest of the twentieth century.[8]

Certainly, a large part of what damned Bryant to faint praise in the twen-
tieth century was the rise of a canon of American poetry that, after Matthies-
sen, assumed Emerson as touchstone for the proto-modern poetics of Dick-
inson and Whitman. The reasons for Emerson's increased importance to
intellectual history were multiple, but Bryant's decline may explain an aspect
of that history not often discussed: as Bryant was feminized and dubbed imi-
tative, cast as the poet of his time rather than the poet of the future, so most
nineteenth-century American verse was increasingly cast as "conventional"
and out of date. Karen Kilcup has suggested that nineteenth-century review-
ers "killed American poetry," and Joan Shelley Rubin has suggested that
nineteenth-century American poetry never really died, but some nineteenth-
century American poets have certainly fared better than others.[9] The truth is
that Emerson's poetry was not very important to American poetics, though
his ideas about the ideal lyricism of poetry were. Bryant's poetry, on the other
hand, *was* as important to the history of American poetics as the residual
traces of his prominence imply. Pearce's and Matthiessen's comments betray
a defensiveness in relation to Bryant that we may want to examine more care-
fully: what's so wrong with Europe and "the want of male principle"? How
could Bryant, of all poets, pose a threat to White American manhood, even
to "the male principle in American genius"? What, exactly, was he so busy
teaching his contemporaries, and why did that lesson come to seem so stuck
in the past?

Ironically, in addition to Pearce's understanding of all American poetry as
"the drive toward modernism" and Matthiessen's desire to establish American
originality and Whitmanian masculine "procreant urge" as preconditions of
the new discipline of American literary studies, the affectively overdetermined
motive for the demotion of Bryant in twentieth-century academic literary
criticism may also have been a reaction to his prominence in American literary
education in the late nineteenth and at least the first half of the twentieth
century. In 1926, fifteen years before Matthiessen pronounced Bryant's poetry
dead on arrival, Vachel Lindsay published an essay titled "What It Means to

Be a Poet in America." In defense of his own position as modern American poet, Lindsay complained that nineteenth-century American poets, and Bryant in particular, were responsible for the fact that "there is no word in America more hated than the word 'poet.'" The evidence can be found, Lindsay claimed, in "the art store panel of the portraits of dead poets":

> It is hung up all over the land, from the first-reader rooms to the little seminar rooms for the postgraduates at the great universities. This art-store panel is a picture of seven senile, spiteful, educated, overbearing old gentlemen with long whiskers and long hair, and the atmosphere of executioners. They all look like the kind of quick workers that would steal pennies from a dead child's eyes. I have seen the pictures of most of these men in their youth. They were handsome boys, regular sheiks; they really looked like the young miniatures of Shelley and Keats and Byron.
>
> But think of the atrocity of making a small boy memorize "Thanatopsis, A Meditation on Death," then of telling him it was written by William Cullen Bryant at eighteen! Even if the youth had poetry in his soul, he would swear a secret and eternal vendetta against the name of poet forever. And is he, by way of apology, shown a picture of William Cullen Bryant at eighteen, before he was educated, charming, debonair, sheiklike, the Apollo Belvedere of his day? No; he is shown a picture of William Cullen Bryant that is ferocity itself, with gray hair all down his back and whiskers that go on forever. So poor little Willy Smith is only waiting to meet one of those poets down an alley, and hopes to have a gun handy. . . . Could any angel from heaven then persuade that small boy that "Thanatopsis" is poetry? Death is no poem to rub into babies, nor should they be bothered with puffy, self-important, overeducated, toothless, malevolent old bullies.
>
> Bryant and all the others have been hated by the typical young American ever since they went into the textbooks, and will continue to be hated unless they are thrown out of the textbooks, and until that art-store panel of the long-haired frights is destroyed forever.[10]

As the *Norton* cover attests, Bryant has not yet been "thrown out of the textbooks," but he has certainly been thrown out of accounts of the genealogy of American lyric. So have most of the poets in the mass-produced series of portraits of "long-haired frights" to which Lindsay referred, a panel that did indeed hang in countless American schoolrooms ("from the first-reader rooms to the little seminar rooms for the postgraduates at the great universities"), libraries, and homes for much of the twentieth century. The portrait

FIGURE 4.2. The American Schoolroom Poets, or "The Worthies." Provenance unknown. Collection of the Author.

was generally referred to as a picture of "the worthies" or simply as "Our Poets," and it was usually composed of six (rather than seven) oval busts of nineteenth-century gray-haired White literary men (Figure 4.2).[11]

Bryant does indeed have the longest whiskers in the bunch, perhaps to indicate that he was the oldest and earliest of these "Schoolroom" or "Fireside" poets. Lindsay singles him out for derision since, as Angela Sorby has written, "he was the most culturally conservative of the schoolroom poets," and in 1926, still one of the most revered (thus his central place next to Longfellow).[12] But Lindsay's complaint is not about Bryant's own cultural politics, exactly. Once upon a time, Lindsay imagines, Bryant looked like a gorgeous naked Apollo Belvedere or a "regular sheik," a "handsome boy," really "like the young miniatures of Shelley and Keats and Byron." True, he did write a dreary poem about death, and by the late nineteenth century, that poem had become a standard text for memorization and recitation in the expanding public school system. But the real problem with the word "poet" according to Lindsay was that it had been made to refer to dead White "puffy, self-important, overeducated, toothless" American men like William Cullen Bryant rather than to classically sexy, vaguely Orientalized, forever young, and revolutionary British Romantics.[13] The way forward for the modern poet was clear.

Lindsay may have represented an eccentric view, but such attempts to distance modern poets from nineteenth-century American "dead poets" began before the poets people like Lindsay called "ours" actually died, and this attempt at distancing had become the general rule by the second and third decades of the twentieth century. This was so much the case, in fact, that by 1915 Van Wyck Brooks began to wax nostalgic:

What emotions pass through an hereditary American when he calls to mind the worthies who figured in that ubiquitous long paneled group of "Our Poets" which occupied once so prominent a place in so many domestic interiors? Our Poets were commonly six in number, kindly, gray-bearded, or otherwise grizzled old men. One recalls a prevailing six, with variations. . . . Frankly, we feel in ourselves, we are no longer so fortunate as in those days. It could really have been said of us then, as it cannot now be said at all, that as a folk we had won a certain coherence.[14]

If we put Brooks's explicitly racist nostalgia beside Lindsay's vitriol, a picture of Bryant's importance to the history of American lyric begins to come into view. By half-imagining that Bryant could be recuperated if he were recast as a young British Romantic, Lindsay was actually registering what had happened to Bryant's poem over a century after it was first published in 1817: initially received as a daring Lake School experiment (Richard Henry Dana is reported to have exclaimed "*That* was never written on this side of the water!" when the manuscript was first read to him), "Thanatopsis" became the sort of poem by the sort of poet that gave nineteenth-century American poetry a bad name.[15]

The fact that Lindsay was the author of "The Congo: A Study of the Negro Race" (1914), a poem that gave modern American poetry a bad name, is more than an irony here.[16] By the time that Sterling Brown called Lindsay's poem "that monstrosity" in his 1973 address at Williams College, "The Congo" was considered too racist to be included in textbooks and anthologies.[17] Like Brown, Bryant attended Williams, and like Lindsay, he was a "progressive" political thinker who wrote verse that has not only come to seem stuck in an earlier literary age but also stuck in that age's racism. In fact, just about everyone has come to agree with Lindsay that Bryant is outdated; but if Bryant's antiquity has been taken for granted in the history of American poetry, his role in the establishment of a White American poetics as well as his role in ushering in literary criticism's later replacement of that poetics with the White British Romanticism Bryant was accused of imitating have remained unacknowledged. We can see in Lindsay the beginnings of a genealogy of modern American poetics that is still surprisingly current: if that poetry can be imagined in relation to Shelley and Keats and Byron rather than in relation to Wheatley and Bryant and Longfellow and Horton and Whitfield and Plato and John Greenleaf Whittier and Frances Ellen Watkins Harper, it might recover its good name.

In fact, it did. Comic as it may seem, by the 1930s the idea that British Romanticism was where modern American poetry began would become a critical paradigm—so much so that Cleanth Brooks could write of modern poetry in 1939 that "we are witnessing (or perhaps have just witnessed) a critical revolution of the order of the Romantic Revolt."[18] What Brooks meant was that "Romantic poetry"—*British* Romantic poetry—"thus foreshadows the characteristic structure" of modern poetry in English, a perspective that allowed Brooks (and many American literary critics who have followed in his wake) to go one step further than Lindsay in simply erasing the embarrassing old grizzled bullies who interrupted that vision of modern poetry as an all-White current flowing from Wordsworth to Eliot or from Shelley to Stevens with a little authentically American Emerson and Whitman in between. Lindsay was right that Bryant was a young Romantic, but what Lindsay did not realize—and what no one else seems to have realized since—is that Bryant's intimate identification with and practice of Anglo-Romanticism turned American poetics in a direction these twentieth-century writers were following rather than resisting. Bryant's abstraction of the British Romantic poetics he has been accused of merely borrowing had lasting effects on the lyricization of transatlantic poetics, which is to say, on current ideas of Romantic lyric (specifically on versions of "the" Romantic lyric taught in American English departments) and on the naturalization of lyric reading. Bryant's lyricized racism is and was inherent in the very Romantic-Englishness of the forms he used to establish what it was and is to be a poet in America. Reactions like Lindsay's were symptoms of an emergent modern aversion to the moribund whiteness of that genealogy, an aversion cast as attraction to its source. I will go on to suggest that Bryant's poems were often about that predicament—that is, about whiteness and its precarious, dangerously fragile, defensive, and above all fictively continuous presence in the American landscape.

Of course, this defensiveness, too, was overdetermined. As Anna Brickhouse and Kirsten Silva Gruesz have made abundantly clear, Bryant's anglicization of American poetry occurred at the same time that he was immersed in the translation, edition, and critical review of Mexican and Cuban literature, much of which was published in Philadelphia.[19] When the Cuban poet José Martí wrote about Bryant ten years after his death, he commended him as "illustrious" and "socratic," but complained that "as a poet, a white poet, in the comfortable style of Wordsworth," this "excessively gentle" North American was "not like those unfortunate and glorious ones who nourish themselves on their own entrails."[20] What Martí meant was that Bryant was not Whitman, but also that he was not José María Heredia, the Cuban poet Martí called "the first poet of America" and that Bryant (that other first poet of America) has been credited with befriending and translating. But if Martí was right that Bryant was too gentle and too White and too Anglo, Brickhouse points out that "he was emphatically wrong about the geographical and linguistic scope of the poet's literary sensibility. In fact, Bryant's formal poetic orientation toward Europe overshadowed a compelling, hemispherically American dimension within the story of his career, a multilingual literary consciousness."[21] This is to say that Bryant's anglicization of American poetics was meant to signify what Brickhouse calls "a broader cultural agenda that his own intellectual circles described as a kind of literary manifest destiny," since "his writings on Latin American and U.S. hispanaphone topics often propounded a broader Anglo-Saxonist and expansionist ideology in which a glorious U.S. paragon of democracy and civilization" would efface the traces of the Spanish colonization of the Americas with "an indomitable English."[22]

In his preface to *The Book of American Negro Poetry* in 1922, James Weldon Johnson noticed something else about Bryant's Spanish translations. In discussing Plácido, whom he calls "the greatest of all the Cuban poets," Johnson focuses on the celebrated sonnet written the night before the revolutionary's execution by Spanish colonial officers. "Plácido's sonnet to his mother has been translated into every important language," Johnson writes, as a way to emphasize the Black Cuban poet's notoriety; "William Cullen Bryant did it in English." Bryant's name seems to assure the sonnet's North American importance, but then Johnson's focus turns from poet to translator:

> Bryant's translation totally misses the intimate sense of the delicate subtlety of the poem. The American poet makes it a tender and loving farewell of a son who is about to die to a heart-broken mother; but that is not the kind of farewell that Plácido intended to write or did write.
>
> The key to the poem is in the first word, and the first word is the Spanish conjunction *Si* (if). The central idea, then, of the sonnet is, "If the sad fate which now overwhelms me should bring a pang to your heart, do not weep, for I die a glorious death and sound the last note of my lyre to you." Bryant either failed to understand or ignored the opening word, "If," because he was not familiar with the poet's history.[23]

As Johnson goes on to explain, the "delicate subtlety of the poem" has everything to do with the "history" that Bryant totally missed: "Plácido's father was a Negro, his mother was a Spanish white woman" who abandoned him. The poet's appeal to his mother becomes for Johnson a Black man's appeal to a White interlocutor tone deaf to both the poem and its history—that is, tone deaf to the racial politics of transatlantic poetics. Johnson actually retranslates the poem in order to underline his point: Plácido's poem is part of the history of Black poetics of which White readers—and especially White poets like Bryant—have been ignorant. As we saw in Delany's attribution of Whitfield's poem to a fictional "Placido," the revolutionary inspiration of the Cuban poet had informed the American Black radical poetic tradition for over half a century when Johnson finally corrected Bryant's translation. But as Whitfield's variations on Bryant's English stanzas also suggest, the poetics of whiteness that Bryant crafted was not just based on ignorance but on design.

As Johnson implied, that design depended not only on Bryant's explicit anglicization of his Spanish American sources, and, as we shall see, on his lyricization of the American genres of the figure of "the vanishing Indian" in the midst of the escalation of the state-sponsored Indigenous genocide, but also on an antiblackness so fundamental to the poetics that Bryant appropriated from British Romanticism that it need not say its name. The poet's racism was, as we shall see, explicit in relation to the Indigenous people he called "savages," but his antiblack racism was only occasionally visible in casual remarks in his correspondence. Yet Johnson is right that Bryant's poetry is deeply informed by a forceful *un*acknowledgment of the presence of African Americans in the Americas, despite his newspaper's famously antislavery stance. "Thanatopsis," the "survey of death" that made the young Bryant famous after his father sent the manuscript to the editors of the *North American Review*, ends with a telling directive:

> So live, that when thy summons comes to join
> The innumerable caravan, which moves
> To that mysterious realm, where each shall take
> His chamber in the silent halls of death,
> Thou go not, like the quarry-slave at night,
> Scourged to his dungeon, but sustained and soothed
> By an unfaltering trust, approach thy grave,
> Like one who wraps the drapery of his couch
> About him, and lies down to pleasant dreams.[24]

We will return to the racialization of these very Wordsworthian meditative blank verse rhythms, and to the intimate relation of that racialization to Bryant's fondness for what he called "trisyllabic feet in iambic measure," but first it's worth thinking about the figure hiding here in plain sight, the "slave" disguised as ancient history by the quasi-Egyptian "quarry" and vaguely feudal "dungeon." It's just a simile, but it is a simile that Wheatley would have remarked, had she lived to see it: while she encouraged her pre-Revolutionary readers to compare their colonization to her enslavement, Bryant's simile encourages his readers to compare their bourgeois comforts to the compulsory labors of a person deprived of them.

Yet in Bryant's simile, as in his poetics, that deprivation takes place not in antebellum America (where it was happening all the time) but in a past so distant that this person's race and temporality and location are blurry around the edges—or, as Johnson might have said, the poem either ignores or fails to understand this convenient figure. And perhaps this is the point: as Morrison writes, "just as the formation of the nation necessitated coded language and purposeful restriction to deal with the racial disingenuousness and moral frailty at its heart, so too did the literature. . . . Through significant and underscored omissions, startling contradictions, heavily nuanced conflicts . . . one can see that a real or fabricated Africanist presence was critical to [American writers'] sense of Americanness."[25] Through the half-appearance of American slavery as the antithesis of White freedom, Bryant half-acknowledges the frailty at that freedom's heart. This figural and prosodic transformation of racial conflict into a poetics of White individuation under the sign of an appropriated Romantic lyricism would become Bryant's signature, a signature that has remained engraved below the surface of American poetics, like the plaques and statues that dot Manhattan.

In order to bring that faded signature into relief, I will consider here three of Bryant's most famous poems. Each of these poems employs a prosodic strategy that would prove influential for the American poetics of lyricized whiteness. While the figurative structures of apostrophe and personification that have been central to the last two chapters are also central to Bryant's poetics, here I want to foreground the prosody that frames those figures. Just as I have argued that the apostrophic and personifying strategies of Romantic and proto-Romantic American poetics were far from neutral figures but were also racializing strategies, so I have been arguing that prosodic forms racialize the poems they seem to merely structure—and, as we have seen in Wheatley's couplets and Whitfield's Venus and Adonis stanzas and Plato's and Horton's common meter, poets could work with or against that prosodic racialization. While all of those poets worked against the antiblackness embedded within their borrowed prosodies, in this chapter I want to consider the ways in which one influential White poet worked *with* the meters he borrowed from British Romanticism, the ways in which he used prosody to spell out a version of racial continuity—a lyricized poetics constructed against the background of non-White figures. While the study of iambs and trochees is often misrepresented as the study of fixed forms, my understanding of prosody is indebted to the field of critical and historical prosody created by Prins and Martin, a field Martin describes when she writes that "metrical forms circulate, change, and accrue different meanings at different moments, and this is as readable and important in our understanding of the formation of 'poetry' as a concept as the poems themselves."[26]

In the early "To a Waterfowl" (1818), Bryant used a specific prosodic structure borrowed from Robert Southey to craft a Romantic ode so generic that it became a transatlantic sensation, effectively rendering Bryant the "voice" or proto-speaker of and for White Romantic poetics itself. In "An Indian at the Burial-Place of His Fathers" (1824), Bryant used the Venus and Adonis stanza of Wordsworth's "I wandered lonely as a cloud"—the stanza that Pierpont would later use to sustain and Whitfield would later use to parody Bryant's poetics of whiteness—in order to place his poem against a non-White background, thus making its prosodic whiteness distinctly American, and rendering its Indigenous American fictive subject distinctly Anglo. This poem's dramatic colloquy makes an abstract (unnamed and rhetorically hybrid) speaker into the agent of his own fictional cultural transformation. Nine years later, in "The Prairies" (1833), the by-then-famous *New-York Evening Post* newspaper editor Bryant turned the Romantic blank-verse meditation with which he had had such success in "Thanatopsis" into a meditation on the racialization of such cultural transformation—specifically, on the nineteenth-century shift from a racism that depended on theories of monogenesis to an essentialist racism that depended on an emerging theory of polygenesis. At the end of that poem, the poet "in the wilderness alone" is a White man who stands on the mass grave of an implicitly White civilization wiped out by invaders, as indeed the White settlers who were being attacked (or really, resisted) by Black Hawk's assembled warriors as Bryant composed the poem on the Illinois prairies in 1832 feared they would be. This fragile representative person is "missing" in a very different sense than the persons unrepresented in the Black poetics we surveyed in the first part of this book tended to be. While the problem for Whitfield and Horton was the presumptive antiblackness of Romantic apostrophic poetics, and the problem for Wheatley was the presumptive antiblackness of the eighteenth-century poetics of personification that preceded and made Romantic poetics possible, the challenge for Bryant was to differentiate the whiteness of his American poetics from the whiteness of both his eighteenth-century and especially his Romantic models. For Bryant, that project entailed making the non-White background of his poems American by populating it with invisible Black and "vanishing" Indigenous figures. The result was a poetics abstracted by over- rather than underrepresentation: by appropriating the poetics of whiteness in order to distinguish his version of America from the land of Spanish Americans, African Americans, and Native Americans, Bryant's poetry became an image of White-on-White, suspending the threatened White man between non-White worlds. As Lindsay and Mattheissen and others noticed, Bryant's poetry became identified with that vulnerable person, an identification that invited another version of lyric reading, a way of making the prosodic genre of the poem into the genre of the person by making that person's (and that reader's) endangered prosodic whiteness what American poetry was all about.

"Thy solitary way"

My emphasis on Bryant's creation of a poetics of whiteness is hardly a new idea. Jason Rudy has discovered that in 1828, when the first anthology of English-language poetry was published in South Africa, "the opening poem of this volume was written not by an English-speaking emigrant to Britain's Cape Colony but by the American poet William Cullen Bryant."[27] "To a Waterfowl," first published in the *North American Review* in 1818, "was mistaken as an original of the Cape Colony . . . thereby establishing Bryant, anonymously, as the first anthologized writer of English poetry in the South African colony" (48). The truth is that "To a Waterfowl" circulated so extensively in the Anglophone world that its appearance in South Africa is unsurprising (though it is somewhat surprising that it was not recognized as Bryant's), but as Rudy goes on to point out, it is also not surprising that "Bryant reads as a *colonial* poet because his poems are generic congeries" (49). Perhaps Bryant also "reads as a colonial poet" because he followed British prosodic and stanzaic models to the letter. While Bryant's colonial genericism and mimetic prosody got him demoted in modern literary histories that valued formal originality, enthusiastic early reviewers recognized the poem's stanzaic structure as Robert Southey's. Yet by 1845, H. T. Tuckerman could write in an essay on "The Poetry of Bryant" for *The United States Magazine and Democratic Review* that "the very rhythm of the stanzas 'to a Waterfowl,' gives the impression of its flight. Like the bird's sweeping wing, they float with a calm, a majestic cadence to the ear."[28] Apparently, in ten years, "To a Waterfowl" had not only become every White Anglophone emigrant's poem (Rudy also traces publications in Australia, New Zealand, and Canada), but in less than thirty years, it had left its British model behind and was considered its own expressive mimetic form. One of Bryant's most recent biographers goes as far as to call "To a Waterfowl" "a meditative lyric" characterized by "the innovative form" of each quatrain's "alternating tetrameter and pentameter lines."[29] In 1990, Barbara Packer, in trying to make a case for nineteenth-century American landscape poetry as worthy of Romanticists' attention, wrote that "what is new about the poem, what made it seem so fresh and original to its first readers, lies . . . in its form, which manages to break free of the addictive cadences of the blank-verse line or the elegiac quatrain."[30] Yet Bryant's quatrains remain exactly Southey's quatrains, which frame two pentameter lines by a trimeter line at the beginning and another trimeter line at the end of each stanza. Bryant's "To a Waterfowl" begins,

> Whither, 'midst falling dew,
> While glow the heavens with the last steps of day,
> Far, through their rosy depths, dost thou pursue
> Thy solitary way?[31]

Southey's 1799 "The Ebb Tide" begins,

> Slowly thy flowing tide
> Came in, old Avon! scarcely did mine eyes,
> As watchfully I roam'd thy green-wood side,
> Perceive its gentle rise.[32]

In Bryant's lines, Southey's River Avon, signifier of a distinct southwestern British landscape, loses that local distinction and becomes a bird.[33] Yet although the object of address has changed to a generic "waterfowl" (swan? duck? goose? screamer? British? American? Egyptian?), the stanzas are exactly the same. It may have been convenient for readers to forget (or not to know) where they came from, but as it turns out, where they came from matters.

By 1824, "To a Waterfowl" had become such a sensation that a reviewer for *The United States Literary Gazette* wrote that the poem "has been so often quoted, we dare not extract it."[34] Southey's stanza seems to have made the poem recognizable to an Anglo-American transatlantic public as a Lake School production, though the Gazette reviewer actually makes a finer distinction, writing that "some lines in 'The Ages' and in 'Thanatopsis' reminded us rather too strongly of the Lake School; but the ode 'To a Waterfowl,' is a beautiful and harmonious blending of various beauties into one."[35] Though the "various beauties" that Bryant's little poem blended were all borrowed, their combination seems to have struck contemporary readers as something new—and at the same time, as Rudy suggests, as something "generic." The trimeter-pentameter-pentameter-trimeter pattern of the Southey-Bryant quatrains was not common, but the Gazette reviewer makes them less identical to Southey's by placing them in the common genre of "the ode." As we saw in Wheatley's poems, not only does that designation link Bryant to eighteenth-century British poetics, but by the time of this review in 1824, contemporary odes to birds were all the rage: Keats wrote "Ode to a Nightingale" in 1819 and Shelley wrote "To a Skylark" in 1820. Bryant's "To a Waterfowl" was written in 1815, and so preceded those iconic Romantic odes—thus his object of address was not an imitation of one of the second generation Romantics' favorite themes but a prediction of it.[36] Southey's poem is also an ode, if we follow Fry's witty definition of the ode as "a celebratory poem of address in elevated language written on an occasion of public importance—with the proviso, of course, that more often than not it is up to the poet to decide what is 'public' and what is 'important.'"[37] What is clever about Fry's definition is that it elides the difference between the classical or Pindaric ode and the neoclassical eighteenth-century and nineteenth-century Romantic ode. By taking the long view of a history in which odes to returning armies and odes to ideas and odes to rivers and odes to birds could be collapsed into one another, Fry's definition begs the question of the ode's historical status, a blurring that, as Norman Maclean anticipated de Man's equation of lyric and ode by writing in 1952, is built into the term itself:

> The word "ode" has a treacherous history. The word "lyric" was not used until Alexandrian times to designate the body of poetry that has since been so called. . . . From antiquity . . . the word "ode" had a meaning so general as to make it a synonym for lyric poetry, and it was so used until very recent times, when, however, its connotations have become specialized, the word "ode" now calling to mind only a particular kind of lyric—massive, public in its proclamations, and Pindaric in its classical prototype. . . . The reader must also bear in mind that until recently all other kinds of lyrics were often referred to as "lesser odes."[38]

The confusion between ode and lyric that Maclean frames here has a history, but that history may be the reverse of the one Maclean and de Man and others have assumed. As Maclean indicates, both "ode" and "lyric" have "treacherous" genealogies, and both became increasingly bigger and baggier terms for increasingly abstract poetic genres over the course of the eighteenth century—but as lyric began to have a meaning so general that it became a synonym for poetry at the beginning of the nineteenth century, the general meaning of the ode began to be narrowed to "a particular kind of lyric." Taking his stanza from a modest poem from the last year of the eighteenth century, Bryant turned a lesser ode addressed to a particular place and time into an all-purpose nineteenth-century poem that retained just enough of the sense of being "public in its proclamations" that it seemed to be addressed to all places and all times. What Bryant made of Southey's stanza, in other words, was what would come to be recognized as the voice of the generic White Romantic lyric.

This strategy worked so well that it quickly ceased to seem like a strategy at all. In the biography that John Bigelow wrote of his late friend in 1890, he declared that "Bryant was only twenty-one years of age when he wrote this poem, which by many is thought to be the one they would choose to preserve, if all but one of his poems were condemned to destruction."[39] The fantasy of such a destruction is really a way of saying that "To a Waterfowl" still managed to represent at the end of the nineteenth century what an early nineteenth-century Romantic lyric should be, as indeed Bigelow confirmed in a long footnote to his declaration:

> I have from Mr. Parke Godwin [Bryant's son-in-law and first biographer] an incident which belongs to the history of this poem. In a note to me dated Roslyn [Bryant's Long Island summer home], November 6, 1889, he says:—
>
> "Once when the late Matthew Arnold, with his family, was visiting the ever-hospitable county home of Mr. Charles Butler, I happened to spend an evening there. In the course of it Mr. Arnold took up a volume of Mr. Bryant's poems from the table, and turning to me said, 'This is *the* American poet, *facile princeps;*' and after a pause he continued: 'When I first heard of him, Hartley Coleridge (we were both lads then) came into my father's house one afternoon considerably excited and exclaimed, "Matt, do you want to hear the best short poem in the English language?" "Faith, Hartley, I do," was my reply. He then read the poem "To a Waterfowl" in his

best manner. As soon as he had done he asked, "What do you think of that?" "I am not sure but you are right, Hartley; is that your father's?" was my reply. "No," he rejoined, "father has written nothing like that." Some days after he might be heard muttering to himself,

    The desert and the illimitable air,
        Lone wandering, but not lost.[40]

Accounts of Bryant from the late nineteenth century often take this form: Bigelow is recalling a moment in which Godwin was recalling a moment in which Matthew Arnold was recalling the moment of Hartley Coleridge's enchantment with Bryant's lyric, by then understood not as a particular genre but simply as "the best short poem in the English language." It is practically a caricature of White transatlantic poetic transmission: the embedded series of recollections makes Bryant's poem into an exemplary literary artifact, distinctly "American" in Arnold's later estimation, yet also so easily confused with a British Romantic lyric that Arnold could ask whether Samuel Taylor Coleridge had written it. The *coup de grâce* here is Coleridge's son's claim that Bryant's lines so outstrip his father's that they have become their own thing ("father has written nothing like that"). This new genre invites appropriation and reiteration—indeed, it is so memorable that the preeminent Victorian arbiter of literary taste could reiterate its reiteration half a century later. For those in the know, Hartley Coleridge's partiality to Bryant's lines certainly owed something to the fact that he had spent much of his youth in Southey's house, but by the time Arnold remembered overhearing this remediated version surrounded by three sets of scare quotes, "To a Waterfowl" had become not only an exemplary White Romantic lyric but could be considered *better* than any ordinary Romantic lyric. While the capacity to be memorized, appropriated, and reiterated has often been attributed to the lyric as a genre, it is not often attributed to Bryant's appropriation and reiteration of British lyricism, much less recognized as the signature of colonial verse. By the time of Godwin's recollection of Arnold's recollection, to be "the best short poem in the English language" was to be a lyric par excellence, since by 1889, "lyric" had become a generic term for all short poems, thanks in part to an emphasis on lyrical brevity by Coleridge, Hegel, Poe, and indeed by Bryant himself.[41]

What Arnold's little story also indexes is the way in which "the English language" can mystify racialization and level national distinctions, so that Bryant's ode-become-lyric both one-ups and is exchangeable with British Romantic verse. If even Arnold thought that "To a Waterfowl" was "the best short poem in the English language," then Englishness was what the poem could represent—not just to American readers, but to British connoisseurs. It is this doubleness—this structure of appropriation—that racializes the poem. The object of address that defines the ode could also come to define a White transatlantic public educated to identify with that object of address. That education was the office of the eighteenth- and nineteenth-century ode in its many manifestations, but Bryant's little ode takes that preliminary education as its subject. It does this by making the generic waterfowl a "figure" from the beginning:

> Vainly the fowler's eye
> Might mark thy distant flight to do thee wrong,
> As, darkly painted on the crimson sky,
>   Thy figure floats along.

(ll. 5–8)

If we root for the potential victim of the fowler's gun, that vulnerability is quickly distanced and aestheticized, as a sunset scene is "painted" for us. We then begin to *read* this painting, since reading is what figures are for. That reading begins as a question:

> Seek'st thou the plashy brink
> Of weedy lake, or marge of river wide,
> Or where the rocking billows rise and sink
>   On the chafed ocean-side?

(ll. 9–12)

This sort of question is a performance of a reading: it is not actually a question for the bird any more than Southey's questions are for the Avon or Keats's questions are for the nightingale or urn or season or Shelley's questions are for the skylark. The streamlining of ode into lyric in "To a Waterfowl" means that the shared psychic space of the public Bryant's genre brings into being would become the addressees of "English language" Romantic poetry—or of American poetry as optimistically Anglo rather than as, say, Scots or German or French or Yoruba or Sudanese or Cherokee or Ojibwe or Pequot or Spanish or Mexican or Cuban.

The figure of address on which this form depends thus represents the communal impulse of a displaced colonial Anglo-Romanticism. Here apostrophe does exactly the racialized social work that nineteenth-century Black poets exposed or resisted or struggled within, the work of fabricating whiteness. In chapter 2, I emphasized (or allowed nineteenth-century Black poets to emphasize) that the political consequences of this version of White anglocentric American apostrophic lyric allowed poets like Pierpont and Bryant to create a shared poetic world—a genre—that we all recognize quite easily. I invoked Berlant's recasting of the post-structuralist understanding of apostrophe as rhetorical animation, a revision worth repeating here. In apostrophic address, according to Berlant, the addressee

> is animated in speech as distant enough for a conversation but close enough to be imaginable by the speaker in whose head the entire scene is happening. But the condition of projected possibility . . . creates a fake present moment of intersubjectivity in which, nonetheless, a performance of address can take place. . . . Apostrophe therefore . . . is actually a turning back, an animating of a receiver on behalf of the desire to make something happen *now* that realizes something *in the speaker*, makes the speaker more or differently possible, because she has admitted, in a sense, the importance of speaking for, as, and to, two—but only under the condition, and illusion, that the two are really (in) one.[42]

One of the interesting things about the genericism of "To a Waterfowl" is that Bryant does not even pretend to animate the bird. From the poem's first line, the poem is clearly about "realizing something *in the speaker*." While Horton's 1828 variations on Shelley's apostrophic surrender recognize the potential dangers of the interpellation that Berlant describes, Bryant's 1818 variations on Southey recognize that there is only one, not two, in the first place. In "To a Waterfowl," the "fake moment of intersubjectivity in which nonetheless, a performance of address can take place" is for Bryant not really a moment of intersubjectivity at all. As the South African and British responses suggest, this performance is all about the figure that was fast becoming the generic form of Romantic apostrophe, and that form is acknowledged as figurative from the poem's first line. This meta-performance makes the illusion of agency embodied by the speaker not only the voice of the British colonies or of Britannia herself but of White men under the sign of their generic, mutual understanding, since "the two are really (in) one" from the beginning, the sum of a doubled and redoubled whiteness.

The popularity of the poem testified to the success of this apparently innocuously lyricized form of address in achieving this understanding, and that

popularity was based in part on the explicit lesson "To a Waterfowl" offered
the readers who understood themselves as its real interlocutors:

> There is a Power whose care
> Teaches thy way along that pathless coast—
> The desert and illimitable air—
> Lone wandering, but not lost.

(ll. 13–16)

The young Hartley Coleridge liked this message, as did the young Arnold, as
did the many readers who "so often quoted" the poem well into the twentieth
century. What T. E. Hulme called Romanticism's "spilt religion" is on the sur-
face of Bryant's lines, which manage to combine all divinity into one unnamed
"Power" as generic as the waterfowl and the poem itself.[43] The fact that the
first decades of the nineteenth century were in fact full of very specific
religions—which, in New England, primarily meant many specific versions of
Christianity—that were often in conflict with one another made the even
younger Bryant swerve into a suspension of all religious reference in "Thana-
topsis," which came to be known as "the Pagan poem."[44] The first version of
"Thanatopsis" was written in 1811 and published (after Bryant's father found
the manuscript in the family home) in the North American Review in 1817, a
year before "To a Waterfowl" (written in 1815) was published in the same jour-
nal. It's not a stretch to imagine that the placement of "To a Waterfowl" was
meant to compensate for some of the dismay that accompanied the reception
of "Thanatopsis," reassuring the transatlantic readership of the North American
Review that the figure addressed in and as the poem they were reading was
itself guided by "a Power" they could believe in without worrying that such
belief would divide one reader from another, British from American readers,
colonist from colonized, church from church. It is then no accident that the
most beautiful lines in the poem, the lines that Hartley Coleridge knew by
heart, follow this reassurance with a grammatical wobble, as "desert" shifts
from possible noun to an adjective modifying the "illimitable air," a mimetic
flourish that demonstrates the lesson learned when the "pathless" landscape
is read as only apparently pathless by design.

First identified with the bird addressed as "not lost," the oriented reader can
now turn to join the poet, in effect occupying both sides of the apostrophe.
From this double perspective, we can encourage the object of our common
care to believe what we now believe, our shared psychic optimism focused on

the bird's ability to find the path we have already found, or that has been found for us:

> All day thy wings have fanned,
> At that far height, the cold, thin atmosphere,
> Yet stoop not, weary to the welcome land,
>   Though the dark night is near.
>
> And soon thy toil shall end;
> Soon shalt thou find a summer home, and rest.
> And scream among thy fellows; reeds shall bend,
>   Soon, o'er thy sheltered nest.

(ll. 17–24)

The language of labor in these lines is surprising. The lone bird begins as a figure of free flight, is transformed into a figure that models guidance by being invisibly guided, and then shape-shifts into the figure of a "weary" worker, whose "toil shall end" not just at the end of a long day at the office but in "a summer home" complete with fraternal parties. It is tempting to read these lines biographically, since when they were written in 1815 Bryant was working as a newly minted country lawyer, very unhappy with the terms of his daily grind. A less biographical reading might understand these lines as addressed to the newly emergent early nineteenth-century liberal individual subject coming to terms with the predicament of his alienated labor (a reading often offered in relation to British Romanticism). This is a strange predicament indeed to attribute to a flying bird. The poem so efficiently frames our figurative reading of the bird as our own capacity for poetic flight that these lines seem out of place, and indeed that disjunction may be their point. The questions that signaled a process of interpretation or reflection just two stanzas earlier have turned into the opposite of questions and the inverse of interpretation. The poet now seems to know the answers the bird-worker needs to know; yet as soon as these answers are offered, the bird disappears:

> Thou'rt gone, the abyss of heaven
> Hath swallowed up thy form; yet, on my heart
> Deeply has sunk the lesson thou has given,
>   And shall not soon depart.

(ll. 25–28)

And so "the lesson" shifts again: the prospect of comfort and release from toil that we (or the poet) offer the laboring bird becomes a scene of instruction the poet himself incorporates, a bird-form he has swallowed as "the abyss of heaven" has "swallowed up" the bird. Or not quite swallowed—what "has sunk" into the poet's heart is a reading (the root sense of lesson, or *lectio*) of the abstraction of a figure, a "form" we can make of what we will. The charges of didacticism often leveled by modern readers against this poem are obviously well founded, but what is less often noticed is that the poem takes such didacticism as its subject: with each stanza, Bryant makes "the lesson" of the bird-as-apostrophic-imaginary-reader-believer-worker-guide a little more general, and thus a little more White, as stanza by stanza the bird becomes a more and more portable anthropomorphic abstraction, a more and more detached lyric form. If this poem is a generic lyric about a generic poet's generic faith in a generic water-bird understood as a figure for a generic poetic ideal, then its didacticism resides in its instruction on how to read such a poem. On this view, the last stanza is not the punch line but an afterthought:

> He who, from zone to zone,
> Guides through the boundless sky the certain flight,
> In the long way that I must tread alone,
> Will lead my steps aright.

> (ll. 29–32)

We have seen similar echoes of Psalm 119 ("Order my steps in thy word: and let not any iniquity have dominion over me") in Wheatley's "On Messrs. Hussey and Coffin" and in Pierpont's and Whitfield's allusions to Bryant in their apostrophes to the North Star. We can all agree that "aright" is not a beautiful word on which to end "the best short poem in the English language," but it makes explicit the didactic frame that each stanza has built: here at the end of the poem the first-person pronoun (what de Man and Johnson would call "the fiction of the spoken voice") emerges for the first time, as the poet repeats the basics of the lesson the poem takes as its subject, and the basics are just that—an outline or abstract form that commits poet and reader to no particular interpretation or faith or profession in order to mutually agree to believe in poetry, especially in poetry "in the English language."[45] Wherever the "solitary way" that the bird begins by pursuing and the poet ends by pursuing leads, there is no direction that is not right because all directions can be counted on to move from trimeter to pentameter to pentameter to trimeter, from a to b to rhyming a and b.

In the end, the waterfowl's flight "from zone to zone" is not only going nowhere because the words for its origin and destination are the same (and because that word begins with the last letter of the alphabet, as if the limit of the poem's tracking device has been reached) but because each stanza is the same, and those repeated stanzas are themselves a repetition of Southey's stanzas. By following the pattern of Southey's stanzas to the letter, the poet's metrical feet step "aright" because they so exactly match the steps of his British model. What is reassuring about this ending is that the lonely "I" at the end of the poem is actually in good company: assurance of providential guidance may be the lesson the bird has taught him, but if so, it is a lesson his stanzas have known all along, since they exemplify in their structure an argument by design. Modern readers would call the figure who comes to claim that lesson at the end of the poem "the lyric I" or "the speaker" (as when a 1991 commentator on Robert Frost's "Design," a poem Frost described as his answer to "To a Waterfowl," wrote that Bryant's "speaker assures himself that both the perilous and distant flight of a bird and his own steps will be carefully guided by God"), but readers in 1818—or 1828 or 1832 or 1845—would have referred to this figure simply as the poet.[46] Yet the "I" in "To a Waterfowl" is not Bryant, exactly, in the sense that he is not a particular White man but a generic White man, the representative of the imaginary or potential anglocentric transatlantic public the poem addresses. Like everything else in this poem, the first-person expression in the last stanza is pure form without content: it is what we all feel if we feel what White men guided by British poetics say they feel, at home and "aright" in the anglicized poetic world the poem makes its own and "our poet" makes our own.

"To a Waterfowl" followed a British Romantic pattern, but as an exemplary English lyric, it also *became* an anglicized pattern that later lyric readers and writers on both sides of the Atlantic could follow. William Wordsworth's "To a Skylark" (composed in 1825 and first published in 1827) might be read as an attempt to combine Shelley's errantly gorgeous 1820 poem of that title with Bryant's tamer and by then ubiquitous "To a Waterfowl" (the phrase "pilgrim of the sky" in Wordsworth's first line may be the giveaway). Wordsworth used Shakespeare's six-line Venus and Adonis stanza to apostrophize his skylark as a Shelleyan "Ethereal Minstrel" that could nevertheless become a Bryant-like "Type of the wise who soar, but never roam; / True to the kindred points of Heaven and Home!" Since Bryant's poem was published two years before

Shelley's, it is entirely possible that even Shelley's poem began as a response to Bryant, though I have been unable to find any British reprintings of "To a Waterfowl" before 1823. Since transatlantic Romanticism has usually been thought to travel from east to west rather than from west to east, the fairly obvious connections between these poems have gone unremarked. That said, later American poets may have noticed them: John Ashbery composed a cento (a poem made entirely of lines taken from other poets) titled "To a Waterfowl" in 1961 and published it in the second issue of *Locus Solus*. That poem takes lines from Donne, Milton, Longfellow, Tennyson, Coleridge, Shelley, Johnson, Keats, Arnold, Shakespeare, Spenser, Stevens, Wyatt, Blake, Byron, Pound, Thomas, Dryden, Whitman, Campion, Waller, Yeats, Eliot, Hopkins, Browning, Cowper, Collins, Marvell, Meredith, Swinburne, Hardy, and Bryant himself. It is a chorus of White male Anglo-American poetry, a chorus gathered beneath the title of the poem that Bryant wrote in order to assemble that chorus for future practitioners of White poetics.

Like April Snow

There is much more to say about the uptake of "To a Waterfowl" as a performance of the Anglo-colonial lyric identity it was designed to perform, but in order to explore another aspect of the racialized structure of Bryant's lyric address, I want to turn to another poem that uses British Romantic stanzas in a colonial context to somewhat different effect—specifically, to represent a speaking figure distinct from the poet and also distinctly not Anglo. Bryant's "An Indian at the Burial-Place of His Fathers" was first published in 1824, and is most famous as the source of an epigraph in James Fenimore Cooper's *The Last of the Mohicans* (1826). The poem shares what Lora Romero so aptly characterized in Cooper as "the historical sleight-of-hand crucial to the topos of the doomed aboriginal: it represents the disappearance of the native as not just natural but as having already happened."[47] That genocidal rationalization is even more obvious in Bryant's poem than it is in Cooper's novel, but what might be less obvious about this poem is the way in which it achieves this representation by way of the Romantic lyricism—particularly the Romantic stanza—it takes from Wordsworth. "An Indian" begins with the romantically educated "I" that "To a Waterfowl" withholds until its end:

> It is the spot I came to seek—
>   My father's ancient burial-place,

Ere from these vales, ashamed and weak,
   Withdrew our wasted race.
It is the spot—I know it well—
Of which our old traditions tell.[48]

If Bryant's generic waterfowl was guided "from zone to zone" by a British Romantic stanzaic pattern that turned a lesser ode into a Romantic lyric, here Bryant's generic Indian is guided by a different British Romantic stanzaic pattern toward a differently abstracted verse genre: the lyricized dramatic monologue. Though that genre is usually traced from what M. H. Abrams called Romantic "colloquy," its vogue would not emerge until the Victorian period in England, so Bryant was conducting an early experiment.[49] Why? In July 1824, Bryant wrote to Dana that "the only poems that have any currency at present are of a narrative kind—light stories in which love is a principal ingredient. Nobody writes epic and nobody reads didactic poems; and as for dramatic poems they are out of the question. In this uncertainty what is to be done?"[50] What Bryant did that year was to write a poem that implies an epic theme, that traces (like "To a Waterfowl") the outlines of a didactic lesson, that depends on a narrative that is anything but a light love story, and that is staged as a drama. If in "To a Waterfowl," a White male proto-speaker emerges in the last stanza, in "An Indian at the Burial-Place of His Fathers," the non-White male dramatic character speaks to us directly in every line of the poem. Or does he? We know that this figure is not the poet because the title of the poem sets this speaker's fictional stage (Who? "An Indian"; Where? "The Burial-Place of His Fathers"), but also because by the fourth line of the poem this dramatic character identifies himself as the generic representative and apparently lone survivor of "our wasted race." Identified by race rather than tribe, Bryant's nameless Indian is more radically genericized than his waterfowl (though both figures are designated by indefinite articles), and of course that racializing deracination carries higher stakes. Here the first-person plural pronoun clearly indexes an imagined community to which "we" do not belong. But how do we know that? To whom does this last Indian speak? To return to Johnson, if "apostrophe situates its fictive entities in the field of direct address, so that the spoken voice is what knits the utterance together," then what are the fictive entities this nameless tribeless Indian's voice knits together? And why is he speaking English? As "To a Waterfowl" became a transatlantic genre contingent on a structure of anglicized White interpellation, so "An Indian" adapts a British Romantic model in order to address readers who recognized that model as their own lyricized interpellation, their own shared psychic space of optimism. Since "An Indian" speaks in a version of Wordsworth's famous six-line "Daffodils" stanza (the stanza of "I wandered lonely as a cloud," a stanza Wordsworth inherited from Shakespeare's Venus and Adonis stanza, which, we recall, Pierpont adopted in order to ally himself with this White tradition and Whitfield adopted in order to critique it), Anglo-identified readers could be reassured that this speaker was our poet after all: he may be an Indian, but his poetry is White.

This may just be a way of saying what Romero and others have said about the literature of the vanishing Indian: the spectacular violence of the decade that led up to the Indian Removal Act of 1830 could be aestheticized, excused, and erased by writers like Cooper and Bryant because they turned people into literature. That is certainly true, but by making his representative vanishing Indian speak in the "Daffodils" stanza, Bryant was not only posing as literary apologist for state-sponsored violence but was also fashioning a poetics that made what Brickhouse calls "an indomitable English" American *poetry* seem the inevitable and natural result of such violence. In Cooper's novel, that Anglo-American domination is narrated and thematized as America's answer to the French and British Romantic novel, but in Bryant's poem, it is enacted in the structure of the stanza itself; the plot of Cooper's novel was first Bryant's poetic material, and Bryant's poem was first the poetic material of Wordsworth's most famous single lyric. Wordsworth's poem (written in 1804, published in 1807, and revised in 1815) begins,

> I wandered lonely as a Cloud
> That floats on high o'er Vales and Hills,
> When all at once I saw a crowd,
> A host, of golden Daffodils;
> Beside the Lake, beneath the trees,
> Fluttering and dancing in the breeze.[51]

As you can see, Bryant's stanza borrows the ababcc structure of Wordsworth's stanza.[52] As you can also see, Bryant alters Wordsworth's stanza just a little by making his fourth line a trimeter rather than a tetrameter (Wordsworth's lines are all tetrameters). The effect of this repetition in variation in "An Indian" is to give the dramatic monologue the *gravitas* of a British poetic genealogy and at the same time to inflect that genealogy just slightly with a folksy difference (since hymns and ballads were commonly associated with tetrameter/trimeter variation). Thus the nameless tribeless Indian speaks with Wordsworthian authority about the "spot" he has chosen as subject, but he also speaks with the authority of the folk Wordsworth so often made his subjects in *Lyrical Ballads*. Subject as well as object, representer as well as stuff of representation, Bryant's doubly Wordsworthian Indian is a character formed prosodically by what Martin has called "the ballad theory of civilization," which she describes as the nineteenth-century appetite for poems in which "the peripheral is elevated as the primitive and brought into the whole fabric of the nation as an imagined common past of the colonizing nation. . . . An imagined innocent past, a purer primitive poetics in the guise of 'ballad.'"[53] That version of the ballad (which occupied the long nineteenth century in a process that Cohen has called "balladization") followed the outlines traced by early Romantic theories of "primitive" or "pure poetry"—the turn to expressivist aesthetic theory at the end of the eighteenth century to which Abrams famously attributed the emergence of "the lyric as poetic norm."[54] Of the early British Romantics, Abrams wrote that "the defining character of all these poets was that they composed from nature, hence spontaneously, artlessly. . . . Like the aborigines in whose outcries, extorted by passion, poetry had originated, these men were said to poetize under the stress of personal feeling."[55] The trick of Bryant's poem then is to make the fantasy poetics of the "primitive" Indian into a pure White version of the Romantic lyric, since by taking the stanza of Wordsworth's most recognizable single poem, Bryant could make his Indian actually speak *as a lyrical ballad*—as the personification of a poetry simultaneously aboriginal and indomitably English, both elegiacally primitive and optimistically modern.

What I am suggesting is that Bryant was indeed "the American Wordsworth," but also that the phrase that has damned him to faint praise in the history of American poetry should be literalized to acknowledge the version of Romantic lyricism that helped to create the "imagined common past" of American poetics that Bryant has come to represent. By making the "primitive" speak in the language of the lyricized ballad, Bryant made his doomed aboriginal into a version of what Romantic poetry would say if it could speak for itself. "I wandered lonely as a cloud" was not one of the *Lyrical Ballads*, but since it was so popular on both sides of the Atlantic, it could function as a moment of recognition instantiated in discourse—that is, as a genre. But what genre? As in "To a Waterfowl," the genre Bryant made out of Wordsworth's materials was a hot take on its sources, an abstraction of more than one earlier verse genre: of a genre recognizable in 1824 simply as "Wordsworth" (or, as we saw in the earlier *Gazette* review, as "a Lake School production"), of a signature stanzaic genre recognizable as anglocentric (given the dependence of Words-worth's stanza on Shakespeare's stanza), of a genre reminiscent of the ballad (the genre McGill has so felicitously dubbed "the literary form of nonliterary verse"), of a genre that had not yet become the dramatic monologue, of an emerging genre of "the doomed aboriginal" (a genre practiced on both sides of the Atlantic, including by Southey, but especially by Bryant's friends Wash-ington Irving, Cooper, Fitz-Greene Halleck, and Robert Charles Sands, as well as by Lydia Sigourney and several contemporary Poetesses), and of neoclassi-cal verse genres, especially georgic and pastoral elegy.[56]

In "An Indian at the Burial-Place of His Fathers," what Bryant was really fashioning out of all these genres was an indomitably anglocentric perspective on poetics, a genre in which the representative White American man could stand for all kinds of poems at once. While Wordsworth's wandering "I" hap-pens upon a prospect that surprises and delights him, and Bryant's "I" has fi-nally found "the spot" that saddens and enrages him, what these perspectives share is a relation between the one and the many, between a single figure gaz-ing and a depopulated landscape that is the object and subject of his gaze. A century before the idea of "the Romantic lyric" was coined by the practices of lyric reading and modern criticism, Bryant performed the outlines of what that genre would become. In effect, the poem represents that new genre from the inside out but also from the outside in:

> A white man, gazing on the scene,
>> Would say a lovely spot was here,
> And praise the lawns, so fresh and green,
>> Between the hills so sheer.
> I like it not—I would the plain
> Lay in its tall old groves again.

(ll. 13–18)

Don't make the mistake of regarding this landscape as a Romantic poem, Bry-ant's Indian warns us. "A white man" will make that mistake, and so will miss the history buried beneath the prospect, the old culture hidden beneath the new agriculture:

> But now the wheat is green and high
>> On clods that hid the warrior's breast,
> And scattered in the furrows lie
>> The weapons of his rest;

And there, in the loose sand, is thrown
Of his large arm the mouldering bone.

(ll. 43-48)

What the Indian seems to be telling us is that he knows something the White man does not know about this Romantic landscape, since this is, after all, "the burial-place of *his* fathers." Yet in order to describe what is buried beneath the scene "a white man" may mistake for innocent nature, the authority the Indian invokes is Virgil's first *Georgic*, which ends, "A time shall come when in those lands, as the farmer toils at the soil with crooked plough, he shall find javelins eaten up with rusty mould, or with his heavy hoes shall strike on empty helms, and marvel at the giant bones in the upturned graves."[57] The White man's mistake turns out not to be in looking at this landscape as Romantic poetry but in misreading his georgic Wordsworth. As Kevis Goodman has argued, Wordsworth's version of the georgic does not (like "a white man") turn history into nature but "points rather to a failure of reception and recognition, a problematic inability—sometimes refusal—to know what has been turned up *as* history."[58] If, as Goodman writes, "Virgil imagined his own violent present as the future's past," the problem for Bryant's Indian is to imagine his own violent present as a history only a White Anglo-Romantic poet could write.[59]

So while Virgil's farmer comes upon the past that is Virgil's present, and Wordsworth's georgic modernity insists upon the past inherent in an only apparently pastoral nineteenth-century present, Bryant's White man embodies both present racial violence and a future of White supremacy:

Ah, little thought the strong and brave
    Who bore their lifeless chieftain forth—
Or the young wife that weeping gave
    Her first-born to the earth,
That the pale race, who waste us now,
Among their bones should guide the plough.

(ll. 49-54)

Repeating the figure from Virgil once again, Bryant makes it clear that Virgil's farmer has become an entire "pale race," and that unlike the innocent Virgilian farmer who merely discovers the remnants of an earlier culture by accident, that race is the agent of the Indian's "primitive" culture's extinction. But "race" and "culture" are slippery terms here, and their slipperiness is the problem.

Though ideas of culture as (in Raymond Williams's phrase) "a whole way of life" had been circulating for a long time by the early nineteenth century, the early twentieth-century ethnographic invention of the culture concept was in this poem's future, and in 1824 the idea of "race" as ethnically marked genealogy that dated from the early modern period had just begun to shift toward the scientific racism that would preoccupy the later nineteenth century.[60] By turning his Virgilian and Wordsworthian figure into a proto-racial representative, Bryant blurs the difference between past, present, and future by blurring the genre of that difference. In the most beautiful lines in the poem, genocide is not described as dramatic or epic or georgic violence but as pastoral elegy:

> They waste us—ay—like April snow
>   In the warm noon, we shrink away;
> And fast they follow, as we go
>   Toward the setting day—
> Till they shall fill the land, and we
> Are driven into the Western sea.

(ll. 55–60)

As Cavitch has written, these explicitly pastoral elegiac lines certainly seem "to naturalize anti-Indian violence even though white agency in Indian displacement is an explicit theme in the poem."[61] Molly McGarry points to the sources of this rhetorical contradiction more starkly:

> Christian missionaries would write elegies to vanished Indians, using increasingly pastoral metaphors that mystified both the fact of disease and the effect of warfare. . . . Employing naturalized language to efface the ravages of disease and starvation among the Iroquois, Thoroughgood Moore, a missionary from the Society for the Propagation of the Gospel in Foreign Parts, wrote in 1705: "They waste away, and have done so ever since our arrival among them (as they say themselves) like snow against the sun, so that very probably forty years hence there will scarce be an Indian seen in our America." Though melancholic, this image demands no more accountability than the melting of snow in spring.[62]

By putting an early eighteenth-century missionary's phrase into a fictional Indigenous man's mouth, Bryant makes that fictive representative non-White person proclaim his own disappearance in the discourse of those responsible for it. How can the poem hope to have it both ways?

If an individual can be turned into a "race," then the race that Virgil's farmer represents can be made to stand in for the history of Western culture, a history that, in a Wordsworthian turn, Bryant insists we recognize as the poetic history of a common whiteness. Cavitch is certainly right that this poem demonstrates a "fluency in the motifs of pastoral elegy," as well as in the motifs of eighteenth-century georgic, but it also demonstrates a fluency in the narrative of Western progress that both Virgil and Wordsworth came to represent for an emerging New World poetics of White supremacy. Though the poem ends with the Indian's warning that "The realm our tribes are crushed to get / May be a barren desert yet," the sources of Bryant's poetics reassure his reader that this progress is guaranteed. Published six years before Andrew Jackson signed the Indian Removal Act into law, "An Indian at the Burial-Place of His Fathers" imagined its own violent present as a future in which English Romantic poetry (here indexed by the ending couplet of Wordsworth's "Daffodils"/Shakespeare's "Venus and Adonis" stanza) will bind us all in a White poetic community, a public the unnamed Indian's speaking voice knits together in an accumulating and expanding psychic space made possible by the rhymed continuity from "get" to "yet." As both Pierpont and Whitfield knew when they adapted the stanza after Bryant, that abstract space is the optimistic projection of a shared potential after Western expansion, after Congress passes the Indian Removal Act (six years later), after the embrace of the discourse of Manifest Destiny (twenty years later), after the genocide (that is ongoing). If we are members of that new poetic world, we know that the future is ours because the Indian's pessimism alienates him from us, marking the difference between "his fathers" and "our poets," bringing into being the racial difference the poem itself performs.[63]

The Forms of Being

On January 4, 1830, Bryant, as new editor of the *New-York Evening Post*, began contributing editorials in support of Jackson's "visionary" stance on Indigenous "removal." As Andrew Galloway has put it,

> Bryant's long career as chief editor at the *New York Evening Post* was inaugurated by his columns in favor of Indian Removal, for which he argued in the *Post* from January to May 1830. His editorship helped found the New York "liberal" tradition: adamantly antislavery and pro-Abolition, adamantly prounion, adamantly proimmigrant, and adamantly in favor of (decorous)

freedom of speech. But Bryant's editorials argued that the "Red-man" had to move, for his own good and that of "civilization," and the quickly following poem "The Prairies" treats this as a historical inevitability.[64]

Galloway (who has done us all a great service by being the first to reprint Bryant's editorials on "Indian Removal") here exemplifies the difficult position in which modern readers of "The Prairies" (composed in 1832, first published in 1833, and revised in 1834) tend to find themselves. Anyone who has taught this poem to undergraduates will recognize the perplexity with which new readers encounter its unmistakable argument: did "the father of American poetry" really think that "'the Red-man' had to move, for his own good and for that of 'civilization'"? Did he actually agree with Jackson that "to preserve this much-injured race," that "race" must be segregated from "our" race? Though Galloway's emphasis on Bryant's "adamantly" held progressive political positions makes it seem unlikely, he did. Further, in "The Prairies," Bryant shifted the eighteenth-century theory of Universal History he had adopted in "The Ages" in 1821 toward an emerging nineteenth-century theory of history that was not (as Hannah Arendt put it) one "immortalizing" and "uninterrupted development" of "the human race" but that instead assigned different histories to different races.[65] Stephen Jay Gould has called this 1830s development in differential racial theory "the American school of ethnology," though these theories did not add up to just one "school" exactly, since they were actually a motley array of competing ideas.[66] What unified these ideas was the coincidence of the removal violence with what Rusert has described as White "anxieties over the abolitionist movement and the strengthening political mobilization of free black communities in urban areas across the Northeast."[67] In the short term, this new racist American ethnology allowed Bryant to substitute a story of polygenesis—of different races with different histories—for older racist theories that depended on a narrative of monogenesis, of a single human race that took (because of biblical curse or climate or circumstance or hard luck) various forms. In "The Prairies," that consequential shift in the American theory of racialization turned into a consequential shift in the American theory of poetics.

The White "liberal tradition" that Galloway rightly attributes to Bryant as public intellectual did extend to a politics that was modeled on inclusion (antislavery, prounion, proimmigrant), but Bryant's support of the Removal Act was not (as Galloway implies) the curiously bad political choice of an otherwise nice progressive guy, not an exception to but a condition of the poet's liberal views. The "historical inevitability" of Indigenous extinction in "The Prairies" was not just a detail. By devoting a long poem in blank verse to the Western landscape from which Indigenous people were in the process of being violently displaced, the poet becomes the solitary figure who finds himself at the end of the poem "in the wilderness alone," now recognizable as a prototype of the White fugitive subject, a negative image of the abstract speaker of modern lyric reading. That subject's public was something new in 1833, since its genre was determined by an address to an imagined community of similarly isolated and alienated White liberal individuals, a poetic public composed of what a century later Adorno would call "human beings between whom the barriers had fallen." For Adorno, that sense of shared alienation accomplished by modern lyric was the consequence of the shared loss of communal life under industrial capitalism; for Bryant, it was the consequence of the shared cost of White communal life under the racialized conditions of slavery and settler colonialism—of what Morrison called "the racial disingenuousness and moral fragility" at the heart of American literature. In Bryant's version of the communal impulse that informed American White shared alienation, someone had to die. The White public this poet addressed would need (or be allowed) to share both the public grief for and the public disavowal of that loss.

In his last editorial in support of the Removal Act, Bryant wrote that the president "was confident that the only possible method of preserving the Indian race, and of elevating Indian character, was to remove them from the vicinity of the whites, until their gradual civilization could be effected" (748). Why would "the Indian race" need to be "preserved" long enough to allow for such "gradual civilization" to take place (Bryant specifies that as little as "fifty years might accomplish the work")? As all of Bryant's editorials made clear, he considered such "preservation" necessary because he disagreed with the many opponents of the Removal Act that "the red men are pure, spotless, injured beings; white men, cruel, mercenary, and relentless," or that "the Indians under their own government form a sort of Eutopia: while the laws of Georgia are calculated to produce only anarchy and ruin." No, Bryant wrote, "we [the newspaper's public editorial 'we'] are not entire believers in the immaculate beauty of the Indian character" (716). Bryant's second *Post* editorial emphasizes this point by insisting that "such a race could not exist in contact with a civilized community" (747). A decade later, echoing the discourse of eighteenth-century Christian missionaries like Moore, Bryant would observe that "the destiny of the red race while in the presence of the white" would lead to "decay and gradual extinction, even under circumstances apparently the most favorable to its preservation."[68] What is remarkable about these remarks is not their racism or their exceptional aggression, since the *Post* editor and the president and many Americans had those things in common. Although modern readers are often incredulous and Galloway, who reprints the editorials, apologizes for them as exceptions in the career of an otherwise progressive editor, and other critics, like Jules Zanger, continue to be dismayed by "an uncharacteristic political cast and, more significantly, an uncharacteristic employment of the poem as a rhetorical political instrument" in Bryant's stance on removal, what has gone unremarked is that a new polygenetic theory of civilizational racism made both Bryant's new editorial and new poetic eloquence possible.[69] That new virulent theory of race made it possible for the father of American poetry to realize the project of the earlier poems we have considered, since in "The Prairies," Bryant explicitly and influentially lyricized poetic address as the White man's burden.

Yet the beginning of the poem appears innocent of all this history and theory—indeed, its deictic opening also claims to be innocent of poetry:

> These are the gardens of the Desert, these
> The unshorn fields, boundless and beautiful,
> For which the speech of England has no name—
> The Prairies.[70]

The initial version of these lines, published in the New York *Knickerbocker Magazine* in December 1833, emphasized that this pastoral innocence preceded human history:

> These are the Gardens of the Desert, these
> For which the speech of England has no name—
> The boundless unshorn fields, where lingers yet
> The beauty of the earth ere man had sinned—
> The Prairies. (410)

In the 1834 revised poem, Bryant made his lines better by deleting the explicit allusion to Milton. Yet since no poet writing in English blank verse in the early nineteenth century could not be indebted to Milton, the first lines of the revision get to keep English poetics without keeping English poetry—or so it seems. In his 1830 sonnet to Cole, Bryant urged the British-born painter to keep the "wilder image" of America "bright" during his European tour. "The Prairies" makes a point of opposing that brighter, wilder image to "the speech of England" (the word is actually from the Latin via old French), but from the beginning something about the scene the traveling poet points to ("These . . . these . . .") is a little off. The sophisticated New Yorker telling readers of a New York magazine about his trip to the wild West wants it both ways: his blank verse hails readers who know that "these" fields are being aesthetically framed for them, and yet we are asked to pretend to share the poet's immediate encounter with this "unshorn" landscape. That dramatic fiction is not the same fiction of address experienced by Mill's invisible listener to the lament of a prisoner in a solitary cell or by the unacknowledged audience for a soliloquy or for the accidental witness to a highlander singing a song to himself. From the first word of "The Prairies," Bryant directly addresses a contemporary literary periodical-reading public that likes scenes of travel and appreciates a finely tuned trochee within an iambic line. That poet willingly sees through the eyes of the poet—not an anonymous "speaker," but the view of the famous William Cullen Bryant himself. Thus in the next lines when

> . . . I behold them from the first,
> And my heart swells, while the dilated sight
> Takes in the encircling vastness, Lo! they stretch

(ll. 4–6)

toward us and away from the poet (in a preview of the 1976 Saul Steinberg cover of the *New Yorker*, "View of the World from 9th Avenue"), the definite article joins Bryant's gaze on the prairies to his readers' virtual gaze from Manhattan facing west. The trisyllabic foot "Lo! they stretch" mimetically stretches the line and winks at readers who, like Bryant's friend Dana, accused Bryant of using trisyllabics "a little too frequently, perhaps, for what is familiar."[71] For attentive readers still, Bryant's habit of varying blank verse lines can be annoying: in 1990, Barbara Packer wittily remarked that "'Thanatopsis' might almost have been written to demonstrate how many spondees a blank verse line can sustain."[72] In the *Knickerbocker* in 1833, that sustained series of metrical variations was a bravura literary performance in a poem that was not incidentally also performance of the new Anglo-American "we" such verse could sustain.

That metropolitan literary crowd not only appreciated the ins and outs of blank verse but also knew something about the representation of apparently innocent American landscapes. As the poem's sixth line stretches from iamb to amphibrach, the landscape stretches into and then beyond the frame of a New York Sketch Club painting:

In airy undulations far away,
As if the ocean, in his gentlest swell,
Stood still, with all his rounded billows fixed,
And motionless forever.—Motionless?—
No—they are all unchained again. The clouds
Sweep over with their shadows, and, beneath,
The surface rolls and fluctuates to the eye;
Dark hollows seem to glide along and chase
The sunny ridges.

(ll. 7–15)

These lines turn a scene that could be painted, framed, and hung ("motionless forever") into a moving panorama, or in Bryant's way of describing the effect, "the truth is, painting and sculpture are, literally, imitative arts, while poetry is only metaphorically so."[73] Unlike any of the landscapes painted by Cole and Durand and others, Bryant's prairie landscape is inhuman yet animate: poetry can do what painting cannot do, since the poet can make his unpopulated (or, as it will turn out, *de*populated) landscape *move*.

Yet what we now recognize as the ecological fragility of the prairies (only one per cent of tallgrass prairie remains in the United States today; the state of Illinois once held over thirty-five thousand square miles of prairie and now holds about three) becomes cultural fragility in "The Prairies." Bryant wrote the poem after a trip to Illinois to visit his brothers in 1832. When he returned to New York (in the middle of a cholera epidemic), Bryant wrote to Dana that

these prairies, of a soft fertile soil, and a smooth undulating surface . . . covered with high thinly growing grass, full of weeds and gaudy flowers, and destitute of bushes or trees, perpetually brought to my mind the idea of their having been once cultivated. They looked to me like the fields of a race which had passed away, whose enclosures and habitations had decayed. . . [74]

"The fields of a *race* that had passed away"? The poem's performative special effects seem to have been anticipated by a different fantasy of animation: why would "the boundless unshorn fields" suggest an earlier state of cultivation? Why would Bryant have confused natural fragility with cultural fragility?

Unlike the great majority of Bryant's poems, "The Prairies" has attracted a number of critical readings over the last few decades, all devoted to answering that question. John Hay has nominated Bryant as an early practitioner of what Ursula Heise has termed "*eco-cosmopolitanism*, an approach toward achieving a 'sense of planet' by stressing the connections between more immediately familiar natural places and cultural processes." As Bryant's "views evolved," Hay writes, "the prairies became for him a powerful symbol of damaging human activity rather than a unique natural ecosystem."[75] I have been suggesting that "The Prairies" hems nature in with culture from its first line, and that it continues, by way of its blank verse variations and enjambments (to which we shall return), to make "the unshorn fields, boundless and beautiful" into boundless fields of Anglo-lyricization. The "damaging human activity" of which Hay thinks the prairies became a symbol is also the property of a White poetics that worried over the sources of that damage and that nominated English verse as its survivor. As Gruesz has pointed out, the apostrophe to the "Breezes of the South" that move the "unchained" landscape put that landscape on a continuum with "the palms of Mexico and the vines / Of Texas," thus encouraging, Gruesz writes, "a mutability in territorial boundaries, both the west and to the south of the United States" that prefigured the doctrine of Manifest Destiny.[76] Yet as Gruesz also points out, "the conquest of foreign time in 'The Prairies' is as significant as the conquest of foreign space, [since] the same southern breezes that infuse the prairie with movement bring the waft of an unseen history to the speaker's imagination" (49). In the context of our reading of Bryant's poetic historiography, perhaps we are now in a position to see that this only apparently naturally occurring history *was* foreseen and that the difference between "the speaker's imagination" and the poet's intention makes a big difference in how we understand the poetics of history and the history of poetics embedded in "The Prairies."

The recent readings of "The Prairies" all call the "I" that enters the poem in its fourth line "the speaker." Of course they do. Bryant's readers in the 1830s had not learned this concept, but I have been arguing that Bryant's poetics joined the poetics of Plato, Whitfield, Horton, and Wheatley in inaugurating an early shift toward it. Yet if we anachronistically assume that this "speaker" or "persona" is distinct from the poet and is present from the beginning of "The Prairies," we will not notice that shift taking place. In "To a Waterfowl," we traced that shift in the generically lyricized ode; in "An Indian at the Burial-Place of His Fathers," we traced that shift in the lyricized dramatic colloquy or proto-dramatic monologue of a racially marked persona; in "The Prairies," we have begun to trace it in the eloquent New York White poet's blank verse depiction of the western frontier. In all of these instances, the figure of an abstract lyric "speaker" distinct from the poet begins to emerge. But "The Prairies" differs from the earlier Bryant poems we have considered so far, since it seems to have no specific Anglo-Romantic stanzaic model other than the blankness of blank verse, and since the abstraction of the poet into a generic figure in this slightly later poem was the consequence of a new American and deeply racist theory of history.

That is why it is important to notice that when what Gruesz calls "an unseen history" is revealed under the surface of the prairie landscape, we recognize the "I" who reveals it to us as the poet rather than as a dramatic persona. The only way to believe the story this poem will go on to tell is to rely on the poet and newspaper editor's authority:

> As o'er the verdant waste I guide my steed,
> Among the high rank grass that sweeps his sides
> The hollow beating of his footsteps seems
> A sacrilegious sound. I think of those
> Upon his rest he tramples. Are they here—
> The dead of other days?—and did the dust
> Of these fair solitudes once stir with life
> And burn with passion?

(ll. 34–41)

As Bryant's letter to Dana emphasized the "thinly growing grass, full of weeds and gaudy flowers, and destitute of trees," this description's emphasis on the tallgrass prairie as a "waste" full of "rank grass" makes the fields seem less "boundless" and "beautiful" than they did at first, and when the traveling cosmopolitan poet on horseback asks whether "they" are "here—/ The dead of other days," we are taken aback and hooked. This city poet's trip west just got a little gothic and a little more interesting, and recognizably so, since the *siste viator* ("Stop, traveler") trope common to the graveyard elegy also invokes the genre of Bryant's early success in "Thanatopsis." As Cavitch writes, in "Thanatopsis," Bryant sought "to embed his numerous borrowings from Gray and others in a matrix of blank verse, casual diction, prosaic rhythms, republican principles, and American topography."[77] "The Prairies" again winks at its New York audience by alluding to the borrowings, blank verse, diction, rhythms, principles, and topography of "Thanatopsis," and so we are meant to under-

stand that this will also be a poem about mass death. In "Thanatopsis," we are
told that

> All that tread
> The globe are but a handful to the tribes
> That slumber in its bosom.—Take the wings
> Of morning, pierce the Barcan wilderness,
> Or lose thyself in the continuous woods
> Where rolls the Oregon, and hears no sound,
> Save his own dashings—yet the dead are there:
> And millions in those solitudes.[78]

The rhyme between "These fair solitudes" of "The Prairies" and the "millions
in those solitudes" of Bryant's youthful poetic sensation would have been hard
to miss in 1833. In "Thanatopsis," the global "tribes" buried everywhere, from
the North African ("Barcan") desert to the Northwest Territory of North
America, are alone together in a transhistorical and transplanetary universal
historical mass grave; in "The Prairies," "these fair solitudes" index a very spe-
cifically located mass grave of a very specific vanished race with its own very
specific history. Or so the prairie landscape itself tells us:

> Are they here—
> The dead of other days? ...
> 　... Let the mighty mounds
> That overlook the rivers, or that rise
> In the dim forest crowded with old oaks,
> Answer. A race, that long has passed away,
> Built them;—a disciplined and populous race
> Heaped, with long toil, the earth, while yet the Greek
> Was heaving the Pentelicus to forms
> Of symmetry, and rearing on its rock
> The glittering Parthenon.

> 　　　　　　　　　(ll. 38–39, 41–49)

When the mounds become the speaker of Bryant's poem, what they say is
what a lot of people in North America in the 1830s wanted to hear. While read-
ers of this poem today usually require an introduction to why "the mighty
mounds" in the midwestern and southeastern United States would contain the
answer to the poet's question, Bryant's contemporaries required no such

explanation.[79] As Hay writes, "spurred by reports from frontier expeditions following the Louisiana Purchase, the growing fascination in and exploration of the Indian mounds of the Midwest in the early decades of the century contributed to a full-blown mythology of the ancient Moundbuilders: a civilized race, separate from modern Native Americans, whose heartland empire flourished and fell long before the arrival of Columbus" (479). Gordon Sayre calls the popular attention the mounds attracted in the early nineteenth century "mounds mania," and, as Hay and others have pointed out, Bryant was counting on this mania to guarantee a popular audience for his poem.[80] That fad was part of what Patrick Brantlinger has called "extinction discourse," a "specific branch of the dual ideologies of imperialism and racism—a 'discursive formation,' to use Foucauldian terminology."[81] That discursive formation ran deep in the early decades of the nineteenth century, as we can see in Bryant's casual fantasy in his letter to Dana. Indeed, President Jackson himself drew on it in his famous speech to Congress in 1830, a speech that both letter and poem echo:

> To follow to the tomb the last of his race, and to tread on the graves of extinct nations, excites melancholy reflections. But true philanthropy reconciles the mind to these vicissitudes, as it does to the extinction of one generation to make room for another. In the monuments and fortresses of an unknown people, spread over the extensive regions of the west, we behold the memorials of a once powerful race, which was exterminated, or has disappeared, to make room for the existing savage tribes. Nor is there anything in this, which, upon a comprehensive view of the general interests of the human race, is to be regretted.[82]

Notice the eloquent turn Jackson takes in turning mourning to "philanthropy" and polygenetic extinction theory to the older, more comfortable monogenetic theory of regeneration of a unified "human race." The debate over whether this "once powerful race" was "exterminated" or simply "disappeared" is left undecided in Jackson's appeal. What did it matter? "The existing savage tribes" are clearly not descendants of that race in Jackson's account, and of course his implication is that their turn for extinction is at hand. As Jackson's speech makes clear, that narrative of Indigenous extinction included a story of Indian responsibility for a previous genocide. Indeed, Bryant's poem emphasizes the story of what happened to the "unknown people" who preceded "the existing savage tribes," of what became of the "disciplined and populous race" who were building the beginnings of a civilization that rivaled that of ancient Greece. In that lost world, "lovers walked, and wooed,"

> In a forgotten language, and old tunes,
> From instruments of unremembered form,
> Gave the soft winds a voice. The red man came—
> The roaming hunter tribes, warlike and fierce,
> And the mound-builders vanished from the earth.

(ll. 54–59)

What "the red man" invades is a culture made out of poetry—out of "language," "old tunes," and "instruments"—and that poetry takes the form of "form": like the "forms / of symmetry" that make the mounds comparable to Mount Pentelicus as foundation for the Parthenon, "unremembered form" marks lost civilizational achievement—not a particular achievement, but a genre of progress. Only an abstract idea of what this lost race-become-culture built out of the equivalent of marble survives, and only an abstract idea of its unheard music remains. But these advanced forms did not just disappear; form itself was violently destroyed by the savage tribes:

> All is gone;
> All—save the piles of earth that hold their bones,
> The platforms where they worshipped unknown gods,
> The barriers which they builded from the soil
> To keep the foe at bay—till o'er the walls
> The wild beleaguerer broke, and, one by one,
> The strongholds of the plain were forced, and heaped
> With corpses.

(ll. 64–71)

Bryant's account of the massacre of the mound-builders took its cue from accounts like the anonymous and symptomatic 1816 "On the Aborigines of the Western Country," which stressed that American "aborigines" before the Indian were *"white people."*[83] While Jackson seems to have entertained suggestions like Caleb Atwater's that the mound-builders were farmers of South Asian descent who simply disappeared, or (later President) William Henry Harrison's theory that the mound-builders went to Mexico, Bryant told a story

in which the ancestors of the contemporary Indigenous people Jackson ges-
tured toward as "savage tribes" murdered the more advanced people who pre-
ceded them, and in which those more advanced people were the ancestors of
people like Bryant and President Jackson.[84] As early as 1811, Henry Bracken-
ridge had written after a visit to the Cahokia mounds in southern Illinois that
"if the city of Philadelphia and its environs, were deserted, there would not be
more numerous traces of human existence."[85] Brackenridge implicitly aligned
the mound-builders with modern White Americans, and explicitly insisted
that in any case they were not the "red" people now indigenous to the region.
This insistence marked a departure from what Katy Chiles has called the
"transformable race" theories of the eighteenth century, theories that held that
people could change their race, that climate or disease could alter race over
time.[86] Jefferson's *Notes on the State of Virginia* was still enmeshed in such
"transformable" theories at the end of the eighteenth century, but by 1832,
Bryant was making a clear break from those earlier monogenetic race con-
cepts, though J. H. McCulloh and others had argued in 1829 that the mound-
builders were clearly the forebearers of contemporary Indigenous peoples and
not a separate lost race.[87]

The debate that emerged in the first half of the nineteenth century over the
origins of the mound-builders was itself the debate over the difference be-
tween monogenetic and polygenetic fictions of race, and so gathered energy
from many sources and generated a variety of conflicting possibilities: some
saw the mound-builders as ancestors of the Aztecs, one scholar suggested that
they were Malays, another that they were Egyptians, others that they were
antedeluvians, Polynesians, Greeks, Romans, Israelites, Scandinavians, Welsh,
Scots, and Chinese, still others that they were White men who had been ex-
terminated by "barbarous red men."[88] By 1848, E. G. Squier and E. H. Davis
would use the authority of the new Smithsonian to argue that the mound-
builders were an extinct race connected to Mexico and Peru and unrelated to
contemporary Native Americans.[89] In 1855, Increase Lapham (sponsored by
the American Antiquarian Society) would argue that the mound-builders *were*
the ancestors of modern North American Indigenous people; in 1856, the
Smithsonian and American Antiquarian Society together published another
study in which Samuel F. Haven denied this possibility and scientifically ar-
gued that "with all their characteristics," the mound-builders' "affinities are
found in the early condition of Asiatic races; and a channel of communication
[the Bering Strait] is pointed out through which they might have poured into
this continent."[90] I mention just a few of the abundant (and entertaining)

theories of the origins of the mound-builders not because they are all relevant to Bryant's poem or to the history of American poetics (though they are relevant to the birth of American antiquarianism), but because they not only make it clear that mounds mania had many choices on offer, but that those choices were themselves intricately informed by the relations between emerging concepts of culture and emerging concepts of race, as well as by theories of the history that connected the two. Yet Bryant chose to dwell only on the version most damaging to "the existing savage tribes" at risk in the Removal Act. "The Prairies" abstracts the origins of the mound-builders' "forgotten language" in order to bring the violence of "the red man" into sharper focus. Perhaps that was because when Bryant visited Ohio and Illinois in 1832, many Indigenous people were actively engaged in the series of modern rather than ancient conflicts that became known as the Black Hawk War.

The magical thinking that turned the "unshorn" beauty of the now-extinct tallgrass prairies into the mass grave of a now-extinct race transformed a historical situation that Bryant's letters from Illinois in June 1832 narrate in distressed detail. "I shall be obliged to relinquish my projected route to Chicago," Bryant wrote to his wife, since it "is said to be unsafe in consequence of the neighborhood of the savages." A day later, he wrote to her that

> There is much talk in St. Louis concerning the Indians. The true number killed [in a recent raid] is eleven. The families murdered lived on Rock River to the west of the Illinois river. There were three families, consisting of 15 persons in all. Their bodies were left to be devoured by hogs and dogs. A man has been killed in Buffalo Grove near Galena and it is supposed that an Indian Agent has been murdered by the Savages.[91]

The violence that was one of the immediate consequences of the Removal Act surrounded Bryant as he crossed Illinois, but in "The Prairies" that contemporary violence has been displaced. The prairies that Bryant beheld were not unpopulated; they were so populated by White settlers in conflict with the Indigenous people the Illinois troops were actively displacing that the poet had difficulty crossing them. Bryant was in Illinois near Cahokia just two weeks after Black Hawk attacked the Illinois militia and drove them into retreat, sending panic through the White settler population of the territory. In "The Prairies," that historically immediate violence is turned into the fantasy of a White genocide—which was exactly what the colonizers in 1832 most feared, or at least that was the fear they invoked in defense of their retaliation.

That immediate context is surely why the version of the mound-builders story that Bryant chose out of all the possible stories he could have told was not his mentor Southey's version in *Madoc* (1805), in which the mound-builders are both Welsh and Aztec, or the version of poet Sarah J. Hale, who in her 1823 poem "The Genius of Oblivion" imagined Phoenician lovers who cross the Atlantic and give birth to the mound-builders, or the version in Micah Flint's 1826 poem "The Mounds of Cahokia," in which the poet turns to apostrophize the "long-extinguished race" directly, asking those now buried to

> ... forgive the rude, unhallowed feet,
> Which trode so thoughtless o'er your mighty dead.[92]

Bryant's lines sound a lot like Flint's, but he did not need to borrow from Flint (who, like Bryant, also borrows from Shelley and Virgil) directly to share the popular topos that itself borrowed so much from so many. What is remarkable is that out of these sources, the one that most influenced Bryant's poem was a version of the mound-builders story that came out just months before "The Prairies" appeared in the *Knickerbocker* in December 1833. Josiah Priest's *American Antiquities and Discoveries in the West, Being an Exhibition of the Evidence that an Ancient Population of Partially Civilized Nations Differing Entirely from those of the Present Indians Peopled America Many Centuries Before its Discovery by Columbus, and Inquiries into their Origin, with a Copious Description of Many of their Stupendous Works, Now in Ruins, with Conjectures Concerning What May Have Become of Them* was a best-seller (the 1835 fifth edition boasts that "22,000 volumes of this work have been published within thirty months"), and it gave readers the advantage of surveying an enormous range of theories, concluding definitively that the mound-builders, wherever they first came from, must have been "*white men.*" Priest would go on to become the author of *The Bible Defence of Slavery* (1851), a book that makes the necessity of removing both Black and Indigenous people from an endangered "White America" its subject. An earlier version of this influential two-in-one racism swept the country in *American Antiquities*, in which Priest graphically concluded with a scene depicting "the remnant of a tribe or nation, acquainted with the arts of excavation and defense, making a last struggle against the invasion of an overwhelming foe; where, it is likely, they were reduced by famine, and perished amid the yells of their enemies."[93] Bryant uses the affordances of his genre to echo Priest's sensational surmise and to turn it into a sensational inset narrative:

Haply some solitary fugitive,
Lurking in marsh and forest, till the sense
Of desolation and of fear became
Bitterer than death, yielded himself to die.
Man's better nature triumphed then. Kind words
Welcomed and soothed him; the rude conquerors
Seated the captive with their chiefs; he chose
A bride among the maidens, and at length
Seemed to forget—yet n'er forgot—the wife
Of his first love, and her sweet little ones,
Butchered, amid their shrieks, with all his race.

Thus change the forms of being.

(ll. 74–85)

Bryant here makes his own contribution to mounds mania, prefiguring the fugitive Black figure of antiblack abolitionist verse in the fugitive White figure of anti-Indigenous Removal Act verse. It is a strikingly odd contribution, even given the fantastic theories we have briefly surveyed. Having made contemporary Indigenous people who were themselves under siege the descendants of "the wild beleaguerers" who accomplish the genocide of an implicitly White civilization, Bryant modifies his polygenetic racism in order to restore a version of eighteenth-century Universal History's dynamic of civilizational progress. That desire for progress was not peculiar to Bryant, of course. As Robert Young writes, even Herder's original theory of the *Volksgeist* depended on "a central paradox": "while on the one hand colonization and racial mixture are regarded by Herder as introducing a fatal heterogeneity into traditional culture, on the other hand the cultural education of the human race comes as the result of differences, or cultural mixing and communication, whereby cultural achievements of one culture are grafted on to another."[94] The term "miscegenation" would not be coined in the United States until 1864, and Darwin would not publish *On the Origin of Species by Means of Natural Selection* until 1859, but Bryant here foresees some of the consequences of polygenetic racism and the ways the theory of evolution would take account of them. By moving from a tale of the many to a tale of the one, this section of the poem personalizes the story of mass extinction and gives it a future, albeit in the person of a nameless "fugitive" who marries into the "race" of "the rude conquerors."

This "solitary fugitive" emerges from the dialect of the tribe that the solitary poet has been busy purifying in "The Prairies," since he is a creature of English blank verse. "The rude conquerors" are allowed to join the liberal progressive history of the human race when they show symptoms of "man's better nature," but the way that potential historical progress is written into "The Prairies" is in the punch line to this short tale: "Thus change the forms of being." Again, the word that Bryant uses for the mound-builders' civilized accomplishments abstracts particular cultural production into general cultural ideals, and the result of racial hybridity also seems to produce such "forms," as if hybridity were the natural process of cultural progress. In fact, "grafted" is Herder's (translated) word for the process that seems to contradict the principle of polygenesis: at the end of the Roman Empire, when "barbarians" invade, Herder writes that "everywhere new nations were grafted on the old stock; what buds, what fruits did they produce for mankind?"[95] By turning murdered people into natural cultural "forms" (and not incidentally, by turning mass rape into marriage), Bryant's stunning line does more that justify American state violence against Black Hawk's gathered tribes and all the other murdered and displaced people that populated the prairies he visited: in his poem depicting a landscape populated only by the dead, the poet seeks to eloquently persuade us that this is how both history and poetry naturally work. White people were not committing genocide on the prairies in 1832; blank verse was.

That naturalization of a history of violence as the progress of culture is vividly described in the penultimate section of the poem, in which "arise / Races of living things, glorious in strength. And perish": "the red man," "the beaver," "the bison" have all apparently "withdrawn" from these prairies of their own accord. While

> The bee,
> A more adventurous colonist than man,
> With whom he came across the eastern deep,
> Fills the savannas with murmurings,
> And hides his sweets, as in the golden age,
> Within the hollow oak.

(ll. 108–113)

Nature makes culture at the end of "The Prairies": the beaver "rears his little Venice" far away from "the white man's face," and the colonizing bee restores natural civilization in its westward progress. The bee is Virgilian and Miltonic and Mandevillean, and it is also a figure for what this poem has been doing all along. The bee is a "colonizing trick": it articulates the way in which the success of colonization has already been articulated by the prosody of the poem. But just as "An Indian at the Burial-Place of His Fathers" ends by insisting on its own georgic modernity by invoking Virgil, "The Prairies" is not content with vague allusions to the continuity between classical, British, and American poetics; instead, it emphasizes its own lyric turn on epic Virgil. When Aeneas looks across the river Lethe in the sixth book of the *Aeneid*, he sees the underworld as a colony of bees:

> Souls of a thousand nations filled the air,
> As bees in meadows at the height of summer
> Hover and home on flowers and thickly swarm
> On snow-white lilies, and the countryside
> Is loud with humming.[96]

Virgil uses the metaphor of the bees to naturalize the underworld; Bryant uses the figure of Virgil's colonizing bee to make his history of death eventuate in new life in a new world. But the allusion to Virgil also makes it clear that this new "snow-white" world is haunted. A creature of classical and English poetry, the bee does what Bryant described the English language as doing: "it has grown up, as every forcible and beautiful language has done, among a simple and unlettered people; it has accommodated itself, in the first place, to the things of nature, and, as civilization advanced, to the things of art; and thus it has become a language full of picturesque forms of expression, yet fitted for the purposes of science."[97] For the American poet writing in blank verse, the progress of civilization is guaranteed by the Englishness of English verse itself, since it is itself already "the advance of civilization," and that advance has had its costs since before the founding of Rome.

No English measure made this argument for the progress of English language, White civilization, and culture through a series of stops and starts and rises and falls as eloquently as did blank verse. While the stanzas that Bryant borrowed from Southey and Wordsworth marked some of his most popular poetry as Anglo, the blank verse of "The Prairies" is even more intimately identified with anglocentric prosodic historiography than the prosody of those earlier poems, since it is not associated with any particular British Romantic poem but with the Englishness of English poetry itself. As George Saintsbury would cap off the century by writing, by Bryant's time, blank verse had become "a school of freedom" that liberated poetry in English to become itself, since it had, in the legitimate carrying-out of the great base-principles of English prosody—foot-division with substitution, pause-arrangement with license to shift, and permission of extrametrical syllables at the end only—enriched English verse with such measure as no other language then possessed, and as, in perfection, no other language has ever possessed.[98]

The emphatic variability of the blank verse lines of "The Prairies," their tendency toward trisyllabic endings, their restless shifting of pauses from beginning to middle to two-thirds to three-fourths to period to comma to dash to semicolon, all make them exemplary of the performative meter that Saintsbury described. The form of the lines makes an eloquent argument for the adventure of settler colonialism, ending in a series of enjambments that proved that the American poetic landscape was prosodically destined to be White. As Geoffrey Hartman wrote,

> The halting of the traveler . . . is felt more in the slowed rhythm and meditative elaboration of [the poem's] first lines than as part of the casual frame . . . a countervailing movement is felt at once. . . . As in all blank verse it is the pace (or breathing) which most immediately affects us, and this depends in good part on the distribution of pauses, on subtle organic or meditative haltings . . . a vacillating calculus of gain and loss, hope and doubt . . . distilling from the versification itself, and probably from the informal transitions of one verse paragraph to another, an emotional analogue to the *turn* and *counterturn* of the traditional Sublime Ode.[99]

Hartman was writing about Wordsworth's "Tintern Abbey," but the fact that you might recognize his description of Wordsworth's prosody as the blank verse prosody of "The Prairies" makes my point. To experience blank verse in the way that Saintsbury and Hartman describe it, we need to have what Saintsbury called "an English ear." In blank verse, that ear could be attuned to its national, anglocentric, deeply racialized "freedom."

In addressing his pauses, shifts, stops, and starts to his sophisticated New York reading public, Bryant enlisted them into the very rhythms of the *Volksgeist* of White poetics. Those readers inherit the classical education on which English "foot-division with substitution" was based, and they inherit the natural English intuition that can tell the difference between the turns and counterturns of the Sublime Ode and the rise and fall of blank verse. That metrical inheritance returns us to the theoretical frenzy that surrounded mounds mania: what is the relation between race and culture? What is the difference between culture and civilization? Does historical progress emerge out of grafting one culture onto another? The blank verse of "The Prairies" answers those questions more eloquently than did Josiah Priest's insistence that the mound-builders must have been White because their remnant forms appeared Northern European in origin. If we have appreciated the measure of Bryant's "Greater Romantic Lyric," then we know that the forms of being change because they are destined to turn into *us*.

Robert Shaw has described the history of blank verse as "the rescue" of English poetry "from the state of prosodic anarchy."[100] First employed in the sixteenth century for the translation of Virgil, blank verse did not come into its own until Christopher Marlowe made it the meter of the early modern stage. Shakespeare made it into Shakespeare, of course, and according to Shaw, "blank verse reigned triumphant on the stage until the outbreak of civil war closed the theaters in 1642" (5). Then (or so the story goes) came Milton, who "restored blank verse to epic" and also, not incidentally, made it the object of prosodic analysis and debate for centuries to come. In his essay "The Blank Verse of Milton" (1880), John Addington Symonds summed up the Herderian cast of that arc when wrote that

> blank verse has been the metre of genius, that it is only used successfully by indubitable poets, and that it is no favorite in a mean, contracted, and un-imaginative age. The freedom of the Renaissance created it in England. The freedom of our own century has reproduced it. Blank verse is a type and symbol of our national literary spirit—uncontrolled by precedent or rule, inclined to extravagance, yet reaching perfection at intervals by an inner force and *vivida vis* of native inspiration.[101]

The extravagance of the blank verse of "The Prairies" changed the forms of English literary being into the forms of American literary being, the discursive formation of antiquity, drama, epic, modernity, and verse freedom all at once. As Bryant himself put the case in his essay "On Trisyllabic Feet in Iambic Measure," "the liberty" afforded by blank verse "is an ancient birthright of the poets."[102]

Joseph Harrington has anticipated my argument here by suggesting that the changes that Bryant rang on Romantic poetics inaugurated a new "voice" of American poetry. "Bryant introduced the middle voice into American literature," Harrington writes,

> a voice that later would become a prominent feature of modernist writing. This voice is neither active nor passive, transitive nor intransitive: the forms of being just change. Just as the liberal subject comes to recognition of itself by itself, so too does "America."[103]

I would only add to Harrington's important point that "the middle voice" was a concept created by literary criticism in the 1990s as a tool for interpreting modern narrative; what Bryant was introducing was not a "voice" but a lyricized poetic form in which a single abstract person came to stand for a diverse collection of genres. Harrington's description of the liberal subject's "recognition of itself by itself" actually echoes Hegel's definition of lyric, the genre in which "spirit is pushed back into itself out of its reconciliation of itself with itself."[104] But just as Bryant anticipated and varied the course of Hegelian Universal History, so his blank verse varies the course of Hegelian genre formation. Whereas for Hegel (and the history of literary criticism), the lyric is the perfect expression of the spirit of the age because it is the least material and most subjective genre, for Bryant, the lyricization of several genres eventuates in a subject alienated by the very history that has made this form of being possible. In "The Prairies," those genres included (but were not limited to) loco-descriptive verse, graveyard elegies, *siste viator* poems (often the basis for graveyard elegies), the ode, the georgic, the epic, the popular genre of the mounds tale, Bryant's own signature genre of the mass grave poem, and above all the prosodic genre of English blank verse, which enfolded drama and epic, prose and verse, and thus realized a capacious White spirit of the age. As the "solitary fugitive" hybridizes races and cultures to produce new "forms," so the solitary poet at the end of "The Prairies" turns to us directly and makes his blank verse itself the vehicle of colonial progress, the hybridizing form that changes as it is translated across "the eastern deep." That prosody is neither active nor passive, transitive nor intransitive; it is just the ongoing, liberating birthright of appropriated, unrhymed pentameter. "I listen long," the poet ends, as if he were witness rather than creator,

> . . . and think I hear
> The sound of that advancing multitude
> Which soon shall fill these deserts. From the ground
> Comes up the laugh of children, the soft voice
> Of maidens, and the sweet and solemn hymn
> Of Sabbath worshippers. The low of herds
> Blends with the rustling of the heavy grain
> Over the dark brown furrows. All at once
> A fresher wind sweeps by, and breaks my dream,
> And I am in the wilderness alone.

(ll. 113–123)

Because the trick of the blank verse lines has already naturally (as it were) colonized the prairie landscape, this culminating prophecy in the wilderness lacks drama—or lacks the passion the end of a tale of mass extinction might be expected to incite, though that extinction is this latter-day White agrarian population's condition of future existence. As the poem displaces violence into the fantasy of a vanished White indigenous past, it silences violence in the present and projects colonization into a future in which the souls of a thousand nations fill the air. But William Cullen Bryant cannot be held responsible for the death of those souls, and neither can *we*. The "fresher wind" cannot sweep away the traces of those thousand nations, nor can it erase the probability that the forms of being will continue to change, but the ongoing flow of blank verse reassures us that while this poet may be "alone," this is what history has done to us, since this future of American poetry will never stop being the speech of White men between whom the barriers have fallen, and risen, and fallen.

5

The Poetess

FRANCES ELLEN WATKINS,
HENRY WADSWORTH LONGFELLOW, AND
FRANCES ELLEN WATKINS HARPER

A Specific Vacancy

The first chapters of this book focused on Black Romantic poetics, and in the previous chapter we have just taken a long look at Bryant's representative White Romantic poetics, but I have been arguing all along that the racialized lyricization of American poetry was a dialectical process. In this final chapter, I want to bring the terms of that dialectic closer together, not to create a synthesis between them but instead to emphasize the ways in which these histories were simultaneously mutually defining and neither mutual nor definitive at all. As we have seen, in the first half of the nineteenth century, the poetics of whiteness was defined against non-White figures, and the poetics of blackness was defined against discourses of antiblackness. Black poets after Wheatley inspired the direction of American poetics because the deep design of the social antagonism foundational to America (and not just to America) became the deep design of the poetry that became American lyric. That determination was embedded in a poetics of relation—a relation that could uncannily resemble the brutal dialectic between the feminized figures in the Kara Walker drawing I invoked in chapter 1, figures locked in a struggle that hardly looks like historical progress. If Adorno was right that lyric is the expression of a social antagonism, it is not surprising that the poets most alienated by the gendered and racialized social antagonisms of the late eighteenth and early nineteenth centuries set the terms for that expression, or that those very terms now make the poets that invented them look out of date. What may be surprising is that this invention often took the form of a figure also apparently now out of date: the very nineteenth-century figure of the Poetess.

As the previous chapters have shown, the most remarkable thing about the process of lyricization as we have traced it so far is that the gradual and uneven blurring of verse genres eventuated in a representative abstract person that took the place of those genres. Black Romantics like Horton, Plato, and Whit-field foregrounded that abstract person as the subject generated by the Ro-mantic poetics they inherited, an abstraction that threatened to take the place of actual persons; Wheatley personified the terms of that generic threat, and Bryant arranged those terms around a generic White persona threatened by a non-White American landscape. If "threat" seems like a funny word to attri-bute to poetic figures like apostrophe and personification, and even to stanzaic and prosodic forms, that may be because for the most part the abstractions that resulted from the conflict implicit in nineteenth-century American poet-ics appeared to resolve it. Though Whitfield's heavy-metal performances stand as exceptions to the rule, most of these poets turned opposing forces into a persona that often appeared suspended in a sympathetic pathos of uncertain agency rather than in revolutionary rage or reactionary oppression.[1] That pa-thos of uncertain agency would become Plato's passive undoing of the single subject, Douglass's reappropriation of the appropriated Black fugitive subject, Horton's anguished inhabitation of Romanticism's figuratively fettered subject, Wheatley's depersonification of all figurative subjects, and Bryant's reiteration of Anglo-Romantic figures and prosodies in order to construct a precarious White American lyric subject in the wilderness. All of these poets expressed the result of social conflict as personal abstraction—specifically, as the suspen-sion of personal agency. Of course, the difference between the suspension of personal agency enforced by Horton's or Wheatley's enslavement and the sus-pension of personal agency that appears to let Bryant's settler colonialism off the hook makes all the difference, but what we have begun to see is that the intimate relation between these antagonisms became lyricization's driving force. Nowhere is that force more intimate than in the nineteenth-century figure of the Poetess, the larger-than-life abstraction made to order for the poetics of racial conflict, the figure that appeared to affectively resolve social antagonisms by wiping herself out.

The critical debates that have circled around the Poetess over the past twenty-five years have had their own dialectical quality: while feminist critics who did the crucial work of recovering nineteenth-century women poets have resisted the idea that Poetess verse was not necessarily attached exclusively to women poets, other scholars have emphasized that the separability of the gendered figure from its authors actually proved enormously generative in nineteenth-century verse culture. As Paula Bennett wrote in 2007, "after a century or more in history's dustbin, the Poetess has made a stunning comeback" in the twenty-first century:

> Not only is there an entire website, The Poetess Archive, devoted to this figure, but an ever-increasing number of articles and books, including some by the most prominent scholars in the field, are given over wholly or in part to discussing her. . . . As a result of this inquiry, scholarly interest in nineteenth-century women's poetry, including Poetess poetry, has shifted from addressing it as the stable object of a massive recovery project to understanding it as a discursively-produced set of reading effects fractured along the same lines as the poets themselves.[2]

Bennett both celebrates and laments the recent boom in and critical direction of Poetess studies, not only because she has been personally responsible for a substantial portion of the recovery of nineteenth-century American women's verse, but because she thinks that to characterize all nineteenth-century women poets as Poetesses is to forget how many different kinds of poems "nineteenth-century U.S. women wrote. Writing for a popular literary market . . . these poets wrote hymns and psalms, parodies and satire, odes and elegies, erotic verse and lullabies, work songs and protest poems, screeds and memorials, epics and epyllions, and jingles and riddles. . . . Might it not be more accurate as well as less confusing, to speak of Poetess poems or Poetess thematics, rather than Poetesses per se, especially since these poets did not apply the label to themselves?" (270).

It is a good question. If we define the nineteenth-century Poetess as a nineteenth-century woman poet, then the answer would have to be no. On the other hand, if we define the Poetess as a generic figure that was and is (like gender itself) detachable from the work of any particular poet, a figure defined by this very detachability, then the answer would also have to be no. The nineteenth-century Poetess was not a genre in the sense in which elegies and lullabies and work songs were popular verse genres; the Poetess was instead a trope in a rather pure sense, as definite and slippery as a turn of phrase, a trope that encompassed or turned through many prosodic and rhetorical genres at once. For this reason, it is difficult "to speak of Poetess poems or Poetess thematics," since to do so would imply that the figure is consistent. It isn't—especially since the trope of the Poetess worked differently at different moments over the course of the nineteenth century. How could the Poetess of 1821 be the Poetess of 1891, when everything else about poetry (including the definition of the word itself) had changed in those seventy years? In this chapter, I want to think about the mid-nineteenth-century Poetess as a figure that not only measured but that also helped to effect this change. As Lootens argues in *The Political Poetess*, the "Poetess thrives in a realm of shifting literary (and, of course, political) open secrets, uneasily located between the unspeakable and the all-too-familiar. . . . If the Poetess is a vacancy . . . she is a specific vacancy, and one already possessed of an impressive history."[3]

The idea of the Poetess as the personified vacancy located at the heart of late eighteenth- and nineteenth-century lyricization has been central to this book from its first pages: from Mneme to Wheatley, from Britannia to Plato to Horton to "the want of male principle" in Bryant, the Poetess has been the open secret of many of the poems and poets we have considered so far. I mean "open secret" in Lootens's sense of general epistemological uncertainty, but also in Eve Kosofsky Sedgwick's axiomatic sense of a willed ignorance that structures all the knowledge that surrounds it. I would say of the Poetess what Sedgwick says of the definitional attachment of gender to sexuality, that to understand the Poetess as identical to the woman poet is problematic because

> to use that *fait accompli* as a reason for analytically conflating gender and sexuality [or the Poetess and the woman poet] would obscure the degree to which the fact itself requires explanation. It would also . . . risk obscuring yet again the extreme intimacy with which all these available analytic axes do after all mutually constitute one another: to assume the distinctiveness of the *intimacy* between sex and gender might well risk assuming too much about the definitional *separability* of either of them from determinations of, say, class or race.[4]

Walt Whitman's Poetess poetics took advantage of the inseparability of gender and sexuality from determinations of class and race to *not* separate them, to gather a miscellaneous range of genres and discourses into the largest personal abstraction of the period, an abstraction that has been mistaken for a departure from rather than a grand summation of nineteenth-century American poetics. Whitman's queering of all of the structures of poetics we have surveyed—of apostrophe, of personification, and of course of prosody—extended rather than departed from the poetics that surrounded him. His adoption of the figure of the Poetess enabled that extensive summation, since Whitman learned how to give his exaggerated performance of becoming all of us—Black and White, men and women, rich and poor—from the Poetess verse that specialized in such performances.

That account of Whitman is the stuff of another book. What is important to note here is that Whitman's verse was very much a performance of *White* Poetess poetics, despite its affinities with Black Romanticism. If this were a different book, I would devote this chapter to at least some of the White poets who made Poetess verse the most popular verse of the first half of the century—to anonymous and obscure as well as famous poets like Lydia Howard Huntley Sigourney, whom Kerry Larson describes as "the country's best-selling poet through the 1820s and 1830s," the poet of whom Nina Baym so memorably wrote that if she "had not existed, it would have been necessary to invent her. In fact, she *was* invented."[5] What Baym meant was that as so many women poets began to publish in the first decades of the nineteenth century, "one of their number would inevitably be construed as an epitome of the phenomenon of female authorship" (385). Sigourney's position as "epitome" of feminized poetics did allow her to compose a fierce response to Bryant's genocidal White poetics in her 1841 *Pocahontas*, a verse epic in the same Spenserian stanza that Bryant had adapted from its British Romantic uses in "The Ages" (1821), a meta-Poetess poem that, like so many Poetess poems, represents its titular subject as herself a Poetess. But as Baym indicated, Sigourney was only one of the most visible of the White women poets who published in such profusion in the nineteenth century that, as Socarides has argued, their poetry "was always-already everywhere and nowhere," since as Richards puts it, "the 'poetess' tradition . . . has long been associated with the generic repetition of feminine forms that silence women's attempts to speak as anyone in particular."[6] If that nowhere-yet-everywhere, no-one-in-particular phenomenology of Poetess address sounds a lot like the phenomenology I have attributed to lyric address, that is because, as Richards has so convincingly shown, "the uncanny affinity between poetesses and lyric media marked them as vehicles of cultural transmission. Instead of inscribing their future reception under their proper names, the poetesses grounded their 'fictions of form' in ephemerality, self-dissolution, and ventriloquy."[7] As I have suggested, such dissolution of individual voices into ventriloquized speech would come to define modern lyric, but in the early nineteenth century especially, this disappearing act had the effect of making women poets seem less present than they actually were, since to quote Socarides once again, "erasure was not merely something that was done to women poets, but the result of a set of conventions that once made the circulation of their poetry possible in the first place" (3). Prins, Lootens, Socarides, Jennifer Putzi, Larson, Bennett, Mary Louise Kete, Loeffelholz, Richards, Cristanne Miller, Caroline Gelmi, Elizabeth Renker, Barrett, Eric Gardner, Robert Dale Parker, Monique-Adelle Callahan, Sorby, Jess Roberts, and other scholars of nineteenth-century American women's poetics have done crucial work in making this poetry and its conventions visible, and my argument here owes much to the field we have created together. As Putzi and Socarides write in *A History of Nineteenth-Century American Women's Poetry*, the reconstruction of the history of American women's poetry has signaled "the need for continued revision to the broader paradigms that shape American literary history on the whole."[8] Richards in particular has revised those paradigms by suggesting that Poe was a Poetess, since he was "a male genius figure who impersonate[d] women poets," a figure who allows us to see the ways in which women poets themselves "personif[ied] mimesis."[9] Poe's meta-performance of Poetess meta-performances anticipated and paralleled Whitman's, and these and other nineteenth-century poets' adoption of the Poetess poetics of abstract personification indeed revised the separability of genders, genres, and sexualities.

And races. When Poe and Whitman borrowed the capaciousness of White Poetess poetics, they also borrowed the Poetess's way of resolving racial conflict by absorbing it in person: Sigourney's Pocahontas (1841) dies before she can see the destruction and displacement of her people (which the Poetess recounts in a sweeping final "farewell"), Elizabeth Oakes Smith's "Sinless Child" (1842) sympathizes with all the suffering around her until she dies the night before her own wedding (lest she be transformed from innocent child into adult sexualized woman), Maria White Lowell's "Slave Mother" (1853) prays that her own unowned baby will die, Helen Hunt Jackson's "Story of Boon" (1874) recounts the tale of a woman who impersonates a Siamese sexual slave in order to save the life of her husband and is tortured to death—the catalogue of Poetess performances of personal absorption of and sacrifice to cultural violence goes on and on. In Poetess verse, the intimacies between gender, sexuality, class, and race became intimate indeed. The tendency of White Poetess verse to resolve those intimacies in the annihilation of the women already doomed by them made the Poetess a highly charged specific vacancy in the work of a wide range of poets, a generic figure for the missing person I have located at the heart of nineteenth-century lyricization. Rather than recapitulate the work I and others have done on White women Poetesses, here I want to consider how that overdetermined figure worked in the careers of two apparently very different poets: the Black feminist activist Frances Ellen

Watkins Harper and the White Harvard Professor and best-selling poet of the American nineteenth century, Henry Wadsworth Longfellow.

The fact that these poets would seem to have so little in common is part of my point. While Longfellow himself personified White institutions of poetry in the nineteenth century, Watkins Harper's poetry was aimed against White institutions of poetry and of everything else. While Watkins Harper used the Poetess to frame and objectify the emerging fiction of the lyric speaker in order to work outside that frame, Longfellow used the Poetess to ventriloquize his poems as the voice of everyone and no one, replacing the Poetess's disappearing acts with his own occluded presence in the center of that frame. As work on nineteenth-century American poetics has expanded, these poets have become important to separate histories, but rarely to the same one: as scholars have begun to acknowledge, Watkins Harper was the most influential and most politically radical Black feminist poet of the nineteenth century, and as scholars have long acknowledged but have insufficiently explored, Longfellow was the most influential and least politically radical White poet of the nineteenth century. While Watkins Harper contributed to the process of lyricization by staging a lifelong critique of its effects, Longfellow was, as Poe wrote, "the GREAT MOGUL" of nineteenth-century lyricizers (Poe's word was "imitators"), since he appropriated and remixed not only all contemporary verse genres but also personally laid claim to all of Western literary history in his establishment of the modern discipline of Comparative Literature at Harvard in the 1840s. Both poets relied on the figure of the Poetess to turn genres of poems into genres of persons—but Watkins Harper, even more explicitly than the other Black Romantics we have surveyed, created a poetics devoted to exploding and replacing the racist versions of White feminized personal abstraction that Longfellow coined as the future of modern poetics. By putting these two histories of American poetics together—or really, by considering them as strands in the same history—I hope to demonstrate the ways in which, as Prins writes, the Poetess is "a shifting aesthetic category that is closely linked to historical transformations in modern reading practices," especially to the historical transformation of lyric reading as modern racialized practice.[10]

In order to show how and why, for these as for so many nineteenth-century American poets, the Poetess became a vehicle of racialized lyricization—a mode of cultural transmission, a mediating figure that turned various genres into the specific vacancy of the feminized and vanishing abstract person that would become a template for the modern lyric speaker—this chapter cuts back and forth between Watkins Harper's Black resignification of the Poetess and Longfellow's adoption of the figure. I will begin with a slow reading of "Eva's Farewell," a small lyric written by Frances Watkins in 1854 before she acquired her married name, a reading that will open onto Elizabeth Oakes Smith's "The Sinless Child" (1842), the White Poetess poem from which Longfellow's first popular verse epic *Evangeline: A Tale of Acadie* (1847) also adopted the Poetess's talent for self-erasure. If Watkins's poem contained an implicit critique of both Oakes Smith's White Poetess performance and Longfellow's performative appropriation of the figure, it was explicitly based on the famous scene of the death of "Little Eva" from *Uncle Tom's Cabin* (1852), a novel itself indebted to both Oakes Smith's and Longfellow's innocent White Evangelines. That *mise en abyme* of fictional White feminized innocence was central to all of Longfellow's best-selling poetry, which turned particular verse genres into open-access abstractions of those genres. It was also central to his World Literature project at Harvard, which turned all Western literary traditions into one big, lyricized tradition of White poetics that eventuated in the poetry and scholarship of Longfellow himself. By adopting the trope of the Poetess as figure for his own authorship, Longfellow managed to make that authorship and that tradition appear to belong to *us* rather than to the man Poe liked to print-shout at as "PROFESSOR LONGFELLOW."

I will end by arguing that the influential if unacknowledged consequences of Longfellow's Poetess poetics have obscured the alternative lyricism that Watkins invented around the same time, a lyricism that circumvents and disorganizes the persona of the speaker that would become the basis of modern lyric reading. By turning back to "Eva's Farewell," and then, in a coda, to Watkins's early published poem, "Ethiopia," I will try to discern the expressive outlines of a version of Watkins Harper's poetics that has been hiding all along in plain sight, a version that demands, as Rusert puts it, a "reading method that attempts to run alongside and keep up with the frenzied and dynamic experiments of early black writing and performance."[11] If this split screen promises to be dizzying, that vertigo seems an appropriate response to the racialized conditions of mid-nineteenth-century American poetics, conditions that eventuated in the invention of American lyric.

Eva's Farewell

If, as McGill writes, "critical attention to Harper's fiction and postwar activism has largely eclipsed her antebellum career as a poet and abolitionist," that may be partly because "insofar as 'Frances Ellen Watkins Harper' names a consolidated body of writing, it assimilates her early work to the norms of late nineteenth-century authorship and insists on a single identity across the radical personal and political changes of midcentury."[12] That insistence is ill suited to this writer's early materially miscellaneous and chronologically varying genres and media, McGill argues, and I would add that Watkins Harper's poetry has also proven difficult to assimilate to the norms of modern lyric reading, which has come to insist on a single definition of poetry attached to a single identity across a range of genres, media, and centuries. In fact, Watkins Harper's poetry falls so far outside those norms that early twentieth-century Black literary historians tended to discount her poetry altogether: Benjamin Brawley's *The Negro in Literature and Art in the United States* (1918) devotes barely a page to it, dismissing all the poems as "decidedly lacking in technique"; Redding's 1939 *To Make a Poet Black* laments that Watkins Harper "was apt to gush with pathetic sentimentality over such subjects as wronged innocence, the evils of strong drink, and the blessed state of childhood"; and though Johnson's 1922 *Book of American Negro Poetry* grants that the poems represent "an expression of a sense of wrong and injustice," in his view, all Black poets between Wheatley and Dunbar, especially Watkins Harper, "must be considered more in light of what they attempted than of what they accomplished."[13]

Recent scholarship on Watkins Harper has certainly given the poet more credit, but the early poetry still seems to pose real challenges to readers who think of all poetry as aesthetically elevated personal expression. Frances Smith Foster, whose remarkable scholarship has made the poems newly available to new generations of readers, writes that in her poems before the war, Watkins "played her audience, used her poetry to strike chords of sentiment, to improvise upon familiar themes, and thereby, to create songs more in harmony with what she knew as the dictates of Christianity and democracy. Esoteric displays of technical virtuosity were not only unnecessary but could be detrimental."[14] According to Foster, such concessions became less necessary after the war, when "Frances Harper was performing as an unofficial African-American Poet Laureate," since by then she could address her poetry to an increasingly Black readership.[15] Rebecka Rutledge Fisher and Monique-Adelle Callahan have followed Foster's lead in making ambitious claims for the Reconstruction poetry: Fisher suggests that the vernacular dialect of the "Aunt Chloe" poems in *Sketches of Southern Life* (1872) "seeks redress through its own enunciation and actually reconfigures the possibilities of poetry as representational potentiality," while Callahan suggests that "Harper's work leads us to interrogate poetry as a form of transnational (that is, global) currency—an art form whose emphasis on imagery and linguistic precision provides the building blocks for a restructuring of the symbolic and ideological constructs of national histories."[16]

As the ambitions of Watkins Harper's Reconstruction poetry have become more apparent, according to the very logic of authorial continuity McGill challenges, readers have returned to the antebellum poetry and discovered it to be less harmonious and more politically charged than previously thought. Sandler and Derek Spires both emphasize Watkins's involvement in the Free Produce movement in the late 1850s, which Sandler succinctly describes as "an abolitionist effort to create a marketplace for goods made without the assistance of enforced labor," a "conversion" to practical political economics that Spires suggests Harper experienced on reading Solomon Northrup's *12 Years A Slave* (1854).[17] After that conversion, Spires argues that Watkins Harper moved beyond the "dominant antislavery sentimentalism" that characterized her first two volumes of poems, increasingly embracing a more proactively Black "revolutionary citizenship."[18] These are all steps in the right direction, but it is still worth wondering how and why Watkins's most sentimental early Poetess poems have seemed to so many critics either deficient in "displays of technical virtuosity" or strategically naïve. Wilson is the exception here, suggesting that Watkins's early poetry "sought to ventriloquize her voice through other bodies and form a cadre of interlocutors" (a provocative suggestion to which we will return), but why do most literary critics tend to understand poetic technique as incommensurate with the ability to "strike chords of sentiment"?[19] How might recognizing the ways in which Watkins Harper's "texts carry a particular power to simultaneously describe and defy the limits of Poetess performance itself," as Lootens puts it, expose the limitations of not only the literary critical consensus about how to read the voice of her early poetry but also the literary critical consensus about how to read *poetry's* voice?[20]

Consider "Eva's Farewell," a small poem on which no literary critic has ever commented (figure 5.1). These four quatrains appeared in *Frederick Douglass' Paper* on March 31, 1854, and were reprinted as the final poem in *Poems on Miscellaneous Subjects* the same year—about three years before the publication of *Les Fleurs du Mal*.[21] I reprint the image from Douglass's paper in order to emphasize the ephemerality of this poem's first appearance, but as McGill has discovered, that ephemerality did not belong only to the punctual publication

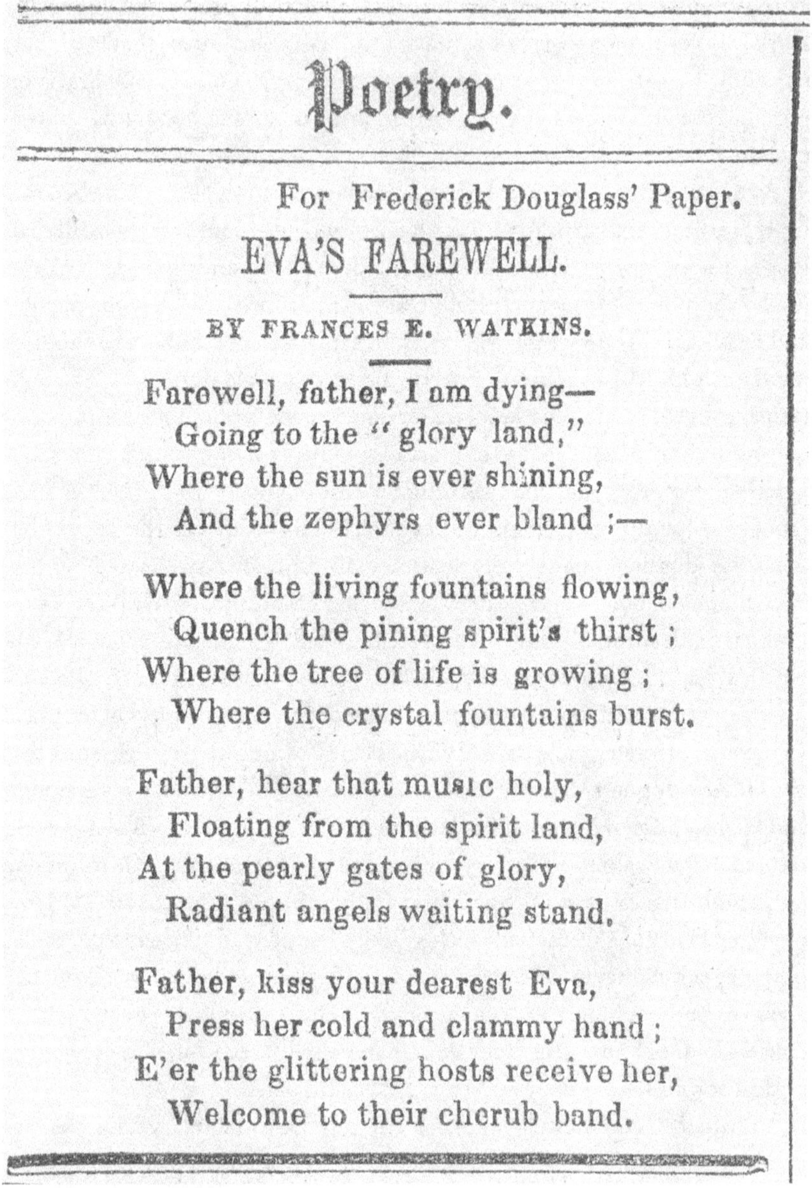

Poetry.

For Frederick Douglass' Paper.
EVA'S FAREWELL.

BY FRANCES E. WATKINS.

Farewell, father, I am dying—
  Going to the " glory land,"
Where the sun is ever shining,
  And the zephyrs ever bland ;—

Where the living fountains flowing,
  Quench the pining spirit's thirst ;
Where the tree of life is growing ;
  Where the crystal fountains burst.

Father, hear that music holy,
  Floating from the spirit land,
At the pearly gates of glory,
  Radiant angels waiting stand.

Father, kiss your dearest Eva,
  Press her cold and clammy hand ;
E'er the glittering hosts receive her,
  Welcome to their cherub band.

FIGURE 5.1. Frances Ellen Watkins, "Eva's Farewell," *Frederick Douglass' Paper,*
March 31, 1854. Photograph courtesy of the American Antiquarian Society.

of the paper, since to call the 1854 book in which "Eva's Farewell" would appear a "book" is to ignore the ways in which it "is more of a pamphlet than a book":

> It is composed of three signatures (forty-eight pages) sewn in a stab binding with a pasted-on paper cover. . . . Published in small print runs in successive batches to be given away or sold at her antislavery lectures, with no copyright notice overleaf, *Poems on Miscellaneous Subjects* bears in its format the traces of a strong relationship to oral performance—to the punctual meetings of reformers bent on miscellaneous reforms that were brought under the umbrella of antislavery, and to the songs that were sung and the songsters that provided a text held in common at these meetings.[22]

In fact, it seems that Watkins's first two books of poetry originated in such formats, marking them as part of not only their immediate occasions but of the publics that made up such occasions. As Johanna Ortner has recently discovered, *Forest Leaves*, Watkins's first book of poems published in Baltimore in the late 1840s, was "lost" for over a century and a half because it looks more like "a pamphlet" than "a book."[23] "Eva's Farewell" has met a similar fate: though it has been included in later reprints and collections of Watkins Harper's poems, this poem seems to belong so completely to its moment—to the profusion of early 1850s multigeneric reenactments of scenes from Stowe's novel, to the emerging Black public of Douglass's newspaper, to the various publics gathered to hear Watkins's political performances—that it has been thought to possess little of its own technical virtuosity or formal integrity. Even the close hermeneutic and pedagogical attention the poems have received since Foster's Feminist Press edition made them available in 1990 has apparently not been focused on "Eva's Farewell," at least not in the case of the anonymous student who annotated the pages of the copy I happened to buy (figure 5.2).

Granted that this is (like the spectral appearance of the Mnemosyne in my preface) at best anecdotal evidence that "Eva's Farewell" has been ignored by even the most devoted students of Watkins Harper's poetics, these pages illustrate the distance between this poem and modern habits of interpretation. Yet if its conventionality, the contingency of its media, its strict hymnal meter, its unoriginal subject matter, and its scene of address work together to make this poem appear to have more in common with "the songs that were sung and the songsters that provided a text in common" for historically specific publics than with transhistorically valuable mid-nineteenth-century lyrics addressed to individual readers located nowhere and everywhere, that may be

FIGURE 5.2. The author's copy of *A Brighter Coming Day: A Frances Ellen Watkins Harper Reader*, ed. Frances Smith Foster. New York: The Feminist Press at the City University of New York, 1990, 74–75.

because this poem's version of lyric is so easy to misrecognize. That ease has a lot to do with the ways in which "Eva's Farewell"—like so many Poetess poems, and so many of the poems in both *Forest Leaves* and *Poems on Miscellaneous Subjects*—takes the poetics of lyric misrecognition as its subject.

If the idea that a mid-nineteenth-century book of poems became a surprise best-seller despite (or perhaps because of) its manipulation of codes of lyric recognition and misrecognition sounds more like a description of *Les Fleurs du Mal* than of *Poems on Miscellaneous Subjects*, that may be because modern literary history has credited Baudelaire with the invention of modern lyric and has not credited Watkins Harper's early poetry with the creation of very much beyond what Johnson called a certain strategic "obviousness."[24] While Benjamin praised Baudelaire as a poet who "envisaged readers to whom the reading of lyric poetry would present difficulties," Watkins's early poetry has been forgiven for envisaging readers to whom the reading of generically feminine, sentimental lyric poetry came all too easily.[25] The miniature replay of what was already by 1854 an iconic scene from *Uncle Tom's Cabin* in "Eva's Farewell" typifies the genres Baldwin complained about in his famous essay about the book he called "Everybody's Protest Novel" (1955):

> Sentimentality, the ostentatious parading of excessive and spurious emotion, is the mark of dishonesty, the inability to feel; the wet eyes of the sentimentalist betray his aversion to experience, his fear of life, his arid heart; and is always, therefore, the signal of secret and violent inhumanity, the mask of cruelty.[26]

If Baldwin's judgment is particularly harsh, you must admit there is something creepy about "Eva's Farewell": in it, a little White girl who in the novel suffers and dies while imploring her enslaver father to alleviate Black suffering becomes the suffering figure with whom we are asked to sympathize. As if that's not enough, Eva is the speaker of this poem, addressing her father while we overhear her dying words in a near-perfect dramatic rendition of Mill's 1833 version of poetry as overheard speech. The racism of this particular triangulation of lyric address indeed feels violently inhumane, if commonly so. And perhaps that is the point. As Berlant wrote, while "the conventional reading of 'Everybody's Protest Novel' sees it as a violent rejection of the sentimental," since "sentimentality is associated with the feminine . . . with hollow and dishonest uses of feeling . . . and with an aversion to the real pain that real experience brings," it may also be the case that "for Baldwin, the narratives and forms of mass culture provide schooling in alternative worlds: its powerful texts do not bind him to the woundedness of his relegation to the inhuman, but provide the conditions to read as a utopian, a mapmaker for new conventions of expression and beyond."[27] What if Watkins was adopting a similarly dialectical view of femininized sentiment by appearing to embrace and inhabit the White mask of the Poetess, while actually creating alternative worlds? If so, then might her portrayal of the mass cultural persona of the dying Eva have provided the conditions for her—or for her publics—to imagine new conventions of lyric expression?

That rhetorical question may seem like a wishful and modernizing stretch, since everything about "Eva's Farewell" makes an argument in the other direction: rather than a Baldwinesque critique of the racial politics of sentimentalism, the poem seems a perfect representation of and for what Berlant calls "the first mass cultural intimate public in the United States," a form of "women's culture" distinguished "by a view that the people marked by femininity already have something in common."[28] The poem hails this White intimate mass feminized public in the voice of the character of little Evangeline herself—though that voice turns out to be a chorus. Both the hymnal meter and the illuminated landscape of Revelations 21 ("living fountains flowing," "pearly gates of glory," "radiant angels waiting," "glittering hosts") characterize that chorus as not only Evangeline's but as evangelical, despite the moment when the child Stowe called "the little evangelist" asks her father to "press her cold and clammy hand," a moment that threatens to bring this Protestant Feel Ethic up short in the last stanza. The dying Eva is certainly a White feminized creature of mass Christian culture, but perhaps the "obviousness" of that representation should make us a little suspicious. Whoever comprised this poem's publics in 1854—readers of Douglass's paper, readers of Watkins's "pamphlet," listeners to Watkins's famous oratorical performances, freed or fugitive enslaved people, Black intellectuals like Watkins who had never been enslaved, White abolitionists, readers who needed to be persuaded to embrace abolition, Christians who needed to be reminded of their duty, followers of the Douglass-Delany debate over whether Stowe was friend or foe to Black people (a debate published in the same paper in which "Little Eva" first appeared), Stowe groupies, Watkins groupies—we are not among them. Whoever this poem is addressed to, it is not addressed to us; whatever sentiments it expresses, it is hard to imagine Raymond Williams making an argument for them as *our* own structure of feeling.

Perhaps that is not only because of our historical distance from poems like "Eva's Farewell" but because these sentiments were never *anyone's* structure of feeling. The poem was part of a wave of poems and songs depicting Little Eva's death immediately following the publication of Stowe's novel—so many, in fact, that by 1854 "Eva's Farewell" would have been recognized immediately by those contemporary groups of readers not as a faithful rendition of Stowe's original but as yet another instance of the already well-established Death-of-Little-Eva genre. One of the first iterations of this genre also appeared in *Frederick Douglass' Paper*, published just above the July 23, 1852, installment of *Bleak House*. This earlier Eva lyric begins,

Dry the tears for holy Eva,
With the blessed angels leave her,
Of the form so sweet and fair
Give to earth the tender care.[29]

This poem by Whittier, the nation's premiere White antislavery poet, does not impersonate Eva, as Watkins's poem does; instead, it directly addresses what the paper's headnote describes as the novel's "legion" of sympathetic and now bereaved readers. By the time that Whittier's poem appeared, those readers could already be considered a public constituted by the form of address of the novel itself—a historical public of mourners for a fictional character. The poem is a consolation poem (another popular nineteenth-century verse genre) for Stowe's readers, who were as sad that they had finished the book as they were that Little Eva dies in that book. If publics are functions of genres of address, Whittier's poem is a testament to a new public newly hatched from Stowe's new genre. Whatever genres that public recognized before reading *Uncle Tom's Cabin*, it recognized itself in its own reflection in Whittier's poem, since, as Warner writes, "a public is a space of discourse organized by nothing other than discourse itself. It is autotelic: it exists only as the end for which books are published, shows broadcast, Web sites posted, speeches delivered, opinions produced. It exists *by virtue of being addressed.*"[30]

By addressing a public that had just come into existence in response to the address of Stowe's novel, Whittier's poem joined the *Uncle Tom* plays, pottery, dolls, paintings, songs, broadsides, and games in a networked media landscape that multiplied that address and so multiplied that public. This discourse network was also self-generating and autotelic: the headnote in Douglass's paper describes the poem as a "beautiful little song," and in fact the poem had just been published as sheet music with a score by Manuel Emilio for home recital (figure 5.3). Thanks to the University of Virginia site *UTC in American Culture*, you can listen to a performance of this song.[31] Meanwhile, a month after the publication of Whittier's poem in *Frederick Douglass' Paper*, an ad for the sheet music appeared in the paper next to a similar poem (also printed over an installment of *Bleak House*) titled "Eva's Parting." This Dying Eva poem, by Mary H. Collier, begins,

> I must leave you now, dear father—
>   I seek a fairer shore;
> O, might we go together,
>   Then we should part no more!
> Nay, never weep for Eva—
>   The Blessed calls me home,
> Not long shall we be severed,
>   For I know that you will come.[32]

FIGURE 5.3. "Little Eva, Uncle Tom's Guardian Angel." Sheet music. Boston: J. P. Jewett & Co., 1852. Special Collections, University of Virginia.

Collier's poem adopts the form of address that Watkins would use two years later, since this is Eva's dying speech to her father. Yet unlike Watkins's poem, Collier's poem (also published as sheet music in Boston in 1852) resembles Whittier's poem and song in depicting Eva as the "guardian angel" of Tom and by extension, of all the enslaved people held by the adults who adore her. Unlike the Eva in "Eva's Farewell," this Eva enters "the gates of glory" in the last stanza after asking her father to save Tom because Tom is also a father. Like Whittier's poem, this poem performs the difference between Black and White, enslaved people and enslavers, as a difference that can be bridged by Eva's sacrifice and our sympathy. Like Whittier's poem and Stowe's novel, that sac-

FIGURE 5.4. "Eva to Her Papa," words and music by
George C. Howard. New York: Horace Waters, 1854.
Special Collections, University of Virginia.

rifice and that sympathy enforce the racial difference that Eva's dying apos-
trophic address pretends to figuratively transcend.

With the first *Uncle Tom* play commissioned by George C. Howard and
written by George L. Aiken in 1852, the Death-of-Little-Eva genre became a
multimedia meme. The play starred Howard's four-year-old daughter, "Little
Cordelia Howard" as "the gentle Eva" (figure 5.4). The first version of the play
ended with Little Eva's death rather than with the death of Tom, and so ended
with another song that even more simply and explicitly pleads for Tom's free-
dom as Eva dies. Who could resist this pretty little White girl's appeal? Each

iteration of the Death-of-Little-Eva lyric meme instantiated the difference and distance between Eva and the enslaved people around her; each iteration of the Death-of-Little-Eva lyric meme helped to create a multimedia environment of racial difference, a mass cultural fiction of race. Each iteration of the Death-of-Little-Eva meme thus racialized the public its form of address brought into being, since that fiction required Eva to get whiter and more innocent and younger in every repetition, and it also required that the enslaved people for whom she suffered and died get blacker and more experienced—in particular, Topsy was rendered blacker and less innocent in each iteration. In one broadside ballad version written by Eliza Cook and taken up by the Hutchinson singers, the inhuman cruelty of the Topsy lyrics are suddenly and jarringly humanized by Little Eva's death, as the refrain of "Slavery, forever!" turns strangely to "Humanity, forever!" (figure 5.5). In the Howard production, Topsy was actually played by Little Cordelia Howard's mother in blackface, singing a song painfully titled "Oh! I'se so Wicked" (figure 5.6).

Karen Sánchez-Eppler has made the intriguing suggestion that Stowe may actually have given Topsy her name on the basis of the topsy-turvy doll that was popular before the war and indeed into the twentieth century, a doll that "is two dolls in one: when the long skirts of the elegant white girl are flipped over her head, where her feet should be there grins instead the stereotyped image of a wide-eyed" Black girl.[33] According to Sánchez-Eppler, "pairs of 'Topsy' and 'Little Eva' dolls were marketed by both Sears and Montgomery Ward during the 1930s, and as late as 1950 topsy-turvy versions of Stowe's characters were still being manufactured."[34] Thus the long afterlife of the mass cultural commodified fantasy of feminized racial difference that the figures of Eva and Topsy came to represent parallels rather exactly the afterlife of nineteenth-century fantasies of feminized racial difference in twentieth-century figures of lyric reading, as abstractions of persons came to determine abstractions of poems. The Death-of-Little-Eva meme graphically illustrates the dynamics of that double abstraction, and those dynamics make more sense of "Eva's Farewell": since by 1854, Eva had become the innocent White feminized personification of racial difference, it was that reified fantasy itself that the poem made speak. As Barbara Johnson put it, "the rhetorical figures [like apostrophe and personification] that confer on things some properties of persons" tend to be accompanied by "the parallel process of turning persons into things."[35] That process of reification or commodification makes things like the topsy-turvy doll seem to speak for themselves—not just in Marx's sense in which "the products of labour become commodities, social

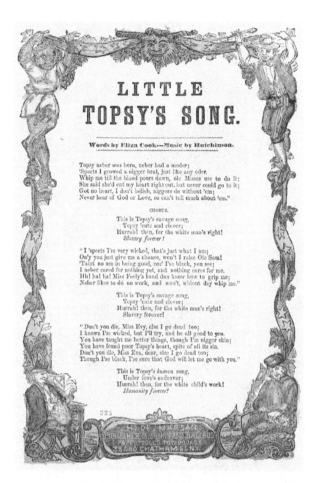

FIGURE 5.5. "Little Topsy's Song," words by Eliza Cook, music by Hutchinson. H. De Marsan, Publisher, 38 & 60, Chatham Street, New York.

things whose qualities are at the same time perceptible and imperceptible by the senses," but in the sense in which lyric poems are thought to "speak."[36] According to Johnson, this reverse process "does not offer itself in the form of a figure, but suggests that figures that increase humanness are by nature working against a decline of humanness and a thingification that go on all the time and have only accelerated with commodity capitalism" (23). Writing at a moment at which "the decline of humanness" had spiraled out of control with the acceleration of racial capitalism, Watkins wove the apostrophic structure of Romantic lyric into a personification of antiblackness that owed

FIGURE 5.6. "Oh! I'se so Wicked, As Sung by Mrs. G. C. Howard in Her Original Character of Topsy." Written by George Howard for performance in his company's dramatization of *Uncle Tom's Cabin*, and "Respectfully Dedicated to G. L. Aiken, Esq.," the author of the play. New York: Horace Waters, 1854. Courtesy Harvard Theatre Collection, The Houghton Library.

its popularity to its guise of White feminized innocence. She then framed that figure in a hymnal meter that would make its mask of cruelty look like a promise of redemption for us all.

We may now be in a better position to attend to what kind of lyric speaker Watkins's dying Eva is. By 1854, Eva was already a person who had been turned into a thing through mimetic, commodified iteration, reiteration, and performance. Of course, as a fictional character, she was never a person, but that fiction of a person had become so fixed by the moment of "Eva's Farewell" that she or it could become a caricature of the lyric speaker, an emerging fiction that Watkins, like Wheatley and Plato and Whitfield and Horton before her (and Dunbar after her), cast as inherently racist. Notice that in contrast to the other examples of the Death-of-Little-Eva genre we have just surveyed, Watkins's poem does not mention race or slavery at all. "Farewell, father! I am dying": Watkins counts on her readers to know the backstory about why Eva is dying, to know that she has been killed by the sins of her own father, by the sins of the peculiar institution of slavery, the wages of which she suffers vicariously. The context of her last words is so obvious that it goes without saying. Those readers would have known that by knowing the novel, of course, but they would also have known that Stowe's Little Eva was already a figure of White feminine vicarious suffering before Stowe made her one, since she shared her youth, her race, and her name with both the title character of Longfellow's blockbuster dactylic hexameter 1847 poem *Evangeline: A Tale of Acadie*, and with the title character of Elizabeth Oakes Smith's 1842 popular Wordsworthian poem, "The Sinless Child". Thus, in addition to voicing the many voices of an emerging mass culture of feminized racist representation, Watkins's Eva may also have been the voice of contemporary White poetics, especially of the poetics associated with the popular abstract form of the Poetess.

Accents Disconsolate

Ten years before Stowe launched Eva into mass cultural stardom, Elizabeth Oakes Smith's long narrative poem "The Sinless Child" was published in the *Southern Literary Messenger* and quickly became another kind of literary sensation altogether.[37] The central figure in the poem is little Eva (as in Stowe, short for Evangeline), a girl who trails clouds of glory,

> A fair-haired girl, of wondrous truth,
>   And blameless from a child,
> Gentle she was, and full of love,
>   With voice exceeding sweet,
> And eyes of dove-like tenderness,
>   Where joy and sadness meet.

(PART I, ll. 3–8)

The shift from past to present tense in Eva's introduction may be the price of a rhyme, or it may mark Eva's entitlement to lyric immortality. Reviewers immediately recognized Eva as close kin of Wordsworth's philosophic song, one critic writing that "the abstract theory developed [in "The Sinless Child"] partakes largely of Wordsworth's philosophy, but in its details, the story displays a fancifulness and glow wholly distinct from the bard of Rydal Mount."[38] "Fancifulness and glow" may or may not be terms of approbation, but the critic was right that the Wordsworthian and Schilleresque Romantic strains in Oakes Smith's poem were only half the story. The other half was the way the figure of Eva joined high Romanticism to sentimental White Poetess verse, since after hundreds of lines depicting the girlchild as perfect sympathetic interpreter of nature's various language, of her widowed mother's grief, of the misery of the poor and disabled, she dies on the eve of "the crowning grace of womanhood," her marriage. Before Eva can become Eve, "her sinless lips" are stilled; "the pure virgin of the soul" becomes at the end of the poem what she always already was, "the vestibule of Heaven," the personification of a poetic ideal.

We might call that ideal "woman" or "lyric" if the "Inscription" that prefaces the poem did not so explicitly make Eva the toggle switch between those terms, the "vestibule" of generically abstract Romantic identities:

> Sweet Eva! Shall I send thee forth, to other hearts to speak?
> With all thy timidness and love companionship to seek?
> Send thee with all thy abstract ways, thy more than earthly tone—
> An exile, dearest, send thee forth, thou, who art all mine own!
>
> Thou fond ideal! vital made, the trusting, earnest, true;
> Who fostered sacred, undefiled, my heart's pure, youthful dew;
> Thou woman-soul, all tender, meek, thou wilt not leave me now
> To bear alone the weary thoughts that stamp an aching brow!
> Yet go! I may not say farewell, for thou wilt not forsake,
> Thou'lt linger, Eva, wilt thou not, all hallowed thoughts to wake?
> Then go; and speak to kindred hearts in purity and truth;
> And win the spirit back again, to Love, and Peace and Youth.

(INSCRIPTION, ll. 1–12)

In these first lines, the poet apostrophizes the poem she has created in the name of the heroine of that poem. This conventional authorial apostrophe both animates Eva and deanimates her, since her "abstract ways" are acknowledged as properties of a poetic fiction, and so her personification must be purely poetic, too. That means that when she is told to "speak to kindred hearts," we know that she is not the one who is speaking. Who is, then? Richards suggests that Eva is "unable to assume a lyric subjectivity" and is therefore "the object rather than the subject of Oakes Smith's third-person narrative poem" (161). Given what I've just said about the later commodification of Stowe's derivative Eva, "object" seems about right, but Oakes Smith's "fond ideal" is not quite the reified figure of feminized lyric sentiment that Stowe's Eva would become. Instead, she is very much an evangelist, not for a strictly Christian message, but for a strictly poetic one. These lines say as much, but they also perform what they say: the fourteener or Latin heptameter structure of the lines in the Inscription presumes both early modern and classical literary ambitions, whereas the common meter of Eva's introduction makes her prosody as "earnest" as the child it describes. Speaking "to other hearts" and "to kindred hearts," Eva is charged with the message of "Love, and Peace, and Youth"—that is, Eva reminds the adult Poetess (whose "weary thoughts . . . stamp an aching brow") of an impossible state of innocence, a state associated with Eva's inhumanity, with her existence as purely poetic ideal. It is this ideal that bears the burden of an impossibly intimate speech. As Larson writes, Oakes Smith insists on "the link between poetry and a supreme Ideality," a link personified by Eva herself.[39] Eva's successful personification of that lyricized ideal made her both popular and portable: like the Poetess, she was an empty figure that could be turned toward different economies of value across rather than in the service of a range of highly charged literary genres. The racial politics that made an innocent White female child seem the perfect vehicle for vicarious personal expression depended on abstraction; the gender politics that made the Poetess seem an ideal representative of such expression also depended on abstraction. Those abstractions were driving forces in the lyricization of American poetry, a process in which ways of reading became more important than what one read, in which the social relations indexed by genre became the social relations transcended by an abstract poetic person—in this case, by a little White girl.[40]

No wonder, then, that the poet who made an academic profession as well as a best-selling body of poetry out of shifting the hierarchies of literary value by shifting the social relations attached to poetic genres adopted both Eva and the pose of the Poetess as his own. When Longfellow's friend Horace Conolly came to him and Nathaniel Hawthorne with the tale of a young woman caught in the eighteenth-century French Canadian diaspora, Longfellow took the idea and ran with it, creating the first of the long narrative, book-length poems that would by 1855 earn him enough money to retire from his position as Smith Professor of Belles Lettres at Harvard.[41] In *Evangeline: A Tale of Acadie* (1847), Longfellow blurred the familiar genre of epic verse narrative, effectively novelizing it, or at least making it very like the sentimental women's novels that his friend Hawthorne complained were flooding the market because of "that damned mob of scribbling women." The success of *Evangeline: A Tale of Acadie* thus drew on the already-established value of Longfellow's popular generic sources, but it also drew on the popular figure of the Poetess, and especially on the already-established character of Oakes Smith's "Sweet Eva" as lyric ideal. It also derived from a much less obviously popular and apparently unlikely source: its thousands of lines were all composed in dactylic hexameter, the meter of classical epic. Received history, narrative poem, sentimental novel, Poetess lyric, the prosody of the Western literary tradition: *Evangeline* collapsed all these genres into the abstract person of its title character, an innocent representative of "the beauty and strength of woman's devotion" and of the Poetess verse devoted to the idea that such devotion can save us all.

Before considering what that peculiar version of lyricization that did not eventuate in a lyric might mean for the gendered racialization of the larger nineteenth-century process, it's important to note that by 1847, Longfellow had already become quite adept at giving readers sophisticated lyricized versions of genres they already knew how to read. In 1840, for example, Longfellow finished "The Wreck of the Hesperus" and wrote to a friend in Rome that "the *National Ballad* is a virgin soil here in New England; and there are good materials. Beside[s] I have a great notion of working on *people's feelings*. I am going to have it printed on a sheet, and sold like *Varses*, with a coarse picture on it."[42] Though published in fancy magazines and a fancy edition of *Ballads and Other Poems* (indeed, as McGill points out, in so many other multimedia formats that it "became a ballad reimagined for mass culture") and never on a cheap broadside, the poem did indeed work on people's feelings, not only as a multimedia sensation and immediate popular favorite but as a standard text for memorization and required inclusion in anthologies of American poetry well into the twentieth century.[43] As an editor at Harper and Brothers wrote during the compilation of *The Home Book of Verse* in 1959, a "few poems like 'The Wreck of the Hesperus' . . . familiar to librarians, teachers and parents from their own childhoods—seem to us really essential: as sugar to catch flies."[44]

The poem that Longfellow joked might be marketed as a broadside ballad *did* come to be marketed over a century later as a National Ballad, as a poem all Americans had in common by the middle of the twentieth century. The irony of this history is that the ballad was not "virgin soil" in New England in 1840. Whittier had been printing literary versions of ballads for over a decade in New England newspapers by the time Longfellow wrote his poem, and of course, broadside ballads had circulated widely in early America since the late seventeenth century, becoming the most popular print genre in the Republic of Letters by the late eighteenth century. Longfellow was not, then, just expressing his "gusto at the prospect of sending his poetry further down the social ladder," as one of his twentieth-century editors has commented, but was expressing his desire to have his poem received as if it were one of the people's "*Varses*" rather than as a poem by Harvard's Professor Longfellow.[45] Longfellow's strategy was to make that *as if* make all the difference, since everyone knew it *was* a poem by Professor Longfellow that looked like a broadside ballad. Longfellow's readers knew how to read ballads, but also felt as if they had special skills in recognizing that "The Wreck of the Hesperus" was not just any broadside ballad. Longfellow's strategy worked. His faux-broadside-ballad came to be treated as a popular ballad by popular demand and his imitation of a genre that had long done many kinds of work across many early American verse cultures came to replace the genre it imitated.

If Longfellow's lyricization of the broadside ballad in "The Wreck of the Hesperus" was exemplary of his ability to adapt a traditional verse genre for his own purposes, it was just a detail in the much larger picture of his lyricizing project. "A Psalm of Life," the poem Longfellow first published in 1838 that became what one scholar calls "the most popular poem ever written in English," bore the subtitle "What the Heart of the Young Man Said to the Psalmist."[46] If twentieth- and twenty-first-century American readers have tended to forget that broadside ballads were the common national American reading matter of the eighteenth and early nineteenth centuries, they have also forgotten that psalm translation, imitation, adaptation and recitation was a national pastime during most of the seventeenth, eighteenth, and early nineteenth centuries. Longfellow's "young man" begins with the now-famous lines (currently reprinted on boxes of Celestial Seasonings herbal tea),

Tell me not, in mournful numbers,
    Life is just an empty dream!
For the soul is dead that slumbers,
    And things are not what they seem.[47]

What his heart is responding to is what everyone in the nineteenth century would have recognized as not just theological doxa but as generic verse doxa: rather than, as in "The Wreck of the Hesperus," imitating a popular verse genre, in "A Psalm of Life" Longfellow framed a generic alternative to a popular verse genre. The "mournful numbers" of the 1640 Bay Psalm Book, for example, were strictly 8/6 quatrains; Longfellow's numbers are the only slightly different 8/7 quatrains, extending the hymnal pattern by just one beat in the alternating trimeter lines (an adjustment that had already become habitual in evangelical American psalmody and hymnody, which is why it shows up in "Eva's Farewell"). The effect of that single beat is to modernize early American psalm meter, thus literalizing in the structure of the poem the injunction of the sixth and seventh stanzas:

> Trust no Future, howe'er pleasant!
>   Let the dead Past bury its dead!
> Act,—act in the living Present!
>   Heart within, and God o'erhead!
>
> Lives of great men all remind us
>   We can make our lives sublime,
> And, departing, leave behind us
>   Footprints on the sands of time.

(WL, VOL. 1, 17)

The call to secular action fictively addressed to "the Psalmist" was directly addressed to readers who had learned to read and write by imitating and translating psalms. "The Wreck of the Hesperus" imitated and ultimately took the place of the broadside ballad in popular American reading culture, but "A Psalm of Life" explicitly posed as the alternative that culture should pursue. By reading the modern verse genre of "A Psalm of Life" rather than reading the common verse genres of popular psalms, Longfellow's American public was invited to imagine itself on the brink of a new and giddy literary practice that would transform everyday life—or would make everyday life make history. At the same time, the modern literary genre of Longfellow's "Psalm" reassured its public that it would do what psalms do, providing advice for living that could be taken away from its context and made portable and adaptable. In fact, Longfellow's "Psalm" takes the portability of its content as its subject, encouraging its readers to "be up and doing / With a heart for any fate"—quite literally any fate, since *what* readers are encouraged to do is left open, a blank order the reader is invited to fill. If psalms were used for many different purposes in early America, Longfellow's "Psalm" was made for all possible purposes, since it could be adapted to "any fate" at will. Longfellow's first hit single was not only framed as a secular alternative to devotional reading, but was itself the best possible example of such reading, since the reader could choose what sort of devotion to pursue. No wonder it is the most popular poem not translated from the Bible ever circulated in English.

Poems like "The Wreck of the Hesperus" and "Psalm of Life" do not just testify to Longfellow's position as "a gentry-class poet in a democratic land," as Matthew Gartner puts it; they also exemplify the winning strategy of all of Longfellow's poetry: it is verse that again and again claims to have been written by everyone and no one.[48] Part of the success of the new lyricized verse genre of *Evangeline* surely derived from the poem's insistence that it was not a poem written by Longfellow at all and that the story it told in the thousands (and thousands) of copies sold could not be found in any book:

> This is the forest primeval. The murmuring pines and the hemlocks,
> Bearded with moss, and in garments green, indistinct in the twilight,
> Stand like Druids of eld, with voices sad and prophetic,
> Stand like harpers hoar, with beards that rest on their bosoms.
> Loud from its rocky caverns, the deep-voiced neighboring ocean
> Speaks, and in accents disconsolate answers the wail of the forest.
>
> This is the forest primeval; but where are the hearts that beneath it
> Leaped like the roe, when he hears in the woodland the voice of the
> huntsman?
> Where is the thatch-roofed village, the home of Acadian farmers—
> Men whose lives glided on like rivers that water the woodlands,
> Darkened by shadows of earth, but reflecting an image of heaven?
> Waste are those pleasant farms, and the farmers forever departed!
> Scattered like dust and leaves, when the mighty blasts of October
> Seize them, and whirl them aloft, and sprinkle them far o'er the ocean.
> Naught but tradition remains of the beautiful village of Grand-Pré.
>
> Ye who believe in affection that hopes, and endures, and is patient,
> Ye who believe in the beauty and strength of woman's devotion,
> List to the mournful tradition, still sung by the pines of the forest;
> List to a Tale of Love in Acadie, home of the happy.

(WL, VOL. 2, 87–88)

Readers did respond in remarkable numbers to the poem that directly addressed them as a fiction of hearing a "mournful tradition" spoken by the trees in "voices sad and prophetic" in thousands of lines containing six perfectly dactylic three-beat feet each. By 1847, Longfellow had already convinced his readers that they could read modern poetry using old models; in *Evangeline*, Professor Longfellow began to teach readers that they no longer needed the old models in order to read their remains. Reading classical meter without having to learn to read Latin or Greek, Longfellow's expanding public also read that the violence of modern warfare and genocide could be understood as natural occurrences, that a community could be "scattered like dust and leaves," and survive only in the poem and the readers that keep "the mournful" tradition alive. As Evangeline journeys from Acadia down the Mississippi to Louisiana and then to Philadelphia, she traces a path from Old World social hierarchies to New World brotherly love, and though her story is tragic, its retelling (and rereading) made it the stuff of a new way of understanding American poetry. If Watkins Harper created a poem in which the fiction of racial difference acquired its own voice, Longfellow created a poetry in which no one has a voice, and thus the poem itself can claim to be the voice of no one and everyone.

Longfellow's most recent biographer writes that he became "the most famous writer in America" the year after *Evangeline*'s publication, but that the reason for the book's unprecedented success has been a matter of some debate.[49] I am suggesting that at least part of the book's appeal can be explained by its close affinity with Poetess verse, an affinity that allowed readers to recognize a kind of poetry they already knew how to read in a new and exciting form that convinced them that, like Evangeline, they could witness the ills of the 1840s "in affection that hopes, and endures, and is patient." Longfellow's Evangeline, like Oakes Smith's Eva, is "an exile" whose "abstract ways" and "more than earthly tone" carry her from place to place and from person to person, sympathizing with each and all—but unlike either Stowe's or Oakes Smith's Evangeline, Longfellow's Evangeline is herself nowhere and everywhere, since after the end of Part I, she is homeless. After the British invade "Acadie, home of the happy" and burn her village of Grand-Pré to the ground, her father dies of grief, and Evangeline's exile becomes abstract indeed, as she searches the American landscape for Gabriel, the man she was destined to marry in a place that no longer exists. This "exile without end, and without an example in story" allows Longfellow to keep his little Eva innocent without following Oakes Smith's precedent or Stowe's later example in killing her while she is still a child; it also allows him to give this innocent a lot of experience. The result is that while both Oakes Smith's and Stowe's Evas are figured as secular saints, Longfellow's Evangeline (known as "Sunshine of Saint Eulalie" in the lost Grand-Pré) becomes a French Canadian Catholic aging saint wandering across North America, fleeing Nova Scotia, floating down the Mississippi (famously, through Louisiana), crossing the prairies to the Ozarks and then traveling back to the northeast, ending up in Philadelphia during the yellow fever epidemic of 1793 (thirty-eight years after the Acadian expulsion). As she goes on her errant way, she ministers to everyone she meets, though she can do little for anyone (including herself) but listen.

In Philadelphia, as "the Sister of Mercy," Evangeline finally finds her Gabriel as he dies in her arms. As Gruesz writes, "the poem does not simply thematize territorial removal and the unassimilable loss of exile; it enacts them on the body of Evangeline."[50] That enactment makes Evangeline another sort of poetic ideal, a Poetess figure that pulls focus on the violence that surrounds her. But unlike other Poetess figures, Longfellow's Evangeline does not absorb that violence in order to resolve it through self-erasure: on the contrary, she is victim of or witness to war, Indigenous displacement, slavery (briefly, from a distance), western expansion, disease, and lots of incidental misery, but her presence has little or no effect on the people and events that surround her. Gruesz suggests that some of the poem's readers might have asked "as did Longfellow and many of his fellow members of the New England intelligentsia—whether their nation's behavior toward Mexico was any more defensible than the expulsions of the Acadians from their Eden, or whether its results would be any less tragic."[51] Kirstie Blair adds that "Evangeline's quest calls to mind three groups of displaced people, all of which loomed large in the American cultural imagination in this period. Firstly, she is compared to a pioneer travelling westwards. Secondly, there are comparisons between Evangeline and displaced Indian tribes, and finally, there are subtle suggestions that her situation parallels that of slaves forced to migrate to the plantations of the deep South."[52]

All of these contemporary conflicts surround the poem, yet Evangeline herself remains oddly untouched by the many forms of (often unacknowledged) violence and "pestilence" that her presence traces across the American landscape (even the yellow fever spares her). Because she embodies "affection that hopes, and endures, and is patient," after the drama of her expulsion from the place and life in which she was destined to "bring to her husband's house delight and abundance, / Filling it with love and the ruddy faces of children," there is no experience that can turn her innocence to either understanding of or resistance to the serial social antagonisms she registers but in which she never becomes enmeshed.

Evangeline's unusual ability to float above or through this chaotic landscape may have something to do with the unusual prosodic orderliness of her "tale." Longfellow himself acknowledged that "to a great many readers the metre must be a stumbling-block," but insisted that he

> could not avoid it. After long deliberation I adopted it as the only one for the kind of poem I wished to write; for it enabled me to speak of familiar household things better than the heroic measure, which some friends urged upon me. Like the flight of the swallow the hexameter soars and sinks at will; now grazing the ground in its long sweep, now losing itself in the clouds.[53]

While one might wonder how Evangeline's journey from disaster to disaster could be understood in terms of "familiar household things," what is striking in this description of hexameter is its lyrically birdlike naturalization of the quantitative meter that was notorious for *not* rolling off English tongues. As Prins writes, "the viability of writing verse in classical meters was an ongoing debate, if not an obsession, among poets and prosodists throughout the Victorian period."[54] This was so much the case that in his early twentieth-century three-volume *History of English Prosody*, George Saintsbury would complain about "the hexameter mania in the middle of the nineteenth century."[55] Longfellow's poem became one focus of that mania, as several British reviewers, including Arnold, objected that *Evangeline*'s hexameters are "much too dactylic," as Prins writes, "a debasement of English hexameter by an American poet who had been parodied in the press as 'Professor Long-and-short-fellow.'"[56]

American reviewers could be even more harsh: in a long essay that appeared in *The American Review* in February 1848, George W. Peck wrote that the hexameters of *Evangeline*

> are the counterparts of
> "Quadrupedante putrem sonitu quatit ungula campum."

> The consequence is, that each line is by itself, and rushes down with a doleful decadence that in a short time carries the reader's courage along with it.[57]

By turning Longfellow's hexameters into a sight-reading of Virgil's Latin, Peck was taking a cue from his close friend Poe, who had staged an increasingly heated defense against the influx of Longfellow's scholarly poetic currency between 1839 and 1845, a flurry that ended in Poe's accusation that Longfellow was "not only a servile imitator, but a most insolent literary thief."[58] Poe himself dubbed this exchange "the Little Longfellow War," and it flared up again in 1848 when Poe anticipated Arnold's complaint that the lines of *Evangeline* were "much too dactylic" by asking his reader to place "a copy of ancient hexameters side by side with a copy (in similar type) of such hexameters as Professor Long-fellow, or Professor Felton, or the Frongpondian Professors collectively, are in the shameful practice of composing 'on the model of the Greek,' [and] it will be seen that the latter (hexameters, not professors) are about one third longer *to the eye*, on an average, than the former."[59] The classicist Cornelius Conway Felton, friend of Longfellow and later president of Harvard, joins Longfellow in Poe's long list of pedants it is best to distrust: you don't need to read Greek to compare their pages to Greek pages in order to see that their hexameters are too long. "The more abundant dactyls make the difference," Poe explains, since "these eminent scholars" don't seem to understand that the hexameter "is a spondaic rhythm varied now and then by dactyls" rather than the other way around.[60] I have written elsewhere about Poe's characteristically perverse em-phasis on hexameter spondees, but the long and short of this particular instance of hexameter mania is that Poe used the prosody of *Evangeline* to accuse the Harvard scholars that Poe called "the Frogpondian Professors" of being so in-vested in their own cultural capital that they could not see the poetry right in front of them. Poe may or may not have been right about the spondees, but he *was* right about Longfellow's investment in a prosody in which there was much more at stake than the lyrical flight of a swallow.

What was this little prosody war all about? In England, Prins writes, "de-bates about translating dactylic hexameter—the metrical form associated with classical epic—were closely linked to the formation of a national literary cul-ture," since "with the rise of the British empire, as England was struggling to accommodate foreignness both within and beyond its national borders, the consolidation of a common language out of heterogeneous elements seemed especially urgent."[61] On this view, hexameter, of all meters, became a British national "metrical imaginary" because the idea that English poetry was the result of a continuous Western literary tradition kept the discordant threat of "foreign-ness" at bay. In the American context, what *Evangeline*'s hexameters kept at bay was different. As Gruesz argues, the poem is all about foreignness, not only the foreignness of Evangeline herself but the assimilated foreignness of the other refugees she encounters along the way, including the Shawnee woman who is a refugee in her own native land (a version of internalized foreignness Longfellow would take up as the central theme of *The Song of Hiawatha* in 1855). And since, as Gruesz writes, "Longfellow's journal entries during the writing of the poem provide suggestive connections between the poem and the news from the Mexican front," it may also be about America's other intimate and ongoing "foreign" war.[62] But it was also surely, as Poe suspected, about Longfellow's own Harvard pedagogy, specifically about Longfellow's attempt to establish a curriculum in modern languages that would complement the established Harvard curriculum in classical languages. Longfellow's early version of Comparative European Literature was based on the German notion of the *Weltliteratur*, or concert of world literatures that Longfellow borrowed from Goethe. This program encouraged the study of a wide variety of cultures with a view toward their progress in forming the synthetic world literature of modern America. As Aamir Mufti has suggested, this synthesis produced a modern version of world literature as a form of "*one-world thinking*," a way of "imagining the world as a *continuous and traversable space*."[63] Just before beginning *Evangeline* in 1847, Longfellow wrote in his journal that "much is said now-a-days of a national literature. Does it mean anything? Such a literature is the expression of national character. We have, or shall have, a composite one, embracing French, Spanish, Irish, English, Scotch, and German peculiarities. Whoever has within himself most of these is our truly national writer. In other words, whoever is the most universal is also the most national."[64] On one hand, Longfellow's understanding of American literature manages to both separate it from the British genealogy that was so conspicuous in Bryant, thus rendering American literature much more cosmopolitan in Longfellow's version than it was in the nationalist versions of so many of his contemporaries; on the other hand, his description of the "national" but also universal "composite" of that cosmopolitan literature is entirely White. If British hexameters promised to keep the empire safe from its non-Western inhabitants, American hexameters promised to keep America safe for its White inhabitants. Gartner notes approvingly that "Longfellow's poetry constructed safe places for women and men seeking shelter."[65] That approval echoes something rather odd that Emerson wrote to Longfellow in 1855: "I have always had one foremost satisfaction in reading your books,—that I am safe. I am in variously skillful hands, but first of all they are safe hands."[66]

Longfellow's pose as Poetess helped him foreground that feeling of safety, allowing him to keep his prosodically skillful manipulation of the structure of that safety in the background. At the end of *Evangeline*, the title character does not become a Poetess, but the poet certainly does:

Still stands the forest primeval; but under the shade of its branches
Dwells another race, with other customs and language.
Only along the shore of the mournful and misty Atlantic
Linger a few Acadian peasants, whose fathers from exile
Wandered back to their native land to die in its bosom.
In the fisherman's cot the wheel and the loom are still busy;
Maidens still wear their Norman caps and their kirtles of homespun,
And by the evening fire repeat Evangeline's story,
While from its rocky caverns the deep-voiced, neighboring ocean
Speaks, and in accents disconsolate answers the wail of the forest.

(WL, VOL. 2, 185–186)

"Thus change the forms of being": whereas in "The Prairies," Bryant's White Romantic male poet claims a theory that requires the extinction of cultures, in Longfellow's poetics, feminized cultures seem to fade away on their own. Though we know the violent history that has led to the replacement of one "race" by another in "the forest primeval," the poet remains oddly innocent of it, his abstract ways miming the perfect Poetess pose of self-erasure. The "deep-voiced, neighboring ocean" and "the wail of the forest" ventriloquize the final hexameters' "accents disconsolate," as if those voices and the maidens that "repeat Evangeline's story" together speak in the voice of the poem itself. It is this composite, universal, pure White lyric speech that Longfellow bequeathed so successfully to literary history that readers still seem to think he was not the one responsible for it.

On Longfellow's death in 1882, Whitman echoed this fiction when he hailed him as the "poet of the mellow twilight of the past in Italy, Germany, Spain, and in Northern Europe—poet of all sympathetic gentleness—and universal poet of women and young people."[67] Over a century later, Angus Fletcher compared the two and lamented that "as a poet, competing for attention in our modern age of anxiety and irony, Longfellow has fallen from his great height"; Dana Gioia (later chair of the National Endowment for the Arts) went further, complaining that "when a literary culture loses its ability to recognize and appreciate genuine poems like 'My Lost Youth' because they are too simple, it has surely traded too much of its innocence and openness for a shallow sophistication."[68] In the last decades of the nineteenth century, Whitman invoked Longfellow as antidote to a "materialistic, self-assertive, money-worshipping" American culture; in the last decade of the twentieth century, literary critics began to invoke Longfellow as antidote to an American literary critical culture that no longer takes poetry to heart, in which poetry has ceased, in Gioia's words, to exercise "a broad cultural influence that today seems more typical of movies or popular music than anything we might imagine possible for poetry."[69] In the first decade of the twenty-first century, Christoph Irmscher argued that we would all "benefit . . . from including Longfellow in the perennial debate about the death (or the survival) of poetry. His example will not only help us clarify what is really at stake . . . it will also give us a better understanding of the hierarchies that still affect us and our thinking about literature and the arts today."[70] I agree, but if we continue to receive Longfellow as the Poetess he pretended to be, as the voice of a vanished tradition that can "win the spirit back again, to Love, and Peace and Youth," we will continue not to see what the history of poetics he so successfully appropriated has done to us.

Unheard Music

Did Watkins Harper see what such influential renditions of White Poetess poetics could do to us? I think she did, since the Eva of "Eva's Farewell" so effectively ventriloquizes the voices of all three of the Evangelines that preceded her: when Eva begins to speak, she speaks as a composite of Oakes Smith's Romantic poetic ideal, Longfellow's appropriation of that ideal as poetry's communal speech, and Stowe's viral representative of both that ideal and its racialized communal imaginary. In all of those precedent poetic media sensations, Evangeline was the innocent White girl who suffered for others, a synecdoche for the Poetess's performance of vicarious sensibility. Because that figure was already embedded in a densely networked multimedia public sphere of print, sound, image, and performance by the middle of the nineteenth century, the readers of Watkins's 1854 poem in *Frederick Douglass' Paper* knew that they were not overhearing the child's private address to her father. They knew that they were reading a public document, the performance of another Poetess vicariously recording the ways in which the lyrical Poetess genre itself had been transformed into the Death-of-Little-Eva genre. Watkins's repetition of what was already a series of repetitions placed on display and signified on the ways in which the Eva genre became a vehicle for an increasingly divided public sphere in the years before the war. That sphere was also being made transatlantically, as an illustration titled "Eva's Farewell" for a fancy 1853 British edition of Stowe's novel indicates (figure 5.7).

EVA'S FAREWELL,

"I'm going to give you all a curl of my hair and when you look upon it think that I loved you and am gone to heaven, and that I want to see you all there."
Vide Uncle Toms Cabin.

FIGURE 5.7. Harriet Beecher Stowe, "Eva's Farewell." London: Printed & Published March 9th, 1853, by Stannard & Dixon, 7, Poland St. The caption reads: "I'm going to give you all a curl of my hair; and when you look upon it think that I loved you and am gone to heaven, and that I want to see you all there."

We don't have any record of Harper reciting "Eva's Farewell" in her political speeches, but it turns out that this little derivative fiercely generic poem also discloses, as McGill writes, "the complex relations of [Watkins Harper's early] poems, and of antislavery poetry more generally" to both visual and oral performance, and so despite—or really because of—its innocent appearance, it might actually help us "to recover the historical importance of the counterhistorical force of poetic address."[71] What would a *counter*-historical version of lyric address look like? Perhaps such a form of address is what Plato, Wheatley, Whitfield, Douglass, Horton, and Watkins Harper were all inventing out of the inherently antiblack apostrophic, personifying, prosodic, and gendered structures of poetics they worked within. That way of thinking about early Black poetics suggests that these poets were part of the Black radical tradition that Cedric Robinson describes when he writes that "harbored in the African diaspora there is a single historical identity that is in opposition to the systemic privations of racial capitalism."[72] I think that's true, but as we have seen, the poetics of a single tradition as vehicle for a single historical identity was the very poetics these poets' work so inventively opposed. In "Eva's Farewell," Watkins's radical Black feminist poetics responded to the White poetics of universal lyric speech by unraveling the idea that poetry expresses a single historical identity. As the process of lyricization in the middle of the nineteenth century began to fold all genres into a large genre of poetry associated with a generic person, began to turn all poems into a large, lyricized idea of poetry, Watkins began to reverse that process. Her counter-historical modern lyric poetics imagined an alternative to the speaking gimmick of racial capitalism that "Eva's Farewell" and the history of modern lyric reading (and, I hope, the many mass-produced images I have displayed here) place at the center of our attention.

By following McGill's lead in refusing to separate the poem from its media, its form from its content, print from reprint, embodied performance from print, or poet from poem, we can begin to see the subtle ways in which Watkins undid the lyricized illusion of a single composite historical identity that Longfellow turned into an institution, the ways in which she bound history to its dialectical companion as Eva was bound to Topsy, as fictions of whiteness were bound to fictions of blackness. History and counter-history, public and counter-public, Poetess and poem, whiteness and blackness occupy the same tiny textual body in "Eva's Farewell." As if its crowd of genres—novelistic character, popular song, newspaper poem, political pamphlet, Death-of-Little-Eva lyric, theatrical performance, doll, Poetess verse, antislavery speech—were not enough for one slight lyric, the body of this poem contains something else as well, but this something else is not exactly either a genre or a person. When Eva begins to speak, she does not beg for Uncle Tom's freedom or offer her golden curls to her servants, but instead invokes recollections of several songs at least some of Watkins's readers or listeners may have known. We do not know if this poem was ever performed or if it was,

---

EVA'S FAREWELL

FAREWELL, father ! I am a dying,
   Going to the " glory land,"
Where the sun is ever shining,
   And the zephyr's ever bland.

Where the living fountains flowing,
   Quench the pining spirit's thirst ;
Where the tree of life is growing,
   Where the crystal fountains burst.

Father ! hear that music holy
   Floating from the spirit land !
At the pearly gates of glory,
   Radiant angels waiting stand.

Father ! kiss your dearest Eva,
   Press her cold and clammy hand,
Ere the glittering hosts receive her,
   Welcome to their cherub band.

FIGURE 5.8. Frances Ellen Watkins, "Eva's Farewell," in Frances Ellen Watkins, *Poems on Miscellaneous Subjects.* Philadelphia: Merrihew and Thompson, printers, 1857. The Library of Congress, Washington, DC.

whether there might have been some kind of cue that would have alerted the audience to listen for these songs, but such a cue *may* have been placed in the 1857 edition of *Poems on Miscellaneous Subjects.* In this edition, Eva's first words have changed just slightly from the 1854 newspaper and pamphlet version of the poem (figure 5.8).

As you can see, in this subsequent (and more widely distributed) version of the poem, the first line has been revised to read, "Farewell, father! I am *a* dying" (emphasis added). The single phoneme's gesture toward the vernacular functions to confuse the whiteness of Little Eva with a "music holy" that seems (because it was) a world away from the musical versions of the Death-of-Little-Eva lyrics that formed the *Uncle Tom* discourse network. In this other world, music exaggerates what Wilson aptly calls the "polyphonic discourse system" that characterizes Watkins Harper's poetics as a whole.[73] By the second line, the quotation marks around "glory land" fully embrace that counter-discourse, a polyphony that begins to resonate somewhere off the page. One of those resonances might be the song variously known as "Glory, Glory," "When I Lay My Burden Down," and "Glory, Glory Hallelujah" (not to be confused with Julia Ward Howe's appropriation of that chorus in the "Battle Hymn of the Republic"), a song for which we have many generic names, though none of them quite fit. After the war, such songs were called "Negro Spirituals" (as in Johnson's 1925 *The Book of American Negro Spirituals*), though Watkins would probably have known them only as "the songs," or as church hymns. Watkins was a free urban woman, so her knowledge of these songs would have been cosmopolitan. That sophisticated distance may be hard for us to imagine, since by now these songs have become so intimately identified with the desire to hear an authentic expression of the sensibility of enslavement; we cannot now unknow them as the songs Du Bois would call "the sorrow songs," the songs to which Frederick Douglass, nine years before *Poems on Miscellaneous Subjects*, applied the adjectives "wild," "rude," and "incoherent," crediting them with his "first glimmering conception of the dehumanizing character of slavery."[74] What Eva says or sings to her father in "Eva's Farewell," in other words, may be a topsy-turvy performance of the music of what Du Bois would call half a century later *The Souls of Black Folk*—but that was after the turn into the twentieth century, when the color line had been drawn to stay and double consciousness was the hermeneutic of the future. In 1854, that future had not yet arrived, so to characterize the music in "Eva's Farewell" proleptically as *the* Black "spiritual" is not quite right, since as Cohen writes in *The Social Lives of Poems in Nineteenth-Century America*, that logic "depends upon substituting an *abstraction of race* . . . for an *abstraction of genre*." The problem with that logic is that "the meaning of spirituals, as well as their power to speak racial experience or transcend time and space, were produced by their circulation through specific institutions, networks, and discourses."[75] When Eva asks her father to "hear that music holy / Floating from the spirit land," she may be ventriloquizing another authorial cue, but that spirit land seems to contain many different kinds of music, and none of it occupies one authorial or textual body.

Once we place "Eva's Farewell" in the polyphonic discourse system that opens out from the unheard music between its lines, the prosody that we thought was so simple turns out to be very complex indeed. Almost every word in this lyric becomes a reverb or riff, as pieces of songs and fragments of sermons and shouts float in and out, never reproduced line by line but invoked as if spectral or offstage. For example, "glory land" might also invoke a hymn now known as "Over in the Glory Land," of which there were and are many versions.[76] Because it was part of a popular hymnal compiled by a Danish immigrant in Texas in 1906, the song has been attributed to James Acuff and Emmett Dean, though ethno-musicologists now think that the song is much older. No one knows for sure. Since its publication at the beginning of the twentieth century, the song has become a standard of New Orleans Black jazz as well as a standard in White Blue Grass performance—in other words, it has followed the raced lines laid out in the Eva lyric meme to the letter. Of the hundreds of versions I have now heard of this song and other songs containing some of the lyrics in this poem (including "Do Lord," which contains the line "I've got a home in glory land," of which I recommend both the Johnny Cash and Big Maybelle versions), of course none can reproduce the music that Watkins and some of her readers might have heard or almost heard between these lines. What we have left of that music are not authentic folk songs, and certainly not songs that coalesce in a single racialized voice, but late traces of a history that "Eva's Farewell" saw coming—a history of appropriation, of racial instantiation, of love and theft. The risks entailed in using folkloric sources collected in the later nineteenth and early twentieth centuries and performed in many places and times for many different reasons are daunting. As Posmentier has suggested, later theorists and collectors of Black cultural production like Du Bois and Hurston "established and maintained" Black lyric history and theory in their creation of "Black ethnographic archives," proving that the project can be worth those risks.[77] It is tempting to speculate that the songs within "Eva's Farewell" contribute to the formation of such an archive, of a single historical identity and genre, but that is not quite what happens in "Eva's Farewell."

These songs may not even have been part of the poem's original soundscape at all—for all we know, they did not exist in 1854. We do have traces of a field shout tied to the seventh line of the poem ("Where the tree of life is growing"), a freedom chant that we know predated Watkins Harper, thanks to the Smithsonian Folkways project.[78] It is tempting to locate that seventh line in such compelling lyricism, but again, Watkins was a free woman who may never have heard such shouts, though she probably heard displaced versions of them in Baltimore and Philadelphia. In the ninth line, the "music holy" may be a clue that we're supposed to be hearing something between the lines here, but then again it may not. By the eleventh line, we might also hear another genre of shout, the "march to heaven," in which the congregation was led through Revelations 21 and through "the pearly gates," a phrase sometimes used to describe the songs themselves, and perhaps used as code for the Underground Railroad. Watkins Harper did work with the Underground Railroad after she was unable to return to Maryland following the passage of the Fugitive Slave Law, so that association makes sense. Since Stowe's novel paid homage to Bunyan's *Pilgrim's Progress*, a text many enslaved and free people knew (and, as Isabel Hofmeyr has suggested, a text that some enslaved people may have known from missionaries in Africa), the pearly gates may also signify the pathetic freedom gained by the enslaved person who does *not* escape, the promise of Heaven's reward earned by the suffering of slavery itself.[79] That is Stowe's promise to Uncle Tom, who has no grave and whose death takes place offstage by torture: "His Lord knows where he lies, and will raise him up, immortal, to appear with him when he shall appear in His glory."[80]

By writing and circulating a poem that turned the Death-of-Little-Eva lyric into a vehicle for songs that Douglass memorably warned could only be understood "within the circle" of enslaved subjects, Watkins invoked a lyricism that escaped the generic limitations of her sources. Rather than reifying the distinction between Black and White, as the Eva meme surely did, Watkins's poem blurred the genres of the emerging racism as well as the emerging racist poetics that would follow the emancipation for which Stowe's Eva was the evangelist. By having her Eva enter a polyphonic discourse network punctuated by the soundscape of people who *had* been made into things, Watkins's poem in effect parodied the post-Hegelian model of the lyric, which is to say that in addition to the many things this now completely unread poem does, it offers us an alternative to the thoroughly Hegelian structure of contemporary lyric theory. Far more radically than Adorno's isolated and reified post-industrial alienated individuals, the people who were bought and sold in 1854 were commodities that *could* speak—not in Marx's metaphorical sense of desire and exchange but in words and song. But to whom were those words and songs addressed? Who could hear them?

The errant, fragmentary lyricism evoked in "Eva's Farewell" is more animate than was the multimedia environment sustained by the multiply commodified Eva lyric, but it is nowhere and everywhere in a very different sense than was nineteenth-century Poetess verse or than modern lyric would promise to become. Whereas Longfellow consolidated the entire Western literary tradition into his own feminized poetic identity, Watkins reified an already-reified figure for feminized poetic identity and created an alternative she invited an unconsolidated and disorganized counter-public to notice, or maybe just imagine. "Eva's Farewell" is not a poem that projects a voice or embodies a compelling or attractive individual consciousness, which we can then hear, or speak, or sing, or try on, or try out, as if it were our own—not unless you think that Eva really is the speaker of this poem. Watkins was not using the Eva genre as a minstrel performance of either Black or White collective recognition, as a mask for the genuine folk, and neither am I. On the other hand, Hegel's and Adorno's suspicion of folk genres was clearly not shared by Watkins: while Adorno had good reason in 1957 to reel away from the consequences of the fantasy of the *Volksgeist*, in 1857, Watkins had every reason to imagine that the songs her poem rang variations on were dying with the people who sang them. She did not objectify a lyric speaker to sing like Topsy as Eva's Black soul; instead, she invoked a world the poem could not represent or record, a disembodied poetry this little lyric could not contain, a music that Eva's infant cruelty could not completely obscure. Some of her readers and listeners may have tuned in to the ambient strains between the words that Eva speaks, and some of those readers and listeners would have known that those strains did not belong to one speaker or one poem or one tradition or one genre or one poet. In "Eva's Farewell," there are so many different forms of address condensed into four hymnal quatrains that what they produce is not an apostrophic or personified or prosodic or gendered or remembered voice but a map for new conventions of lyric expression. Now we just need to learn how to read that map, to trace the deep design of this poem's adventurous silence. This is what it means for a poetics to be historical. And emphatically modern.

The Prophecy

BETWEEN THE LATE EIGHTEENTH CENTURY and the middle of the nine-teenth century, as genres of poems began to be gradually and unevenly replaced by genres of persons, poetic reading publics generated by spontaneous collective generic recognition began to turn into poetic reading publics generated by individual vicarious identification. Over the next two centuries, genres of verse that everyone could recognize were replaced by genres of persons that everyone and no one could recognize. That gradual and uneven exchange would transform all poetry into lyric poetry. For most of the nineteenth century, the figure of the Poetess bridged the transition from verse genre to abstract lyric speaker, since as an explicitly figurative person, she could function as both the generic object of recognition and the personal subject of iden-tification—as both a kind of trans-poem and a kind of trans-person. As the final poem in *Poems on Miscellaneous Subjects*, "Eva's Farewell" split that differ-ence, code-switching between the White mass cultural genres of Evangeline poetics and the fugitive poetics of a Black surplus lyricism that left both the genre of the poem and the genre of the person in its wake. That little poem thus sums up the racialized poetic dialectic that has been the subject of this book: as Black poets abstracted the emerging genres of lyric personhood em-bedded in the discourses of antiblackness, White poets abstracted emerging genres of lyric personhood in order to claim them as their own. But Black poets then made a strange new poetics out of their reiterated alienation from that dialectic itself. This third level of abstraction is not so much a synthesis as it is the basis on which Black poetics, in antagonism with White poetics, pro-duced the conditions for lyricization, and particularly the conditions for the emergence of the abstract modern lyric speaker. In 1854, when this book ends, the production of those conditions was well under way, but it was also just beginning. As an urban queer White working-class poet, Walt Whitman

MRS. FRANCIS E. W. HARPER.

FIGURE C.1. Portrait, "Mrs. Frances E. W. Harper," engraving taken from *The Underground Railroad: A Record of Facts, Authentic Narratives, Letters, &c., Narrating the Hardships, Hair-Breadth Escapes and Death Struggles of the Slaves in their Efforts for Freedom, as Related by Themselves and Others, or Witnessed by the Author,* by William Still. Philadelphia: Porter & Coates, 1872. Courtesy of the American Antiquarian Society, Worcester, Massachusetts.

stepped into those conditions when he self-published the first edition of *Leaves of Grass* in 1855. He certainly assumed the capacious White lyric abstraction that Bryant and Longfellow institutionalized, but he also assumed the anti-institutional Black poetics of lyric misrecognition that Wheatley, Horton, Plato, Whitfield, Watkins Harper, and many other not-yet-rediscovered early Black poets had already made into the poetry of the future.

FIGURE C.2. Walt Whitman, front cover, *Leaves of Grass*, 1855.
Courtesy of the Houghton Library, Harvard University Special
Collections.

If we think of Whitman's *Leaves* as prefigured by *Forest Leaves*, Frances Watkins's recently rediscovered first volume of poetry that was published in Baltimore sometime in the latter 1840s, both parts of this claim begin to come into focus: the titles of both books adopt a common metaphor for pages in order to invite readers to think of those pages as parts of nature rather than as parts of us.[1] But both poets also knew that no reader would actually think that way—that given the commonplace nature of the gesture in the 1840s and 1850s, their titles would surround their inaugural pages with the aura of the

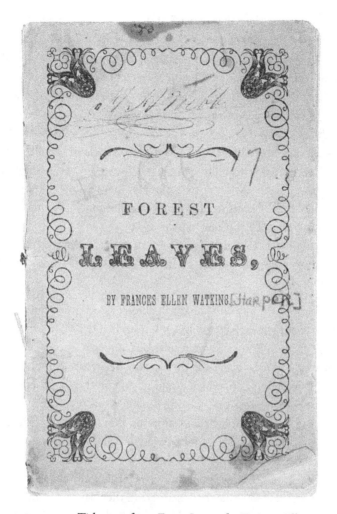

FIGURE C.3. Title page from *Forest Leaves*, by Frances Ellen
Watkins. Baltimore, Maryland, late 1840s. Courtesy of the
Maryland Historical Society [MP3.H294F].

contemporary literary pedigrees these poets did not yet have.[2] The fancy cover
that Whitman made for his *Leaves* makes that point clear (figure C.2). On the
other hand, the paper cover that Watkins did not make for her *Leaves* makes a
very different point (figure C.3). While Whitman (who never had any money)
designed and gold-stamped his branching leaves on green Morocco leather,
Watkins paid a local printer from her domestic servant's salary to produce her
paper-bound pamphlet, for which she probably did not have much choice of

font or decoration. The paper "cover" of the one extant copy of *Forest Leaves* is itself covered by traces of its transmission, by archivists' orange crayons, lead pencils, one green *x*, by someone's signature, by stray stains, and by a librarian's insertion of the poet's married name between square brackets. Unlike the marks, insertions, and autographs inside the rare remaining copies of Whitman's 1855 *Leaves* (the copy in Harvard's Houghton Library is signed by Emerson), the marks on this piece of old paper don't add up to much. This does not look like an important text on which to base any claim about the invention of American lyric. How might we read Watkins's poems as important not because they prefigure Whitman's, but because they tell a story about an invention that, like *Forest Leaves* itself, was itself so common—so transmissible— that it has been hidden all along in plain sight?

As Rusert phrases the question, in view of the open secret of the neglect of early Black print subjects and objects that Johanna Ortner's discovery of *Forest Leaves* exposes,

> might recovery narratives begin to tell different stories, beyond problematic origin narratives, and beyond presumptions that the significance of recovered works is always transparent, obvious, unquestionable? For example, in the case of *Forest Leaves*, is there a way to capture the significance of Harper's first book of poems without relying on the supposedly inherent importance of firstness, or following Kinohi Nishikawa's recent essay, without relying on the tautological assumption that a recovered work of literature is important because it was recovered? Moreover, how do we read an object of the early black print sphere that was published, but did not circulate widely, if at all? How should scholars talk about published works that were not circulated? Like manuscripts? In the terms of counter-publics? Nishikawa suggests that we should be also thinking about the condition of "lostness" of recovered texts, rather than seeking recognition for such works by immediately incorporating (re)discovered works into a predetermined canon, and its associated scholarly narratives. In the words of Leif Eckstrom, how do we know that we even know how to read a work like *Forest Leaves*?[3]

How indeed? My argument in this book has been that we do *not* know how to read a work like *Forest Leaves*, since the norms of lyric reading that Watkins and other early Black poets saw coming now make that work hard to see, even when the evidence of very different social practices, very different relational aesthetics, is staring right at you.

But I have also been arguing that these poets can school us in those prac-tices and those aesthetics, if, as Eckstrom suggests, we learn how to stare back. Consider one final lesson, the first poem in *Forest Leaves* and perhaps Watkins Harper's earliest poem (figure C.4). Everything about this poem seems com-monplace: the common meter, the common abolitionist rhetoric of tyranny, fetters, chains, and redemption, the common feminized, larger-than-life per-sonified figure of an undiscovered country in which such redemption would be possible. As Nadia Nurhussein writes, "whether invoked as a temporally distant primal nation, as an abstract nation of the black race or synecdoche for Africa in general, or as an imaginary locus of biblical or antique nostalgia, the figure of Ethiopia resonates throughout the African American literary tradi-tion." According to Nurhussein, its examples are common:

> Phillis Wheatley, in "To the University of Cambridge, in New-England," refers to herself as an "Ethiop," as does William J. Wilson, using the term as a *nom de plume* for contributions to *Frederick Douglass' Paper*, the *Weekly Anglo-African*, and the *Anglo-African Magazine*; Frances Ellen Watkins Harper and Paul Laurence Dunbar wrote poems entitled "Ethiopia" and "Ode to Ethiopia," respectively. However, as these examples illustrate, ref-erences to Ethiopia as an abstraction, as a metaphoric nationalizing of racial union, were far more common than references to Ethiopia as a con-temporary nation.[4]

On this view, Watkins's poem joins a "common" strain of eighteenth-and-nineteenth-century Black literary "references to Ethiopia as an abstraction." But what kind of common abstraction is "Ethiopia," exactly? And how does this poem frame that abstract undercommons as a scene of reading?[5]

Like many contemporary invocations of Ethiopia as "a metaphoric nation-alizing of racial union," Watkins's poem not only echoes but is structured by Psalms 68:31, the biblical verse that came to be known as "the Ethiopian prophecy." In the King James, Psalm 68:31 reads, "Princes shall come out of Egypt; Ethiopia shall soon stretch out her hands unto God." The verse was so ubiquitous in the eighteenth, nineteenth, and twentieth centuries that Albert Raboteau calls it "without doubt the most quoted verse in black religious history."[6] As Roy Kay has shown, the Ethiopian prophecy is not only a com-mon thread stitching together centuries of Black religious thought and what Nurhussein calls "the African American literary tradition," but also a com-mon thread running through a long history of Black revolutionary and Black nationalist discourse.[7] In eighteenth-century Prince Hall Freemasonry

FOREST LEAVES.

ETHIOPIA.

Yes, Ethiopia, yet shall stretch
Her bleeding hands abroad,
Her cry of agony shall reach
The burning throne of God.

The tyrant's yoke from off her neck,
His fetters from her soul,
The mighty hand of God shall break,
And spurn their vile control.

Redeem'd from dust and freed from chains
Her sons shall lift their eyes,
From cloud capt hills and verdant plains
Shall shouts of triumph rise.

Upon her dark despairing brow
Shall play a smile of peace,
For God hath bent unto her woe
And bade her sorrows cease.

'Neath sheltring vines and stately palms,
Shall laughing children play,
And aged sires with joyous psalms,
Shall gladden every day.

Secure by night, and blest by day
Shall pass her happy hours,
Nor human tigers hunt for prey
Within her peaceful bowers.

Then Ethiopia, stretch, Oh stretch
Thy bleeding hands abroad,
Thy cry of agony shall reach
And find redress from God.

FIGURE C.4. Frances Ellen Watkins, "Ethiopia," third page (and first poem) of *Forest Leaves*. Courtesy of the Maryland Historical Society [MP3.H294F].

(which, as we saw in chapter 2, both Whitfield and Delany invoked in their own revolutionary Black poetics in the middle of the nineteenth century), the verse was adopted as a figure for the Haitian Revolution, Ethiopia stretching her hands not just to God but "from a sink of slavery to freedom and equality" (Kay, 115). In David Walker's *Appeal to the Coloured Citizens of the World* (1829), the specter of Psalm 68:31 hovers over Walker's entire impassioned attempt to generate a revolutionary reading public, an attempt for which he was murdered:

> It is expected that all coloured men, women and children, of every nation, language and tongue under heaven, will try to procure a copy of this Appeal and read it, or get some one to read it to them, for it is designed more particularly for them. Let them remember, that though our cruel oppressors and murderers, may (if possible) treat us more cruel, as Pharaoh did the children of Israel, yet the God of the Ethiopeans, has been pleased to hear our moans in consequence of oppression; and the day of our redemption from abject wretchedness draweth near, when we shall be enabled, in the most extended sense of the word, to stretch forth our hands to the Lord our God, but there must be a willingness on our part, for God to do these things for us, for we may be assured that he will not take us by the hairs of our head against our will and desire, and drag us from our very, mean, low and abject condition.[8]

Walker takes the Ethiopian prophecy out of "her hands," placing it instead in "our hands," thus rendering the imaginary passive feminized figure for "racial union" an active, contemporary communal figure for racial revolution. When the young Frances Ellen Watkins took up Ethiopia's appeal as the opening piece in her first book of poems, she drew on all of these common threads, and she wove them into a poetics of Black feminist lyric collectivity that offered an alternative to the binary opposition between White mass media publics and Black fugitive songs she would go on to so spectacularly frame in "Eva's Farewell." This third path is the future-oriented activist stance she would maintain until her death in 1911, a poetics that answers Walker's appeal to and for a revolution in what is common.

The first stanza of "Ethiopia" might remind you of Whitfield's "YES! Strike Again That Sounding String!"—the poem that Matt Sandler calls "the period's most condensed statement of revolutionary Black lyric theory," published in the *North Star* on March 15, 1850. When I discussed that poem in chapter 2 on the figure of lyric apostrophe, I suggested that the poem reverses the way such apostrophes are supposed to work, since instead of animating their object of address, Whitfield's apostrophes try and fail to animate the subject of that address. Something similar happens in Watkins's "Ethiopia," where the initial "Yes!" may be a way of making the entire poem a dialectical response to Psalm 68:31. Rather than emphasizing the inevitability of the prophecy, the third word in the first line emphasizes its tentativeness: "yet." While Whitfield's poem is very much the poem of the angry male revolutionary, Watkins's poem is a Poetess poem, and like Plato's "To the First of August," it uses a large personification of feminized collective power to show how and why such personifications may disguise uncomfortable truths. As in all of Wheatley's poems, by the last quatrain of "Ethiopia," the personification in and of individual and collective racial union dissolves before our eyes, since this is what history has done to us. The poem is indeed "a particular kind of failure ... a constant economy and mechanics of fugitive making where the subject is hopelessly troubled by, in being emphatically detached from, the action whose agent it is supposed to be." When Watkins reprinted it in 1854 in *Poems on Miscellaneous Subjects*, she did not revise it, but let that dissolution and that detachment stand.

In "Ethiopia," it is not the poet who apostrophizes an imaginary, absent, or dead object or reading public her verse seeks to animate or inspire, but the impossibly abstract person of the poem itself that addresses a power that has not "yet" responded. Yet (so to speak) the second, third, fourth, fifth, and sixth common meter stanzas—that is, the body of the poem—describe a world in which that response *has* already arrived, in which Ethiopia's poetic appeal has done what David Walker's never did: it has produced a world in which Ethiopia can flourish, in which "our very, mean, low and abject condition" has been utterly transformed, in which the terms of antiblack interpellation have been transliterated. If the poem ended here, its horizon would be utopian, since Ethiopia would represent a landscape in which the barriers between poems and persons would have fallen. But that is not what happens in the final quatrain of this poem. Instead, Ethiopia's prophetically plaintive anthem returns, and, as in Horton's verse, Ethiopia shifts from subject to object of address, erupting in a "cry of agony" when forced to relinquish her own momentary transmutation and acknowledge her actual historical situation. This is not a scene of intersubjective confirmation of a self—in fact, it is not a scene of intersubjectivity at all. As Saidiya Hartman has written in a different context, "bound by the fetters of sentiment, held captive by the vestiges of the past, and

cast into a legal condition of subjection—these features limn the circum-
stances of an anomalous, misbegotten, and burdened subject no longer en-
slaved, but not yet free" ([1997], 206). Watkins's Ethiopia is not an innocent
White Poetess like Evangeline or a White Goddess like Mnemosyne or Britan-
nia, but a Black Poetess whose "bleeding hands" testify to her common experi-
ence. Yet the word that is like a bell in the last line of "Ethiopia" promises
something that Ann Plato's, Phillis Wheatley's, George Moses Horton's, and
James Monroe Whitfield's poems never promised. Is it a vision, or a waking
dream? The effect of this poem's final metalyrical address to the figure of Ethio-
pia itself is nothing less than a "redress": a conversion of abstract, apostrophic,
personified, prosodic, and feminized poetic subjection into a never-ending
lyricism of the surplus, an impossible speech that won't stop insisting that
things could be different, that keeps imagining a "then" upon the heels of that
"yet," that stretches toward a rearranged future in which genres of poems and
genres of persons could disappear or be changed at any moment by a muse,
by a goddess, by a star, by a dove of peace, by a girl refined into airy thinness,
by an iamb, by a couplet, by a suffering woman, by a poet, by an American
lyric.

ACKNOWLEDGMENTS

I AM FORTUNATE to have many people and places to thank, and to be able to do so in print. As this book shape-shifted from a book about nineteenth-century American poetry in public to a book about Black poets' interventions in late eighteenth- and early nineteenth-century American poetry in public, it (and I) required a lot of support. The National Endowment for the Humanities, Tufts University, the University of California, Irvine (UCI), and Princeton University all provided valuable research funding. The New York Public Library, the Houghton Library at Harvard, the American Antiquarian Society, the New York Historical Society, the Massachusetts Historical Society, and the British Library provided invaluable archival resources. Audiences at Princeton, Cornell, Johns Hopkins, the University of Chicago, Yale, the University of Cambridge, Northwestern University, the University of Michigan, the University of Notre Dame, SOAS, the University of Maryland, the University of Virginia, the University of Washington, Boston University, the University of Toronto, UCLA, UC Berkeley, UC Riverside, Aalborg University, and elsewhere have made this a much better book.

That is a way of saying that people have been more important than institutions in the development of this project, and it is to a crowd of remarkable individuals that I owe my deepest thanks. First, last, and always, the Historical Poetics Working Group is the lab in which these ideas have been generated and tested, and the HistPoes are also the ideal readers I imagine in my sleep. To Max Cavitch, Michael Cohen, Benjamin Friedlander, Mary Ellis Gibson, Erin Kappeler, Charles LaPorte, Naomi Levine, Tricia Lootens, Meredith Martin, Meredith McGill, Yopie Prins, Jason Rudy, Alexandra Socarides, and Carolyn Williams: *thank you!* For twenty years, our work together has been responsible for everything that is good about my work (the faults are all my own). You each and all know how much this book owes to each and all of you.

What is so mutually enabling about the HistPoes is our ongoing and life-long collaboration, a model of academic labor and joy that is all too rare in the Humanities. I have also been lucky to be able to collaborate with a stunning array of scholars in sustaining the institution known as The English Institute (EI). Frances Ferguson, Deborah Nelson, Sandra Macpherson, Sangeeta Ray, Kirsten Silva Gruesz, Jacqueline Goldsby, David Kurnick, Paul Saint-Amour, Martin Harries, Kyla Wazana Tompkins, of course Meredith McGill and Michael Warner, among so many others over the years, you should know that our conference each year keeps me going. Anne Savarese, my editor at Princeton University Press, has also kept me going. She is everything one dreams an editor could be—responsive, sensible, funny—and she has great ideas! I would also like to thank the two anonymous readers for the Press, who wrote reports that not only recognized this book's intentions but also brilliantly helped to sharpen their focus. In preparing the book for publication, I have had the support of the gifted Jennifer Harris, the ever-resourceful and patient Ellen Foos and Jaden Young, and the life-saving Claire Burdick and Kelana Johnson. No book is the product of only one person's labor.

At UCI, in addition to Rodrigo Lazo, my co-conspirator in all things nineteenth century, Michelle Latiolais, my co-conspirator in all things feminist, Jane Newman, my collaborator in all things comparative, and Rei Terada, my collaborator in all things theoretical, the people who have contributed most to my work are the wonderful group of graduate students I have had the privilege of working with and learning from. Anastasia Baginski, Michael Berlin, Claire Burdick, Fatima Burney, Ashley Call, Austin Carter, Jos Charles, Rose DuCharme, Anna Finn, Andrew Hill, Stephen Howard, Kelana Johnson, Nicholas Joseph, Sharon Kunde, Taylor McCabe, Dana Murphy, Jan Maramot Rodil, Kirsty Singer, Morgan Slade, Scotty Streitfield, Brandon Wild: you are all so awesome. Thank you.

Outside formal collaborations like HistPoe and EI, and settings like the Press and the university, I have also been lucky to collaborate with and be kept going by an enormous range of poets, scholars, and friends, not all of whom I can call by name in even the longest list: Laurien Alexandre, Michael Altman, Emily Apter, Norma Bowles, Suzan Bymel, Margaret Carr, Radiclani Clytus (and the members of the new Gun Cotton Collective), Peter Coviello, Pat Crain, Daniela Hernández Chong Cuy, Craig Dworkin, Lee Edelman, Lisa Gitelman, Jackie Goldsby, Stathis Gourgouris, Brent Hayes Edwards, Terrance Hayes, Diana Henderson, Jonathan Kramnick, Rodrigo Lazo, Joseph Litvak, Dana Luciano, Heather Lukes, Saloni Mathur, Molly McGarry, Sarah Mesle, Edward Mitchell, Aamir Mufti, Jane Newman, Alan Page, Neni Panourgiá, Andrew

Parker, Marjorie Perloff, Adela Pinch, Henrik Rehbinder, Matt Sandler, Caleb Smith, Stefanie Sobelle, Rei Terada, Tony Vidler, Ivy Wilson—you have all helped me so much. Michael Warner has the great gift of making all his friends smarter; he has made me smarter, too. Lauren Berlant had the gift of making all her friends pay attention. I am distracted by how much I miss her. Carolyn Williams can take one's thoughts and twist them around her own faster than anyone I have ever known. Meredith Martin makes me feel as if I can do anything, and that we can do even more together. Meredith McGill is the most generous intellectual friend anyone could have; I owe most of this book to conversations with her.

My lovely sister, Julia Valente, deserves a lot of credit for sustaining me through the writing of this book. I hereby give it to her (and to the great Frank Valente, who sustains us all). Our mother, Eunice Evelyn Mills Harris, passed away before she could see this book, but her shining example made everything possible. Bill Harris remains an example of how good a person can be. Karsten Harries, Elizabeth Langhorne, Lisa, Peter, Roman, Ute, and all of our collective kids have made me feel at home at last. This book is dedicated to Martin Harries, Sadye Walker, Walker Mills, and Yopie Prins. It is also dedicated to the memory of Elizabeth Wanning Harries. Betsey Harries also passed away just as this book began to see the light. I wish she were still around to read it, not least because you could always count on her to tell you exactly what she thought. She was the feminist teacher and scholar I aspire to be. Sadye and Walker have grown up while I was writing this book. I could not be prouder of the radiant, creative, loving people they have become. They are my daily inspiration, my dusk and my dawn. Like all my work, this book reflects a deep and lifelong collaboration with Yopie Prins, who anticipated every word I wrote and spelled it back to me, letter by letter; the words I have to thank her she already knows. I wish I had the words to thank Martin Harries. To say that he has made this book and my life possible is not to say half enough; it's a good thing that the other half we don't have to say. That said, I promise to spend the rest of my life trying.

Parts of chapter 2 first appeared in *Critical Inquiry* (Summer 2022, Volume 48, Number 4) and *Modern Language Quarterly* (September 2020, Volume 81, Number 3). Part of chapter 4 first appeared in *New Literary History* (Autumn 2018, Volume 49, Number 4). My thanks to these journals for permission to publish that material here.

NOTES

Preface. Mnemosyne

1. Phillis Wheatley, *The Writings of Phillis Wheatley*, ed. Carretta, 29. Carretta suggests that in Samuel Boyse, *A New Pantheon: Or, Fabulous History of the Heathen Gods, Heroes, Goddesses, &c . . .* (London 1753), Mneme was "the muse of memory, the daughter of Jupiter and Mnemosyne" (164), but given this poem's invocation of "ye sacred Nine," it seems more likely that "Mneme" is short for Mnemosyne herself.

2. In the order in which they appear in my sentence, these are the first lines of "Ode on a Grecian Urn" and "Bright star, would I were as steadfast as thou art" by John Keats (*Complete Poems*, 1982); "To a Skylark," by Percy Bysshe Shelley (*Complete Poetry*, 2000–); "To a Skylark," by William Wordsworth (*The Poems, Volume Two*, 1977); and "The Tyger," by William Blake (*The Complete Poems*, 2007).

3. Roughly in order, this list might include but not be limited to Roy Harvey Pearce, *The Continuity of American Poetry* (1961); F. O. Matthiessen, *American Renaissance: Art and Expression in the Age of Emerson and Whitman* (1941); Harold Bloom, *Poetry and Repression: Revisionism from Blake to Stevens* (1976); Charles Altieri, *Postmodernisms Now: New Essays on Contemporaneity in the Arts* (1998); and Jennifer Ashton, *From Modernism to Postmodernism: American Poetry and Theory in the Twentieth Century* (2005).

4. A notable exception to this rule would be George Hutchinson's admirable *The Harlem Renaissance in Black and White* (1995).

5. Joan R. Sherman, *Invisible Poets: Afro-Americans of the Nineteenth Century* (1974), xv. It has been almost fifty years since Sherman offered this provocation, and scholars of nineteenth-century poetics are just beginning to respond.

6. See especially Matt Sandler, *The Black Romantic Revolution: Abolitionist Poets at the End of Slavery* (2020), and Ivy Wilson, *Specters of Democracy: Blackness and the Aesthetics of Politics in the Antebellum U. S.* (2011). Several scholars have done important work on individual poets such as Watkins Harper and Horton, and Wilson has edited new collections of the work of both James Monroe Whitfield and Albery Allson Whitman, but what I mean here is that the reassessment of the range and variety of Black poetics in the period as a whole is just beginning.

7. On the historical formation of American literary studies, see Gerald Graff and Michael Warner, *Professing Literature: An Institutional History* (1987). On the project of undisciplining literary studies, see Ronjaunee Chatterjee, Alicia Mireles Christoff, and Amy R. Wong, "Undisciplining Victorian Studies" (2020).

8. On Wheatley's involvement in the arrangements for the publication of her book in London, see Vincent Carretta, *Phillis Wheatley: Biography of a Genius in Bondage* (2011), 85–108.

9. As Carretta explains, this letter was not exactly anonymous, since it was signed by one "L." and includes correspondence from "Your very humble servant, PHILLIS." See *Phillis Wheatley: Biography of a Genius in Bondage* (2011), 84–85.

10. June Jordan, "The Difficult Miracle of Black Poetry in America or Something Like a Sonnet for Phillis Wheatley" (1986), 257.

11. J. Saunders Redding, *To Make a Poet Black* (1939; 1988), 11.

12. Theodor Adorno, "On Lyric Poetry and Society" in *The Lyric Theory Reader* (2014), 344.

13. J. Paul Hunter, "Formalism and History: Binarism and the Anglophone Couplet" (2000), 119.

14. Hunter makes this point as well when he offers "what we might call an elementary reminder of intellectual history, what we might call the Hegelian Ghost, which hovers over antithetical structures for modern readers in a way it did not for Dryden, Rochester, Behn, and the generations that immediately followed them. Not Necessarily Synthesis might be our mantra when we hit these antitheses." "Formalism and History" (2000), 116.

15. Lisa Gitelman, *Paper Knowledge: Toward a Media History of Documents* (2014), 2. Gitelman's version of genre is actually a definition we have come up with together. See 151 n. 4 for her acknowledgment of our collaboration.

16. Reuben Brower, "The Speaking Voice" (1951; 2014), 213. It's worth noting that Brower's focus on "the voice we hear in a lyric" speaks volumes about that focus in the criticism of his students Helen Vendler and Paul de Man.

17. Max Cavitch, "The Poetry of Phillis Wheatley in Poetry's Recollective Economies" (2014), 221. We will come back to Cavitch's emphasis on nineteenth-century abolitionist editions of Wheatley, and on the Knapp edition in particular, in chapter 3.

18. M. A. Richmond, *Bid the Vassal Soar: Interpretive Essays on the Life and Poetry of Phillis Wheatley (ca. 1753–1784) and George Moses Horton (ca. 1797–1883)* (1974), xi, viii.

19. For "locus of impossible speech," see Saidiya Hartman, "Venus in Two Acts" (2008), 3. Hartman actually credits the phrase to Stephen Best in an unpublished essay, "The African Queen," 3 n. 8.

20. Ronald A. T. Judy, *(Dis)Forming the American Canon: African-Arabic Slave Narratives and the Vernacular* (1993), 1.

21. See Judy as well for what such a triangulation might mean for re- or un-reading Hegel via Kant as a model of European modernity. Moten's trilogy extends and re-imagines Judy's foundational insights, as does Rei Terada in her recent *Metaracial: Hegel, Antiblackness, and Political Identity* (2022).

22. Meredith McGill, *American Literature and the Culture of Reprinting, 1834–1853* (2003), 9. Karl Marx's discussion of commodity fetishism is the subject of the first chapter of *Capital, Volume One* (1867).

23. Honorée Fanonne Jeffers, *The Age of Phillis* (2020), 183. Cavitch makes the important point that Knapp was an incorporationist rather than a colonizationist, so this ideology shifts between the 1834 and 1838 editions.

24. Quoted in Robert C. Jones. Jr., "The Power of Books," *News@TheU*, University of Miami, Coral Gables, April 24, 2019: https://news.miami.edu/stories/2019/04/the-power-of-books.html.

Chapter One. What History Does to Us

1. James W. C. Pennington, "To the Reader," in *Essays; Including Biographies and Miscellaneous Pieces, in Prose and Poetry by Ann Plato* (1841; 1988), xvii.

2. Of course, the fact that you could be anyone is the definition of a public. As Michael Warner writes, "a public is a relation among strangers," even though "strangers can be treated as already belonging to our world. More: they must be." See *Publics and Counterpublics* (2002), 75. For a provocative reading of the importance of stranger intimacy to what he calls "antiracist stranger humanism," see Lloyd Pratt, *The Stranger's Book: The Human of African American Literature* (2016).

3. Frances Smith Foster *Written by Herself: Literary Production by African American Women, 1746–1892* (1993), 53. Fred Moten, *Black and Blur* (2017), vii. This is actually a condensation of the first sentences of the first book in Moten's trilogy, *consent not to be a single being*. These words describing Pennington's preface in my preface also preface Moten's work, and this "unremitting" series is actually prefaced by an essay by Nathaniel Mackey (as the title of Moten's trilogy is prefaced by a line from Édouard Glissant). Moten's unedited sentences read, "The essays in *Black and Blur* attempt a particular kind of failure, trying hard not to succeed in some final and complete determination either of themselves or of their aim, blackness, which is, but so serially and variously, that it is given nowhere as emphatically as in rituals of renomination, when the given is all but immediately taken away. Such predication is, as Nathaniel Mackey says, 'unremitting'—a constant economy and mechanics of fugitive making where the subject is hopelessly troubled by, in being emphatically detached from, the action whose agent it is supposed to be." See Nathaniel Mackey, "Destination Out" (2000), 814.

4. For "scene of subjection," see Saidiya Hartman, *Scenes of Subjection: Terror, Slavery, and Self-Making in Nineteenth-Century America* (1997); for "a world in which things would be different," see Theodor Adorno, "On Lyric Poetry and Society" (1957/2014), 341.

5. It probably goes without saying that it is more common for critics of modern poetics to make the opposite point. See, for example, *The Plural of Us: Poetry and Community in Auden and Others* (2017), in which Bonnie Costello writes that poets "have said 'we' to create community rather than to divide groups or impose majority" (1).

6. The Schomburg Library of Nineteenth-Century Black Women Writers has now made many poets available in modern editions; we may not know how to read them, but at least they are in print (though, alas, not in paperback or in digital editions). As a point of comparison, consider the fact that in the compendious *Encyclopedia of American Poetry*, edited by Eric L. Haralson in 1998, Plato does not appear at all. Her poems also make no appearance in the widely used 1993 Library of America anthology, *American Poetry: The Nineteenth Century*, edited by John Hollander.

7. Mary Loeffelholz, *From School to Salon: Reading Nineteenth-Century Women's Poetry* (2004), 4.

8. There are forty-eight extant copies listed in the WorldCat database, many in the United States and United Kingdom, but there are also a few in libraries in Spain, Canada, and New Zealand.

9. Meredith McGill, "Frances Ellen Watkins Harper and the Circuits of Abolitionist Poetry" (2012), 73.

10. Joanna Brooks, "The Unfortunates: What the Life Spans of Early Black Books Tell Us about Book History" (2012), 41.

11. Evie Shockley, *Renegade Poetics: Black Aesthetics and Formal Innovation in African American Poetry* (2011), 9. She continues, "Black aesthetics are a function of the writing process, are contingent, and must be historicized and contextualized with regard to period and place, and with regard to the various other factors that shape the writer's identity, particularly including gender, sexuality, and class as well."

12. As we shall see, Plato's biographer Ron Welburn makes this point as a way to measure the "contrasts in cultural investment" between Plato's poems on Indigenous subjects and her poems on Black subjects. See Welburn, *Hartford's Ann Plato and the Native Borders of Identity* (2015), 33.

13. All citations of Plato's poems are from the 1988 reprint edition of her 1841 *Essays: Including Biographies and Miscellaneous Pieces, in Prose and Poetry* in The Schomburg Library of Black Women Writers. Plato (1841; 1988), 114.

14. Bernstein, "The Difficult Poem," in *Attack of the Difficult Poems: Essays and Inventions* (2011), 5. The first year of the publication of *Poetry* magazine was 1912.

15. For a concise account of the exclusion of nineteenth-century American poetry (with the routine exceptions of Whitman and Dickinson) from modern literary study, see Joseph Harrington, "Why American Poetry Is Not American Literature" (1986). The racialized and gendered dimensions of this erasure are more complicated than Harrington's critical history allows, as Erin Kappeler argues in "Editing America: Nationalism and the New Poetry" (2014).

16. Terrance Hayes, "American Sonnet for My Past and Future Assassin," in *American Sonnets for My Past and Future Assassin* (2018), 5. For an example of a recent all-White version of the history of nineteenth-century American poetry, see Karen K. Kilcup, *Who Killed American Poetry? From National Obsession to Elite Possession* (2019).

17. Sherman (1974), xv. In addition to Redding (1939), see Benjamin Brawley, *The Negro in Literature and Art in the United States* (1918); Sterling Brown, *Negro Poetry and Drama* (1937); and Jean Wagner, *Black Poets of the United States*, trans. Kenneth Douglas (1973). Johnson's *Book of American Negro Poetry* (1922) is in many ways a separate case. Johnson does work harder than anyone else in the first half of the twentieth century to incorporate nineteenth-century Black poets into the history of American poetry, though he also writes that "it is a long way from the plaints of George Horton to the invectives of Claude McKay, from the obviousness of Frances Harper to the complexness of Anne Spencer" (36). Johnson's narrative always casts nineteenth-century Black poetry as deficient in *modernism*.

18. For a sustained meditation on the arbitrary distinction between poetry and prose, see Craig Dworkin, *Radium of the Word* (2020), 21–47.

19. Kwame Anthony Appiah, "The Case for Capitalizing the *B* in Black," *Atlantic*, June 18, 2020. https://www.theatlantic.com/ideas/archive/2020/06/time-to-capitalize-blackand-white /613159/.

20. Virginia Jackson, "Lyric," *The Princeton Encyclopedia of Poetry and Poetics* (2012), 826.

21. Kirsten Silva Gruesz, *Ambassadors of Culture: The Transamerican Origins of Latino Writing* (2002), xii.

22. Manu Samriti Chander, *Brown Romantics: Poetry and Nationalism in the Global Nineteenth Century* (2017), 91.

23. Stephen Best, *None Like Us: Blackness, Belonging, Aesthetic Life* (2018), 1.

24. Mae Gwendolyn Henderson, "Speaking in Tongues: Dialogics, Dialectics, and the Black Woman Writer's Literary Tradition" (2000), 352.

25. Frederick Douglass, "What to the Slave Is the Fourth of July?" (1852), in *Douglass: Speeches and Writings* (2022), 431.

26. Wilson, *Specters of Democracy: Blackness and the Aesthetics of Politics in the Antebellum U.S.* (2011), 15; Claudia Rankine, *Just Us: An American Conversation* (2020), 33; Frank Wilderson III, *Afropessimism* (2020); Joseph Rezek, "The Racialization of Print" (2020).

27. For Sylvia Wynter's eloquent exposure of "the referent-we" as the pronoun that came to define the White male genre that came to count as "the" human (and I would add, "the" lyric), see *Sylvia Wynter: On Being Human as Praxis*, ed. McKittrick (2015), 24, 27, 33–34, 38–39, 44–45, 56–58, 68, 70–73.

28. Émile Benveniste, *Problems in General Linguistics* (1971), 217.

29. Zakiyyah Iman Jackson, *Becoming Human: Matter and Meaning in an Antiblack World* (2020), 18.

30. Katherine Clay Bassard, *Spiritual Interrogations: Culture, Gender, and Community in Early African American Women's Writing* (1999), 82.

31. Nicholas Hudson, "From 'Nation' to 'Race': The Origin of Racial Classification in Eighteenth-Century Thought" (1996), 258.

32. James Brewer Stewart, "Modernizing 'Difference': The Political Meanings of Color in the Free States, 1776–1840" (Winter 1999), 693.

33. James W. C. Pennington, *A Text Book of the Origin and History, &c.&c. of the Colored People* (1841). On "the curse theory," see Ibram Kendi, *Stamped from the Beginning: The Definitive History of Racist Ideas in America* (2016).

34. See Britt Rusert, *Fugitive Science: Empiricism and Freedom in Early African American Culture* (2017), 44–50.

35. Ta-Nehisi Coates, *Between the World and Me* (2015), 7.

36. Rusert (2017), 48.

37. Katie Trumpener, *Bardic Nationalism: The Romantic Novel and the British Empire* (1997).

38. Best (2018), 1.

39. Hortense Spillers, "Mama's Baby, Papa's Maybe: An American Grammar Book" (1987/2003), 203.

40. On the shifting fortunes of common meter, see Lucía Martínez Valdivia, "Mere Meter: A Revised History of English Poetry" (2019).

41. Hartman (1997), 65.

42. Before C.L.R. James published his famous *The Black Jacobins: Toussaint L'Ouverture and the San Domingo Revolution* (1938), he wrote a play in 1934 entitled *Toussaint L'Ouverture: The Story of the Only Successful Slave Revolt in History; A Play in Three Acts* (reprinted by Duke University Press in 2012).

43. Marlene L. Daut, *Tropics of Haiti: Race and the Literary History of the Haitian Revolution in the Atlantic World, 1789–1865* (2015), 3.

44. See Cedric Robinson, *Black Marxism: The Making of the Black Radical Tradition* (1983), 158–159.

45. Julius S. Scott, *The Common Wind: Afro-American Currents in the Age of the Haitian Revolution* (2018), 118.

46. See David Waldstreicher, "The Mansfieldian Moment: Slavery, the Constitution, and American Political Traditions" (2013). For an extended consideration of the relation between

this moment and the *Zong* massacre, see Ian Baucom, *Specters of the Atlantic: Finance Capital, Slavery, and the Philosophy of History* (2005).

47. J. R. Kerr-Ritchie, *Rites of August First: Emancipation Day in the Black Atlantic World* (2007), 1. Kerr-Ritchie does not discuss Plato or many of the poets who wrote poems in the First of August genre of occasional verse for these public celebrations, but he does discuss Pennington's participation in several such occasions.

48. Lauren Berlant, *The Queen of America Goes to Washington City: Essays on Sex and Citizenship* (1997), 223.

49. M. NourbeSe Philip, *Zong!: As Told to the Author by Setaey Adamu Boateng* (2008).

50. Meredith McGill, "The Poetry of Slavery" (2016), 125.

51. David Waldstreicher, "The Wheatleyan Moment" (2011).

52. Simon Gikandi, *Slavery and the Culture of Taste* (2011), xviii.

53. Meredith Martin, *The Rise and Fall of Meter: Poetry and English National Culture, 1860–1930* (2012), 4.

54. Max Cavitch, "Slavery and Its Metrics" (2011), 99.

55. Michael Warner, *Publics and Counterpublics* (2002), 11–12.

56. Yopie Prins, "Poetess" in *The Princeton Encyclopedia of Poetry and Poetics* (2012), 1051.

57. Eliza Richards, *Gender and the Poetics of Reception in Poe's Circle* (2004), 1.

58. Alexandra Socarides, *In Plain Sight: Nineteenth-Century American Women's Poetry and the Problem of Literary History* (2020), 3.

59. Virginia Jackson and Yopie Prins, "Lyrical Studies" (1999), 523.

60. Tricia Lootens, *The Political Poetess: Victorian Femininity, Race, and the Legacy of Separate Spheres* (2017), 7.

61. Welburn, (2015), 34.

62. James Baldwin, "The White Man's Guilt" (1965), in *Baldwin: Collected Essays* (1998), 722–723.

63. See Ezra Tawil, *The Making of Racial Sentiment: Slavery and the Birth of the Frontier Romance* (2008).

64. Tiffany Lethabo King, *The Black Shoals: Offshore Formations of Black and Native Studies* (2019), x.

65. Barbara Johnson, *Persons and Things* (2008), 15.

66. Herbert Tucker, "Dramatic Monologue and the Overhearing of Lyric" (1985), 242.

67. Caroline Gelmi, "The Speaker, Photographed: Paul Laurence Dunbar's *Poems of Cabin and Field*" (2020), 73.

68. Sonya Posmentier, "Lyric Reading in the Black Ethnographic Archive" (2018), 57.

69. Phillip Brian Harper, *Abstractionist Aesthetics: Artistic Form and Social Critique in African American Culture* (2015), 4.

70. John Stuart Mill, "Thoughts on Poetry and Its Varieties" (1833/1981), 348.

71. Emily Dickinson, *The Poems of Emily Dickinson* (1999), #764 (fascicle 34).

72. Virginia Jackson, *Dickinson's Misery: A Theory of Lyric Reading* (2005), 233.

73. Susan Stewart, "Lyric Possession" (1995), 41. In a later essay on "My Life Had Stood," Stewart suggests that the "speaker" of the poem is a dog—specifically, "a hunting dog." See Susan Stewart, "On ED's 754/764" (2014), 263.

74. Zora Neale Hurston, "How It Feels to Be Colored Me" (1928/1995), 828.

75. Claudia Rankine, *Citizen: An American Lyric* (2014), 52–53.

76. For the intimate relation between racialization and abstraction, see Harper.

77. Posmentier (2018), 69.

78. Claudia Rankine, Beth Loffreda, and Max King Cap, eds., *The Racial Imaginary: Writers on Race in the Life of the Mind* (2015), 22.

79. Gitelman (2014), 2.

80. Fred Moten, "Taste Dissonance Flavor Escape: Preface for a Solo by Miles Davis" (2007), 243. On the relation of figures of constraint to lyric theory, see also Andrea Brady, *Poetry and Bondage: A History of Lyric Constraint* (2021). Brady and I seem to agree on the importance of figures of "unfreedom" in lyric history and theory, but my argument here is that those figures have a deeply designed history in American poetics, since their referent is not free-floating but always essentially antiblack.

81. Claudia Rankine "The First Person in the Twenty-First Century" (2021), 135–136.

82. Rankine (2020), 335.

83. Kamran Javadizadeh, "The Atlantic Ocean Breaking on Our Heads: Claudia Rankine, Robert Lowell, and the Whiteness of the Lyric Subject" (2019).

84. Evie Shockley, "Race, Reception, and Claudia Rankine's 'American Lyric'" (2016).

85. Adorno (1957/2014), 339.

86. Walter Benjamin, "On Some Motifs in Baudelaire" (1939), 327, 328.

87. G.W.F. Hegel, *Aesthetics: Lectures on Fine Art* (1975), 2: 971.

88. This is the sort of punctual, event-based literary history that this book is arguing against, but the dates here have been considered turning points for various histories of American poetics. In rough order, they include the date of the last poem in this book, Frances Ellen Watkins Harper's "Eva's Farewell," the end of the Civil War and the assassination of Abraham Lincoln, the turn into the twentieth century, the date of publication of Du Bois's *The Souls of Black Folk*, the date of the first issue of *Poetry* magazine, the date of the publication of *The Waste Land*, the beginning of the "Post-45" postwar period, the beginning of half a century of financial "crisis," and the attack on the World Trade Center on September 11, 2001.

89. Adorno (1957/2014), 350.

90. Paul de Man, "Lyric and Modernity" (1983), 173.

91. Jonathan Culler, *Theory of the Lyric* (2015), 2.

92. John Keene, "White Silences: The Lyric Theory Reader Panel @ACLA 2014," *J's Theater*: http://jstheater.blogspot.com/2014/04/white-silences-lyric-theory-reader.html.

93. Dorothy Wang, *Thinking Its Presence: Form, Race, and Subjectivity in Contemporary Asian American Poetry* (2014), xx. Wang was actually with Keene when they approached me after the special session on *The Lyric Theory Reader* at the 2014 ACLA. I am grateful to them both for starting a conversation.

94. Sonya Posmentier, *Cultivation and Catastrophe: The Lyric Ecology of Modern Black Literature* (2017), 4.

95. Anthony Reed, *Freedom Time: The Poetics and Politics of Black Experimental Writing* (2014), 7.

96. Zadie Smith, "What Do We Want History to Do to Us?" (2020), 10.

97. I have just "recited" in translated verbatim the famous "Angel of History" passage from Benjamin's "Theses on the Concept of History," a series of fragments he wrote just before his

suicide. After I wrote that passage, I encountered Jesse McCarthy's beautiful reading of it as a figure for the way that "of all the cultural forces in the social fabric, black intellectuals tend to have the shortest reach." He then reads Benjamin's figure, as I do, through Kara Walker's audacious work and Zadie Smith's inventive reading of that work. See Jesse McCarthy, "Venus and the Angel of History" in *Who Will Pay Reparations on My Soul?* (2021), 34–50. See also, of course, Walter Benjamin, "Theses on the Concept of History" (1940), in *Illuminations* (1968), 253–264.

98. Stephanie Burt, *the poem is you: 60 Contemporary American Poets and How to Read Them* (2016), 4.

99. Michael Cohen, *The Social Lives of Poems in Nineteenth-Century America* (2015), 1.

100. Roger Chartier, "Laborers and Voyagers: From the Text to the Reader," trans. J. A. Gonzalez (1992), 50. As Nan Z. Da writes, "the quotation is taken from Roger Chartier's reflections on the challenge of drawing sociological conclusions about reading. Chartier enlists Michel de Certeau's phenomenology of everyday life to modulate the sociology of literature from bibliographic inventory-taking to the reconstruction of the sociology of reading. A historian who attends to reading's circumstantial 'actualization' in embodied practice is someone who reconstructs the variables of interpretive communities and distinguishes what is actually read from what is available for reading," "Other People's Books" (2020), 495 n. 1.

101. Frances Barton Gummere, *Democracy and Poetry* (1911). Of Whitman, for example, Gummere wrote, "He cannot be the poet of democracy in its highest ideal who rejects the democratic idea of submission to the highest social order, to the spirit of the laws, to that imagined community" (127). For a discussion of Gummere's influential version of lyric imagined community, see my essay "The Cadence of Consent: Francis Barton Gummere, Lyric Rhythm, and White Poetics" (2019). For an eye-popping view of Gummere's unacknowledged importance in the racialized formation of early twentieth-century American poetics, see Erin Kappeler, "Editing America: Nationalism and the New Poetry" (2014).

102. Barbara Johnson, "Apostrophe, Animation, and Abortion" (1987), in *The Lyric Theory Reader* (2014), 530.

103. Brent Hayes Edwards, "The Seemingly Eclipsed Window of Form: James Weldon Johnson's Prefaces" (1998), 596.

104. Housten Donham and Fred Moten, "POETRY BEGINS WITH THE WILLINGNESS TO SUBORDINATE WHATEVER THE HELL IT IS THAT YOU HAVE TO SAY": AN INTERVIEW W/ FRED MOTEN, *Open House*, 20 July 2015.

105. Reed (2014), 8.

Chapter Two. Apostrophe, Animation, and Racism

1. For the concept of genres dependent on a "silent responsive understanding" or a "responsive understanding with a delayed reaction," see M. M. Bakhtin, "The Problem of Speech Genres" (1986), 69.

2. Walt Whitman, "Apostroph." Since this poem appeared only in the 1860 edition of *Leaves of Grass* (Boston: Thayer and Eldridge, 1860), the best place to read it is on the page images available on the Walt Whitman Archive: https://whitmanarchive.org/published/LG/1860/poems/4.

3. As Barbara Johnson wrote of Whitman's poem, "So central to the poetic function is apostrophe that in Whitman's 1860 edition of *Leaves of Grass*, a poem called 'Apostroph.' prefaced

the section titled 'Chants Democratic,' as if an apostrophe were a kind of strophe" "Toys R Us: Legal Persons, Personal Pronouns, Definitions," in *Persons and Things* (2008), 8. As my reader can already tell, much of what and how I think about poetry—especially about apostrophic poetry—is indebted to Johnson, so I am happy to say that I introduced her to "Apostroph." at the 2001 English Institute meeting at Harvard.

4. Anahid Nersessian, *The Calamity Form: On Poetry and Social Life* (2020), 133. I cite Nersessian here not because her view of apostrophe is new or singular but because she is intentionally summing up various formalist accounts of what she calls "the work of Romantic lyric" (132). Her version of apostrophe aims to represent the view of the field of British Romanticism over the past four decades.

5. Jonathan Kramnick's response to what he calls the "deconstructive" legacy of this sensationally animating view of apostrophe is to suggest that eighteenth-century and Romantic apostrophes often aimed for the antithetical effect: "the apostrophizing poet speaks to something that is just here and does so in the precise formal manner of that thing's existence: he or she creates a poem that is the world it describes, that makes or joins up with or adds parts to an environment in which one might live." See Jonathan Kramnick, *Paper Minds: Literature and the Ecology of Consciousness* (2018), 84. Kramnick's critique of the post-structuralist hypostasis of apostrophe might be called radically eco-formalist (in contrast to Nersessian's eco-formalist embrace of that received hypostasis). As will be evident, my critique of both the post-structuralist and the formalist versions of apostrophe is historicist, but post-structuralism and formalism are part and parcel of that historicism. For the best account I know of the inevitable entanglement of historicism and formalism in Romantic studies, see Frances Ferguson, *Solitude and the Sublime: The Romantic Aesthetics of Individuation* (1992).

6. John Pierpont, "Hymn for the First of August," *The Antislavery Poems of John Pierpont* (1843), 52. It's worth noting that the publisher of Pierpont's volume was the Garrisonian printer Oliver Johnson, so the version of abolitionism promoted by the poems would have been obvious to readers before they opened the book. Pierpont's daughter's son was John Pierpont Morgan, founder of J. P. Morgan & Company, later J. P. Morgan Chase. Morgan (who preferred to be called "Pierpont") was not only an originator of the modern American banking industry but also a driving force behind the industrial consolidation of the United States.

7. Paul de Man, "Lyrical Voice in Contemporary Theory: Riffaterre and Jauss" (1985), 61.

8. Jonathan Culler, "Apostrophe," in *The Pursuit of Signs: Semiotics, Literature, Deconstruction* (1981), 141–142.

9. Erving Goffman, *Forms of Talk* (1981), 124–157. Goffman's discussion of "a change in footing" is especially relevant to the workings of apostrophe (literally, turning aside): "A change in footing implies a change in the alignment we take up to ourselves and the others present as expressed in the way we manage the production or reception of an utterance. A change in our footing is another way of talking about a change in our frame for events. Participants over the course of their speaking constantly change their footing, these changes being a persistent feature of natural talk," 128.

10. Barbara Johnson, "Apostrophe, Animation, Abortion" (1987/2014), 529.

11. Lauren Berlant, *Cruel Optimism* (2011), 25–26.

12. Johnson (1987/2014), 529; Berlant (2011), 24.

13. As I mentioned in this book's introduction, Tucker's great essay on "Dramatic Monologue and the Overhearing of Lyric" was originally published in *Lyric Poetry: Beyond the New*

Criticism in 1985 and is reprinted in *The Lyric Theory Reader* (2014). As Barbara Johnson's essay "Apostrophe, Animation, and Abortion" (1987) paved the way for the way in which I am reconsidering the racialization of lyric apostrophe, so Tucker's essay paved the way for the way in which I am thinking here about the racialization of the lyric speaker.

14. Jared Hickman, *Black Prometheus: Race and Radicalism in the Age of Atlantic Slavery* (2017), 194. Hickman discusses Pierpont's poem at length, but interestingly, not its appropriation of Black North Star discourse as such, or Black poets' reappropriation of that discourse. He does discuss James Russell Lowell's desire to become "the antislavery poet that Pierpont already was" (185), and he does argue that the North Star "comes to center a heretical cosmography" (214), but in his account, White and Black poetic cosmographies seem to be complementary rather than conflicting.

15. Pierpont (1843), 29.

16. For an illuminating discussion of the stanza's acquisition of a Shakespearean proper name in the early modern period, see Elizabeth Scott-Bauman and Ben Burton, "Shakespearean Stanzas? *Venus and Adonis, Lucrece,* and Complaint" (2021).

17. Bryant's "The Indian Girl's Lament" first appeared in the *New York Review* in January 1825. Before that, "An Indian at the Burial-Place of His Fathers" was published in the *United States Literary Gazette* on August 1, 1824. To say that these poems were reprinted and recirculated widely over the next few decades would be an understatement.

18. Lethabo King (2019), 1.

19. Bryant's "Hymn to the North Star" was first published in the *United States Literary Gazette* on January 15, 1825. See *The Life and Works of William Cullen Bryant*, Volume III (1883), 123.

20. Actually, the continuing success of Pierpont's poem in speaking to and for a liberal White public was literalized when Yale, his alma mater, carved a line from "The Fugitive Slave's Apostrophe to the North Star" beneath a bow window of Branford College. See Mark Alden Branch, "Thy Light and Truth Shall Set Me Free," *Daily Snap*, 19 August 2015.

21. Eric Lott, *Love and Theft: Blackface Minstrelsy and the American Working Class* (1993), 6.

22. Ann Laura Stoller, *Carnal Knowledge and Imperial Power: Race and the Intimate in Colonial Rule* (2002), 159.

23. On the relationship between Douglass and Delany, see Robert S. Levine, *Martin Delany, Frederick Douglass, and the Politics of Representative Identity* (1997).

24. Henry Louis Gates Jr., *The Signifying Monkey: A Theory of African-American Literary Criticism* (1988). Of the many ways in which Gates's foundational text has been elaborated and built upon over the past three decades, his emphasis on the "speakerly" text is overdue for reconsideration. This is not the place for that reconsideration, so I will just say that in relation to Whitfield's poetics, Gates's account of his book's beginning in James Snead's Yale seminar on parody is wildly suggestive (1).

25. In Douglass's famous account of his name, his mother gives him the surname "Bailey," though that was not the name of his (probably) White father or of any of the White men who thought they owned him. When he arrives in New Bedford under the alias "Johnson," he asks the abolitionist Nathan Johnson to choose a less common name for him, and Johnson suggests that he be called Douglass because he "had just been reading The Lady of the Lake." See Douglass, *Narrative of the Life of Frederick Douglass, an American Slave: Written by Himself* (1845), 112.

26. Daniel Hack, *Reaping Something New: African American Transformations of Victorian Literature* (2017), 24.

27. For a provocative account of the figure of apostrophe as a problem of racialized personal abstraction, especially in public (that is, stranger-oriented) forms of address, see Pratt (2016).

28. Again, the notable exception to this rule is Sandler (2020).

29. Arlene Balkansky, "Discover Poetry in Old News!" 30 April 2020 https://blogs.loc.gov /headlinesandheroes/2020/04/.

30. Rowan Ricardo Phillips's remarkable *When Blackness Rhymes with Blackness* (2010) includes a chapter on Douglass as lyric poet *manqué*; I am suggesting instead that Douglass was an early critic of the lyricizing tendencies of a fundamentally racist American poetics.

31. David W. Blight, *Frederick Douglass: Poet of Freedom* (2018), 191.

32. For the definition of counter-publics as "publics . . . defined by their tension with a larger public," see Warner (2002), 56–63.

33. James M. Whitfield, "The North Star," *North Star*, 21 December 1849, 4. See also Whitfield (2011), 96.

34. Eliza Cook, "The Poor Man's Friend," in *The Poetical Works of Eliza Cook* (1856), 338.

35. Adams actually wrote the lines on "Freedom's hallowed shade" in a private album in 1842, and they weren't published until his death in 1848. Adams was a famous abolitionist (he defended the *Amistad* rebels), and Whitfield wrote "Lines on the Death of John Quincy Adams" in tribute to him in 1849. Campbell's poetry became popular in the United States after the success of *Gertrude of Wyoming: A Pennsylvanian Tale* (1809). See Thomas Campbell, "Hallowed Ground," in *Poems of Thomas Campbell* (1904), 141.

36. Ivy Wilson calls such maneuvers in Whitfield's poems "particularly recombinant forms of double voicing." Wilson (2011), 74.

37. See https://hymnary.org/text/o_may_our_sympathizing_breast_breasts.

38. Andrew Jackson, *Narrative and Writings of Andrew Jackson, of Kentucky* (1847), 15.

39. Hickman (2017), 206. As I have noted, Hickman's focus on the secularization of Black cosmography differs from my focus on Black poetics, but I am grateful for his scholarship on racialized stargazing in the nineteenth century, and particularly for introducing me to Jackson's narrative.

40. Hartman, *Lose Your Mother: A Journey Along the Atlantic Slave Route* (2007), 170.

41. Ivy Wilson, "P.S.: A Coda," *in Unsettled Stated: Nineteenth-Century American Studies*, ed. Dana Luciano and Wilson (2014), 310.

42. Levine and Wilson, "Black Nationalism and Emigration," in *The Works of James M. Whitfield: "America" and Other Writings by a Nineteenth-Century African American Poet* (2011), 101.

43. Whitfield (2011), 41. On "the colonizing trick," see David Kazanjian, *The Colonizing Trick: National Culture and Imperial Citizenship in Early America* (2003).

44. Levine and Wilson (2011), 74.

45. In fact, there were many more than two of these layers, as Whitfield well knew. According to the Library of Congress, the history of the melody of Smith's song was not just borrowed from "God Save the Queen," but has a more complicated history of borrowing, sharing, appropriation, and sampling, including a claim in 1740 that it was originally written as "God Save Great George the King," a song that borrowed its melody from British, French, and Swiss

sources. Before it reached the United States, that melody underwrote the national anthems of six countries, including Denmark, Prussia, and Lichtenstein. In colonial America, the melody accompanied a hymn dedicated to George Whitefield, the minister credited with inspiring the African American church (and the subject of Phillis Wheatley's transatlantic debut), a tribute to George Washington, and several popular songs. See https://www.loc.gov/item/ihas .200000012/. This is all to say that Whitfield did not just echo Smith and/or Britannia, but extended a long transatlantic history of revision and riff.

46. Whitfield, letter to Douglass, 25 September 1853, in Whitfield (2011), 95. In an article in the *North Star* on August 10, 1849, a reporter described Whitfield's recitation of the poem at a First of August celebration in Buffalo that year.

47. Whitfield (2011), 129.

48. Whitfield's friend and fellow Prince Hall Freemason Delany actually wrote a book about some of the cosmology associated with nineteenth-century Black Freemasonry. See Delany, *The Origin and Objects of Ancient Freemasonry* (1853).

49. Carolyn Williams, *Gilbert and Sullivan: Gender, Genre, Parody* (2011), 9.

50. I do mean "Black radical tradition" in Cedric Robinson's sense that "a civilization maddened by its own perverse assumptions and contradictions is loose in the world. A Black radical tradition formed in opposition to that civilization and conscious of itself is one part of the solution" (Cedric J. Robinson, *Black Marxism: The Making of the Black Radical Tradition* [1983], 318). I am suggesting that Whitfield's poetics framed that maddened civilization as a way of offering a solution in opposition.

51. Pierpont (1843), 34.

52. That exposure is even more remarkable in the tendency of White abolitionist publications to reprint "The Slaveholder's Address" without its companion piece. See, for example, the abolitionist gift book that the poet John Greenleaf Whittier helped to compile in 1840, *The North Star: The Poetry of Freedom, by Her Friends*. Whittier (1840).

53. Martin R. Delany, *Blake; or, the Huts of America*, ed. Jerome McGann (2017), 136, 133.

54. McGann, introduction to Delany (2017), xxv.

55. Britt Rusert, *Fugitive Science: Empiricism and Freedom in Early African American Culture* (2017), 168–169.

56. As Rodrigo Lazo writes, "invoking the rights of black and indigenous populations to justify a takeover of Cuba, [*Blake*] inverted the racist notions that fueled filibustering expeditions by calling for Anglo-Saxon or white Creole territorial control" (Rodrigo Lazo, *Writing to Cuba* [2005], 158). Lazo goes on to explain the centrality of the figure of Plácido not only to Delany but also to other Black intellectuals in the 1840s and 1850s responding to Cuban anticolonial agitation. But Lazo thinks that Delany's substitution of (the unaccented) Placido for the historical Plácido (Gabriel de la Concepción Valdés) and especially his substitution of Whitfield's poetry for Plácido's poetry also "erases the local Cuban conditions of composition" (162) of the original, and diminishes the novel's revolutionary ambition. Thus, while I am suggesting that Delany's appropriation recognizes the revolutionary potential of Whitfield's poetics, it simultaneously misrecognizes the revolutionary potential of Plácido's poetics. Bryant's English translation of Plácido may have had something to do with that misrecognition, as we shall see in chapter 4.

57. I am printing the poem as it appears in Whitfield (2011), 77, and as it first appeared in the *North Star*, March 15, 1850, 4. When he reprints it in *Blake*, Delany prints Whitfield's quatrains

as three octets and one twelve-line stanza written by Placido, perhaps to disguise the original's very Anglo-American tetrameter quatrains.

58. As Moten writes, "black performance has always been the ongoing improvisation of a kind of lyricism of the surplus—invagination, rupture, collision, augmentation. This surplus lyricism . . . is what a lot of people are after when they invoke the art and culture—the radical (both rooted and out there, immanent and transcendent) sensuality—of and for my people. It's a lyricism that Marx was trying to get to when he envisioned theoretical senses. It's what that which is called the avant-garde desires whether it accepts or rejects that name." Fred Moten, *In the Break: The Aesthetics of the Black Radical Tradition* (2003), 26.

59. Sandler (2020), 101.

60. Included in Joan R. Sherman, *The Black Bard of North Carolina: George Moses Horton and His Poetry* (1997), 75.

61. Johnson (1987; 2014), 533.

62. Sandler (2020), 64.

63. McGill, "The Poetry of Slavery" (2016), 125.

64. Paul Fry, *The Poet's Calling in the English Ode* (1980), 274.

65. Deidre Shauna Lynch, *Loving Literature: A Cultural History* (2018), 247.

66. David Walker, *Appeal to the Colored Citizens of the World* (1829; 2000).

67. Percy Bysshe Shelley, *Prometheus Unbound, a Lyrical Drama in Four Acts; with Other Poems* (1820; 2000), 222.

68. Fry (1980), 204.

69. Sandler reprints the entire poem, "Let Us Go: A Song for the Emigrant," from the January 1867 issue of the American Colonization Society's publication *The African Repository*. See Sandler (2020), 84.

70. George Moses Horton, *The Poetical Works of George Moses Horton, The Colored Bard of North Carolina* (1845).

71. George Moses Horton, "Individual Influence" (2017), 1244–1250. We all owe Senchyne a debt of gratitude for his discovery and publication of this astonishing manuscript.

72. Sylvia Wynter and Katherine McKittrick, "Unparalleled Catastrophe for Our Species? Or, to Give Humanness a Different Future: Conversation" in *Sylvia Wynter: On Being Human as Praxis* (2015), 31.

73. Joshua Bennett, *Being Property Once Myself* (2020), 12.

74. Horton, *Naked Genius*, rev. and comp. Will H. S. Banks, Capt. 9th Mich. Cav. (1865), iii. *Naked Genius* is now so rare that Sherman (1997) performed a great service in reprinting some of it and in including the young captain Will Banks's letters. Matt Sandler has done us all an even greater service by putting the 1982 Chapel Hill Historical Society facsmile of the book up online as an open-access pdf file: https://static1.squarespace.com/static/55774e9fe4b05114f3f2831c/t/57852e71c534a5bdead073b6/1468345971886/Naked+Genius.PDF.

75. Faith Barrett, *To Fight Aloud is Very Brave* (2012), 226, 250.

76. Redding, *To Make a Poet Black* (1939), 18; Sterling Brown, *Negro Poetry and Drama* (1937), 7. The tendency of early twentieth-century Black literary historians to disidentify with Horton is striking.

77. Sandler (2020), 63. I only argue with Sandler because his work on Horton is so compelling.

78. See Horton, *Naked Genius* (1865), 51. In this last book, the poem is simply titled "Liberty."

79. David Lowry Swain Papers, Southern Historical Collection, University of North Carolina, Chapel Hill, Folder 12.

Chapter Three. Personification

1. I say "probably" because of course Wheatley's origins and early life are matters of guesswork. For an informed version of such guesswork, see Vincent Carretta, *Phillis Wheatley: Biography of a Genius in Bondage* (2–11), 1–12. For a prolonged meditation on the political risks and charges of such guesswork, see Hartman, *Lose Your Mother: A Journey along the Atlantic Slave Route* (2007).

2. Barbara Jordan, "The Difficult Miracle of Black Poetry in America or Something Like a Sonnet for Phillis Wheatley" (1986), 253. Christina Sharpe, *In the Wake: On Blackness and Being* (2016), 52–53.

3. Dana Murphy, "Praisesong for Margaret Walker's *Jubilee* and the Phillis Wheatley Poetry Festival" (2020), 299. Although this article is not all about Phillis Wheatley, Murphy's embrace of this poet's "everlasting literary life" announces a thrilling new direction for Wheatley/Peters/Phillis studies (Murphy prefers to animate the latter dead name).

4. That source is Margaretta Matilda Odell's "memoir" of the poet she never knew in *Memoir and Poems of Phillis Wheatley, a Native African and a Slave. Dedicate to the Friends of the Africans* (1834). On Odell's unreliability as narrator, see Jeffers (2020), 167–189.

5. The sentence belongs to Henry Louis Gates, the general editor of the series, and it is as significant for its claims about "the Afro-American literary tradition" as it is for its claim that Wheatley's single book founded that tradition.

6. James Weldon Johnson (1922), 17. What Johnson actually writes is that "by some sort of conspiracy she has been kept out of most of the books, especially the text-books on literature used in the schools. Of course, she is not a *great* American poet—and in her day there were no great American poets—but she is an important American poet."

7. See Samantha Pinto, *Infamous Bodies: Early Black Women's Celebrity and the Afterlives of Rights* (2020), 31–64.

8. See Jeffers (2020), 167–189. Jeffers is passionate about the need to reply to the antiblack circulation of Peters under her enslaved rather than her free married name, the name of the White man she did not choose rather than of the Black man she did, and she is right. I call her "Wheatley" here because that is the name that has been attached to the reception of the poetry, but surely Jeffers makes a fundamental point about the name of the historical person.

9. Ann Plato, "Lines, Written Upon Being Examined in School Studies for the Preparation of a Teacher," (1841/1988), 94.

10. Phillis Wheatley, "On Recollection," in Carretta, ed. *The Writings of Phillis Wheatley* (2019), 77.

11. Kenny J. Williams, Introduction, Plato (1988), xlix.

12. Bassard (1999), 73.

13. The line is from *Henry VIII*, Act IV, Scene 2. It may or not be the source of the John Keats's famous epitaph, but the two young American poets' adoption of it is suggestive in all kinds of ways.

14. This is Michel Foucault's way of posing the question of "What Is an Author?"—though, with characteristic irony, he takes the question from Samuel Beckett. See "What Is an Author?" (1978).

15. Virginia Jackson, "The Poet as Poetess" (2012), 63.

16. Henry Louis Gates, *The Trials of Phillis Wheatley* (2003), 75–76.

17. Redding (1939), 11.

18. Gates (2003), 89. It is worth noting that Gates's little book on Wheatley first took the form of the Thomas Jefferson Lecture in the Humanities at the Library of Congress in March 2002, as Gates begins the book by noting (1).

19. Paul Gilroy, *The Black Atlantic: Modernity and Double Consciousness* (1993), 79.

20. James Weldon Johnson (1922), 19.

21. See David Scott, *Conscripts of Identity: The Tragedy of Colonial Enlightenment* (2004).

22. Paul de Man, "Anthropomorphism and Trope in Lyric" in *The Rhetoric of Romanticism* (1984), 261–262. De Man was basing a high-stakes argument about "the possibility of lyric" on one poem by Baudelaire, a poet already credited with the invention of modern lyric. I am basing such an argument on a couple of poems by Wheatley, a poet already credited with inaugurating "the Afro-American literary tradition," but never credited with the invention of modern lyric. It's worth noting that de Man does not use the definite article, and neither do I.

23. Lord Byron, *Don Juan* (1821) beginning of third canto, invoked in the online Oxford Reference definition of invocation: https://www.oxfordreference.com/view/10.1093/acref /9780199208272.001.0001/acref-9780199208272-e-611#.

24. Anne Carson, "Sappho Shock," in *Dwelling in Possibility* (1997), 223–229.

25. Jesse McCarthy, "Venus and the Angel of History," in *Who Will Pay Reparations on My Soul?* (2021), 78.

26. Kramnick, *Paper Minds* (2018), 57.

27. Julie Ellison, *Cato's Tears and the Making of Anglo-American Emotion* (1999), 117.

28. See David Hall, *Lived Religion in America: Toward a Theory of Practice* (1997), vii–xiii.

29. Phillis Wheatley, "On Recollection," *Writings*, ed. Carretta (2019), 29.

30. Herbert Tucker, "Changes of Address: Epic Invocation in Anglophone Romanticism" (2017), 126.

31. John C. Shields, *Phillis Wheatley and the Romantics* (2010), 46–47.

32. Geoffrey Hartman, "On Traumatic Knowledge and Literary Studies" (1995), 552.

33. Anne-Lise François, *Open Secrets: The Literature of Uncounted Experience* (2007), xv, 19.

34. Cathy Caruth, *Unclaimed Experience: Trauma, Narrative, and History* (1996).

35. Hartman (2008), 14.

36. Sigmund Freud, "Screen Memories" (1899).

37. As I noted in my first chapter, *consent not to be a single being* is the title of Fred Moten's trilogy that begins with *Black and Blur* (2017), but the phrase is Édouard Glissant's: see "One World in Relation: Édouard Glissant in Conversation with Manthia Diawara" (2011), 4–19. Both Glissant's and Moten's variations on the phrase are endlessly suggestive when thinking about Wheatley.

38. Morrison's reflections on rememory have been posthumously re-collected with other lectures and speeches in *Mouth Full of Blood: Essays, Speeches, Meditations* (2020). The challenge this concept poses to the genres of narrative fiction is evident in Morrison's novel *A Mercy* (2008), the novel she based on a Wheatley-like figure. For an extended meditation on this challenge, see

Farrah Jasmine Griffin, *Read Until You Understand: The Profound Wisdom of Black Life and Literature* (2021).

39. Toni Morrison, *Beloved* (1987), 43.

40. Johnson (2008), 17.

41. Ibid., 18.

42. "Memoir" in *Memoir and Poems of Phillis Wheatley, A Native African and a Slave. Also Poems by a Slave*. Boston: Isaac Knapp, 1838, 11–12. Because this is a reprint of the 1834 George W. Light edition, readers may have known that Odell was the author of this memoir, but in the Knapp edition, it is not signed.

43. Carra Glatt, "'To Perpetuate Her Name': Appropriation and Autobiography in Margaretta Matilda Odell's Memoir of Phillis Wheatley" (2020), 145–176.

44. Jennifer Rene Young, "Marketing a Sable Muse: Phillis Wheatley and the Antebellum Press" (2011), 219.

45. Joanna Brooks, "Our Phillis, Ourselves" (2010), 17.

46. *Memoir and Poems* (1838), 7. Like the *Memoir*, the introduction to the Knapp edition is unsigned.

47. The Burns poem that made the "philibeg an' tartan plaid" line famous is "The Jolly Beggars: A Cantata," first published in 1799 in a chapbook in Glasgow and reprinted transatlantically throughout the nineteenth century. My thanks to Jennifer Harris for pointing out the subliminal transatlanticism of the slave trade as well as the book trade in this passing allusion. As it turns out, Burns considered a job on a Jamaican plantation.

48. Marsha Watson, "A Classic Case: Phillis Wheatley and Her Poetry" (1996), 127.

49. Heather Keenleyside, *Animals and Other People: Literary Forms and Living Beings in the Long Eighteenth Century* (2016), 24.

50. Steven Knapp, *Personification and the Sublime: Milton to Coleridge* (1985), 4; Adela Pinch, *Strange Fits of Passion: Epistemologies of Emotion, Hume to Austen* (1996), 48.

51. See Saidiya Hartman (1997, 2007, 2008), Fred Moten, (2003, 2017); Frank Wilderson, (2020); Paul Gilroy (1993); Édouard Glissant, (1997).

52. Alexander Pope, trans., *The Iliad* (1720; 1898), xix, 380.

53. Lord Henry Home Kames, *Elements of Criticism* (1762), 64.

54. William Wordsworth, "Wordsworth's Prefaces of 1800 and 1802" (1991), 250.

55. Norman Maclean, "Personification But Not Poetry" (1956), 164.

56. I am not suggesting that Wheatley knew this particular sculpture, but classical scholar that she was, she certainly knew many versions of the scene.

57. Phillis Wheatley, "On Recollection," *Writings*, ed. Carretta, 82.

58. Paula Bennett, "Phillis Wheatley's Vocation and the Paradox of the 'Afric Muse'" (1998), 68.

59. Eric Slauter, *The State as a Work of Art: The Cultural Origins of the Constitution* (2009), 202.

60. Peter Coviello, "Agonizing Affection" (2002), 446.

61. Waldstreicher, "The Wheatleyan Moment" (2011), 537.

62. Joseph Rezek, 'The Print Atlantic: Phillis Wheatley, Ignatius Sancho, and the Cultural Significance of the Book" (2012), 38.

63. Hunter (2000), 119.

64. Thomas Jefferson, *Notes on the State of Virginia* (1787), Query XIV.

65. Gilbert Imlay, *A Topographical Description of the Western Territory of North America* (1793), 185–186.

66. This is the burden of Shields's song in his book *Phillis Wheatley and the Romantics* (2010). Perhaps because of the way Shields makes the argument, the sound literary history behind this claim has not received the attention it deserves.

67. Hartman, *Lose Your Mother* (2007), 30.

Chapter Four. Prosody

1. *The Norton Anthology of American Literature, Volume B, 1820 to 1865*, ed. Nina Baym et al. (2003), 958–959.

2. The cover of *The Norton Anthology of American Literature, Volume B, 1820 to 1865*, has been changed in the most recent editions, but the shorter editions of the anthology retain the *Kindred Spirits* cover for the second volume.

3. After Bryant's death in 1878 (as a result of a fall he took in Central Park), there was discussion of adding a statue of Bryant to Central Park's Poet's Walk. But the statue was (rather controversially) delayed, and Reservoir Square was renamed Bryant Park in 1884. The current New York Public Library building was not built until 1911, and the statue of Bryant behind it in Bryant Park also dates from 1911.

4. For accounts of Bryant's advocacy for the Library, the Park, and the Metropolitan Museum, see both the Godwin and Brown biographies.

5. On the economics of the sale of "Kindred Spirits" in 2005, see Carol Vogel's article for the *New York Times*, "New York Public Library's Durand Painting Sold to Walmart Heiress," May 13, 2005.

6. Cleanth Brooks, *Modern Poetry and the Tradition* (1939), 54; William Ellery Leonard, "Bryant and the Minor Poets," in *The Cambridge History of American Literature* (1917), ed. William Peterfield Trent, John Erskine, Stuart P. Sherman, Carl Van Doren, vol. 1, 267.

7. Roy Harvey Pearce, *The Continuity of American Poetry* (1961), 210, 209.

8. F. O. Matthiessen, *American Renaissance: Art and Expression in the Age of Emerson and Whitman* (1941), 143.

9. Karen Kilcup, Who Killed American Poetry? From *National Obsession to Elite Possession* (2019), 14; Joan Shelley Rubin, *Songs of Ourselves: The Uses of Poetry in America* (2009).

10. Vachel Lindsay, "What It Means to Be a Poet in America," *Saturday Evening Post* 199 (November 13, 1926), 12–13, 45–46, 48.

11. The origin of the mass-produced series of portraits of "Our Poets" is unknown. A panel of six portraits of these men) was issued by L. Prang & Co Fine Art Publishers in Boston in 1894. See "Prang's Latest Pictures," *Watchman* 48 (December 6, 1894), 20. But this is probably one of many—in fact, the mass-produced status of the portraits of authors means that these authors are themselves unauthored. It is probable that the idea for the series was modeled on the early fourteenth-century "Nine Worthies," a series of figures meant to represent the ideals of chivalry, but this is a guess (a guess that would emphasize this portrait as an image with a White, Northern European genealogy). The inclusion of Ralph Waldo Emerson is interesting, since unlike the other "worthies" John Greenleaf Whittier, James Russell Lowell, Henry Wadsworth Longfellow,

William Cullen Bryant, and Oliver Wendell Holmes, Emerson was not primarily known as a popular poet in the nineteenth century.

12. Angela Sorby, *Schoolroom Poets: Childhood, Performance, and the Place of American Poetry, 1865–1917* (2005), 74. Sorby's great book also emphasizes the explicit association of these poets with whiteness, especially in the chapter, "Learning to Be White: John Greenleaf Whittier's *Snow-Bound,*" 35–67. Sorby suggests that the "'schoolroom poets were linked together as such by the turn of the century," but given the appearance of all of these figures in nineteenth-century secondary textbooks, their representative association seems to have begun decades earlier (191).

13. Actually, Lindsay's invocation of the *Apollo Belvedere* is more complicated: as Nell Irvin Painter points out, by the time that Johann Joachim Winckelmann declared the Apollo Belvedere "the embodiment of perfect human beauty" in 1767, it was already the most famous statue in Europe. Painter's point is that as "the white beauty ideal" emerged "as science" in the eighteenth century, this ideal "got the science of race barreling along, with beauty steadily rising as a meaningful scientific category." See Painter, *The History of White People* (2010), 71. The combination of Lindsay's desire to cast Bryant as erstwhile paragon of White beauty, as "a regular sheik" (since, as Painter suggests, White beauty emerged in an orientalist context) and as British Romantic poet *manqué* speaks volumes about the character of Bryant's persistence in the unconscious of modern American poetry. Part of my point here is that this unconscious was also part of the very consciously organized pedagogical dissemination of Bryant about which Lindsay complained, since, as Sorby argues, such poetry taught public school children to be White. On the memorization and recitation of nineteenth-century poems as national racial education, see also Meredith Martin, *The Rise and Fall of Meter* (2012); Catherine Robson, *Heart Beats: Everyday Life and the Memorized Poem* (2012); and Michael C. Cohen, *The Social Lives of Poems in Nineteenth-Century America* (2015).

14. Van Wyck Brooks, *America's Coming-of-Age* (1915), 41–42. Lindsay is clearly riffing on Brooks and slightly displacing Brooks's imaginary all-White pre-twentieth-century "hereditary" American "folk" onto a cosmopolitan White imaginary.

15. Richard Henry Dana's reaction is reported differently by different sources, and sometimes it is attributed to Willard Phillips. In Parke Godwin's version of the story, Phillips read the poem that Bryant's father sent to the magazine, and both men thought that "Thanatopsis" was written by the father rather than the son. In this version, Dana is said to have "remarked, with a quiet smile: 'Ah! Phillips, you have been imposed upon; no one on this side of the Atlantic is capable of writing such verses'" (Godwin, *A Biography of William Cullen Bryant with Extracts from His Private Correspondence* [1883], vol. 1, 150).

16. On modernist reactions to "The Congo," see Rachel Blau DuPlessis, *Genders, Races, and Religious Cultures in Modern American Poetry 1908–1934*, especially chapter 4, "'HOO, HOO, HOO': Some Episodes in the Construction of Modern Male Whiteness" (2001), 81–105.

17. On Sterling Brown's 1973 speech at Williams College, see DuPlessis, (2001), 94.

18. Cleanth Brooks, *Modern Poetry and the Tradition* (1939), viii–ix.

19. See especially Anna Brickhouse, *Transamerican Literary Relations and the Nineteenth-Century Public Sphere* (2004), and Kirsten Silva Gruesz, *Ambassadors of Culture: The Transamerican Origins of Latino Writing* (2002).

20. José Martí, *Obras completas* (1963), 9: 413. Quoted by Brickhouse in *Transamerican Literary Relations and the Nineteenth-Century Public Sphere* (2002), 132.

21. Brickhouse, *Transamerican Literary Relations* (2002), 133–134.

22. Ibid.,142.

23. James Weldon Johnson (1922), 30.

24. Bryant, "Thanatopsis," in *The Life and Works of William Cullen Bryant*, vol. 3: *The Poetical Works of William Cullen Bryant* (1883), ed. Godwin, 20.

25. Toni Morrison, *Playing in the Dark: Whiteness and the Literary Imagination* (1993), 6.

26. Martin (2012), 203.

27. Jason R. Rudy, *Imagined Homelands: British Poetry in the Colonies* (2017), 48.

28. H. T. Tuckerman, "The Poetry of Bryant," *The United States Magazine and Democratic Review* 16 (1845): 191.

29. Gilbert H. Muller, *William Cullen Bryant: Author of America* (2008), 21.

30. Barbara Packer, "'Man Hath No Part in All This Glorious Work': American Romantic Landscapes," in *Romantic Revolutions: Criticism and Theory*. ed. Kenneth R. Johnston, et al. (1990), 147.

31. Bryant, "To a Waterfowl," in *The Life and Works of William Cullen Bryant*, vol. 3: *The Poetical Works of William Cullen Bryant*, ed. Godwin (1883), 26.

32. Robert Southey, "The Ebb Tide," in *Poetical Works of Robert Southey, Esq.*, vol. 13, *Minor Poems of Robert Southey* (1823), 53.

33. There are several River Avons (Avon means "river" in Welsh, so in effect these rivers are called "River River"), but Southey was from Bristol, readers assumed that the Bristol Avon was the river invoked in this poem.

34. "Poems, by William Cullen Bryant," in the *United States Literary Gazette* (April 1, 1824), 9. Bryant helped found this magazine, so it is no surprise that the magazine's first volume contains such a favorable review of his first collected volume of poems.

35. "Poems, by William Cullen Bryant" (1824), 8.

36. Because "To a Waterfowl" was not published in the *North American Review* until March 1818, there has been some confusion about the place and date of composition in 1815. See William Cullen Bryant II, "The Waterfowl in Retrospect," *New England Quarterly* 30, no. 2 (1957), 181–189.

37. Fry (1980), 4–5.

38. Norman, Maclean, "From Action to Image: Theories of the Lyric in the Eighteenth Century," in *Critics and Criticism: Ancient and Modern*, ed. R. S. Crane (1952), 408.

39. John Bigelow, *William Cullen Bryant* (1890), 42.

40. Ibid., 42–43.

41. In his biography of Bryant, Godwin writes that John Bigelow told the Century Club that "Like Horace, like Burns, like Beranger, but unlike most other poets of celebrity, Bryant never wrote any long poems. I once asked him why. He replied: 'There is no such thing as a long poem.' His theory was that a long poem was as impossible as a long ecstasy." Godwin, *A Biography of William Cullen Bryant*, vol. 1 (1883), 186.

42. Berlant (2011), 25–26.

43. T. E. Hulme, "Romanticism and Classicism," in *Romanticism: Points of View*, ed. Robert F. Gleckner and Gerald E. Enscoe (1936; 1962), 58. On the importance of this sort of generalization of religious feeling in the Romantic period, see Colin Jager, *Unquiet Things: Secularism in the Romantic Age* (2015).

44. Apparently, the idea that "Thanatopsis" was Bryant's "pagan poem" remained controversial for the entire century: in the publication from the Bryant Centennial in Cummington, Massachusetts, in 1894, it is reported that "Beecher in a discourse delivered soon after the poet's death, pronounced 'Thanatopsis' a pagan poem." *Bryant Centennial, Cummington: August the Sixteenth 1894* (Cummington, MA: Clark W. Bryan Company Printers, 1894), 37.

45. See Johnson, *Persons and Things* (2008), and de Man, "Lyrical Voice in Contemporary Theory" (1985).

46. Mordecai Marcus, *The Poems of Robert Frost: An Explication* (Ann Arbor: University of Michigan Press, 1991), 152.

47. Lora Romero, *Home Fronts: Domesticity and Its Critics in the Antebellum United States* (1997), 35.

48. William Cullen Bryant, "An Indian at the Burial-Place of His Fathers," in *The Life and Works of William Cullen Bryant*, vol. 3, *The Poetical Works of William Cullen Bryant*, ed. Godwin (1883), 93.

49. M. H. Abrams uses the word "colloquy" to describe the "dramatized" conversation between the Romantic poet and his (always his) subjects over and over in *Natural Supernaturalism: Tradition and Revolution in Romantic Literature* (1971). For example, of *The Prelude*, Abrams writes that "the whole poem is written as a sustained address to Coleridge.... The solitary author often supplements this form with an interior monologue, or else carries on an extended colloquy with the landscape in which the interlocutors are 'my mind' and 'the speaking face of earth and heaven'" (74). What Abrams is pointing to is the emerging idea of the dramatic lyric speaker in Romantic poetry. In "Dramatic Monologue and the Overhearing of Lyric," Herbert F. Tucker argues that the Victorian dramatic monologue took up this "lyric" Romantic colloquy and turned it toward the fiction of the poetic speaker that would become the foundation of New Critical lyric reading. "What is poetry? Textuality a speaker owns," Tucker writes: "The old kind of self-expressive lyricism is dead: Long live the Speaker King!" ("Dramatic Monologue and the Overhearing of Lyric," in *Lyric Poetry: Beyond New Criticism* [1985], 242). I am arguing here that Bryant—and nineteenth-century American poetics more generally—is the missing link in the emergence of "the Speaker King," and that considering this link means considering the racialization of the figure of the speaker.

50. *The Letters of William Cullen Bryant*, vol. 1, *1809–1836*, ed. William Cullen Bryant II and Thomas G. Voss (1975), 158.

51. William Wordsworth, *Poems, in Two Volumes, and Other Poems, 1800–1807*, ed. Jared Curtis (1983), 207.

52. On the Venus and Adonis stanza as "the most popular sextain, consisting of a heroic quatrain and couplet rhyming *ababcc* in iambic pentameter," see "Venus and Adonis Stanza" in *The Princeton Encyclopedia of Poetry and Poetics*, ed. Roland Greene et al. (2012), 1506.

53. Meredith Martin, "'Imperfectly Civilized': Ballads, Nations, and Histories of Form" (2015), 348.

54. M. H. Abrams, "The Development of the Expressive Theory of Poetry and Art," in *The Mirror and the Lamp* (1953), 84. On "balladization," see Cohen (2015), 136–163.

55. Abrams (1953), 83. On "pure poetry," see also Maclean, "From Action to Image" (1952), 413–414.

56. On the ballad as "the literary form of nonliterary verse," see McGill, "What Is a Ballad? Reading for Genre, Format, and Medium" (2016), 1. In a letter to his wife dated April 29, 1824, Bryant wrote of a dinner party at Robert Sedgwick's "in a company of *authors*. Mr. Cooper the

novelist, Mr. Halleck author of Fanny—Mr. Sands author of Yamoyden," at which the writers seem to have conferred about their mutual project to popularize the "doomed aboriginal" theme (*The Letters of William Cullen Bryant*, vol. 1, 154).

57. Virgil, *Georgics* (trans. 1988), I. ll. 493–497.

58. Kevis Goodman, *Georgic Modernity and British Romanticism: Poetry and the Mediation of History* (2004), 110.

59. Ibid., 1.

60. On the genealogy of the race concept, see Rusert, *Fugitive Science* (2017), and Painter, *The History of White People* (2010). See Marc Manganaro, *Culture, 1922: The Emergence of a Concept* (2002), for an introduction to the history of the culture concept. The original definition of the culture concept is usually attributed to E. B. Tylor, who wrote in 1871 that culture is "that complex whole which includes knowledge, belief, art, morals, law, custom, and any other capabilities and habits acquired by man as a member of society" (Tylor, *Primitive Culture: Researches into the Development of Mythology, Philosophy, Religion, Art, and Custom* [New York: Gordon Press, 1871], 1). Tylor's definition is still posted as the current Wikipedia definition of "culture": http://en.wikipedia.org/wiki/Culture.

61. Max Cavitch, *American Elegy: The Poetry of Mourning from the Puritans to Whitman* (2007), 130–131. Cavitch's reading is by far the most beautiful this poem has received.

62. Thoroughgood Moore, as cited by Molly McGarry in *Ghosts of Futures Past* (2008), 71.

63. In a remarkable appropriation of Bryant's poem titled "The Indian Requiem," published in the *Indian Teepee* in 1927, a Yuma poet named Arsenius Chaleco reworked many of Bryant's lines, breaking apart the Wordsworthian stanzas and shifting the pronouns so that the poem ends "And realms our tribes were crushed to get / May be our barren desert yet." The poem is included by Robert Dale Parker in his collection *Changing Is Not Vanishing: A Collection of American Indian Poetry to 1930* (Philadephia: University of Pennsylvania Press, 2011), 341–342. Parker represents Chaleco's poem as an original composition rather than as a pastiche of a poem by Bryant, and in doing so he follows a history of reception inaugurated by the note from William Tompkins that appeared beneath the poem's original publication: "In my humble opinion it [Chaleco's poem] ranks with the greatest of sorrow songs of any race, and I am happy to give it to the Teepee, and welcome any Indian poems" (quoted 341). The nonrecognition of the once very visible Bryant poem, the alternative recognition of racial representation in Tompkins's adoption of W. E. B. Du Bois's genre of "sorrow songs" to describe the poem, and Chaleco's very differently alienated adjustment of Bryant's lines are the stuff of another essay. My thanks to Claire Burdick, who first pointed out to me that Chaleco's poem is an adaptation of Bryant's. Her own essay on her discovery is forthcoming.

64. Andrew Galloway, "William Cullen Bryant's American Antiquities: Medievalism, Miscegenation, and Race in 'The Prairies'" (2010), 727.

65. On Bryant's version of eighteenth-century Universal History in the Spenserian stanzas of "The Ages" (1821), see my essay, "Bryant; or, American Romanticism" (2008).

66. Stephen J. Gould, *The Mismeasure of Man* (1996).

67. Rusert (2017), 9.

68. Bryant, *Prose Writings* 2, 77.

69. Jules Zanger, "The Premature Elegy: Bryant's 'The Prairies' as Political Poem," in *Interface: Essays on History, Myth and Art in American Literature*, ed. Daniel Royot (Montpellier: Université de Montpellier, 1984), 13–20.

70. William Cullen Bryant, "The Prairies," in *The Life and Works of William Cullen Bryant*, vol. 3, *The Poetical Works of William Cullen Bryant*, ed. Godwin (1883), 228 (1834 version).

71. Godwin (1883), 277.

72. Packer (1990), 255.

73. Bryant, "Lectures on Poetry," *Prose Writings*, 5.

74. Bryant, *Letters*, vol. 1, 360.

75. John Hay, "A Poet of the Land: William Cullen Bryant and Moundbuilder Ecology" (2015), 479.

76. Gruesz (2002), 49.

77. Cavitch (2007), 123.

78. William Cullen Bryant, "Thanatopsis," in *The Life and Works of William Cullen Bryant*, vol. 3, *The Poetical Works of William Cullen Bryant*, ed. Godwin (1883), 19.

79. While I am dwelling here on nineteenth-century myths of the "moundbuilders," for an account of actual Mississippian culture that busts those myths, see Philip H. Round's "Mississippian Contexts for Early American Studies," *Early American Literature* 53, no. 2 (2018), 445–473.

80. See Gordon Sayre, "The Mound Builders and the Imagination of American Antiquity in Jefferson, Bartram, and Chateaubriand" (1998), 225–249.

81. Patrick Brantlinger, *Dark Vanishings: Discourse on the Extinction of Primitive Races, 1800–1930* (2003), 1.

82. For the full text of President Andrew Jackson's speech to Congress on December 6, 1830, see https://www.archives.gov/milestone-documents/jacksons-message-to-congress-on-indian-removal.

83. Hay (2015), 485.

84. Ibid., 485.

85. Ibid., 480.

86. See Katie Chiles, *Transformable Race: Surprising Metamorphoses in the Literature of Early America* (2014).

87. See J. D. McCulloh, Jr., *Researches, Philosophical and Antiquarian, Concerning the Aboriginal History of America* (Baltimore: Fielding Lucas, Jr., 1829).

88. Robert Silverberg, *Mound Builders of Ancient America: The Archeology of a Myth* (1968), 83–84.

89. Stephen Williams, *Fantastic Archeology: The Wild Side of North American Prehistory* (1991), 47.

90. Ibid., 50.

91. Bryant, *Letters*, vol. 1, 340.

92. It is unlikely that Bryant would have known Flint's 1826 poem, since its popular circulation really began when it was included in William T. Coggeshall, ed., *Poets and Poetry of the West* (Columbus, OH: Follett, Foster and Company, 1860), 57–58.

93. Josiah Priest, *American Antiquities and Discoveries in the West, Being an Exhibition of the Evidence that an Ancient Population of Partially Civilized Nations Differing Entirely from those of the Present Indians Peopled America Many Centuries Before its Discovery by Columbus, and Inquiries into their Origin, with a Copious Description of Many of their Stupendous Works, Now in Ruins, with Conjectures Concerning What May Have Become of Them* (Albany, NY: Printed by Hoffman and White, 1831), 177.

94. Robert Young, *Colonial Desire: Hybridity in Theory, Culture, and Race* (1995), 41.

95. Cited by Young (1995), 41.

96. Virgil, *The Aeneid*, trans. Robert Fitzgerald (New York: Vintage Random House, 1990), 184. Fitzgerald's late twentieth-century blank verse might be considered an extension of the history I trace here, though Bryant translated Virgil into heroic couplets as a boy, since the English *Aeneid* with which he was most familiar was Dryden's 1697 translation.

97. "On Poetry in Its Relation to Our Age and Country" was the third of Bryant's "Lectures on Poetry" at the New York Atheneum in April 1825, shortly after his arrival in New York. See *The Life and Works of William Cullen Bryant*, vol. 5, *Prose Writings*, ed. Godwin (1883), 34.

98. George Saintsbury, *History of English Prosody*, vol. 2 (1910), 199.

99. Geoffrey Hartman, *Wordsworth's Poetry 1787–1814* (1971), 27.

100. Robert Shaw, *Blank Verse: A Guide to Its History and Use* (2007), 33, 6.

101. John Addington Symonds, "Blank Verse," in *Sketches and Studies of Southern Europe* (1880), 361–362.

102. Bryant, "On Trisyllabic Feet in Iambic Measure," in *The Life and Works of William Cullen Bryant*, vol. 5, *Prose Writings*, ed. Godwin (1883), 67. All of the poets cited as examples of this "liberty" in Bryant's essay are of course White British men.

103. Joseph Harrington, "Re-Birthing 'America': Philip Freneau, William Cullen Bryant, and the Invention of Modern Poetics" (1996), 272.

104. *Hegel's Aesthetics*, trans. T. M. Knox (1975), 517–518.

Chapter Five. The Poetess

1. "Heavy metal" is Matt Sandler's (conversational) phrase for Whitfield's poetics, and it is just right.

2. Paula Bennett, "Was Sigourney a Poetess? The Aesthetics of Victorian Plenitude in Lydia Sigourney's Poetry" (2007), 270.

3. Tricia Lootens, *The Political Poetess* (2017), 3, 5.

4. Eve Kosoksy Sedgwick, *Epistemology of the Closet* (1990), 31.

5. Kerry Larson, "The Passion for Poetry in Lydia Sigourney and Elizabeth Oakes Smith" (2017), 53; Nina Baym, "Reinventing Lydia Sigourney" (1990), 1.

6. Alexandra Socarides, *In Plain Sight: Nineteenth-Century Women's Poetry and the Problem of Literary History* (2020), 1; Eliza Richards, *Gender and the Poetics of Reception in Poe's Circle* (2004), 1.

7. Richards (2004), 3.

8. Jennifer Putzi and Alexandra Socarides, eds., *A History of Nineteenth-Century American Women's Poetry* (2017), 12.

9. Richards (2004), 1.

10. Yopie Prins, "Poetess," in *The Princeton Encyclopedia of Poetry and Poetics*, 1052.

11. Rusert (2017), 19.

12. Meredith McGill, "Frances Ellen Watkins Harper and the Circuits of Abolitionist Poetry," in *Early African American Print Culture*, ed. Lara Langer Cohen and Jordan Stein (2012), 56.

13. Benjamin Brawley, *The Negro in Literature and Art in the United States* (1918), 75; Redding (1939), 40; Johnson (1922), 24, 19.

14. Frances Smith Foster, *A Brighter Coming Day: A Frances Ellen Watkins Harper Reader* (1990), 30.

15. Ibid., 237.

16. See Rebecka Rutledge Fisher, "Remnants of Memory: Testimony and Being in Frances E. W. Harper's *Sketches of Southern Life*" (2008), 71; Monique-Adelle Callahan, "Frances Harper and the Poetry of Reconstruction," in Putzi and Socarides, *A History of Nineteenth-Century Women's Poetry* (2017), 343.

17. Sandler (2020), 122. Derrick R. Spires, *The Practice of Citizenship: Black Politics and Print Cultures in the Early United States* (2019), 210.

18. Spires (2019), 216, 210.

19. Wilson (2011), 63.

20. Lootens (2017), 181.

21. Frances Ellen Watkins, *Poems on Miscellaneous Subjects* (Boston: J. B. Yerrinton & Son, Printers, 1854), 32.

22. McGill, "Frances Ellen Watkins Harper and the Circuits of Abolitionist Poetry" (2012), 57.

23. Joanna Ortner, "Lost No More: Recovering Frances Ellen Watkins Harper's *Forest Leaves*," *Commonplace: The Journal of Early American Life* (2015): http://commonplace.online /article/lost-no-more-recovering-frances-ellen-watkins-harpers-forest-leaves/.

24. J. W. Johnson (1922), 36.

25. Walter Benjamin, "Some Motifs in Baudelaire," in *The Lyric Theory Reader* (1939/2014), 327.

26. James Baldwin, "Everybody's Protest Novel," in *The Price of the Ticket: Collected Nonfiction, 1948–1985* (1985), i–xx.

27. Lauren Berlant, *The Female Complaint: The Unfinished Business of Sentimentality in American Culture* (2008), 58, 60.

28. Ibid., viii–ix.

29. John Greenleaf Whittier, "Little Eva," *Frederick Douglass' Paper* (Rochester, NY), July 23, 1852, 4.

30. Warner, *Publics and Counterpublics* (2002), 67.

31. See http://utc.iath.virginia.edu/songs/littlevaf.html.

32. Mary H. Collier, "Eva's Parting," *Frederick Douglass' Paper* (Rochester, NY), August 13, 1852, 4.

33. Karen Sánchez-Eppler, *Touching Liberty: Abolition, Feminism, and the Politics of the Body* (1993), 133.

34. Sánchez-Eppler (1993), 174 n. 2.

35. Johnson, *Persons and Things* (2008), 23.

36. Karl Marx, *Capital*, vol. 1, in *The Marx-Engels Reader* (1978), 320.

37. Elizabeth Oakes Smith, "The Sinless Child", *Southern Literary Messenger* (January 1842), 86–89; (February 1842), 121–129. A revised longer version was published in *The Poetical Writings of Elizabeth Oakes Smith* (New York: J. S. Redfield, 1845), 15–84. There seem to be many reprint book volumes of the single poem as well; I have one that is four and a half inches long by three inches wide with gilt edges, a convenient size for a pocket or purse (New York: John Keese, 1843). Line numbers here are from the Keese edition.

38. The reviewer is H. T. Tuckerman, quoted in Richards (2004), 161.

39. Larson, "The Passion for Poetry in Lydia Sigourney and Elizabeth Oakes Smith" (2017), 53.

40. On the shift from hierarchies of genre to hierarchies of reading, see Leah Price, *The Anthology and the Rise of the Novel: From Richardson to George Eliot* (2000), 156.

41. Charles C. Calhoun, *Longfellow: A Rediscovered Life* (2004), 180.

42. Longfellow to George W. Greene, 5 January 1840, in *Letters of Henry Wadsworth Longfellow*, ed. Andrew Hilen, 6 vols. (1966–1982), vol. 2, 203.

43. McGill, "What Is a Ballad?" (2016), 175.

44. The memo is cited by Joan Shelley Rubin in *Songs of Ourselves: The Uses of Poetry in America* (2007), 248.

45. Lawrence Buell, ed., Introduction to *Henry Wadsworth Longfellow, Selected Poems* (1988), xviii.

46. Robert L. Gale, *A Henry Wadsworth Longfellow Companion* (2003), 202.

47. Henry Wadsworth Longfellow, *The Works of Henry Wadsworth Longfellow*, ed. Samuel Longfellow, 14 vols. (1886), 16. Henceforth cited as *WL*.

48. Matthew Gartner, "Becoming Longfellow: Work, Manhood, and Poetry" (2000), 61.

49. Calhoun (2004), 190.

50. Gruesz (2002), 92.

51. Gruesz (2002), 94.

52. Kirstie Blair, "Accents Disconsolate: Longfellow's *Evangeline* and Antebellum Politics" (2011), 21.

53. Longfellow to Robert Bigsby, 20 September 1848, *The Letters of Henry Wadsworth Longfellow*, ed. Andrew Hilen, 4 vols. (1966–1972), vol. 3, 180.

54. Yopie Prins, "Victorian Meters," in *The Cambridge Companion to Victorian Poetry*, ed. Joseph Bristow (2000), 100.

55. Saintsbury, *History of English Prosody*, III (1910), 207.

56. Yopie Prins, "Metrical Translation: Nineteenth-Century Homers and the Hexameter Mania," in *Nation, Language, and the Ethics of Translation*, ed. Sandra Bermann and Michael Wood (2005), 238.

57. George W. Peck, "A Review of Mr. Longfellow's *Evangeline*," *American Review*, February 1848, 6.

58. Edgar Allan Poe, *Essays and Reviews*, ed. G. R. Thompson (1984), 777.

59. Ibid., 69.

60. Ibid., 69.

61. Prins, "Metrical Translation" (2005), 229.

62. Gruesz (2002), 90.

63. Aamir Mufti, *Forget English!: Orientalisms and World Literatures* (2016), 5. Mufti argues that "*a genealogy of world literature leads to Orientalism*" (19), and in the American context that is certainly true, since Longfellow derives his version of the *Weltliteratur* from Goethe, but it is also true that in the American context, Orientalism becomes a hermeneutic for Black and Indigenous subjects.

64. Entry for 6 January 1847, cited in *Life of Henry Wadsworth Longfellow, with Extracts from His Journals and Correspondence*, ed. Samuel Longfellow, 3 vols. (Boston: Ticknor, 1886), vol. 2, 73–74.

65. Gartner (2000), 67.

66. Emerson to Longfellow, 25 November 1855, cited in Samuel Longfellow, *Life of Henry Wadsworth Longfellow*, 3 vols. (1886), vol. 2, 265.

67. Walt Whitman, "Death of Longfellow," in Justin Kaplan, ed., *Specimen Days. Walt Whitman: Poetry and Prose* (New York: Library of America, 1996), 941–942.

68. Angus Fletcher, "Whitman and Longfellow: Two Types of the American Poet" (1991), 139; Dana Gioia, "Longfellow in the Aftermath of Modernism," in Jay Parini, ed., *The Columbia History of American Poetry* (1993), 85.

69. Gioia (1993), 65.

70. Christoph Irmscher, *Longfellow Redux* (2006), 5–6.

71. McGill (2012), 57.

72. Cedric Robinson, *Black Marxism* (1983), 317.

73. Wilson (2011), 72.

74. Frederick Douglass, *Narrative of the Life of Frederick Douglass, an American Slave* (New York: Penguin Classics, 2014), 27.

75. Cohen (2015), 201.

76. You can listen to an amazing version of the song in one of Odetta's last performances at https://www.youtube.com/watch?v=BLfE7p75g2g.

77. See Sonya Posmentier, "Lyric Reading in the Black Ethnographic Archive" (2018), 55–84.

78. You can listen to a modern performance of that shout produced for the Smithsonian at https://folkways.si.edu/the-seniorlites/you-got-a-right-to-the-tree-of-life/african-american-music-gospel-sacred/music/track/smithsonian.

79. See Isabel Hofmeyr, *The Portable Bunyan: A Transnational History of the Pilgrim's Progress* (2003).

80. Harriet Beecher Stowe, *Uncle Tom's Cabin; or, Life Among the Lowly* (1852/1896), 500.

Coda. The Prophecy

1. Johanna Ortner's discovery of *Forest Leaves* is so new and so remarkable that Watkins Harper scholarship is just beginning to process what it means for an understanding of her career as well as for an understanding of early Black print culture more generally. The essays in *Common Place* 16, no. 2 (Summer 2016), devoted to this discovery make a great start.

2. These pages were not Whitman's debut in print, of course, but in each of the editions of *Leaves of Grass*, Whitman tended to stage the book as a debut. Many scholars have made both this point and the point about the *au courant* literary leaves about Whitman. See especially Ed Folsom, "Whitman Making Books/Books Making Whitman," *Walt Whitman Archive* (2005), https://whitmanarchive.org/criticism/current/anc.00150.html.

3. Britt Rusert, "'Nor Wish to Live the Past Again': Unsettling Origins in Frances Ellen Watkins Harper's *Forest Leaves*," *Common Place* 16, no. 2 (Summer 2016), http://commonplace.online/article/nor-wish-to-live-the-past-again-unsettling-origins-in-frances-ellen-watkins-harpers-forest-leaves-2/. The allusion to Kinohi Nishikawa is to "The Archive on Its Own: Black Politics, Independent Publishing, and *The Negotiations*," *MELUS* 40, no. 33 (Fall 2015), 76–201. Rusert's citation of Leif Eckstrom is from personal correspondence, though since I have

also benefited from personal exchanges with Leif Eckstrom over many years, I will say that I recognize the wisdom.

4. Nadia Nurhussein, *Black Land: Imperial Ethiopianism and African America* (2019), 6. Nurhussein's fascinating book is more interested in the challenge to such representations when Ethiopia did assert itself as a contemporary nation, but her analysis is suggestive for the prehistory of that assertion in abstract instances like Watkins's invocation in "Ethiopia." On Wilson's "Ethiop," see Radiclani Clytus, "Visualizing in Black Print: The Brooklyn Correspondence of William J. Wilson aka 'Ethiop'" (2018).

5. On the concept of the undercommons as a defense against the fact that "politics is an ongoing attack on the common—the general and generative antagonism—from within the surround," see Stefano Harney and Fred Moten, *The Undercommons: Fugitive Planning and Black Study* (2013), 17.

6. Albert Raboteau, *A Fire in the Bones: Reflections on African-American Religious History* (1995), 42.

7. Roy Kay, *The Ethiopian Prophecy in Black American Letters* (2011). Kay's book is not written for literary or critical race theory scholars, but for historians of religion; though the book lags in argument and terminology (oddly, Black people are referred to as "Negroes" in 2011), it remains a resource in its meticulous scholarship.

8. David Walker, *Appeal to the Coloured Citizens of the World* (1829/2000), 2. This note prefaces the "Preamble" in the third edition of Walker's *Appeal*.

SELECTED BIBLIOGRAPHY

Abrams, M. H. 1953. *The Mirror and the Lamp: Romantic Theory and the Critical Tradition*. Oxford: Oxford University Press.

———. 1971. *Natural Supernaturalism: Tradition and Revolution in Romantic Literature*. New York: W. W. Norton & Company.

Adorno, Theodor. 1957/reprint 2014. "On Lyric Poetry and Society," trans. Shierry Weber Nicholson. In *The Lyric Theory Reader*, ed. V. Jackson and Y. Prins. Baltimore, MD: Johns Hopkins University Press, 339–350.

Altieri, Charles. 1998. *Postmodernisms Now: New Essays on Contemporaneity in the Arts*. State College, PA: Penn State University Press.

Appiah, Kwame Anthony. 2020. "The Case for Capitalizing the B in Black," *The Atlantic*, June 18, 2020: https://www.theatlantic.com/ideas/archive/2020/06/time-to-capitalize-blackand-white/613159/.

Ashton, Jennifer. 2005. *From Modernism to Postmodernism: American Poetry and Theory in the Twentieth Century*. Cambridge: Cambridge University Press.

Bakhtin, Mikhail M. 1986. *Speech Genres and Other Late Essays*, trans. Vern W. McGee. Austin: University of Texas Press.

Baldwin, James. 1985. *The Price of the Ticket: Collected Nonfiction, 1948-1985*. New York: St. Martin's Press.

———. 1998. *Baldwin: Collected Essays*. New York: Library of America.

Barrett, Faith. 2012. *To Fight Aloud Is Very Brave: American Poetry and the Civil War*. Amherst and Boston: University of Massachusetts Press.

Bassard, Katherine Clay. 1999. *Spiritual Interrogations: Culture, Gender, and Community in Early African American Women's Writing*. Princeton, NJ: Princeton University Press.

Baucom, Ian. 2005. *Specters of the Atlantic: Finance Capital, Slavery, and the Philosophy of History*. Durham, NC: Duke University Press.

Baym, Nina. 1990. "Reinventing Lydia Sigourney." *American Literature* 62, no. 3, 385–404.

Benjamin, Walter. 1939/reprint 2014. "On Some Motifs in Baudelaire," translated by Harry Zohn. In *The Lyric Theory Reader*, ed. V. Jackson and Y. Prins. Baltimore, MD: Johns Hopkins University Press, 327–338.

———. 1940/1968. *Illuminations: Essays and Reflections*, trans. Harry Zohn. New York: Schocken Books.

Bennett, Joshua. 2020. *Being Property Once Myself: Blackness and the End of Man*. Cambridge, MA: The Belknap Press of Harvard University Press.

Bennett, Paula. 1998. "Phillis Wheatley's Vocation and the Paradox of the 'Afric Muse.'" *PMLA* 113, no. 1, 64–76.

———. 2007. "Was Sigourney a Poetess? The Aesthetics of Victorian Plenitude in Lydia Sigourney's Poetry." *Comparative American Studies* 5, no. 3, 270.

Benveniste, Émile. 1971. *Problems in General Linguistics*, trans. Mary Elizabeth Meek. Coral Gables, FL: University of Miami Press.

Berlant, Lauren. 1997. *The Queen of America Goes to Washington City: Essays on Sex and Citizenship*. Durham, NC: Duke University Press.

———. 2008. *The Female Complaint: The Unfinished Business of Sentimentality in American Culture*. Durham, NC: Duke University Press.

———. 2011. *Cruel Optimism*. Durham, NC: Duke University Press.

Bernstein, Charles. 2011. "The Difficult Poem." In *Attack of the Difficult Poems: Essays and Inventions*. Chicago: University of Chicago Press, 3–7.

Best, Stephen. 2018. *None Like Us: Blackness, Belonging, Aesthetic Life*. Durham, NC: Duke University Press.

Bigelow, John. 1890. *William Cullen Bryant*. Boston: Houghton Mifflin.

Blair, Kirstie. 2011. "Accents Disconsolate: Longfellow's *Evangeline* and Antebellum Politics," *LEAR: Literature of the Early American Republic* 3.

Blake, William. 2007. *Blake: The Complete Poems*, ed. W. H. Stevenson. London: Routledge.

Blight, David. 2018. *Frederick Douglass: Prophet of Freedom*. New York: Simon & Schuster.

Bloom, Harold. 1976. *Poetry and Repression: Revisionism from Blake to Stevens*. New Haven, CT: Yale University Press.

Brady, Andrea. 2021. *Poetry and Bondage: A History and Theory of Lyric Constraint*. Cambridge: Cambridge University Press.

Brantlinger, Patrick. 2003. *Dark Vanishings: Discourse on the Extinction of Primitive Races, 1800–1930*. Ithaca, NY: Cornell University Press.

Brawley, Benjamin. 1918. *The Negro in Literature and Art in the United States*. New York: Duffield & Company.

Brickhouse, Anna. 2004. *Transamerican Literary Relations and the Nineteenth-Century Public Sphere*. Cambridge: Cambridge University Press.

Brooks, Cleanth. 1939. *Modern Poetry and the Tradition*. Chapel Hill: University of North Carolina Press.

Brooks, Joanna. 2010. "Our Phillis, Ourselves." *American Literature* 82, no. 1, 1–28.

———. 2021. "The Unfortunates: What the Life Spans of Early Black Books Tell Us about Book History." In *Early African American Print Culture*, ed. Lara Langer Cohen and Jordan Stein. Philadelphia: University of Pennsylvania Press, 40–52.

Brooks, Van Wyck. 1915. *America's Coming-of-Age*. New York: B. W. Huebsch.

Brower, Reuben. 1951/reprint 2014. "The Speaking Voice." In *The Lyric Theory Reader*, ed. V. Jackson and Y. Prins. Baltimore, MD: Johns Hopkins University Press, 211–218.

Brown, Charles H. 1971. *William Cullen Bryant: A Biography*. New York: Charles Scribner's Sons.

Brown, Sterling. 1937. *Negro Poetry and Drama*. Washington, DC: The Associates in Negro Folk Education.

Bryant, William Cullen. 1883. *The Life and Works of William Cullen Bryant*, six volumes, ed. Parke Godwin. New York: D. Appleton.

———. 1975. *The Letters of William Cullen Bryant*, vol. 1, *1809–1836*, ed. William Cullen Bryant II and Thomas G. Voss. New York: Fordham University Press.

Burt, Stephanie. 2016. *the poem is you: 60 Contemporary Poets and How to Read Them*. Cambridge, MA: The Belknap Press of Harvard University Press.

Calhoun, Charles C. 2004. *Longfellow: A Rediscovered Life*. Boston: Beacon Press.

Callahan, Monique-Adele. 2017. "Frances Harper and the Poetry of Reconstruction." In Putzi and Socarides, eds., *A History of Nineteenth-Century American Women's Poetry*, 329–344.

Campbell, Thomas. 1904. *Poems of Thomas Campbell*, selected and arranged by Lewis Campbell. New York: The Macmillan Company.

Carretta, Vincent. 2011. *Phillis Wheatley: Biography of a Genius in Bondage*. Athens: University of Georgia Press.

Carson, Anne. 1997. "Sappho Shock." In *Dwelling in Possibility: Women Poets and Critics on Poetry*, ed. Yopie Prins and Maeera Schreiber. Ithaca, NY: Cornell University Press, 223–229.

Caruth, Cathy. 1996. *Unclaimed Experience: Trauma, Narrative, and History*. Baltimore, MD: Johns Hopkins University Press.

Cavitch, Max. 2007. *American Elegy: The Poetry of Mourning from the Puritans to Whitman*. Minneapolis: University of Minnesota Press.

———. 2011. "Slavery and Its Metrics." In *The Cambridge Companion to Nineteenth-Century American Poetry*, ed. Kerry Larson. Cambridge: Cambridge University Press, 94–112.

———. 2014. "The Poetry of Phillis Wheatley in Slavery's Recollective Economies, 1773 to the Present." In *Race, Ethnicity, and Publishing in America*, ed. Cécile Cottenet. London: Palgrave Macmillan, 210–230.

Chander, Manu Samitri. 2017. *Brown Romantics: Poetry and Nationalism in the Global Nineteenth Century*. Lewisburg, PA: Bucknell University Press.

Chartier, Roger. 1992. "Laborers and Voyagers: From the Text to the Reader," trans. J. A. Gonzalez. *Diacritics* 22, no. 2, 49–61.

Chatterjee, Ronjaunee, Alicia Mireles Christoff, and Amy R. Wong. 2020. "Undisciplining Victorian Studies," *Los Angeles Review of Books*, July 10, 2020: https://www.lareviewofbooks.org /article/undisciplining-victorian-studies/.

Chiles, Katie. 2014. *Transformable Race: Surprising Metamorphoses in the Literature of Early America*. New York: Oxford University Press.

Clytus, Radiclani. 2018. "Visualizing in Black Print: The Brooklyn Correspondence of William J. Wilson aka 'Ethiop.'" *J19: The Journal of Nineteenth-Century Americanists* 6, no. 1 (Spring), 29–66.

Coates, Ta-Nehisi. 2015. *Between the World and Me*. New York: Spiegel & Grau.

Cohen, Michael. 2015. *The Social Lives of Poems in Nineteenth-Century America*. Philadelphia: University of Pennsylvania Press.

Cook, Eliza. 1856. *The Poetical Works of Eliza Cook*. Philadelphia: W. P. Hazard.

Costello, Bonnie. 2017. *The Plural of Us: Poetry and Community in Auden and Others*. Princeton, NJ: Princeton University Press.

Coviello, Peter. 2002. "Agonizing Affection." *Early American Literature* 7, no. 3, 439–468.

Culler, Jonathan. 1981. *The Pursuit of Signs: Semiotics, Literature, Deconstruction*. Ithaca, NY: Cornell University Press.

———. 2015. *Theory of the Lyric*. Cambridge, MA: Harvard University Press.

Da, Nan Z. 2020. "Other People's Books." *New Literary History* 51, no. 3, 475–500.

Daut, Marlene L. 2015. *Tropics of Haiti: Race and the Literary History of the Haitian Revolution in the Atlantic World, 1789–1865*. Liverpool: Liverpool University Press.

Delany, Martin. 1853. *The Origin and Objects of Ancient Freemasonry: Its Introduction to the United States and Legitimacy among Colored Men*. Philadelphia: W. S. Haven.

———. 1859, 1861–1862/2017 reprint. *Blake; or, The Huts of America*, ed. Jerome McGann. Cambridge, MA: Harvard University Press.

De Man, Paul. 1983. "Lyric and Modernity." In *Blindness and Insight: Essays in the Rhetoric of Contemporary Criticism*. Minneapolis: University of Minnesota Press, 166–186.

———. 1984. "Anthropomorphism and Trope in Lyric." In *The Rhetoric of Romanticism*. New York: Columbia University Press, 237–262.

———. 1985. "Lyrical Voice in Contemporary Theory." In *Lyric Poetry: Beyond New Criticism*, ed. Chaviva Hošek and Patricia Parker. Ithaca, NY: Cornell University Press.

Dickinson, Emily. 1999. *The Poems of Emily Dickinson*. Variorum Edition. 3 volumes. Cambridge, MA: The Belknap Press of Harvard University Press.

Donham, Housten, and Fred Moten. "POETRY BEGINS WITH THE WILLINGNESS TO SUBORDINATE WHATEVER THE HELL IT IS THAT YOU HAVE TO SAY": AN INTERVIEW W/ FRED MOTEN. *Open House*, 20 July 2015.

Douglass, Frederick. 1845. *Narrative of the Life of Frederick Douglass, An American Slave*. Boston: The Anti-Slavery Office.

———. 2022. *Douglass: Speeches and Writings*. Ed. David W. Blight. New York: Library of America.

DuPlessis, Rachel Blau. 2001. *Genders, Races, and Religious Cultures in Modern American Poetry, 1908–1934*. Cambridge: Cambridge University Press.

Dworkin, Craig. 2020. *Radium of the Word: A Poetics of Materiality*. Chicago and London: Univeristy of Chicago Press.

Edwards, Brent Hayes. 1998. "The Seemingly Eclipsed Window of Form: James Weldon Johnson's Prefaces." In *The Jazz Cadence of American Culture*, ed. Robert O'Meally. New York: Columbia University Press, 580–601.

Ellison, Julie. 1999. *Cato's Tears and the Making of Anglo-American Emotion*. Chicago: University of Chicago Press.

Ferguson, Frances. 1992. *Solitude and the Sublime: The Romantic Aesthetics of Individuation*. London and New York: Routledge.

Fisher, Rebecka Rutledge. 2008. "Remnants of Memory: Testimony and Being in Frances E. W. Harper's *Sketches of Southern Life*." *ESQ: A Journal of the American Renaissance* 54, nos. 1–4, 55–74.

Fletcher, Angus. 1991. "Whitman and Longfellow: Two Types of the American Poet." *Raritan* 10, no. 4, 131–145.

Folsom, Ed. 2005. "Whitman Making Books/Books Making Whitman," *Walt Whitman Archive*: https://whitmanarchive.org/criticism/current/anc.00150.html.

Foster, Frances Smith, ed. 1990. *A Brighter Coming Day: A Frances Ellen Watkins Harper Reader*. New York: The Feminist Press at the City University of New York.

———. 1993. *Written by Herself: Literary Production by African American Women, 1746–1892*. Bloomington: Indiana University Press.

Foucault, Michel. 1978. "What Is an Author?" *Language, Counter-Memory, Practice: Selected Essays and Interviews*, trans. Donald F. Bouchard and Sherry Simon, ed. Donald Bouchard. Oxford: Basil Blackwell.

François, Anne-Lise. 2007. *Open Secrets: The Literature of Uncounted Experience*. Stanford, CA: Stanford University Press.

Freud, Sigmund. 1899. "Screen Memories." In *The Standard Edition, of the Complete Psychological Works of Sigmund Freud*, ed. James Strachey. London: The Hogarth Press, 3: 301–322.

Fry, Paul. 1980. *The Poet's Calling in the English Ode*. New Haven, CT: Yale University Press.

Galloway, Andrew. 2010. "William Cullen Bryant's American Antiquities: Medievalism, Miscegenation, and Race in 'The Prairies.'" *American Literary History* 22, no. 4, 724–751.

Gartner, Matthew. 2000. "Becoming Longfellow: Work, Manhood, and Poetry." *American Literature* 72, no. 1, 59–86.

Gates, Henry Louis, Jr. 1988. *The Signifying Monkey: A Theory of African-American Literary Criticism*. Oxford: Oxford University Press.

———. 2003. *The Trials of Phillis Wheatley: America's First Black Poet and Her Encounter with the Founding Fathers*. New York: Basic Books.

Gelmi, Caroline. 2020. "The Speaker, Photographed: Paul Laurence Dunbar's *Poems of Cabin and Field*." *J19: The Journal of Nineteenth-Century Americanists* 8, no. 1, 67–95.

Gikandi, Simon. 2011. *Slavery and the Culture of Taste*. Princeton, NJ: Princeton University Press.

Gilroy, Paul. 1993. *The Black Atlantic: Modernity and Double Consciousness*. New York: Verso Books.

Gioia, Dana. 1993. "Longfellow in the Aftermath of Modernism." In *The Columbia History of American Poetry*, ed. Jay Parini. New York: Columbia University Press, 64–96.

Gitelman, Lisa. 2014. *Paper Knowledge: Toward a Media History of Documents*. Durham, NC: Duke University Press.

Glatt, Cara. 2020. "'To Perpetuate Her Name': Appropriation and Autobiography in Margaretta Matilda Odell's Memoir of Phillis Wheatley." *Early American Literature* 55, no. 1, 145–176.

Glissant, Édouard. 1997. *Poetics of Relation*, trans. Betsy Wing. Ann Arbor: University of Michigan Press.

———. 2011. "One World in Relation: Édouard Glissant in Conversation with Manthia Diawara," trans. Christopher Winks. *Journal of Contemporary African Art* 28 (Spring), 4–19.

Godwin, Parke. 1883. *A Biography of Henry Wadsworth Longfellow with Extracts from His Private Correspondence*. 2 volumes. New York: D. Appleton.

Goffman, Erving. 1981. *Forms of Talk*. Philadelphia: University of Pennsylvania Press.

Goodman, Kevis. *Georgic Modernity and British Romanticism: Poetry and the Mediation of History*. Cambridge: Cambridge University Press.

Gould, Stephen J. 1996. *The Mismeasure of Man*. New York: W. W. Norton & Company.

Graff, Gerald, and Michael Warner. 1987. *Professing Literature: An Institutional History*. Chicago: University of Chicago Press.

Griffin, Farrah Jasmine. 2021. *Read Until You Understand: The Profound Wisdom of Black Life and Literature*. New York: W. W. Norton & Company.

Gruesz, Kirsten Silva. 2002. *Ambassadors of Culture: The Transamerican Origins of Latino Writing*. Princeton, NJ: Princeton University Press.

Gummere, Francis Barton. 1911. *Democracy and Poetry*. Boston: Houghton Mifflin Company.

Hack, Daniel. *Reaping Something New: African American Transformations of Victorian Literature*. Princeton, NJ: Princeton University Press.

Hall, David. 1997. *Lived Religion in America: Toward a Theory of Practice*. Princeton, NJ: Princeton University Press.

Haralson, Eric L., ed. 1998. *Encyclopedia of American Poetry*. Chicago and London: Fitzroy Dearborn Publishers.

Harney, Stefano, and Fred Moten. 2013. *The Undercommons: Fugitive Planning and Black Study*. New York: Autonomedia.

Harper, Frances Ellen Watkins. 1988. *Complete Poems of Frances E. W. Harper*, ed. Maryemma Graham. *The Schomburg Library of Nineteenth-Century Black Women Writers*. New York: Oxford University Press.

Harper, Phillip Brian. 2015. *Abstractionist Aesthetics: Artistic Form and Social Critique in African American Culture*. New York: New York University Press.

Harrington, Joseph. 1996a. "Re-Birthing 'America': Philip Freneau, William Cullen Bryant, and the Invention of Modern Poetics." In *Making America/Making American Literature*, ed. A. Robert Lee and W. M. Verhoeven. Amsterdam: Rodopi, 249–274.

———. 1996b. "Why American Poetry Is Not American Literature." *American Literary History* 8 (Fall), 496–515.

Hartman, Geoffrey. 1971. *Wordsworth's Poetry, 1787–1814*. New Haven, CT: Yale University Press.

———. 1995. "On Traumatic Knowledge and Literary Studies." *New Literary History* 26, no. 3, 537–563.

Hartman, Saidiya. 1997. *Scenes of Subjection: Terror, Slavery, and Self-Making in Nineteenth-Century America*. Oxford: Oxford University Press.

———. 2007. *Lose Your Mother: A Journey Along the Atlantic Slave Route*. New York: Farrar, Straus and Giroux.

———. 2008. "Venus in Two Acts." *Small Axe*, Number 26, 12, no. 2, 1–14.

Hay, John. 2015. "A Poet of the Land: William Cullen Bryant and Moundbuilder Ecology." *ESQ: A Journal of the American Renaissance* 61, no. 3, 474–511.

Hayes, Terrance. 2018. *American Sonnets for My Past and Future Assassin*. New York: Penguin Books.

Hegel, G.W.F. 1975. *Aesthetics: Lectures on Fine Art*, trans. T. M. Knox. Oxford: Clarendon Press.

Henderson, Mae Gwendolyn. 2000. "Speaking in Tongues: Dialogics, Dialectics, and the Black Woman Writer's Literary Tradition." In *African American Literary Theory: A Reader*, ed. Winston Napier. New York: New York University Press, 102–112.

Hickman, Jared. 2017. *Black Prometheus: Race and Radicalism in the Age of Atlantic Slavery*. Oxford: Oxford University Press.

Hofmeyr, Isabel. 2003. *The Portable Bunyan: A Transnational History of the Pilgrim's Progress*. Princeton, NJ: Princeton University Press.

Hollander, John, ed. 1993. *American Poetry: The Nineteenth Century*. 2 volumes. New York: Library of America.

Horton, George Moses. 1845. *The Poetical Works of George Moses Horton, The Colored Bard of North Carolina*. Hillsborough, NC.

———. 1865. *Naked Genius*, rev. and comp. Will H. S. Banks, Capt. 9th Mich. Cav. Raleigh, NC: Wm. B. Smith & Co.

———. 2017. "Individual Influence." *PMLA* 132, no. 5, 1244–1250.

Hošek, Chaviva, and Patricia Parker, eds. 1985. *Lyric Poetry: Beyond New Criticism*. Ithaca, NY: Cornell University Press.

Hudson, Nicholas. 1996. "From 'Nation' to 'Race': The Origin of Racial Classification in Eighteenth-Century Thought." *Eighteenth-Century Studies* 29, no. 3, 247–264.

Hulme, T. E. 1936/1962. "Romanticism and Classicism." In *Romanticism: Points of View*, ed. Robert F. Gleckner and Gerald E. Enscoe, 2nd ed. Englewood Cliffs, NJ: Prentice-Hall, 55–65.

Hunter, J. Paul. 2000. "Formalism and History: Binarism and the Anglophone Couplet." *MLQ: Modern Language Quarterly* 61, no. 1, 109–129.

Hurston, Zora Neale. 1928/reprint 1995. "How It Feels to Be Colored Me." In *Zora Neale Hurston: Folklore, Memoirs, & Other Writings*, ed. Cheryl A. Wall. New York: Library of America, 826–829.

Hutchinson, George. 1995. *The Harlem Renaissance in Black and White*. Cambridge, MA: The Belknap Press of Harvard University Press

Imlay, Gilbert. 1793. *A Topographical Description of the Western Territory of North America*. London: Samuel Campbell, no. 37, Hanover Square.

Irmscher, Christoph. 2006. *Longfellow Redux*. Urbana: University of Illinois Press.

Jackson, Andrew. 1847. *Narrative and Writings of Andrew Jackson, of Kentucky; Containing an Account of His Birth, and Twenty-Six Years of His Life While a Slave; His Escape; Five Years of Freedom, Together with Anecdotes Related to Slavery; Journal of One Year's Travels; Afric-American Astronomers, etc. Narrated by Himself; Written by a Friend*. Syracuse, NY: Daily and Weekly Star Office.

Jackson, Virginia. 2005. *Dickinson's Misery: A Theory of Lyric Reading*. Princeton, NJ: Princeton University Press.

———. 2008. "Bryant; or, American Romanticism," in *The Traffic in Poems*, ed. Meredith McGill. New Brunswick, NJ: Rutgers University Press, 185–204.

———. 2012a. "Lyric." In *The Princeton Encyclopedia of Poetry and Poetics*, fourth edition, ed. Roland Greene et al. Princeton, NJ: Princeton University Press, 826–834.

———. 2012b. "The Poet as Poetess." In *The Cambridge Companion to Nineteenth-Century American Poetry*, ed. Kerry Larson. Cambridge: Cambridge University Press, 54–76.

———. 2019. "The Cadence of Consent: Francis Barton Gummere, Lyric Rhythm, and White Poets." In *Critical Rhythm: The Poetics of a Literary Life Form*, ed. Ben Glaser and Jonathan Culler. New York: Fordham University Press, 87–105.

Jackson, Virginia, and Yopie Prins. 1999. "Lyrical Studies." *Victorian Literature and Culture* 27, no. 2, 521–530.

———, eds. 2014. *The Lyric Theory Reader: A Critical Anthology*. Baltimore, MD: Johns Hopkins University Press.

Jackson, Zakiyyah Iman. 2020. *Becoming Human: Matter and Meaning in an Antiblack World*. New York: New York University Press.

Jager, Colin. 2015. *Unquiet Things: Secularism in the Romantic Age*. Philadelphia: University of Pennsylvania Press.

James, C.L.R. 1938. *The Black Jacobins: Toussaint L'Ouverture and the San Domingo Revolution*. London: Secker & Warburg.

Javadizadeh, Kamran. 2019. "The Atlantic Ocean Breaking on Our Heads: Claudia Rankine, Robert Lowell, and the Whiteness of the Lyric Subject." *PMLA* 134, no. 3, 475–490.

Jeffers, Honorée Fanonne. 2020. *The Age of Phillis*. Middletown, CT: Wesleyan University Press.

Johnson, Barbara. 1987/reprint 2014. "Apostrophe, Animation, and Abortion." In *The Lyric Theory Reader*, ed. V. Jackson and Y. Prins. Baltimore, MD: Johns Hopkins University Press, 529–540.

———. 2008. *Persons and Things*. Cambridge, MA: Harvard University Press.

Johnson, James Weldon. 1922. *The American Book of American Negro Poetry*. New York: Harcourt, Brace, and Company.

Jordan, June. 1986. "The Difficult Miracle of Black Poetry in America or Something Like a Sonnet for Phillis Wheatley," *Massachusetts Review* 27, no. 2, 252–262.

Judy, Ronald A. T. 1993. *(Dis)Forming the American Canon: African-Arabic Slave Narratives and the Vernacular*. Minneapolis: University of Minnesota Press.

Kames, Henry Home, Lord. 1762. *Elements of Criticism*. Edinburgh: Printed for A. Miller, London, and A. Kincaid & J. Bell, Edinburgh.

Kappeler, Erin. 2014. "Editing America: Nationalism and the New Poetry." *Modernism/modernity* 21, no. 4, 899–918.

Kay, Roy. 2011. *The Ethiopian Prophecy in Black American Letters*. Gainesville: University Press of Florida.

Kazanjian, David. 2003. *The Colonizing Trick: National Culture and Imperial Citizenship in Early America*. Minneapolis: University of Minnesota Press.

Keats, John. 1982. *Complete Poems*. Ed. Jack Stillinger. Cambridge, MA: Harvard University Press.

Keene, John. 2014. "White Silences: The Lyric Theory Reader Panel @ ACLA 2014." *J's Theater*: http://jstheater.blogspot.com/2014/04/white-silences-lyric-theory-reader.html.

Keenleyside, Heather. 2016. *Animals and Other People: Literary Forms and Living Beings in the Long Eighteenth Century*. Philadelphia: University of Pennsylvania Press.

Kendi, Ibram X. 2016. *Stamped from the Beginning: The Definitive History of Racist Ideas in America*. New York: Nation Books.

Kerr-Ritchie, J. R. 2007. *Rites of August First: Emancipation Day in the Black Atlantic World*. Baton Rouge: Louisiana State University Press.

Kilcup, Karen K. 2019. *Who Killed American Poetry? From National Obsession to Elite Possession*. Ann Arbor: University of Michigan Press.

King, Tiffany Lethabo. 2019. *The Black Shoals: Offshore Formations of Black and Native Studies*. Durham, NC: Duke University Press.

Knapp, Isaac, ed. 1838. *Memoir and Poems of Phillis Wheatley, A Native African and a Slave. Also Poems by a Slave*. Boston: Isaac Knapp, 1838.

Knapp, Steven. 1985. *Personification and the Sublime: Milton to Coleridge*. Cambridge, MA: Harvard University Press.

Kramnick, Jonathan Brody. 2018. *Paper Minds: Literature and the Ecology of Consciousness*. Chicago: University of Chicago Press.

Larson, Kerry, ed. 2011. *The Cambridge Companion to Nineteenth-Century American Poetry*. Cambridge: Cambridge University Press.

————. 2017. "The Passion for Poetry in Lydia Sigourney and Elizabeth Oakes Smith." In *A History of Nineteenth-Century Women's Poetry*, ed. Jennifer Putzi and Alexandra Socarides. Cambridge: Cambridge University Press, 53–67.

Lazo, Rodrigo. 2005. *Writing to Cuba: Filibustering and Cuban Exiles in the United States*. Chapel Hill: University of North Carolina Press.

Leonard, William Ellery. 1917. "Bryant and the Minor Poets." In *The Cambridge History of American Literature*, ed. William Peterfield Trent, John Erskine, Stuart P. Sherman, and Carl Van Doren. New York: G. P. Putnam's Sons, 1917, vol. 2, chapter v, 260–283.

Levine, Robert. 1997. *Martin Delany, Frederick Douglass, and the Politics of Representative Identity*. Chapel Hill: University of North Carolina Press.

Loeffelholz, Mary. 2004. *From School to Salon: Reading Nineteenth-Century American Women's Poetry*. Princeton, NJ: Princeton University Press.

Longfellow, Henry Wadsworth. 1886a. *Life of Henry Wadsworth Longfellow, with Extracts from His Journals and Correspondence*, ed. Samuel Longfellow. 3 volumes. Boston: Ticknor and Fields.

————. 1886b. *The Works of Henry Wadsworth Longfellow*, ed. Samuel Longfellow. 14 volumes. Boston: Houghton Mifflin.

Lootens, Tricia. 2017. *The Political Poetess: Victorian Femininity, Race, and the Legacy of Separate Spheres*. Princeton, NJ: Princeton University Press.

Lott, Eric. 1993. *Love and Theft: Blackface Minstrelsy and the American Working Class*. Oxford: Oxford University Press.

Luciano, Dana, and Ivy G. Wilson, eds. 2014. *Unsettled States: Nineteenth-Century American Literary Studies*. New York: New York University Press.

Lynch, Deidre Shauna. 2018. *Loving Literature: A Cultural History*. Chicago: University of Chicago Press.

Mackey, Nathaniel. 2000. "Destination Out." *Callaloo* 23, no. 2, 814.

Maclean, Norman. 1952. "From Action to Image: Theories of the Lyric in the Eighteenth Century." In *Critics and Criticism: Ancient and Modern*, ed. R. S. Crane. Chicago: University of Chicago Press, 408–462.

————. 1956. "Personification But Not Poetry." *ELH* 23, no. 2, 163–170.

Manganaro, Marc. 2002. *Culture, 1922: The Emergence of a Concept*. Princeton, NJ: Princeton University Press.

Martin, Meredith. 2012. *The Rise and Fall of Meter: Poetry and English National Culture*. Princeton, NJ: Princeton University Press.

————. 2015. "'Imperfectly Civilized': Ballads, Nations, and Histories of Form." *ELH* 82, no. 2, 345–363.

Marx, Karl. 1867/reprint 1978. *Capital*, vol. 1, in *The Marx-Engels Reader*, ed. Robert C. Tucker. New York: Norton, 1978.

Matthiessen, F. O. 1941. *American Renaissance: Art and Expression in the Age of Emerson and Whitman*. New York: Oxford University Press.

McCarthy, Jesse. 2021. *Who Will Pay Reparations on My Soul?* New York: Liveright/W. W. Norton. & Company.

McGarry, Molly. 2008. *Ghosts of Futures Past: Spiritualism and the Cultural Politics of Nineteenth-Century America*. Berkeley: University of California Press.

McGill, Meredith. 2003. *American Literature and the Culture of Reprinting, 1834–1853*. Philadelphia: University of Pennsylvania Press.

———, ed. 2008. *The Traffic in Poems: Nineteenth-Century Poetry and Transatlantic Exchange*. New Brunswick, NJ: Rutgers University Press.

———. 2012. "Frances Ellen Watkins Harper and the Circuits of Abolitionist Poetry." In *Early African American Print Culture*, ed. Lara Langer Cohen and Jordan Stein. Philadelphia: University of Pennsylvania Press, 53–74.

———. 2016. "The Poetry of Slavery." In *The Cambridge Companion to Slavery in American Literature*, ed. Ezra Tawil. Cambridge: Cambridge University Press, 115–136.

———. 2016. "What Is a Ballad? Reading for Genre, Format, and Medium." *Nineteenth-Century Literature* 71, no. 2, 156–175.

McKittrick, Katherine, ed. 2015. *Sylvia Wynter: Being Human as Praxis*. Durham, NC: Duke University Press.

Mill, John Stuart. 1981. "Thoughts on Poetry and Its Varieties." In *Autobiography and Literary Essays*, vol. 1, *The Collected Works of John Stuart Mill*, ed. John M Robson and Jack Stillenger. Toronto: University of Toronto Press, 341–366.

Morrison, Toni. 1987. *Beloved*. New York: Alfred A. Knopf.

———. 1993. *Playing in the Dark: Whiteness and the Literary Imagination*. New York: Vintage Reprint Edition.

———. 2020. *Mouth Full of Blood: Essays, Speeches, Meditations*. London: Random House UK.

Moten, Fred. 2003. *In the Break: The Aesthetics of the Black Radical Tradition*. Minneapolis: University of Minnesota Press.

———. 2007. "Taste Dissonance Flavor Escape: Preface for a Solo by Miles Davis." *Women and Performance: A Journal of Feminist Theory* 17, no. 2, 217–246.

———. 2017. *Black and Blur*. Durham, NC: Duke University Press.

Mufti, Aamir. 2016. *Forget English!: Orientalisms and World Literatures*. Cambridge, MA: Harvard University Press.

Muller, Gilbert H. 2008. *William Cullen Bryant: Author of America*. Albany: State University of New York Press.

Murphy, Dana. 2020. "Praisesong for Margaret Walker's *Jubilee* and the Phillis Wheatley Poetry Festival." *African American Review* 53, no. 4, 299–313.

Nersessian, Anahid. 2020. *The Calamity Form: On Poetry and Social Life*. Chicago: University of Chicago Press.

Nishikawa, Kinohi. 2015. "The Archive on Its Own: Black Politics, Independent Publishing, and *The Negotiations*," *MELUS* 40, no. 33 (Fall 2015): 76–201.

Nurhussein, Nadia. 2019. *Black Land: Imperial Ethiopianism and African America*. Princeton, NJ: Princeton University Press.

Ortner, Johanna. 2015. "Lost No More: Recovering Frances Ellen Watkins Harper's *Forest Leaves*." *Common Place: The Journal of Early American Life* 15, no. 4 (Summer 2015): http://commonplace.online/article/lost-no-more-recovering-frances-ellen-watkins-harpers-forest-leaves/.

Packer, Barbara. 1990. "'Man Hath No Part in All This Glorious Work': American Romantic Landscapes." In *Romantic Revolutions: Criticism and Theory*. ed. Kenneth R. Johnston, et al. Bloomington: Indiana University Press, 250–268.

Painter, Nell Irvin. 2010. *The History of White People*. New York: Norton & Company.

Parker, Andrew. 2010. "The Poetry of the Future; or, Periodizing the Nineteenth Century." *Modern Language Quarterly* 71, no. 1: 75–85.

Parker, Robert Dale, ed. 2011. *Changing Is Not Vanishing: A Collection of American Indian Poetry to 1930*. Philadelphia: University of Pennsylvania Press.

Pearce, Roy Harvey. 1961. *The Continuity of American Poetry*. Princeton, NJ: Princeton University Press.

Pennington, James W. C. 1841. *A Text Book of the Origin and History, &c. &c. of the Colored People*. Hartford, CT: L. Skinner, Printer.

Philip, M. NourbeSe. 2008. *Zong!: As Told to the Author by Setaey Adamu Boateng*. Middletown, CT: Wesleyan University Press.

Phillips, Ricardo Rowan. 2010. *When Blackness Rhymes with Blackness*. Champaign, IL, and London: Dalkey Archive Press.

Pierpont, John. 1843. *The Anti-Slavery Poems of John Pierpont*. Boston: Oliver Johnson.

Pinch, Adela. 1996. *Strange Fits of Passion: Epistemologies of Emotion, Hume to Austen*. Stanford, CA: Stanford University Press.

Pinto, Samantha. 2020. *Infamous Bodies: Early Black Women's Celebrity and the Afterlives of Rights*. Durham, NC: Duke University Press.

Plato, Ann. 1841. *Essays; Including Biographies and Miscellaneous Pieces, in Prose and Poetry*. Hartford, CT: Printed for the Author.

———. 1988. *Essays; Including Biographies and Miscellaneous Pieces, in Prose and Poetry*. New York and Oxford: Oxford University Press.

Poe, Edgar Allan, 1984. *Essays and Reviews*, ed. G. R. Thompson. New York: Library of America, 1984.

Pope, Alexander, trans. *Pope's Translation of Homer's Iliad Books I VI XXII XXIV*, ed. with introduction and notes by William Tappan. Boston: The Athenaeum Press, 1898.

Posmentier, Sonya, 2017. *Cultivation and Catastrophe: The Lyric Ecology of Modern Black Literature*. Baltimore, MD: Johns Hopkins University Press.

———. 2018. "Lyric Reading in the Black Ethnographic Archive." *American Literary History* 30, no. 1, 55–84.

Pratt, Lloyd. 2016. *The Stranger's Book: The Human of African American Literature*. Philadelphia: University of Pennsylvania Press.

Price, Leah. 2000. *The Anthology and the Rise of the Novel: From Richardson to George Eliot*. Cambridge: Cambridge University Press

Prins, Yopie. 1999. *Victorian Sappho*. Princeton, NJ: Princeton University Press.

———. 2000. "Victorian Meters." In *The Cambridge Companion to Victorian Poetry*, ed. Joseph Bristow. Cambridge: Cambridge University Press, 89–113.

———. 2005. "Metrical Translation: Nineteenth-Century Homers and the Hexameter Mania." In *Nation, Language, and the Ethics of Translation*, ed. Sandra Bermann and Michael Wood. Princeton, NJ: Princeton University Press, 2005, 229–256.

————. 2012. "Poetess." In *The Princeton Encyclopedia of Poetry and Poetics*, fourth edition, ed. Roland Greene et al. Princeton, NJ: Princeton University Press, 1051–1054.

Putzi, Jennifer, and Alexandra Socarides, eds. 2017. *A History of Nineteenth-Century American Women's Poetry*. Cambridge: Cambridge University Press.

Raboteau, Albert. 1995. *A Fire in the Bones: Reflections on African-American Religious History*. Boston: Beacon Press.

Rankine, Claudia. 2001. "The First Person in the Twenty-First Century." In *After Confession: Poetry as Autobiography*, ed. Kate Sontag and David Graham. Minneapolis: Graywolf Press, 132–136.

————. 2014. *Citizen: An American Lyric*. Minneapolis: Graywolf Press.

————. 2020. *Just Us: An American Conversation*. Minneapolis: Graywolf Press.

Rankine, Claudia, Beth Loffreda, and Max King Cap, eds. 2015. *The Racial Imaginary: Writers on Race in the Life of the Mind*. Albany, NY: Fence Books.

Redding, J. Saunders. 1939/reprint 1988. *To Make the Poet Black*. Ithaca, NY: Cornell University Press.

Reed, Anthony. 2014. *Freedom Time: The Poetics and Politics of Black Experimental Writing*. Baltimore, MD: Johns Hopkins University Press.

Rezek, Joseph. 2012. "The Print Atlantic: Phillis Wheatley, Ignatius Sancho, and the Cultural Significance of the Book." In *Early African American Print Culture*, ed. Lara Langer Cohen and Jordan Stein. Philadelphia: University of Pennsylvania Press, 19–39.

————. 2020. "The Racialization of Print." *American Literary History* 32, no. 3, 417–445.

Richards, Eliza. 2004. *Gender and the Poetics of Reception in Poe's Circle*. Cambridge: Cambridge University Press.

Richmond, M. A. 1974. *Bid the Vassal Soar: Interpretive Essays on the Life and Poetry of Phillis Wheatley (ca. 1753–1784) and George Moses Horton (ca. 1797–1883)*. Washington, DC: Howard University Press.

Robinson, Cedric. 1983/reprint 2000. *Black Marxism: The Making of the Black Radical Tradition*. Chapel Hill: University of North Carolina Press.

Robson, Catherine. 2012. *Heart Beats: Everyday Life and the Memorized Poem*. Princeton, NJ: Princeton University Press.

Romero, Lora. 1997. *Home Fronts: Domesticity and Its Critics in the Antebellum United States*. Durham, NC: Duke University Press.

Round, Philip H. 2018. "Mississippian Contexts for Early American Studies." *Early American Literature* 53, no. 2, 445–473.

Rubin, Joan Shelley. 2009. *Songs of Ourselves: The Uses of Poetry in America*. Cambridge, MA: Harvard University Press.

Rudy, Jason R. 2017. *Imagined Homelands: British Poetry in the Colonies*. Baltimore, MD: Johns Hopkins University Press.

Rusert, Britt. 2016. "'Nor Wish to Live the Past Again': Unsettling Origins in Frances Ellen Watkins Harper's *Forest Leaves*," *Common Place* 16, no. 2 (Summer 2016): http://commonplace.online /article/nor-wish-to-live-the-past-again-unsettling-origins-in-frances-ellen-watkins-harpers -forest-leaves-2/.

————. 2017. *Fugitive Science: Empiricism and Freedom in Early African American Culture*. New York: New York University Press.

Saintsbury, George. 1910. *A History of English Prosody from the Twelfth Century to the Present Day*, vols. 1–3. London: Macmillan Co.

Sánchez-Eppler, Karen. 1993. *Touching Liberty: Abolition, Feminism, and the Politics of the Body*. Berkeley: University of California Press.

Sandler, Matt. 2020. *The Black Romantic Revolution: Abolitionist Poets at the End of Slavery*. London and New York: Verso.

Sayre, Gordon. 1998. "The Mound Builders and the Imagination of American Antiquity in Jefferson, Bartram, and Chateaubriand." *Early American Literature* 33, no. 3, 225–249.

Scott, David. 2004. *Conscripts of Identity: The Tragedy of Colonial Enlightenment*. Durham, NC: Duke University Press.

Scott, Julius S. 2018. *The Common Wind: Afro-American Currents in the Age of the Haitian Revolution*. New York: Verso.

Scott-Bauman, Elizabeth, and Ben Burton. 2021. "Shakespearean Stanzas? *Venus and Adonis*, *Lucrece*, and *Complaint*." *ELH* 88, no. 1, 1–26.

Sedgwick, Eve Kosoksky. 1990. *Epistemology of the Closet*. Berkeley: University of California Press.

Senchyne, Jonathan. 2017. Introduction to George Moses Horton, "Individual Influence," *PMLA* 32, no. 5, 1244–1250.

Sharpe, Christina. 2016. *In the Wake: On Blackness and Being*. Durham, NC: Duke University Press.

Shaw, Robert. 2007. *Blank Verse: A Guide to Its History and Use*. Athens: Ohio University Press.

Shelley, Percy Bysshe. 2000. *The Complete Poetry of Percy Bysshe Shelley*. Ed. Donald H. Reiman and Neil Fraistat. Baltimore, MD: Johns Hopkins University Press.

Sherman, Joan R. 1974. *Invisible Poets: Afro-Americans of the Nineteenth Century*. Urbana: University of Illinois Press.

———. 1997. *The Black Bard of North Carolina: George Moses Horton and His Poetry*. Chapel Hill: University of North Carolina Press.

Shields, John C. 2010. *Phillis Wheatley and the Romantics*. Knoxville: University of Tennessee Press.

Shockley, Evie. 2011. *Renegade Poetics: Black Aesthetics and Formal Innovation in African American Poetry*. Iowa City: University of Iowa Press.

———. 2016. "Race, Reception, and Claudia Rankine's 'American Lyric.'" *Los Angeles Review of Books*, January 6, 2016.

Silverberg, Robert. 1968. *Mound Builders of Ancient America: The Archeology of a Myth*. Greenwich, CT: New York Graphic Society, Ltd.

Slauter, Eric. 2009. *The State as a Work of Art: The Cultural Origins of the Constitution*. Chicago: University of Chicago Press.

Smith, Zadie. 2020. "What Do We Want History to Do to Us?" *New York Review of Books*, February 27, 2020.

Socarides, Alexandra. 2020. *In Plain Sight: Nineteenth-Century American Women's Poetry and the Problem of Literary History*. Oxford: Oxford University Press.

Sorby, Angela. 2005. *Schoolroom Poets: Childhood, Performance, and the Place of American Poetry, 1865–1917*. Durham, NC: University of New Hampshire Press.

Spillers, Hortense. 1987/reprint 2003. "Mama's Baby, Papa's Maybe: An American Grammar Book." In *Black, White, and in Color: Essays on American Literature and Culture.* Chicago: University of Chicago Press, 203–229.

Spires, Derek R. 2019. *The Practice of Citizenship: Black Politics and Print Cultures in the Early United States.* Philadelphia: University of Pennsylvania Press.

Stewart, James Brewer. 1999. "Modernizing 'Difference': The Political Meanings of Color in the Free States, 1776–1840." *Journal of the Early Republic* 19 (Winter), 691–712.

Stewart, Susan. 1995. "Lyric Possession." *Critical Inquiry* 22, no. 1, 34–63.

———. 2014. "On ED's 754/764." *New Literary History* 45, no. 2, 253–270.

Stoler, Ann Laura. 2002. *Carnal Knowledge and Imperial Power: Race and the Intimate in Colonial Rule.* Berkeley: University of California Press.

Symonds, Jon Addington. 1880. "Blank Verse." In *Sketches and Studies of Southern Europe.* New York: Harper & Brothers, 325–382.

Tawil, Ezra, 2008. *The Making of Racial Sentiment: Slavery and the Birth of the Frontier Romance.* Cambridge: Cambridge University Press.

Terada, Rei. 2022. *Metaracial: Hegel, Antiblackness, and Political Identity.* Chicago and London: University of Chicago Press.

Trumpener, Katie. 1997. *Bardic Nationalism: The Romantic Novel and the British Empire.* Princeton, NJ: Princeton University Press.

Tucker, Herbert. 1985. "Dramatic Monologue and the Overhearing of Lyric." In *Lyric Poetry: Beyond New Criticism,* ed. C. Hošek and P. Parker. Ithaca, NY: Cornell University Press, 226–246.

———. 2017. "Changes of Address: Epic Invocation in Anglophone Romanticism." In *The Call of Classical Literature in the Romantic Age,* ed. K. P. Van Anglen and James Engall. Edinburgh: Edinburgh University Press, 126–150.

Valdivia, Lucía Martínez. 2019. "Mere Meter: A Revised History of English Poetry." *ELH* 86, no. 3, 555–585.

Virgil. 1988. *Georgics.* Ed. Richard F. Thomas. 2 vols. Cambridge: Cambridge University Press.

Wagner, Jean. 1973. *Black Poets of the United States: From Paul Laurence Dunbar to Langston Hughes,* trans. Kenneth Douglas. Urbana: University of Illinois Press.

Waldstreicher, David. 2011. "The Wheatleyan Moment." *Early American Studies* 9, no. 3, 522–551.

———. 2013. "The Mansfieldian Moment: Slavery, the Constitution, and American Political Traditions." *Rutgers Law Journal* 43, no. 3 (Fall/Winter 2013), 471–486.

Walker, David. 1829/2000. *Appeal to the Coloured Citizens of the World,* ed. Peter H. Hinks. University Park: Pennsylvania State University Press.

Wang, Dorothy. 2014. *Thinking Its Presence: Form, Race, and Subjectivity in Contemporary Asian American Poetry.* Stanford, CA: Stanford University Press.

Warner, Michael. 2002. *Publics and Counterpublics.* New York: Zone Books.

Watkins, Frances Ellen. Late 1840s. *Forest Leaves.* Baltimore, Maryland.

———. 1854. *Poems on Miscellaneous Subjects.* Boston: J. B. Yerrinton & Son, Printers.

Watson, Marsha. 1996. "A Classic Case: Phillis Wheatley and Her Poetry." *Early American Literature* 31, no. 2, 103–132.

Welburn, Ron. 2015. *Hartford's Ann Plato and the Native Borders of Identity.* Albany: State University of New York Press.

Wheatley, Phillis. 2019. *The Writings of Phillis Wheatley*, ed. Vincent Carretta. Oxford: Oxford University Press.

Whitfield, James Monroe. 2011. *The Works of James M. Whitfield: America and Other Writings by a Nineteenth-Century African American Poet*, ed. Robert S. Levine and Ivy G. Wilson. Chapel Hill: University of North Carolina Press.

Whitman, Walt. 1860. *Leaves of Grass*. Boston: Thayer and Eldrige. Available in *The Walt Whitman Archive*, gen. ed. Matt Cohen, Ed Folsom, and Kenneth M. Price: http://www .whitmanarchive.org.

Whittier, John Greenleaf, ed. 1840. *The North Star: The Poetry of Freedom, by Her Friends*. Philadelphia: Merrihew and Thompson.

Wilderson, Frank III. 2020. *Afropessimism*. New York: Liveright, W. W. Norton & Company.

Williams, Carolyn. 2011. *Gilbert and Sullivan: Gender, Genre, Parody*. New York: Columbia University Press.

Williams, Stephen. 1991. *Fantastic Archeology: The Wild Side of North American Prehistory*. Philadelphia: University of Pennsylvania Press.

Wilson, Ivy. 2011. *Specters of Democracy: Blackness and the Aesthetics of Politics in the Antebellum U.S.* Oxford: Oxford University Press.

———, ed. 2014. *Whitman Noir: Black America and the Good Gray Poet*. Iowa City: University of Iowa Press.

Wordsworth, William. 1977. *The Poems: Two Volumes*, ed. John O. Hayden. New Haven, CT: Yale University Press.

———. 1983. *Poems, in Two Volumes, and Other Poems, 1800–1807*, ed. Jared Curtis. Ithaca, NY: Cornell University Press.

———. 1991. "Preface 1800 Version (with 1802 variants)." In *Lyrical Ballads*, ed. R. L. Brett and A. R. Jones. New York: Routledge, 233–258.

Wynter, Sylvia. 2015. *Sylvia Wynter: On Being Human as Praxis*, ed. Katherine McKittrick. Durham, NC: Duke University Press.

Young, Jennifer Rene. 2011. "Marketing a Sable Muse: Phillis Wheatley and the Antebellum Press." In *New Essays on Phillis Wheatley*, ed. John C. Shields and Eric C. Lamore. Knoxville: University of Tennessee Press, 209–246.

Young, Robert. 1995. *Colonial Desire: Hybridity in Theory, Culture, and Race*. London: Routledge.

INDEX

Note: Page numbers in italic type indicate illustrations.

abolition: antiblack, 10, 12, 74, 85; British, 28–30; Douglass and, 76; Horton and, 95, 98; Knapp's *Memoir and Poems of Phillis Wheatley* and, 8–10; Pierpont and, 68, 71–74, 85, 255n6; Plato's "To the First of August" and, 21–30; publics for poems associated with, 15, 237. *See also* slavery

abortion, 70–71

Abrams, M. H., 163, 165, 265n49

abstraction: Adorno on, 20; Barbara Johnson on, 120; Bryant and, 146, 160, 165, 176; Ethiopia as, 237; of genre into form, 7, 10; Longfellow and, 196–97, 214, 218; lyric characterized by, 9, 20, 32, 43–44, 63, 66, 80, 88, 98, 101, 146, 171, 188, 191, 196, 232; as means of racialization, 32, 39–40, 43, 57, 66, 76, 87–88, 90, 98, 105, 151, 169, 176, 181, 184, 191, 213; Poetess as, 33–35, 191–95, 197, 211–13, 224, 232; simple, 12; "the speaker" as, 4, 7, 20, 32, 37–40, 53, 57, 98, 150, 171, 176, 232; Watkins Harper's critique of, 61–62, 196. *See also* lyric; lyricization; race; racialization

Acuff, James, 229

Adams, John Quincy, 78, 257n35

address: Adorno on, 50, 171; apostrophe as figure of, 7, 59, 69–101, 105, 240; Barbara Johnson on, 69–70; Berlant on, 70–71, 157; counterhistorical force of, 226; Culler on, 50–51, 69; genres of, 21, 32, 201; "O!" as Romantic signifier of, 64–66; in Plato's

"To the First of August," 21–26; problems inherent in, 13; publics constituted by, 13, 20, 20, 56–58, 68, 157, 205, 208; racialization of, 72, 76, 82–88, 110, 156, 171–72, 203; transformation of, in invention of American lyric, 3–4, 7, 40–41, 48, 63, 66, 98; in Watkins Harper's "Eva's Farewell," 231. *See also* apostrophe; publics; "the speaker"

Adorno, Theodor, 5, 6, 20, 49–50, 56, 171, 190, 230–31

The African Repository (magazine), 95

Aiken, George L., *Uncle Tom's Cabin* (play), 207, 210

alienation: Black poets and, 20, 49, 66, 82, 87–89, 232; as definition of modern lyric, 49–51, 109, 171, 202; in Wheatley's poetry, 107, 125, 138

American Antiquarian Society, 180

American Colonization Society, 10

American poetry: Bryant's role and status in, 140–42; developments in, 3–4, 16; Eurocentric histories of, 139–40, 142; genre of the poem vs. genre of the person, 3–4, 20, 33, 58, 66, 87–88, 103, 151, 191, 232; Longfellow's role and status in, 196–97, 218, 224; lyricization into a single genre of, 3–4, 17–18, 21, 39, 57, 63, 101, 154, 188, 197–98, 226, 232; modern canon of, 3, 16, 48, 139–46; persons/subjects connected to, 8, 20, 32; public nature of early, 3, 8, 15,

A NOTE ON THE TYPE

This book has been composed in Arno, an Old-style serif typeface in the classic Venetian tradition, designed by Robert Slimbach at Adobe.

CPSIA information can be obtained
at www.ICGtesting.com
Printed in the USA
JSHW051531301122
34081JS00004B/4